Strategic Issues in Finance

i

Strategic Issues in Finance

Edited by Keith Ward

Butterworth-Heinemann Ltd
Linacre House, Jordan Hill, Oxford OX2 8DP

 A member of the Reed Elsevier plc group

OXFORD   LONDON   BOSTON
MUNICH   NEW DELHI   SINGAPORE   SYDNEY
TOKYO   TORONTO   WELLINGTON

First published 1994

British Library Cataloguing in Publication Data
Strategic Issues in Finance. – (Management Reader Series)
  I. Ward, Keith II. Series
  658.15

ISBN 0 7506 0996 6

Composition by Genesis Typesetting, Laser Quay, Rochester, Kent
Printed and bound in Great Britain by Clays, St Ives plc

Contents

Preface

The major rationale underlying the production of this readings book is a concern that many people with a deep interest in finance have never read the key original articles and journal papers, on which the wealth of modern financial theory and practice is built. Finance is a relatively modern subject in its own right, having developed over the last forty years, or so, out of mainstream financial economics. However, the original seminal articles in this area are now incorporated in a very summarized form in the plethora of textbooks and developmental material, which has resulted from the massive conceptual and empirical research produced in the relatively short period which finance has had a separate discipline.

Consequently, no apology whatsoever is made for reproducing in this readings book several of the key journal papers which still form the bedrock of modern financial theory. Reading the original ideas of the academics, and some practitioners, which changed the way in which the role of finance is perceived, analysed and applied can only enhance the understanding of anyone truly interested in this fascinatingly complex area of business. It should enable a full appreciation of the underlying assumptions incorporated within these models, which are increasingly taken as 'givens' in the modern world of global financial markets.

In addition to these original thinking 'seminal' articles, the book also attempts to incorporate a sample of the applied development and empirical testing work which has been undertaken in more recent years. The selection is restricted due to a chronic shortage of space (some of the major review articles would fill an entire book on their own) and, as editor, I take complete responsibility for any apparent bias which you, as the reader, may feel has come through in the articles included. If this bias should be felt to include an absence of the more esoteric and mathematical developments in this area, I am sure that many readers may feel an inward sense of relief; I have based the selection on my own sense of practical relevance and comprehension!

The editorial chapter is intended as a guide through both the book and the development of the entire subject, but, inevitably, a degree of my personal views will have come through in the way certain areas are treated and commented upon. I hope that my own very strong views on the immense practical relevance and importance of financial strategy to modern businesses will not distort your appreciation of the assembled material.

I am extremely grateful to all the learned journals which have given permission for their articles to be included but, most importantly, I am indebted to the stimulating and exciting work that my worldwide colleagues in this area have produced, some of which is incorporated in this single volume.

Keith Ward

Part 1
Introduction

1 Introduction and editor's overview

Increasing shareholder value

A key objective of most commercially-based businesses is to deliver financial return which at least matches the expectations of the investors in the business. (How these expectations are arrived at is considered later in the book.) Indeed if the actual return achieved only just equals the expected return, the investors can be regarded as merely having swapped a present cash flow (the cost of their investment) for an equally valuable future cash flow (the actual return achieved). In real terms therefore the investor is no better off and shareholder value is only created if the actual return exceeds the investor's expected or required rate of return. This concept is absolutely central to the idea of creating shareholder value, as is developed in the first article in Part Two by A. Shapiro.

The first issue is that, in a perfectly competitive market, it is impossible for any business consistently to achieve above normal rates of return on its investments, because competitive responses in such a market will remove the opportunity for such a super profit or 'economic rent', as Shapiro terms it. Thus it is only possible to invest in projects with a positive net present value on a discounted cash flow basis if there are imperfections in the competitive arena which can be exploited successfully by a particular business. It is now well understood that the main thrust of competitive strategies is to develop, and then to maintain, such sources of 'sustainable competitive advantage'. This is the main thrust of Shapiro's article and the many company examples given also dramatically illustrate how competitive advantages can change over time. Several of the success stories in 1985 are experiencing severe difficulties now and some are even fighting for survival; this issue is not limited to Shapiro's paper as it is equally true for the contemporaneous publications of Porter or Peters and Waterman to which Shapiro refers.

However, the thrust of this book is not competitive strategy but the role of financial strategy and Shapiro's article is included as the opening contribution for three reasons not directly related to the paper's main objectives. First, by emphasizing the significant role of 'sustainable competitive advantages' in the product/market areas (i.e. the particular goods and services sold by the company and the customers to whom they are sold), the paper highlights the relatively limited potential role for pure financial strategy in creating true shareholder value. Finance can at best have a second order value impact on the value of the company. Further, as sustainable competitive advantages can only be developed and maintained through exploiting market imperfections, it is necessary to consider the relative state of perfection in financial markets in order to understand the degree and type of imperfections which may be exploitable.

There is no doubt that there are imperfections in financial markets; obvious examples being taxation, inflation and transaction costs. One of the major problems encountered in developing any theory of finance is how these imperfections can be taken into account within the theoretical framework. As will be seen throughout the papers in the book, the major theoretical advances have been developed under assumptions of perfect competition. A significant criticism of them by practitioners is that the theories do not respond well to the inclusion of the inevitable imperfections of the real world. A good example of this is the capital asset pricing model, dealt with in Part Three and which considers the investors' required rate of return. Most textbook treatments of this topic do not mention taxation, but the differential impact of taxation among classes of investors and across financial markets could distort the expected theoretical relationship between risk and return. Similarly in the area of capital structure, considered in Part Four, the tax deductibility of interest expense has created problems for the theorists; leading F. Modigliani and M.H. Miller to publish a correction article to their original ground-breaking paper.

Second and more significant is the clear way in which Shapiro's paper illustrates how financial capital markets already reflect expectations in the prices applied to financial assets. The article opens with a discussion of thirteen USA-based companies which consistently outperformed their sector and the overall stock market over a decade in terms of return on equity. However, their very consistency in turning in such good financial results meant that the total returns to their investors over the same period were by no means so outstanding; indeed, in some cases, the investors' return was significantly below that achieved from the market as a whole. In other words, at the beginning of the period investors could expect or predict that these companies would outperform the average company with a similar risk profile and therefore 'the expected high ROE is already priced out or capitalized by the market'. The challenge facing these companies was, of course, that if they had failed to sustain their high ROE, which flowed from their successful development of a sustainable competitive advantage, the total return to their investors would have been considerably lower and could even have become significantly negative over this period. This might appear to be a harsh penalty to a company which may have only reverted to being 'average', but this is inevitable when market prices are based on expectations. This highlights two important aspects of any financial strategy which will be returned to later in the book; it is important that companies not only properly understand the implications of investors' current expectations but also take a pro-active role in managing those expectations so as to ensure that they do not become unrealistic. The impact on a company of failure to achieve what were clearly unrealistic expectations (especially when considered with the clarity of vision granted by the benefits of hindsight) can be both very rapid and dramatic. It also reiterates the logic that shareholder value is only enhanced by achieving actual rates of return which exceed the expectations which are already incorporated in the current market price.

The third reason for including the Shapiro paper is that it indicates the importance for shareholder value of cash flow measures rather than accounting measures such as profit, earnings per share and return on equity. The financial markets have proved themselves quite adept at dealing with the apparent contradictions which can arise when the accounting results appear to show an improving performance which is not borne out in terms of the cash flows of the business. Indeed a key element in a sound valuation process is the ability to reconcile any discrepancies between the valuations generated by using the accounting earnings for the business and the present value of the forecast future cash flows. As already stated the critically important *positive* net present values which are needed to enhance shareholder value will normally only be achieved from sustainable competitive advantages and this should focus attention on a key strategic role for the finance function. It should seek to identify and explain the sources of all the positive net present values which are currently being achieved by the company and which are claimed to be achievable in new investment proposals. After all, these should develop into the most important *assets* of the business and should be developed and maintained so as to optimize their value.

The Shapiro paper provides a strategic overview of the role of finance in enhancing shareholder value, which enables our review of the development of financial theory to be made in an appropriate context.

It seems logical to start with an attempt to understand investors' behaviour and how investors' demands or expectations are set. One of the earliest ground-breaking pieces of work in this area was carried out by Markowitz and the second article in Part Two represents a very early publication of his work on portfolio selection. The paper starts by challenging the simple maxim that investors merely do or should 'maximize discounted return' and dismissing it because it does not match with observed behaviour. Observation of actual behaviour shows that investors prefer to invest in a range of assets rather than concentrating exclusively on the *one* which they believe would generate the highest discounted present value. 'Hence any investment theory has to argue in favour of a diversified portfolio if it is not to be self-evidently unsound.'

The justification for investment in such a diversified portfolio is based on the reduction in risk which can be achieved. Risk is measured in terms of the potential volatility in the expected returns from the investment. Markowitz argued that the variance on any portfolio cannot be greater than the variance on any component of the portfolio and would normally be significantly less. As the returns from securities are intercorrelated, diversification cannot eliminate all risk. The degree of risk reduction is determined by the level of correlation among the securities in the portfolio (which is measured by the co-variances among the securities). This analysis was used to develop a concept of an efficient investment portfolio based on the essential trade-off between expected return and the associated risk.

The next major theoretical step, covered in Part Three, was to be the development of a model predicting this risk/return trade-off relationship for the capital markets in total.

Capital asset prices – developing a model of the capital market

The development of portfolio theory highlighted the need for a method of predicting the way in which capital markets would respond to the risks associated with any particular investment. Markowitz's work had already indicated that there were really two elements in the total risk associated with individual components of a portfolio because, even in the most completely diversified portfolio (i.e. a portfolio comprising an appropriately weighted mix of all available investments), not all of the risk can be removed. Another fundamental element of the accepted theory was that rational investors required an increase in expected return in order to compensate for an increase in their perceived level of risk; in other words, required return is positively correlated with risk. In addition there is a time associated cost (the pure interest rate) with even a completely risk free investment. It must be remembered that risk is defined as volatility in the returns received from any investment; hence, a risk free investment provides an absolutely certain level of return, but even this must be positive in order to compensate investors for giving up the immediate alternative use of their funds.

During the early 1960s a model was developed which tried to relate the total expected return on a given asset to the risk free level of return and the additional premium required to compensate for the specific risk of the asset. It is a sign of the increasing interest in the theory of finance that a similar theory was independently derived by three people at around the same time. One of these papers is published as the first article in Part Three but the work of J. Treynor and J. Lintner in this area should not be forgotten. W.F. Sharpe's theory is based on the portfolio theory logic that an investor will make investment choices based on only two parameters: the expected value or return from each investment and its standard deviation. Investors are assumed to prefer more wealth to less but to be risk-averse, i.e. they demand increasing returns in order to undertake riskier investments.

The theory is also based on an assumption of equilibrium in capital markets and this condition itself requires two further assumptions. The market must have a common pure rate of interest, which enables *all* investors to borrow or lend funds on equal terms. Second, it is assumed that there is homogeneity of investor expectations, i.e. that all investors agree on the expected return from each potential investment, and on their standard deviations and correlation coefficients. Sharpe's analysis showed that there should be a linear relationship between the risk of any diversified investment portfolio and its expected return, under these equilibrium conditions, but it also used the two elements of risk in a much more specific way. It was argued that part of the risk of an investment is caused by its correlation to a well-diversified efficient portfolio of risky assets; this component of the risk was entitled the 'systematic' risk (or 'market' risk) and is caused by changes in the level of economic activity. The remainder of the risk, not surprisingly christened the 'unsystematic' component (or 'specific' or 'unique' risk), can be diversified away by a rational, risk-averse investor. As a consequence, an efficient capital market will not compensate investors for bearing unnecessary risks (i.e. the unsystematic component) which means that the risk premium will be driven by the asset's systematic risk level. Although not explicitly stated as such in Sharpe's original 1964 paper this relationship is now most commonly referred to as:

$$K_E = K_F + \beta \ (K_M - K_F)$$

Where K_E = the required rate of return on a particular investment (also known as the cost of equity capital)

K_F = the risk free rate of return or pure interest rate

β = the systematic risk of the particular investment

K_M = the required rate of return on the stock market as a whole (strictly speaking, this should be the return on an efficient portfolio from all possible risky assets, i.e. not just publicly quoted equity shares)

The relevance of any theory should be tested by comparing its predicted outcomes with reality and Sharpe rapidly attempted to do this with his new theory, which is normally referred to as the Capital Asset Pricing Model (CAPM). This initial empirical research is included as the second article in Part Three in which Sharpe immediately highlighted one of the fundamental problems associated with validating theories in this area. The CAPM theory is based on the '*expected* returns from assets and the associated risks', while what can be empirically measured is, of course, the *actual* return achieved; 'clearly, actual results may differ considerably from the predictions made by investors at the time they purchase assets'. Another potential problem was identified in that results over several years are needed to estimate expected rates of return and standard deviations, but investors' required return for risk free investments and their required incremental return for bearing risk may change over time.

Notwithstanding these considerable problems, Sharpe used a ten-year analysis of the returns from thirty-four USA mutual funds in which he took the average actual rate of return as an estimate of the expected rate of return and the standard deviation of this actual return as an estimate of the predicted risk. In other words, the assumption was that investors' predictions were proved right in both dimensions; also it was assumed that all the mutual funds were operating efficient portfolios. The conclusions drawn from the analysis were that there *was* a positive correlation between risk and return, and that, to a degree, estimates of the risk free rate and the actual risk premium could be made for the period under consideration. However, as Sharpe admitted, 'there is no a priori reason to assume that these rates will *characterize any future period*'. He then went on to challenge one of the underlying tenets of the theory, i.e. the linear relationship between risk and return. This had been based on the assumed ability of investors to borrow and lend unlimited amounts of money at the risk free rate. Where the consequent investments were in high risk assets, their ability to borrow at a risk free rate must be called into question and it would not be surprising therefore to see the slope of the line turn into an increasingly upward curve as the risk associated with the asset increased. Some tendency towards this result was reported by Sharpe but the effect could easily have been due to other factors.

Clearly this major new theory was deserving of much empirical evaluation, which it has undoubtedly received, but the fundamental difficulties associated with the measurement of actual returns and volatilities rather than the required 'expectations' of investors have proved insurmountable. In fact, much of the research has focused on removing some or all of the restrictive assumptions required for the development of the basic CAPM theory.

One of the major theoretical developments from this basic capital asset pricing model was published in 1976 by S.A. Ross as the Arbitrage Theory of Capital Asset Pricing; this paper is included as the third article in Part Three. Ross also attacked the basic tenet of the linear relationship between risk and return; his model had the added attraction that it was not dependent upon market equilibrium and did not subscribe any particular significance to the 'market portfolio'. However, the resulting model suffered from the problems that investors still had to have 'essentially identical expectations and agreement on the β coefficients' and, more significantly, that the factors required to turn the formula into a practical predictive model were, to all intents and purposes, not calculable from observable data. The CAPM has remained the subject of much academic research and a wide range of derivatives have been proposed and tested. However, as stated in the next article in Part Three by D.W. Mullins, the basic CAPM remained in 1982, and still does today, the most popular basis in the major, developed capital markets for assessing the required rate of return for risky investments.

This paper considers the practical use of the CAPM within a business; i.e. in assessing the required rate of return on any proposed investment. The required rate of return should take into account the risk associated with the project which, under the CAPM, could be assessed by 'computing' (or guessing!) the appropriate β for the specific capital project. The practical problems involved in assessing the future volatility in the returns of any particular investment proposal should not be underestimated. However, it can also be argued that even an approximation of the associated risk should enable the company to make a better estimate of the appropriate risk adjusted required rate of return.

Mullins' article also states another key theory which underlies much of modern financial theory, but which is not explicitly covered by any of the papers included in this book. This is the theory that capital markets are efficient, but this efficiency is meant in a particularly technical form in that 'relevant information about companies is quickly and universally distributed and absorbed'. There are three classical forms of this theory of efficient markets, which are normally described as the weak form, the semi-strong, and the strong form. In very brief terms the weak form assumes that all historical financial information is already reflected in current share prices. Hence it would be impossible, on a consistent basis, to earn a super profit by carrying out financial analysis on the historical trends of share prices; i.e. 'chartism' is a waste of time. This position can be paraphrased as financial markets following a random walk over time, where the direction and strength of the next movement cannot be predicted by those moves in the past. It is very interesting that even this weak definition of market efficiency is now challenged by the newly emerging chaos theory of financial markets, which postulates that markets do have a form of memory (albeit a very complex one based on the dynamics of fractal geometry).

In its semi-strong form, the theory of efficient markets can be stated as indicating that a current share price incorporates *all* publicly available information regarding the company. Hence *fundamental* external security analysis cannot be expected to deliver a consistent level of super profit. This clearly has important implications for the securities industry which, however, have apparently been ignored by those professional fund managers who practise active management strategies in attempts to 'beat the market'. A yet more dramatic conclusion can be drawn from the strong form of the theory because this states that all 'knowable' information is incorporated in the current share price. This would mean that even investors with private 'insider' information would find it impossible to outperform the overall market on a consistent basis.

Not surprisingly these theories of efficient markets have been the subject of countless research studies in attempts to explore which, if any, form really applies to modern financial markets. What *may* appear surprising is that, in a book which purports to deal with the major theoretical developments in the field of finance, no articles relating to theories of efficient markets are included. Let me, very briefly, try to justify this. First, these theories only purport to describe the behaviour of markets in general and hence their proponents can always ignore case histories of particular investors who have consistently outperformed the market as 'statistical irrelevancies'. As the market in total always, by definition, performs to its own average, it is difficult to falsify the theory that markets are efficient. Second, the theory is based on information available at a given moment in time with sudden price movements presumed to be due to the availability of new information; again this is difficult to test empirically. Third, this theory does not claim to be able to predict or forecast the price of any individual share at any point in time. It only works for markets in total and there is no presumption that the incorporation of the available information (at whichever level) results in the share being traded at the 'right' price, merely that its resulting price is 'unbiased'. In summary, it can be asserted that the level of 'efficiency' of capital markets has little, if any, implication for the financial strategy of any particular company, which is the main thrust of this book.

Returning to the Mullins article, it has been included as it provides a good summary of the potential practical applications of the CAPM from the perspective of companies. This indicates that an estimate of the investors' risk adjusted cost of equity capital for a company should be a prerequisite for any of the company's financial managers involved in investment decision making criteria, if any objective of enhancing shareholder value is claimed by the company. The paper also includes a table illustrating systematic and unsystematic risks which is an area which often seems to create a surprising degree of confusion. Finally, the article also briefly compares the CAPM as a measure of the cost of equity with the simplest version of the dividend growth model which is the subject of the next part of the book.

Dividends or growth: the continuing puzzle

One of the apparent conundrums of financial theory is represented by the following two statements. The current price of a share represents the present value of the expected future dividend stream. Dividend policy is irrelevant in terms of determining the current share price. An invitation to reconcile these statements is a relatively common examination question in certain finance courses.

The first statement is uncontentious as long as the company is assumed to have an infinite life, i.e. there is no reason to assume that the company will be liquidated in the foreseeable future with the net proceeds of liquidation being distributed to the shareholders. Even then, if this final liquidation distribution is classified as a dividend for the purposes of the valuation model, the first statement is still valid. The second statement has been the subject of much greater academic debate, with an original justification being proposed by J.T.S. Porterfield in 1959; this article is included as the first entry in Part Four.

Porterfield starts from the very basic statements that 'the objective of a publicly owned company should be to maximize the return on its owners' investment' and that 'stockholders can realize a return in two ways – from dividends and from appreciation in the market value of their holdings'. He goes on to demonstrate that 'stock dividends', like share splits and bonus issues, have no intrinsic value to shareholders and consequently should result in no change in the total value of the company. A similar analysis is applied to rights issues in order to show that there is no 'giveaway' or added value in the apparent discount at which rights issues are sold to existing shareholders. This is now reflected in the way in which rights issues are accounted for; i.e. by splitting the rights into an offer of shares at the full market price combined with a bonus issue of the remaining shares representing the discount in the offer. The effect of this accounting practice is to restate the earnings per share figures for previous years at lower levels due to the increase in the 'equivalent' number of issued shares caused by the bonus element in a rights issue.

More dramatically, Porterfield argues that cash dividends similarly *should* have no impact on the share price as they merely represent the payment to the shareholders of something they already 'own'. Therefore, the resulting reduction in the asset position of the company should result in an equivalent reduction in the share price. Conversely it is argued that the payment of no cash dividend at all should not harm shareholders because the retained earnings should be reflected in a higher share price. Any shareholders who desire a cash inflow from their investment could sell an appropriate portion of their shares and still retain an equivalently valued net investment (i.e. fewer shares but with a higher price each). Porterfield does mention the issue of tax in passing and raises the possible arguments of applying a higher discount rate to retained earnings because of the risks associated with retention or the lack of attractive reinvestment opportunities on the part of the company; however, he finds 'none of them completely convincing'. His conclusion is that companies should seek to determine whether their stock 'sells mainly on the basis of dividends paid or on the basis of earnings retained', and acknowledges that 'corporate images are not immutable'.

This article had already been pre-dated by the publication of a valuation model which set out a theoretical framework for including both the current dividend yield and the future capital growth which should be created from the retained earnings. M.J. Gordon and E. Shapiro's 1956 paper is included as the second article in Part Four and builds on the work of J.B. Williams back in 1932. Once again, their argument starts from the premise that 'the objective of a firm is the maximization of the value of the stockholders' equity', and they use the *then* accepted relationship that 'this objective is realized in capital budgeting when the budget is set so as to equate the marginal return on investment with the rate of return at which the corporation's stock is selling in the market'. The major thrust of their paper was that the existing measurements of this rate of return (which were the dividend yield and the earnings yield) failed to recognize that 'a share's payments can be expected to grow'.

They used the present value of the future dividend stream derivation of current share prices to arrive at the required rate of return (i.e. the required rate of return is the discount rate applied to the future expected dividend stream). However, as long as the future dividend stream is an apparently random series of payments, it is impossible to derive a meaningful, practical formula for this required rate of return. Gordon and Shapiro made two simplifying assumptions: first, the company is expected to retain a constant proportion of its after-tax profits (which, of course, also implies that a constant proportion is paid out as dividends); second, the company is expected to generate a constant rate of return on the book value of its common equity (which, of course, includes the retained earnings). The result of these simplifying assumptions is that future dividends will be expected to grow at a constant compound rate (which is equal to the retention ratio multiplied by the rate of return on equity) and a very simple expression for the required rate of return on equity (K_E) can be derived:

$$K_E = \frac{D}{P} + g$$

where D is the current annual dividend payment
$\quad\quad$ P is the current share price
and $\quad$ g is the rate at which the dividend is expected to grow.

The assumptions underlying this formula mean that the expected future rate of growth in dividends is really only an extrapolation of the current position, and this growth rate is not only uniform and compound but also projected to continue to infinity. However, the strength of the discounting technique is that it reduces the impact of such long-term future projections. The authors also suggest that other methods of deriving an estimate of the future growth rate of dividends (such as the average of the past rate of growth in dividends) could be tried. However it is arrived at, there is a strong argument made in the article that this growth orientated required rate of return on equity capital should be used in establishing the minimum rate of return needed for internally financed capital investment projects. Their conclusion is that a company's dividend policy should be dictated by the availability of investment projects with expected rates of return above the required rate of return on shareholders' funds. Equilibrium (i.e. indifference on the part of investors) is reached when the marginal return on investment (which should fall if the funds available for reinvestment are increased) equals the required rate of return (i.e. cost of equity). Gordon and Shapiro actually state that 'changing the dividend so as to equate "these" should maximize the price of the stock'; thus they are very clearly arguing that dividend policy does make a difference to the share price. They also end by stating that the required rate of return varies with the dividend rate, due to a change in the risk perception of the investor.

In 1959, Gordon published a follow-up paper, also included in Part Four, which attempted some empirical testing of the dividend growth model. The evidence was not conclusive but the paper also developed the theoretical argument as to why the dividend payout ratio affects the share price. This hinged on the argument that the cost of equity is an increasing function of the retention rate; i.e. that there is an inverse correlation with the dividend payout ratio. If the discount rate applied to future cash inflows is affected by the dividend policy, it is clear that the dividend policy will affect the share price.

This paper provoked a very aggressive responsive from other academics, most notably F. Modigliani and M.H. Miller who took strong exception to the whole argument that dividend policy had an impact on share prices. Their basic line was consistent with their own earlier conceptual work on capital structure, which is considered in Part Five, but, unfortunately, their 1961 paper is too long to be included. In its place, a later paper by M. Brennan from 1971 has been included because this not only considers the original counter arguments, but also includes the continuing dialogue which ensued. Modigliani and Miller's (M–M) argument starts from the assumption that a company's investment policy is decided upon independently of its dividend policy. This means that, if insufficient retained earnings are available, the company will need to raise additional capital from either its existing shareholders or new investors. Gordon's model had effectively ignored additional injections of capital as it was considering the sustainable organic growth rate of the company. M–M argued that Gordon's conclusion was based on a confounding of the effects of dividend policy and investment policy; this accusation was 'refuted' by Gordon. M–M's contention was that the company could obtain the benefit of any additional attractive investment projects (on the basis that a company should invest in *all* those projects expected to generate a rate of return in excess of the company's cost of capital) by raising new shares rather than by reducing dividends. Since this increased investment policy should add value to the total company, the existing shareholders would benefit, even if they did not provide the additional financing.

As stated at the beginning of Brennan's article, 'the issue between these opposing views cannot be settled by resort to experience, for the fundamental reason that the above hypotheses relate to the effects of dividend policy in perfect capital markets, whereas of course actual securities markets suffer from several imperfections'; in other words, empirical research will not prove things either way! The theoretical debate still continues with some academics, like Brennan, coming down on the side of Modigliani and Miller due to their separation of investment decisions and dividend policy; some textbooks unfortunately make this choice without properly acquainting their readers with the other side of the debate. However, the Gordon and Shapiro original model is still widely quoted and used, and a wide range of more sophisticated variants have been developed and are applied in capital markets. Thus, linear growth and two or more stage growth models now exist, and the assumption of infinite growth has been removed from many of these updated versions.

One area of relevant empirical research on dividend policy is with regard to the way in which dividend policies are established. Some original work was done on this by J. Lintner in 1956, but once again space does not allow the inclusion of the whole paper. However, it is well referred to in the 1985 paper by H.K. Baker et al. which is included in Part Four and this paper provides some updated research which is consistently structured around Lintner's earlier work. Lintner's main conclusions were that dividend policy was normally established so as to pay a steady (i.e. not violently fluctuating) stream of income to shareholders and was set as a first priority rather than after considering the reinvestment opportunities available to the company. The later research did not conflict with these findings and also highlighted that senior company executives believe that dividend policy has an impact on the total value of the company's equity, as well as signalling to the market the future intentions and expectations of the company. Baker et al.'s research did not seek to identify why executives believe dividend policy is important or in which way it affects share valuation, but this issue may highlight the key difference between the conflicting theoretical positions. Modigliani and Miller's position is based on an assumption of unlimited access to capital for all financially attractive investment projects, without any costs being associated with raising this capital; in a perfectly efficient market, their position can be supported. Gordon's position is based on an assumption that investors will apply a higher discount rate to higher reinvested profits (i.e. a lower dividend pay-out ratio) as they will perceive this strategy as incurring higher risk. Under M–M's theoretical position, the company only reinvests in projects where it can earn a return equal to the shareholders' cost of capital and the company has access to a potentially unlimited supply of such projects. (It must be remembered that, in a perfectly competitive market, it will be impossible to earn on a sustainable basis a super profit, i.e. a return in excess of that demanded by the investor.) Hence there would theoretically be no need for investors to apply a higher discount rate as the risk is not increased.

However, in reality companies do not perceive themselves as having an unlimited pool of financially attractive projects (on a risk adjusted basis) and they equally do not have access (on a 'no-cost' fund raising basis) to unlimited additional finance. Consequently, dividend policies could/should be driven by the relative availability of attractive reinvestment opportunities and this expectation could/should be reflected in the market's reaction to changes in dividend policy on the part of the company.

As a last contribution to this part of the book, R.C. Higgins' article on 'How Much Growth can a Firm Afford?' is included. Higgins uses the concept of sustainable growth in an interesting way by introducing the impact of inflation on the 'real' sustainable growth rate of a business. An amended version of the organic sustainable growth rate for a company is generated, but this formula still assumes a target debt:equity ratio for the company which must be maintained in the long term. The article also considers alternative strategies when the internally generated sustainable growth rate is found to be unacceptable and these include changing the dividend pay-out ratio, raising new equity, or altering the capital structure of the company. The introduction of capital structure is a good linkage into Part Five of the book, which deals with this subject in depth.

Is there an optimum capital structure?

The issue of the impact of capital structure on the return required by both equity investors in the company and lenders to the company (i.e. the rate of interest charged) and the related net impact on the value of the company has been one of the most debated areas of financial theory. However, due to practical problems it has not been as comprehensively researched and the debate as to whether there is an optimum capital structure for a particular company continues today.

The classical paper on this subject by F. Modigliani and M.H. Miller is included as the first article in Part Five of the book. Despite being originally published in 1958, it is still reverentially referred to in almost every textbook on finance; even by those who challenge its conclusions or propose alternative theoretical frameworks. Their analysis, which developed three basic 'propositions' regarding the relationship between capital structure and the value of a company's equity, was based on several important underlying assumptions which are unfortunately often disregarded when the resulting theory is discussed in other finance texts. A first assumption is that the value of any company can be calculated by reference to 'the *average* value over time of the earnings stream' from the company and the 'market rate of capitalization for the expected value of the uncertain earnings streams from the company'. This requires the explicitly stated assumptions that the shares in these companies are 'traded in perfect markets under conditions of atomistic competition', and that these shares can be classified into homogeneous groupings which are substitutes for each other. It also excludes any assumption of inbuilt trend (e.g. growth in earnings over a finite period) in these earnings, unless such growth is somehow allowed for in the market capitalization rate. The use of this market capitalization rate also assumes that the expected value earnings stream represents a perpetual annuity. The main thrust of the paper is to develop a model describing the impact of allowing companies to incorporate debt financing into their capital structure. Using an arbitrage model, the first proposition argues that investors can adjust their personal investment portfolios to replicate any given level of company gearing or leverage. Consequently, given a further important assumption that the company cost of borrowing and the investors' cost of borrowing are identical, the 'market value of any firm is independent of its capital structure and is given by capitalizing its expected return at the rate appropriate to its class' (i.e. its risk rating). This proposition can be more clearly restated as 'the *average* cost of capital to any firm is completely independent of its capital structure and is equal to the capitalization rate of a pure equity stream of its class'. The arbitrage model used is dependent upon the existence of an exactly equivalent set of investments in terms of expected returns and risk profiles and differing only in terms of capital structure, as well as the assumption of equal debt funding costs.

From this first proposition, the paper develops Proposition II which is that, 'the expected yield of a share is equal to the appropriate capitalization rate for a pure equity (funded) stream in the class (i.e. risk category), plus a premium related to financial risk equal to the debt to equity ratio times the gap between the equity capitalization rate and the cost of debt'. This proposition argues that there is a linear increase in the required return on a share in a leveraged company, compared to its unleveraged equivalent, so that the level of increase is simply proportional to the degree of leverage in the company.

The impact of this second proposition would be to make it impossible for a company to increase value for its shareholders by adjusting its capital structure, because the change in the required return would exactly offset the change in return which should be achieved from such a change. For example, it would only be logical for a company to borrow funds (at, say, 10 per cent per annum) if it had identified uses for those funds which were expected to generate a return in excess of the borrowing costs (say, 15 per cent per annum); consequently the use of debt finance *should* result in an increase in the return on the *equity* funds invested in the business. However, the increase in the leverage ratio of the company *will* result in a proportional increase in the required return on this equity due to an increased perception of risk on the part of the shareholders. If these two impacts exactly counterbalance each other, as they should given the underlying assumption of perfectly functioning capital markets, the particular capital structure of a company will not affect the value of the equity in the company. Thus the theoretical result of this proposition should not be regarded as too surprising.

However, as stated in their paper, these propositions were significantly at odds with accepted views at this time. Therefore, they were worthy of empirical observations and testing; this raises the very important issue of the difficulty of testing such propositions in the real capital markets. At first sight their third proposition appears a more attractive opportunity for empirical investigation, as it states that 'the cut-off point for investment in the firm will in all cases be the market capitalization rate for the company and will be completely unaffected by the type of security used to finance the investment'. If companies did not apply this rate of return for investment decisions, it might be possible to detect changes in the value of the company; however, these investment decisions are based on expected returns whereas only actual returns can be observed and, often, the required rate of return used internally by the company is not disclosed to the shareholders. It is also important to remember that Modigliani and Miller were not saying that the types of financial instrument used to finance any particular investment were of no importance to the company; their argument was that they were irrelevant to the evaluation of the decision as to whether to invest or not.

Following the publication of this original paper, Modigliani and Miller produced an article in 1963 which corrected errors in this original work relating to the impact of taxation on the cost of debt. They had accepted that the distortion caused by the tax deductibility of interest expenses for companies would 'prevent the arbitrage process from making the value of all firms in a given class proportional to the expected returns generated by their physical assets', but their original adjustment for this distortion was wrong. The 1963 paper, which is included as the second article in Part Five, corrected the detailed equations used to describe all three propositions for their updated view of the impact of taxation. The impact of the amendments was not to destroy the main thrust of their arguments, but the scale of their difference from traditional thinking was reduced somewhat. For example, the corrected statement is that a firm's value is independent of its capital structure except for the value added by the present value of the tax shields on interest. In the second paper, reference is also made (albeit obliquely) to the now commonly used expression – weighted average cost of capital.

This work on capital structure has proved remarkably resilient as can be evidenced by its still very high occurrence as a reference in modern writings. The third article in Part Five, which dates from 1984, uses these papers as a major base and also gives a brief review of how the subject had developed in the ensuing twenty years, including the absence of effective research testing. However, the main reason for including S. Myers' paper is that it advances an alternative framework to try to explain the actual behaviour of companies with regard to their capital structures. The traditional view of capital structure was that companies established 'a target debt to value ratio and gradually moved towards it'. Under the alternative 'pecking order' framework, advanced by G. Donaldson in 1961 as Myers notes, the company has no well-defined target debt to value ratio but does have an established hierarchy of preferred sources of funding which places new equity issues at the bottom of the list.

Myers' paper starts with a clear summary of the 'developed' view of Modigliani and Miller's theory which includes an initial increase in the market value of the firm when debt financing is introduced, due to the value of the tax shelter available on interest payments. At the other extreme, the market value of the company can be driven down because an excessive level of debt gives rise to concerns regarding the possibility of financial distress or bankruptcy, with the consequent associated costs. These opposite impacts indicate that there should, in an ideal world, be an optimum debt to equity structure for any company.

The 'pecking order' theory is developed from a practical analysis of how companies are observed to behave and Myers gives a brief review of the supporting literature. However, the development in this paper is the proposal of a theoretical foundation to this theory, which is based on the existence of 'asymmetric information'. Asymmetric information simply means that managers have a far better level of information regarding the actual current performance and future prospects for the company than investors; in particular, managers 'know' whether the shares in the company are currently undervalued or overvalued. This asymmetry will affect the behaviour of both parties regarding the type of funding which will be offered to, and taken up by, investors. It also suggests the role of dividend policy as a signalling device by managers.

The theory is an attempt to explain the observed tendency for companies to prefer internal resources (i.e. retained earnings which is of course equity) to external, and why if external sources are used companies tend to raise debt. In the article it is admitted that this theory does not explain all behaviours which can be observed, but it does represent an alternative to the normal view.

More complex and sophisticated financial products

The continuing debates regarding the impact of capital structure and dividend policies on equity values have not been aided by the difficulty of conducting valid empirical research with which to support the alternative conceptual arguments. This can be contrasted with the development of the financial markets for derivatives where, it can be argued, the dramatic growth in the volumes of traded options and other financial derivative products has been significantly helped by the advances in valuation frameworks and detailed models.

Varying types of pricing models for options had been around since 1900 when F. Black and M. Scholes, in 1973, published their version of a valuation model for call options on non-dividend paying equity shares. (This paper is included as the first article in Part Six, unfortunately space does not allow the inclusion of the contemporaneous paper by R. Merton which also developed a rational theory of option pricing.) This restriction to shares which generated no cash income to their holders was important, as the valuation of options on income producing assets is more complicated. (It should be remembered that, according to Modigliani and Miller and many others, cash dividend payments are irrelevant to the overall value of the investment but, even under their theory, significantly do affect option values. Option holders do not receive the cash dividends but the price of the assets, which they have a right to buy in the future at a fixed exercise price, should fall by a corresponding amount; hence the value of their option declines.)

The value drivers for options are relatively straightforward; the problem is to turn these value drivers into a predictive mathematical relationship. An option is a right to buy or sell an asset within a specified period of time at a given price (the exercise or striking price of the option). Clearly the length of the period involved (the unexpired life of the option) has a significant impact on the value of an option, but the real advantage of an option is that it enables the holder to defer the buy or sell decision until they have seen which way, and to what extent, the price of the asset moves. Consequently the unexpired life of the option must be related to the volatility of the asset price per time period, and these factors will combine to determine the value of the option. However, an option will only be exercised if the asset price crosses the exercise price (i.e. a call option is only exercised if the asset price is above the exercise price, otherwise the option is simply allowed to lapse; conversely for a put option), and therefore the relationship between the exercise price and the current asset price is also a factor in determining the value of the option. This exercise price is only paid or received when the option is actually exercised, so that the relevant comparison is between the present value of the exercise price (using the risk free cost of money as the discount rate) and the current asset price.

Black and Scholes based their valuation model on these underlying value drivers but they needed to make several simplifying assumptions in order to derive a balanced hedge position incorporating inverse positions in the stock and a weighted number of the options on the stock from which their famous model was developed. Their original derivation relied on the use of stochastic calculus but subsequently their formula has been derived using less complex mathematics. This work has in fact shown that the Black Scholes option valuation model (which is based on continuous variables) is a special limiting case of a more generally binomially based model which can be applied to discrete time periods. Once again space precludes the inclusion of these later models such as that developed in 1979 by Cox, Ross and Rubinstein. Black and Scholes also discussed the relevance of option theory to the valuation of many other types of corporate financial instruments and this concept is now widely used and accepted; e.g. the equity in a leveraged company can be regarded as a call option on the assets of the company with an exercise price equal to the required principal repayment of the debt. (In fact in the case of an interest bearing debt instrument, a complex or compound option is created which is an option on an option etc. because each interest payment can be regarded as giving the shareholders an option.) They conceded in their article that their valuation formula was not valid for complex options such as are created by convertible bonds or preference shares.

Not surprisingly, the Black and Scholes option valuation model generated a great deal of work in this area and their model was developed, generalized, and modified in attempts to take account of many of the simplifications and restrictions within the original framework. A major challenge was in applying this framework to the valuation of convertible bonds because, as well as being an increasingly common capital market product, they involve a dual option of either conversion into equity at the option of the holder or of a call redemption option on the part of the issuer. (This call redemption option is normally subject to restrictions of either time and/or market value of the underlying financial product, such as the equity into which the bond would convert.) This problem was tackled by M. Brennan and E. Schwartz and their paper is included as the second article in Part Six. They attempted to develop optimal call and conversion strategies in the case of interest bearing convertible bonds issued by dividend paying companies; in other words in a much less restricted environment than used for the development of the original formula.

The basis for their argument is that each party (i.e. the issuer and the investor) 'pursues an optimal strategy and expects the other party to do the same'; what is described as 'symmetric market rationality'. The optimal strategies are clearly diametrically opposed in that the investor will seek a conversion strategy which maximizes the value of the bond while the issuer will try to minimize the value of the bond through the exercise of their call redemption option. Their analysis derived boundaries for the valuation of the convertible bond as each of the value drivers changes in value and hence in overall impact; by applying detailed numerical analysis to the specifics of any case, Brennan and Schwartz demonstrate how a valuation could be derived for even complicated convertible bonds.

This is an area which has seen a great deal of applied research due to the massive values of derivatives which are traded on a daily basis. However, even the application of powerful computer models cannot guarantee the achievement of a consistent super profit from such trading, because the market value will be primarily driven by perceptions of risk and future volatility (not by the historic levels which can be analysed). This dependence upon value drivers which *cannot* be measured is one of the great attractions of finance as an area of study; long may it continue so that finance remains an exciting enigma with many more questions than answers despite an increasing wealth of empirical research.

Part 2
Increasing Shareholder Value

2 Corporate strategy and the capital budgeting decision

A. C. Shapiro

The decade 1974 through 1983 was a dismal one for American business in general. It began with the deepest economic decline since the Depression and ended with national recoveries from back-to-back recessions in the early 1980s. Yet throughout these dark years, 13 companies on the Fortune 500 list of the largest US industrial companies were money-making stars, earning consistently high returns. These firms averaged at least a 20 percent return on shareholders' equity (ROE) over this ten-year span. (To gain some perspective, a dollar invested in 1974 at a compound annual rate of 20 percent would have grown to $6.19 by the end of 1983, a healthy return even after allowing for the effects of inflation.) Moreover, none of these firms' ROE ever dipped below 15 percent during this difficult period.

The 13 were led by a profit superstar, American Home Products, whose ROE not only averaged 29.5 percent during the 1974–83 decade, but also has held above 20 percent for 30 straight years. To appreciate the significance of such a feat, one dollar invested at 20 percent compounded annually would be worth over $237 at the end of 30 years.

What type of firm can achieve such a remarkable record? Far from being the prototypical high-tech firm or a lucky oil company, American Home Products is the low-profile producer of Anacin, Chef Boy-Ar-Dee pasta products, Brach's candy, and Gulden's mustard, in addition to prescription drugs and non-drug products such as cardiovascular drugs, oral contraceptives, and infant formula.

In general, high technology firms were not well represented among the 13, which included just IBM and two pharmaceutical companies, SmithKline Beckman and Merck. IBM, moreover, with an average ROE of 20.5 percent, ranked only 11th out of the 13, far behind such low-tech firms as Dow Jones (26.3%), Kellogg (24.8%), Deluxe Check Printers (24.1%), and Maytag (23.1%). It was even less profitable than a steel company (Worthington Industries – 23.9%) and a chemical firm (Nalco Chemical – 21.5%)).

The demonstrated ability of a firm such as Deluxe Check Printers – a firm on the trailing edge of technology, described as a 'buggy whip company threatened with extinction by the "checkless society"' – consistently to earn such extraordinary returns on invested capital must be due to something more than luck or proficiency at applying sophisticated techniques of investment analysis. That something is the knack for creating positive net present value (NPV) projects, projects with rates of return in excess of the required return. The scarcity of this skill is attested to by the fact that aggregate profits of $68.8 billion for the Fortune 500 in 1983 were, in real terms, 22 percent below the $43.6 billion earned in 1974, a recession year. Keep in mind also that the Fortune 500 have been disciplined savers, re-investing over $300 billion of retained earnings in their businesses over the ten-year period. This massive reinvestment alone should have produced considerably higher real earnings than 1974's.

This evidence notwithstanding, it is usually taken for granted that positive NPV projects do exist and can be identified using fairly straightforward techniques. Consequently, the emphasis in most capital budgeting analyses is

---

13 Stars of the Decade 1974–1983

Company	*Average ROE 1974–1983*	*Total return to investors 1974–1983**
American Home Products	**29.5%**	**6.6%**
Dow Jones	26.3%	29.8%
Mitchell Energy	**26.0%**	**26.4%**
SmithKline Beckman	25.4%	19.7%
Kellogg	**24.8%**	**13.3%**
Deluxe Check Printers	24.1%	13.4%
Worthington Industries	**23.9%**	**41.7%**
Maytag	23.1%	14.5%
Merck	**21.9%**	**3.8%**
Nalco Chemical	21.5%	11.4%
IBM	**20.5%**	**11.3%**
Dover	20.3%	26.6%
Coca-Cola	**20.3%**	**2.9%**
Median total return to investors for the 13:	13.4%	
Median total return to investors for the Fortune 500:	13.6%	

* Total return to investors as calculated by *Fortune*, April 30, 1984. It includes both price appreciation and dividend yield to an investor and assumes that any proceeds from cash dividends, the sale or rights and warrant offerings, and stock received in spinoffs were reinvested at the end of the year in which they were received. The return reported is the average annual return compounded over the ten-year period.

Although the 13 have earned extraordinary returns on shareholders' equity capital, Exhibit 1 shows that returns to the shareholders themselves have been less than earthshaking. This is consistent with the efficient market hypothesis, the idea that prices of traded securities rapidly reflect all currently available information. Since the high return on equity capital earned by the 13 is not news to investors – these firms have consistently been outstanding performers – investors back in 1974 had already incorporated these expectations in their estimations of firm values. This means that a firm's expected high ROE is already "priced out" or capitalized by the market at a rate that reflects the anticipated riskiness of investing in the company's stock. As a result, investors will earn exceptional returns only if the firm turns out to do even better than expected, something that by definition is not possible to predict in advance. The fact that the 13's median annual total return to investors (stock price appreciation plus reinvested dividends) of 13.4 percent is almost identical to the Fortune 500's median return of 13.6 percent indicates that investor expectations about the relative performances of both groups of firms were subsequently borne out.

This illustrates the key distinction between operating in an efficient financial market and operating in product and factor markets that are less than perfectly competitive. One can expect to consistently earn excess returns only in the latter markets; competition will ensure that excess returns in an efficient market are short-lived. However it is evident from the generally dismal performance of the Fortune 500 that it is no mean trick to take advantage of those product and factor market imperfections that do exist.

on estimating and discounting future project cash flows. Projects with positive net present values are accepted; those that fail this test are rejected.

It is important to recognize, however, that selecting positive NPV projects in this way is equivalent to picking under-valued securities on the basis of fundamental analysis. The latter can be done with confidence only if there are financial market imperfections that do not allow asset prices to reflect their equilibrium values. Similarly, the existence of economic rents – excess returns that lead to positive net present values – is the result of monopolistic control over product or factor supplies (i.e. 'real market imperfections').

It is the thesis of this article that generating projects likely to yield positive excess returns is at least as important as the conventional quantitative investment analysis. This is the essence of corporate strategy: creating and then taking advantage of imperfections in product and factor markets. Thus, an understanding of the strategies followed by successful firms in exploiting and defending those barriers to entry created by product and factor market imperfections is crucial to any systematic evaluation of investment opportunities. For one thing, it provides a qualitative means of identifying, or ranking, ex ante those projects most likely to have positive net present values. This ranking is useful because constraints of time and money limit the number and range of investment opportunities a given firm is likely to consider.

More important, a good understanding of corporate strategy should help uncover new and potentially profitable projects. Only in theory is a firm fortunate enough to be presented, at no effort or expense on its part, with every available investment opportunity. Perhaps the best way to gain this understanding is to study a medley of firms, spanning a number of industries and nations, that have managed to develop and implement a variety of value-creating investment strategies. This is the basic approach taken here.

The first section discusses what happens to economic rents over time, and thus to opportunities for positive NPV projects, in a competitive industry. The second section considers in more detail the nature of market imperfections that give rise to economic rents and how one can design investments to exploit those imperfections. The third section presents the available evidence on the relationship between various competitive advantages and rates of return on invested capital. The fourth introduces a normative approach to strategic planning and investment analysis. The fifth and final section deals with the rationale and means for domestic firms to evolve into multinational corporations.

Competitive markets and excess returns

A perfectly competitive industry is one characterized by costless entry and exit, undifferentiated products, and increasing marginal costs of production. These undifferentiated products, also known as commodities, are sold exclusively on the basis of price. In such an industry, as every student of micro-economics knows, each firm produces at the point at which price equals marginal cost. Long-run equilibrium exists when price also equals average cost. At this point, total revenue equals total cost for each firm taken individually and for the industry as a whole. This cost includes the required return on the capital used by each firm. Thus, in the long run, the actual return on capital in a competitive industry must equal the required return.

Any excess return quickly attracts new entrants to the market. Their additional capacity and attempts to gain market share lead to a reduction in the industry price and a lowering of returns for all market participants. In the early 1980s, for example, the high returns available in the video-game market, combined with the ease of entry into the business, attracted a host of competitors. This led to a red-ink bath for the industry in 1983, followed by the exit of a number of firms from the industry. Conversely, should the actual return for the industry be below the required return, the opposite happens. The weakest competitors exit the industry, resulting in an increase in the industry price and a boost in the overall return on capital for the remaining firms. This process, which is now taking place in the oil refining business, continues until the actual return once again equals the required return.

The message from this analysis is clear: the run-of-the-mill firm operating in a highly competitive, commodity-type industry is doomed from the start in its search for positive net present value projects. Only firms that can bring to bear on new projects competitive advantages that are difficult to replicate have any assurance of earning excess returns in the long run. These advantages take the form of either being the low-cost producer in the industry or being able to add value to the product – value for which customers are willing to pay a high (relative to cost) price. The latter type of advantage involves the ability to convert a commodity business into one characterized by products differentiated on the basis of service and/or quality. By creating such advantages, a firm can impose barriers to entry by potential competitors, resulting in a less-than-perfectly competitive market and the possibility of positive NPV projects.

Barriers to entry and positive net present value projects

As we have just seen, the ability to discourage new entrants to the market by erecting barriers to entry is the key to earning rates of return that consistently exceed capital costs. If these barriers did not exist, new competitors would enter the market and drive down the rate of return to the required return. High barriers to entry and the threat of a strong reaction from entrenched competitors will reduce the risk of entry and so prolong the opportunity to earn excess returns.

This analysis suggests that successful investments (those with positive NPVs) share a common characteristic: they are investments that involve creating, preserving, and even enhancing competitive advantages that serve as barriers to entry. In line with this conclusion, the successful companies described by Thomas Peters and Robert Waterman in their best seller, *In Search of Excellence*, were able to define their strengths – marketing, customer contact, new product innovation, low-cost manufacturing, etc. – and then build on them. They have resisted the temptation to move into new businesses that look attractive but require corporate skills they do not have.

A clearer understanding of the potential barriers to competitive entry can help to identify potential value-creating investment opportunities. This section now takes a closer look at the five major sources of barriers to entry – economies of scale, product differentiation, cost disadvantages, access to distribution channels, and government policy – and suggests some lessons for successful investing.[1]

Economies of scale

Economies of scale exist whenever a given increase in the scale of production, marketing, or distribution results in a less-than-proportional increase in cost. The existence of scale economies means that there are *inherent cost advantages in being large*. The more significant these scale economies, therefore, the greater the cost disadvantage faced by a new entrant to the market. Scale economies in marketing, service, research, and production are probably the principal barriers to entry in the mainframe computer industry, as GE, RCA, and Xerox discovered to their sorrow. It is estimated, for example, that IBM spent over $5 billion to develop its innovative System 360, which it brought out in 1963. In natural resource industries, firms such as Alcan, the Canadian aluminum company, and Exxon are able to fend off new market entrants by exploiting economies of scale in production and transportation.

High capital requirements go hand-in-hand with economies of scale. In order to take advantage of scale economies in production, marketing, or new product development, firms must often make enormous up-front investments in plant and equipment, research and development, and advertising. These capital requirements themselves serve as a barrier to entry; the more capital required, the higher the barrier to entry. This is particularly true in industries such as petroleum refining, mineral extraction, and mainframe computers.

A potential entrant to a market characterized by scale economies in production will be reluctant to enter unless the market has grown sufficiently to permit the construction and profitable utilization of an economically-sized plant. Otherwise, the new entrant will have to cut price to gain market share, destroying in the process the possibility of abnormal profits. By expanding in line with growth in the market, therefore, entrenched competitors can preempt profitable market entry by new competitors.

---

[1] See, for example, Michael E. Porter 'How Competitive Forces Shape Strategy', *Harvard Business Review*, March–April 1979, pp. 137–145 for a good summary and discussion of these barriers to entry and their implications for corporate strategy.

Consider, for example, the economics of the cement industry. The low value-to-weight ratio of cement makes the cement business a very regional one; beyond a radius of about 150 to 200 miles from the cement plant, the costs of transport become prohibitive unless cheap water or rail transportation is available. At the same time, the significant economies of scale available in cement production limit the number of plants a given region can support. For instance, suppose that demand in a land-locked region is sufficient to support only one or two modern cement plants. By expanding production and adding substantial new capacity to that already available, a firm can significantly raise the price of market entry by new firms and make plant expansion or replacement by existing competitors look much less attractive. This type of move obviously requires a longer timeframe and the willingness to incur potential losses until the market grows larger.

Scale economies are all-important in the grocery retailing business, on the level of the individual store as well as the city-wide market. Whether a store has $100,000 or $10,000,000 in annual sales, it still needs a manger. In addition, the cost of constructing and outfitting a supermarket doesn't increase in proportion to the number of square feet of selling space. Thus, the ratio of expenses to sales exhibits a significant decline as the volume of sales rises.

Similarly, whether it has 10 percent or 25 percent of a given market, a supermarket chain has to advertise and supply its stores from a warehouse. The higher the share of market, the lower the advertising cost per customer, the faster the warehouse will turn over its inventory, and the more likely its delivery trucks will be used to capacity. These cost efficiencies translate directly into a higher return on capital.

The relationship between the market dominance of a supermarket chain in a given market and its profitability is evident in the relative returns for firms following contrasting expansion strategies. Chains such as Kroger and Winn-Dixie, which have opted for deep market penetration in a limited geographic area (ranking number 1 or 2 in almost all their major markets), have realized returns on equity that far exceeded their equity costs. On the other hand, chains such as A&P and National Tea, which expanded nationally by gaining toe-hold positions in numerous, though scattered markets, have consistently earned less than their required returns.

Computer store chains, to take another example, also enjoy significant economies of scale. These show up in the form of lower average costs for advertising, distribution, and training. Even more important, they receive larger discounts on their products from the manufacturers.

LESSON #1: *Investments that are structured to fully exploit econo-mies of scale are more likely to be successful than those that are not.*

Product differentiation

Some companies, such as Coca-Cola and Procter and Gamble, take advantage of *enormous advertising expenditures* and *highly-developed marketing skills* to differentiate their products and keep out potential competitors wary of the high marketing costs and risks of new product introduction. Others sell expertise and high-quality products and service. For example, Nalco Chemical, a specialty chemical firm, is a problem-solver and counselor to its customers while Worthington Industries, which turns semifinished steel into finished steel, has a reputation for quality workmanship that allows it to charge premium prices. As indicated in the introduction to this article, both have been handsomely rewarded for their efforts, with average equity returns exceeding 20 percent annually from 1974 to 1983.

Pharmaceutical companies have traditionally earned high returns by developing unique products that are protected from competition by patents, trademarks, and brand names. Three outstanding examples are SmithKline Beckman's Tagamet, for treating stomach ulcers, and Hoffman-La Roche's tranquilizers, Librium and Valium. American Home Products also owes a great deal of its profitability to several patented drugs.

Similarly, the development of technologically-innovative products has led to high profits for firms such as Xerox and Philips (Netherlands). A fat R&D budget, however, is only part of the activity leading to commercially successful innovations. To a great extent, the risks in R&D are commercial, not technical. Firms that make technology pay off are those that closely link their R&D activities with market realities. They always ask what the customer needs. Even if they have strong technology, they do their marketing homework. This requires close contact with customers, as well as careful monitoring of the competition. Studies also indicate that top management involvement is extremely important in those firms that rely heavily and effectively on technology as a competitive weapon. This requires close coordination and communication between technical and business managers.

Failure to heed that message has led to Xerox's inability to replicate its earlier success in the photocopy business. In addition to its revolutionary copier technology, Xerox developed some of the computer industry's most important breakthroughs, including the first personal computer and the first network connecting office machines. But, through a lack of market support, it has consistently failed to convert its research prowess into successful high-tech products.

Service is clearly the key to extraordinary profitability for many firms. The ability to differentiate its computers from others through exceptional service has enabled IBM to dominate the worldwide mainframe computer business with a market share of over 75 percent. Similarly, Caterpillar Tractor has combined dedication to quality with outstanding distribution and after-market support to differentiate its line of construction equipment and so gain a commanding 35 percent share of the world market for earth-moving machinery. American firms, such as the auto companies, that have been somewhat lax in the area of product quality have fallen prey to those Japanese firms for which quality has become a religion.

What may not be obvious from these examples is that it is possible to differentiate anything, even commodity businesses such as fast food, potato chips, theme parks, candy bars, and printing. The answer seems to be quality and service as companies like McDonald's, Disney, Frito-Lay, Mars, and Deluxe Check Printers have demonstrated. Cleanliness and consistency of service are the hallmarks of Disney and McDonald's, with both rating at the top of almost everyone's list as the best mass service providers in the world. Similarly, it is said that at Mars plants are kept so clean one can 'eat off the factory floor'.

High quality work and dependability have helped Deluxe Check Printers flourish in a world supposedly on the verge of doing without checks. It fills better than 95 percent of orders in two days, and ships 99 percent error free.

Frito-Lay's special edge is a highly-motivated 10,000 person sales force dedicated to selling its chips. They guarantee urban supermarkets and rural mom and pop stores alike a 99.5 percent chance of a daily call. Although they get only a small weekly salary, the sales people receive a 10 percent commission on all the Lay's, Doritos, and Tostitos they sell. So they hustle, setting up displays, helping the manager in any way possible, all the while angling for that extra foot of shelf space or preferred position that can mean additional sales income. There are also tremendous side benefits to close contact with the market. Frito can get a market test rolling in ten days and respond to a new competitive intrusion in 48 hours.

A similar level of service is provided by Sysco, a $2 billion firm in the business of wholesaling food to restaurants and other institutional business. It is a very mundane, low-margin business – one where low cost is seemingly all that matters. Yet, behind its slogan, 'Don't sell food, sell peace of mind', Sysco earns margins and a return on capital that is the envy of the industry. Even in that business, a large number of customers will pay a little more for personalized service. And in a low-margin business, a little more goes a long way.

Sysco's secret was to put together a force of over 2,000 'marketing associates' who assure customers that '98 percent of items will be delivered on time'. They also provide much more, going to extraordinary lengths to produce a needed item for a restauranteur at a moment's notice. Chairman John Baugh summed it up as follows:

The typical food service company picks a case of frozen french fries out of the warehouse and drops it on the restaurant's back porch. Where is the skill in that?

Where is the creativity? Service isn't a free lunch. The price tag (and cost) is higher; but even at the lower end of the market, most customers (not all, to be sure) will pay some additional freight for useful service.[2]

Other firms have made their owners wealthy by understanding that they too are *selling solutions to their customers' problems*, not hardware or consumables. John Patterson, the founder of National Cash Register, used to tell salesmen: 'Don't talk machines, talk the prospect's business'. Thomas Watson, the founder of IBM, patterned his sales strategy on that admonition. Thus, while other companies were talking technical specifications, his salesmen were marketing solutions to understood problems, such as making sure the payroll checks came out on time.

These days, Rolm Corp., a leader in the crowded market for office communications systems, is taking a page out of IBM's book. It has built up a service force of over 3,400 employees whose main job is to reassure customers mystified by the complexities of modern technology, while selling them more equipment. The common strategic vision and approaches of the two firms may help explain why IBM, when it decided to enter the telecommunications business, did so by acquiring Rolm (in 1984) rather than another firm.

The contrast between the approaches followed by IBM and DEC is particularly revealing. DEC has developed excellent narrow-purpose mini-computers, trusting that application solutions can be developed by others to justify advanced technology. That simple strategy – selling machines on their merits to scientists and engineers – worked spectacularly for two decades, turning DEC into the world's second-largest computer company. One consequence of that strategy, however, is that DEC never needed to and never did develop the kind of marketing orientation IBM is noted for.

The advent of the personal computer, which can perform many of the functions of a minicomputer at a fraction of the cost, has underscored the shortcomings inherent in DEC's product- rather than market-oriented strategy. As its traditional business has stagnated, DEC has attempted to reposition itself to compete in the nimble new world of personal computers. But it has failed thus far to adapt marketing and sales strategies to the new, less technically-sophisticated customers it has tried to attract.

The results are painfully obvious. On October 18, 1983, DEC's stock nose-dived 21 points after it announced that quarterly earnings would be 75 percent lower than the year before. Thus far at least, IBM, and its strategy of utilizing proven technology to market solutions to known problems, has prevailed in the marketplace.

---

[2] Quoted in *Forbes*, October 11, 1982, p. 58.

LESSON #2: Investments designed to create a position at the high end of anything, including the high end of the low end, differentiated by a quality or service edge, will generally be profitable.

Cost disadvantages

Entrenched companies often have cost advantages that are unavailable to potential entrants, independent of economies of scale. Sony and Texas Instruments, for example, take advantage of the *learning curve* to reduce costs and drive out actual and potential competitors. This concept is based on the old adage that you improve with practice. With greater production experience, costs can be expected to decrease because of more efficient use of labor and capital, improved plant layout and production methods, product redesign and standardization, and the substitution of less expensive materials and practices. This cost decline creates a barrier to entry because new competitors, lacking experience, face higher unit costs than established companies. By achieving market leadership, usually by price cutting, and thereby accumulating experience faster, this entry barrier can be most effectively exploited.

Proprietary technology, protected by legally-enforceable patents, provides another cost advantage to established companies. This is the avenue taken by many of the premiere companies in the world, including 3M, West Germany's Siemens, Japan's Hitachi, and Sweden's L.M. Ericsson.

Monopoly control of low-cost raw materials is another cost advantage open to entrenched firms. This was the advantage held for so many years by Aramco (Arabian-American Oil Company), the consortium of oil companies that until the early 1980s had exclusive access to low-cost Saudi Arabian oil.

McDonald's has developed yet another advantage vis-à-vis potential competitors: it has already acquired, at a relatively low cost, many of the best fast-food restaurant locations. Favorable locations are also important to supermarkets and department stores.

A major cost advantage enjoyed by IBM's personal computer is the fact that software programs are produced first for it since it has a commanding share of the market. Only later – if at all – are these programs, which now number in the thousands, rewritten for other brands. Companies that don't develop IBM look-alikes must either write their own software, pay to have existing software modified for their machines, or wait until the software houses get around to rewriting their programs.

Sometimes, however, new entrants enjoy a cost advantage over existing competitors. This is especially true in industries undergoing deregulation, such as the airlines and trucking. In both of these industries, regulation long insulated firms from the rigors of competition and fare wars. Protected as they were, carriers had little incentive to clamp down on costs. And still they were quite profitable. The excess returns provided by the regulatory barrier to entry were divided in effect between the firms' stockholders and their unionized employees.

Deregulation has exposed these firms to new competitors not saddled with outmoded work rules and high-cost employees. For example, new low-cost competitors in the airline industry, such as People's Express and Southwest Airlines, have much lower wages (about half of what big airlines pay) and more flexible work rules (which, for example, permit pilots to load baggage and flight attendants to man reservations phones).

One firm that managed to stay ahead of the game is Northwest Airlines. For years, Northwest has been run as if competition were fierce, while still making the most of the protections of regulations. It gained a reputation for fighting labor-union demands and hammered away to increase productivity. As a result, Northwest's overhead costs are only about 2 percent of total costs, compared with about 5 percent for major competitors. Similarly, its labor costs are about two-thirds the industry average. Consequently, it is the most efficient of the major airlines, which has greatly enhanced its competitive position.

LESSON #3: Investments aimed at achieving the lowest delivered cost position in the industry, coupled with a pricing policy to expand market share, are likely to succeed, especially if the cost reductions are proprietary.

Access to distribution channels

Gaining distribution and shelf space for their products is a major hurdle that newcomers to an industry must overcome. Most retailers of personal computers, for example, limit their inventory to around five lines. Currently, over 200 manufacturers are competing for this very limited amount of shelf space. Moreover, the concentration of retail outlets among chains means that new computer makers have even fewer avenues to the consumer. This presents new manufacturers with a Catch-22: you don't get shelf space until you are a proven winner, but you can't sell until you get shelf space.

Conversely, well-developed, better yet unique, distribution channels are a major source of competitive advantage for firms such as Avon, Tupperware, Procter and Gamble, and IBM. Avon, for example, markets its products directly to the consumer on a house-to-house basis through an international network of 900,000 independent sales representatives. Using direct sales has enabled Avon to reduce both its advertising expenditures and the amount of money it has tied up in the business. Potential competitors face the daunting task of organizing, financing, and motivating an equivalent sales force. Thus, its independent representatives are the entry barrier that allows Avon consistently to earn exceptional profit margins in a highly competitive industry. Similarly, the sales forces of Frito-Lay, Sysco, and IBM help those firms distribute their products and raise the entry barrier in three very diverse businesses.

Conversely, the lack of a significant marketing presence in the US is perhaps the greatest hindrance to Japanese drug makers attempting to expand their presence in the UK. Marketing drugs in the US requires considerable political skill in maneuvering through the US regulatory process, as well as rapport with American researchers and doctors. This latter requirement means that pharmaceutical firms must develop extensive sales forces to maintain close contact with their customers. There are economies of scale here: the cost of developing such a sales force is the same, whether it sells one product or one hundred. Thus, only firms with extensive product lines can afford a large sales force, raising a major entry barrier to Japanese drug firms trying to go it alone in the US.

One way the Japanese drug firms have found to get around this entry barrier is to form joint ventures with American drug firms, in which the Japanese supply the patents and the American firms provide the distribution network. Such licensing arrangements are a common means of entering markets requiring strong distribution capabilities. Union Carbide, for example, follows a strategy of using high R&D expenditures to generate a diversified and innovative line of new products. Since each new product line requires a different marketing strategy and distribution network, firms like Union Carbide are more willing to trade their technology for royalty payments and equity in a joint venture with companies already in the industry.

LESSON #4: Investments devoted to gaining better product distribution often lead to higher profitability.

Government policy

We have already seen in the case of the airline, trucking, and pharmaceutical industries that government regulations can limit, or even foreclose, entry to potential competitors. Other government policies that raise partial or absolute barriers to entry include import restrictions, environmental controls, and licensing requirements. For example, American quotas on Japanese cars have limited the ability of companies such as Mitsubishi and Mazda to expand their sales in the US, leading to a higher return on investment for American car companies. Similarly, environmental regulations that restrict the development of new quarries have greatly benefited those firms, such as Vulcan Materials, that already had operating quarries. The effects of licensing restrictions on the taxi business in New York City are reflected in the high price of a medallion (giving one the right to operate a cab there), which in turn reflects the higher fares that the absence of competition has resulted in.

A change in government regulations can greatly affect the value of current and prospective investments in an industry. For example, the Motor Carrier Act of 1935 set up a large barrier to entry into the business as it allowed the Interstate Commerce Commission to reject applicants to the industry. The Act also allowed the truckers themselves to determine their rates collectively, typically on the basis of average operating efficiency. Thus carriers with below-average operating costs were able to sustain above-average levels of profitability. It is scarcely surprising, then, that the major trucking companies pulled out all the stops in lobbying against deregulation. As expected, the onset of trucking deregulation, which greatly reduced the entry barrier, has led to lower profits for trucking companies and a significant drop in their stock prices.

LESSON #5: Investments in projects protected from competition by government regulation can lead to extraordinary profitability. However, what the government gives, the government can take away.

Investment strategies and financial returns: some evidence

Ultimately, the viability of a value-creating strategy can only be assessed by examining the empirical evidence. Theory and intuition tell us that companies which follow strategies geared towards creating and preserving competitive advantages should earn higher returns on their investments than those which do not. And so they do.

William K. Hall studied eight major domestic US industries and the diverse strategies followed by member firms.[3] The period selected for this study was 1975–1979, a time of slow economic growth and high inflation. These were

---

[3] William K. Hall, 'Survival Strategies in a Hostile Environment', *Harvard Business Review*, September-October 1980, pp. 75–85.

especially hard times for the eight basic industries in Hall's study. They all faced significant cost increases that they were unable to offset fully through price increases. In addition, companies in each of these industries were forced by regulatory agencies to make major investments to comply with a variety of health, environmental, safety, and product performance standards. To compound their problems, competition from abroad grew stronger during this period. Foreign competitors achieved high market shares in three of the industries (steel, tire and rubber, and automotive); moderate shares in two others (heavy-duty trucks and construction and materials handling equipment); and entry positions in the other three (major home appliances, beer, and cigarettes).

The net result of these adverse trends is that profitability in the eight basic industries has generally fallen to or below the average for manufacturers in the United States. According to Table 1, the average return on equity for these eight industries was 12.9 percent, substantially below the 15.1 percent median return for the Fortune 1000. A number of firms in these industries have gone bankrupt, are in financial distress, or have exited their industry.

Table 1   Return on equity in eight basic industries: 1975–1979*

Industry	Return on equity	Leading firm	Return on equity
Steel	7.1%	Inland Steel	10.9%
Tire and rubber	**7.4**	**Goodyear**	**9.2**
Heavy-duty trucks	15.4	Paccar	22.8
Construction and materials handling equipment	**15.4**	**Caterpillar**	**23.5**
Automotive	15.4	General Motors	19.8
Major home appliances	**10.1**	**Maytag**	**27.2**
Beer	14.1	G. Heilman Brewing	25.8
Cigarettes	**18.2**	**Philip Morris**	**22.7**
Average – eight industries	**12.9**	*Average – leading companies*	**20.2**
Median – Fortune 1000	**15.1**		

* From William K. Hall, 'Survival Strategies in a Hostile Environment'

Yet this tells only part of the story. As Table 1 also shows, some companies survived, indeed prospered, in this same hostile environment. They did this by developing business strategies geared towards achieving one or both of the following competitive positions within their respective industries and then single-mindedly tailoring their investments to attain these positions:

1 Become the lowest total delivered cost producer in the industry, while maintaining an acceptable service/quality combination relative to competition.
2 Develop the highest product/service/quality differentiated position within the industry, while maintaining an acceptable delivered cost structure.

Table 2 provides a rough categorization of the strategies employed by the two top-performing companies in each of the eight industries studied. In most cases, the industry profit leaders chose to occupy only one of the two competitive positions. Perhaps this is because the resources and skills necessary to achieve a low-cost position are incompatible with those needed to attain a strongly differentiated position.

Table 2   Competitive strategies employed by leaders in eight basic industries*

Industry	Low cost leader	Meaningful differentiation	Both employed simultaneously
Steel	Inland Steel	National	–
Tire and rubber	**Goodyear**	**Michelin (French)**	
Heavy-duty trucks	Ford, Daimler Benz (German)	–	–
Construction and materials handling equipment	–	**John Deere**	**Caterpillar**
Automotive	General Motors	Daimler Benz	–
Major home appliances	**Whirlpool**	**Maytag**	–
Beer	Miller	G. Heilman Brewing	–
Cigarettes	**R. J. Reynolds**	–	**Philip Morris**

* From William K. Hall, 'Survival Strategies in a Hostile Environment'

At least three of the 16 leaders, however, combined elements of both strategies with spectacular success. Caterpillar has combined lowest-cost manufacturing with outstanding distribution and after-sales service to move well ahead of its domestic and foreign competitors in profitability. Similarly, the US cigarette division of Philip Morris has become the industry profit leader by combining the lowest-cost manufacturing facilities in the world with high-visibility brands, supported by high-cost promotion. Finally, Daimler Benz employs elements of both strategies, but in different business segments. It has the lowest cost position in heavy-duty trucks in Western Europe, along with its exceptionally high-quality, feature-differentiated line of Mercedes Benz cars.

Other examples of the benefits of attaining the low-cost position in an industry or picking and exploiting specialized niches in the market abound. For example, the low-cost route to creating positive NPV investments has been successfully pursued in, of all places, the American steel industry. The strategy has involved building up-to-date mini-mills employing non-union workers who earn substantially less than members of the United Steelworkers Union. Mini-mills melt scrap, which is cheaper in the US than anywhere else, and their modern plant and equipment and simplified work practices greatly reduce their need for labor. Chapparal Steel of Midlothian, Texas, a big – and profitable – mini-mill, has pared its labor costs to a mere $29 on a ton of structural steel. This compares with average labor costs of $75 a ton at big integrated US plants.

The chief disadvantage is that their steelmaking capabilities are limited. They can't, for example, make the industry's bread-and-butter item: flat-rolled steel. But in the product areas where mini-mills do compete – rod, bar, and small beams and shapes – big producers have all but surrendered. So, too, have foreign mills. In just two years, Nucor Corp's mini-mill in Plymouth, Utah cut the Japanese share of California's rod and bar market from 50 to 10 percent.

Taking a different tack, Armstrong Rubber Co. has specialized in grabbing small market segments overlooked by its rivals. Today, Armstrong ranks second in industrial tires and second or third in both the replacement market for all-season radials and in tires for farm equipment and off-road recreational vehicles. Its niche-picking strategy relies heavily on the design and production innovations arising from its large investments in research and development.

A number of chemical firms, including Hercules, Monsanto, Dow, and Belgium's Solvay, have attempted to lessen their dependence on the production of commodity chemicals and plastics by investing heavily in highly profitable specialty products for such industries as electronics and defense. These specialty chemicals are typically sold in smaller quantities but at higher prices than traditional bulk commodity chemicals. Perhaps the most successful chemical 'niche-picker' is Denmark's Novo Industri – one of the world's largest producers of enzymes and insulin, and a pioneer in genetic engineering techniques. Novo's continued success is largely due to its ability to find and exploit small but profitable market niches. For instance, industry analysts credit Novo's success at selling enzymes in Japan to the company's ability to outdo even Japanese purity standards and to concentrate on small specialty markets that Japan's chemical giants can't be bothered with. In fact, most of Novo's markets appear too small for giant chemical firms such as Germany's Hoechst or Du Pont to pursue.

James River Corp. has combined cost cutting with product differentiation to achieve spectacular growth and profits in the paper-goods industry, an industry where many companies are struggling to hold their own. Typically,

James River buys other companies' cast-off paper mills and remakes them in its own image. It abandons all or most of the commodity-grade paper operations. It refurbishes old equipment, and supplements it with new machinery to produce specialty products (automobile and coffee filters, airline ticket paper, peel-off strips for Band-Aids, and cereal-box liners) that are aimed at specific markets and provide higher profits with less competition. At the same time, James River cuts costs by extracting wage concessions from workers and dismissing most executives. It also raises the productivity of those employees who stay by allowing many of them to join the company's lucrative *profit-sharing* programs. James River's success in following this two-pronged strategy is reflected in its 1983 net income of $55.1 million, 332 times larger than its 1970 earnings of $166,000.

Designing an investment strategy

Although a strong competitive edge in technology or marketing skills may enable a firm to earn excess returns, these barriers to entry will eventually erode, leaving the firm susceptible to increased competition. Existing firms are entering new industries and there are growing numbers of firms from a greater variety of countries, leading to new, well-financed competitors able to meet the high marketing costs and enormous capital outlays necessary for entry. Caterpillar Tractor, for example, faces a continuing threat from low-cost foreign competitors, especially Japan's Komatsu, which is second in world-wide sales. To stay on top, therefore, a firm's strategy must be constantly evolving, seeking out new opportunities and fending off new competitors.

Xerox clearly illustrates the problems associated with losing a competitive edge. For many years, Xerox was the king of the copier market, protected by its patents on xerography, with sales and earnings growing over 20 percent annually. The loss of its patent protection has brought forth numerous well-heeled competitors, including IBM, 3M, Kodak, and the Japanese, resulting in eroding profits and diminished growth prospects. Xerox has tried to transfer its original competitive advantage in technology to new products designed for the so-called office of the future. However, its difficulties in closely coordinating its R&D and marketing efforts have led to a series of serious, self-confessed blunders in acquisitions, market planning, and product development. For example, as mentioned earlier, the basic technology for the personal computer was developed by Xerox's Palo Alto Research Center in the early 1970s, but it remained for Apple Computer and IBM to capitalize on this revolutionary product.

More recently, Xerox's 1982 acquisition of Crum & Forster, a property and casualty insurance company, has called into question the company's strategy.

It is unclear how Xerox, for whom high technology has been the chief competitive advantage, can earn excess returns in a business in which it has no experience. As we have already seen, firms that stick to their knitting are more likely to succeed than those that don't.

Common sense tells us that, in order to achieve excess returns over time, the distinctive competitive advantage held by the firm must be difficult or costly to replicate. If it is easily replicated, it will not take long for actual or potential competitors to apply the same concept, process, or organizational structure to their operations. The competitive advantage of experience, for example, will evaporate unless a firm can keep the tangible benefits of its experience proprietary and force its competitors to go through the same learning process. Once a firm loses its competitive advantage, its profits will erode to a point where it can no longer earn excess returns. For this reason, the firm's competitive advantage has to be constantly monitored and maintained so as to ensure the existence of an effective barrier to entry into the market. Should these barriers to entry break down, the firm must react quickly either to reconstruct them or build new ones.

Caterpillar has reacted to Komatsu's challenge by attempting to slash its costs, closing plants, shifting productions overseas, forcing union and nonunion workers alike to take pay cuts, eliminating many positions, and pressuring its suppliers to cut prices and speed deliveries. To get lower prices, the company is shopping around for hungrier suppliers, including foreign companies. This is reflected in its philosophy of worldwide sourcing, as described by its director of purchasing: 'We're trying to become international in buying as well as selling. We expect our plants, regardless of where they're located, to look on a worldwide basis for sources of supply.'[4] For example, German and Japanese companies now supply crankshafts once made exclusively in the US.

One important source of extra profit is the quickness of management to recognize and use information about new, lower-cost production opportunities. The excess profits, however, are temporary, lasting only until competitors discover these opportunities for themselves. For example, purchasing the latest equipment will provide a temporary cost advantage, but this advantage will disappear as soon as competitors buy the equipment for their own plants. Only if the equipment is proprietary will the firm be able to maintain its cost advantage. Along the same line, many American electronics and textile firms shifted production facilities to Taiwan, Hong Kong, and other Asian locations to take advantage of lower labor costs there. However, as more firms took advantage of this cost reduction opportunity, competition in the consumer electronics and textiles markets in the US intensified, causing domestic prices to drop and excess profits to dissipate. In fact, firms in

---

[4] As quoted in the *Wall Street Journal* (August 10, 1971), p.1.

competitive industries must continually seize new non-proprietary cost reduction opportunities, not to earn excess returns but simply to make normal profits, or just survive.

Similarly, marketing-oriented firms can earn excess returns by being among the first to recognize and exploit new marketing opportunities. For example, Crown Cork & Seal, the Philadelphia-based bottle-top maker and can maker, reacted to slowing growth in its US business by expanding overseas. It set up subsidiaries in such countries as Thailand, Malaysia, Ethiopia, Zambia, Peru, Ecuador, Brazil, and Argentina. In so doing, as it turns out, they guessed correctly that in those developing, urbanizing societies, people would eventually switch from home-grown produce to food in cans and drinks in bottles.

Profitable markets, however, have a habit of eventually attracting competition. Thus, to be assured of having a continued supply of value-creating investments on hand, the firm must institutionalize its strategy of cost reduction and/or product differentiation. Successful companies seem to do this by creating a corporate culture – a set of shared values, norms, and beliefs – that has as one of its elements an obsession with some facet of their performance in the marketplace. McDonald's has an obsessive concern for quality control, IBM for customer service, and 3M for innovation. Forrest Mars set the tone for his company by going into a rage if he found an improperly wrapped candy bar leaving the plant. In order to maintain its low-cost position in the structural steel market, Chaparral Steel has teams of workers and foremen scour the world in search of the latest production machinery and methods.

Conversely, AT&T's manufacturing orientation, which focused on producing durable products with few options, was well-suited to the regulated environment in which it operated throughout most of its existence. But such an inward-looking orientation is likely to be a significant barrier to the company's ability to compete against the likes of IBM and other market-oriented, high-tech companies that react quickly to consumer demand. Prior to the breakup of AT&T, the manufacturers at Western Electric, AT&T's manufacturing arm, freely decided which products to make and when. They controlled the factories, supplying telephones to a captive market of Bell companies. AT&T was essentially an order taker, no more needing a sales force than any other utility does. There were no competitors forcing quicker market reaction nor any marketers challenging manufacturers' decisions.

Although AT&T claims that it is now 'market-driven', evidence abounds that the company's older, entrenched manufacturing mentality is still dominant. Unless AT&T can change its corporate culture – a difficult and demanding task for any company, much less for a giant set in its ways – and marry manufacturing and marketing, it will have a difficult time competing with firms such as IBM in the office automation and computer businesses it has set its sights on.

The basic insight here is that sustained success in investing is not so much a matter of building new plants as of seeking out lower-cost production processes embodied in these plants, coming up with the right products for these plants to produce, and adding the service and quality features that differentiate these products in the marketplace. In other words, it comes down to people and how they are organized and motivated. The cost and difficulty of creating a corporate culture that adds value to capital investments is the ultimate barrier to entry; unlike the latest equipment, money alone can't buy it.

In the words of Maurice R. (Hank) Greenberg, president of American Insurance Group (AIG), a worldwide network of insurance companies that has enjoyed spectacular success by pioneering in territory relatively unpopulated by competitors, 'You can't imitate our global operation. It's just incapable of being reproduced. Domestically, we have some imitators for pieces of our business, but not the entire business. And in any event, you can only imitate what we've done. You can't imitate what we're thinking. You can't copy what we're going to do tomorrow.'[5]

Corporate strategy and foreign investment

Most of the firms we have discussed are multinational corporations (MNCs) with worldwide operations. For many of these MNCs, becoming multinational was the end result of an apparently haphazard process of overseas expansion. But, as international operations become a more important source of profit and as domestic and foreign competitors become more aggressive, it is apparent that domestic survival for many firms is increasingly dependent on their success overseas. To ensure this success, multinationals must develop global strategies that will enable them to maintain their competitive edge both at home and abroad.

Overseas expansion and survival

It is evident that if one's competitors gain access to lower-cost sources of production abroad, following them overseas may be a prerequisite for domestic survival. One strategy often followed by firms for whom cost is the

---

[5] Wyndham Robertson, 'Nobody Tops A.I.G. in Intricacy – or Daring', *Fortune*, May 22, 1978, p. 99.

key consideration, such as Chapparal Steel, is to develop a global scanning capability to seek out lower-cost production sites or production technologies worldwide.

Economies of scale

A somewhat less obvious factor motivating foreign investment is the effect of economies of scale. We have already seen that in a competitive market, prices will be forced close to marginal costs of production. Hence, firms in industries characterized by high fixed costs relative to variable costs must engage in volume selling just to break even.

A new term has arisen to describe the size necessary in certain industries to compete effectively in the global marketplace: *world scale*. These large volumes may be forthcoming only if firms expand overseas. For example, companies manufacturing products such as mainframe computers that require huge R&D expenditures often need a larger customer base than that provided by even a market as large as the United States in order to recapture their investment in knowledge. Similarly, firms in capital-intensive industries with significant economies of scale in production may also be forced to sell overseas in order to spread their overhead over a higher volume of sales.

To take an extreme case, L.M. Ericsson, the highly successful Swedish manufacturer of telecommunications equipment, is forced to think internationally when designing new products since its domestic market is too small to absorb the enormous R&D expenditures involved and to reap the full benefit of production scale economies. Thus, when Ericsson developed its revolutionary AXE digital switching system, it geared its design to achieve global market penetration.

Many firms have found that a local market presence is necessary in order to continue selling overseas. For example, a local presence has helped Data General adapt the design of its US computers and software to the Japanese market, giving the company a competitive edge over other US companies selling computers in Japan. Data General has also adopted some Japanese manufacturing techniques and quality-control procedures that will improve its competitive position worldwide.

More firms are preparing for global competition. For example, although Black & Decker has a 50 percent market share worldwide in power tools, new competitors like the Japanese are forcing the company to change its manufacturing and marketing operations. Black & Decker's new strategy is based on a marketing concept known as 'globalization', which holds that the world is becoming more homogenized and that distinctions between markets are disappearing. By selling standardized products worldwide, a firm can take advantage of economies of scale, thereby lowering costs and taking business from MNCs that customize products for individual markets. Until recently, the latter strategy of customization was the one that Black & Decker followed; the Italian subsidiary made tools for Italians, the British subsidiary tools for Britons.

By contrast, Japanese power-tool makers such as Makita Electric Works don't care that Germans prefer high-powered, heavy-duty drills and that Americans want everything lighter. Instead, Makita's strategy, which has been quite successful, is based on the notion that if you make a good drill at a low price, it will sell from Brooklyn to Baden-Baden. In response, Black & Decker recently unveiled 50 new power tools, each standardized for world production. It plans to standardize future products as well, making only minimal concessions, which require only minor modifications, to cultural differences.

Knowledge seeking

Some firms enter foreign markets for the purpose of gaining information and experience that is expected to prove useful elsewhere. For instance, Beecham, an English firm, deliberately set out to learn from its US operations how to be more competitive, first in the area of consumer products and later in pharmaceuticals. This knowledge proved highly valuable in competing with American and other firms in its European markets. Unilever, the Anglo-Dutch corporation, learned to adapt to world markets, with impressive results, the marketing skills it acquired in the US through its American affiliate Lever Bros.

In industries characterized by rapid product innovation and technical breakthroughs by foreign competitors, it pays constantly to track overseas developments. The Japanese excel in this. Japanese firms systematically and effectively collect information on foreign innovation and disseminate it within their own research and development, marketing, and production groups. The analysis of new foreign products as soon as they reach the market is an especially long-lived Japanese technique. One of the jobs of Japanese researchers is to tear down a new foreign computer and analyze how it works as a base on which to develop a product of their own that will outperform the original. In a bit of a switch, as pointed out above, Data General's Japanese operation is giving the company a close look at Japanese technology, enabling it quickly to pick up and transfer back to the United States new information on Japanese innovations in the areas of computer design and manufacturing. Similarly, Ford Motor Co. has used its European operations as an important source of design and engineering ideas and management talent.

Designing a global expansion strategy

The ability to pursue systematically policies and investments congruent with worldwide survival and growth depends on four interrelated elements.

1 The first, and the key to the development of a successful global strategy, is to understand and then capitalize on those factors that have led to success in the past. In order for domestic firms to become global competitors, therefore, the sources of their domestic advantage must be transferable abroad. A competitive advantage predicted on government regulation, such as import restrictions, clearly doesn't fit in this category.
2 Second, this global approach to investment planning necessitates a systematic evaluation of individual entry strategies in foreign markets, a comparison of the alternatives, and selection of the optimal mode of entry.
3 The third important element is a continual audit of the effectiveness of current entry modes. As knowledge about a foreign market increases, for example, or sales potential grows, the optimal market penetration strategy will likely change.
4 Fourth, top management must be committed to becoming and/or staying a multinational corporation. Westinghouse demonstrated its commitment to international business by creating the new position of President-international and endowing its occupant with a seat on the company's powerful management committee. A truly globally-oriented firm – one that asks, 'Where in the *world* should we develop, produce, and sell our products and services?' – also requires an intelligence system capable of systematically scanning the world and understanding it, along with people who are experienced in international business and know how to use the information generated by the system.

Summary and conclusions

We have seen that rates of return in competitive industries are driven down to their required returns. Excess profits quickly attract new entrants to the market, lowering returns until actual and required returns are again equal. Thus, the run-of-the-mill firm operating in a highly competitive market will be unable consistently to find positive net present value investments – ones which earn excess returns relative to their required returns. The key to generating a continual flow of positive NPV projects, therefore, is to erect and maintain barriers to entry against competitors. This involves either building defenses against potential competitors or finding positions in the industry where competition is the weakest.

The firm basically has two strategic options in its quest for competitive advantage: it can seek lower costs than its competitors or it can differentiate its product in a number of ways, including high advertising expenditures, product innovation, high product quality, and first-rate service.

Each of these options involves a number of specific investment decisions: construction of efficient-scale facilities and vigorous pursuit of cost reduction through accumulated experience, in the case of cost leadership; if product differentiation is the main goal, the focus is on advertising, R&D, quality control, customer-service facilities, distribution networks and the like. The more an investment widens a firm's competitive advantage and reduces the chances of successful replication by competitors, the greater the likelihood that investment will be successful.

Despite our understanding of the subject matter, it is difficult to give a set of rules to follow in developing profitable investment strategies. If it were possible to do so, competitors would follow them and dissipate any excess returns. One must be creative and quick to recognize new opportunities. Nevertheless, without dictating what should be done in every specific circumstance, there are some basic lessons we have learned from economic theory and the experiences of successful firms. The basic lessons are these:

1 Invest in projects that take advantage of your competitive edge. The corollary is, stick to doing one or two things and doing them well; don't get involved in businesses you are unfamiliar with.
2 Invest in developing, maintaining, and enhancing your competitive advantages.
3 Develop a global scanning capability. Don't be blindsided by new competitors or lower-cost production techniques or locations.
4 Pick market niches where there is little competition. Be prepared to abandon markets where competitors are catching up and apply your competitive advantages to new products or markets.

Assuming that a firm does have the necessary resources to be successful internationally, it must carefully plan for the transfer of these resources overseas. For example, it must consider how it can best utilize its marketing expertise, innovative technology, or production skills to penetrate a specific foreign market. Where a particular strategy calls for resources the firm lacks, such as an overseas distribution network, corporate management must first decide how and at what cost these resources can be acquired. It must then decide whether (and how) to acquire the resources or change its strategy.

Reproduced from Shapiro, A.C. (1985). Corporate strategy and the capital budgeting decision. *Midland Corporate Finance Journal*, Spring, by permission of Midland Bank plc.

3 Portfolio selection[*]

H. M. Markowitz

The process of selecting a portfolio may be divided into two stages. The first stage starts with observation and experience and ends with beliefs about the future performances of available securities. The second stage starts with the relevant beliefs about future performances and ends with the choice of portfolio. This paper is concerned with the second stage. We first consider the rule that the investor does (or should) maximize discounted expected, or anticipated, returns. This rule is rejected both as a hypothesis to explain, and as a maxim to guide investment behavior. We next consider the rule that the investor does (or should) consider expected return a desirable thing *and* variance of return an undesirable thing. This rule has many sound points, both as a maxim for, and hypothesis about, investment behavior. We illustrate geometrically relations between beliefs and choice of portfolio according to the 'expected returns–variance of returns' rule.

One type of rule concerning choice of portfolio is that the investor does (or should) maximize the discounted (or capitalized) value of future returns.[1] Since the future is not known with certainty, it must be 'expected' or 'anticipated' returns which we discount. Variations of this type of rule can be suggested. Following Hicks, we could let 'anticipated' returns include an allowance for risk.[2] Or, we could let the rate at which we capitalize the returns from particular securities vary with risk.

The hypothesis (or maxim) that the investor does (or should) maximize discounted return must be rejected. If we ignore market imperfections the foregoing rule never implies that there is a diversified portfolio which is preferable to all non-diversified portfolios. Diversification is both observed

[*] This paper is based on work done by the author while at the Cowles Commission for Research in Economics and with the financial assistance of the Social Science Research Council.

[1] See, for example, J.B. Williams, *The Theory of Investment Value* (Cambridge, Mass: Harvard University Press, 1938), pp.55–75.

[2] J.R. Hicks, *Value and Capital* (New York: Oxford University Press, 1939), p.126. Hicks applies the rule to a firm rather than a portfolio.

and sensible; a rule of behaviour which does not imply the superiority of diversification must be rejected both as a hypothesis and as a maxim.

The foregoing rule fails to imply diversification no matter how the anticipated returns are formed; whether the same or different discount rates are used for different securities; no matter how these discount rates are decided upon or how they vary over time.[3] The hypothesis implies that the investor places all his funds in the security with the greatest discounted value. If two or more securities have the same value, then any of these or any combination of these is as good as any other.

We can see this analytically: suppose there are N securities; let r_{it} be the anticipated return (however decided upon) at time t per dollar invested in security i; let d_{it} be the rate at which the return on the ith security at time t is discounted back to the present; let X_i be the relative amount invested in security i. We exclude short sales, thus $X_i \geq 0$ for all i. Then the discounted anticipated return of the portfolio is

$$R = \sum_{t=1}^{\infty} \sum_{i=1}^{N} d_{it} \, r_{it} \, X$$

$$= \sum_{i=1}^{N} X_i \left(\sum_{t=1}^{\infty} d_{it} \, r_{it} \right)$$

$R_i = \sum_{t=1}^{\infty} d_{it} \, r_{it}$ is the discounted return of the ith security, therefore

$R = \Sigma X_i R_i$ *where* R_i is independent of X_i. Since $X_i \geq 0$ for all i and $\Sigma X_i = 1$, R is a weighted average of R_i with the X_i as non-negative weights. To maximize R, we let $X_i = 1$ for i with maximum R_i. If several Ra_a, $a = 1, \ldots, K$ are maximum then any allocation with

$$\sum_{a=1}^{K} X a_a = 1$$

maximizes R. In no case is a diversified portfolio preferred to all non-diversified portfolios.[4]

---

[3] The results depend on the assumption that the anticipated returns and discount rates are independent of the particular investor's portfolio.

[4] If short sales were allowed, an infinite amount of money would be placed in the security with highest r.

It will be convenient at this point to consider a static model. Instead of speaking of the time series of returns from the ith security $(r_{i1}, r_{i2}, \ldots, r_{it}, \ldots)$ we will speak of 'the flow of returns' (r_i) from the ith security. The flow of returns from the portfolio as a whole is $R = \Sigma X_i r_i$. As in the dynamic case if the investor wished to maximize 'anticipated' return from the portfolio he would place all his funds in that security with maximum anticipated returns.

There is a rule which implies both that the investor should diversify and that he should maximize expected return. The rule states that the investor does (or should) diversify his funds among all those securities which give maximum expected return. The law of large numbers will insure that the actual yield of the portfolio will be almost the same as the expected yield.[5] This rule is a special case of the expected returns – variance of returns rule (to be presented below). It assumes that there is a portfolio which gives both maximum expected return and minimum variance, and it commends this portfolio to the investor.

This presumption, that the law of large numbers applies to a portfolio of securities, cannot be accepted. The returns from securities are too inter-correlated. Diversification cannot eliminate all variance.

The portfolio with maximum expected return is not necessarily the one with minimum variance. There is a rate at which the investor can gain expected return by taking on variance, or reduce variance by giving up expected return.

We saw that the expected returns or anticipated returns rule is inadequate. Let us now consider the expected returns-variance of returns $(E–V)$ rule. It will be necessary to first present a few elementary concepts and results of mathematical statistics. We will then show some implications of the $E–V$ rule. After this we will discuss its plausibility.

In our presentation we try to avoid complicated mathematical statements and proofs. As a consequence a price is paid in terms of rigor and generality. The chief limitations from this source are (1) we do not derive our results analytically for the n-security case; instead, we present them geometrically for the 3 and 4 security cases; (2) we assume static probability beliefs. In a general presentation we must recognize that the probability distribution of yields of the various securities is a function of time. The writer intends to present, in the future, the general, mathematical treatment which removes these limitations.

We will need the following elementary concepts and results of mathematical statistics:

Let Y be a random variable, i.e., a variable whose value is decided by chance. Suppose, for simplicity of exposition, that Y can take on a finite number of values $y_1, y_2, \ldots, y_N$. Let the probability that $Y = y_1$, be p_1; that $Y = y_2$ be p_2 etc. The expected value (or mean) of Y is defined to be

[5] Williams, *op. cit.*, pp.68, 69.

$$E = p_1 y_1 + p_2 y_2 + \ldots + p_N y_N$$

The variance of Y is defined to be

$$V = p_1 (y_1 - E)^2 + p_2 (y_2 - E)^2 + \ldots + p_N (y_N - E)^2.$$

V is the average squared deviation of Y from its expected value. V is a commonly used measure of dispersion. Other measures of dispersion, closely related to V are the standard deviation, $\sigma = \sqrt{V}$ and the coefficient of variation, σ/E.

Suppose we have a number of random variables: $R_1, \ldots, R_n$. If R is a weighted sum (linear combination) of the R_i

$$R = a_1 R_1 + a_2 R_2 + \ldots + a_n R_n$$

then R is also a random variable. (For example R_1, may be the number which turns up on one die; R_2, that of another die, and R the sum of these numbers. In this case $n = 2$, $a_1 = a_2 = 1$).

It will be important for us to know how the expected value and variance of the weighted sum (R) are related to the probability distribution of the $R_1, \ldots, R_n$. We state these relations below; we refer the reader to any standard text for proof.[6]

The expected value of a weighted sum is the weighted sum of the expected values. I.e., $E(R) = a_1 E(R_1) + a_2 E(R_2) + \ldots + a_n E(R_n)$. The variance of a weighted sum is not as simple. To express it we must define 'covariance'. The covariance of R_1 and R_2 is

$$\sigma_{12} = E\{[R_1 - E(R_1)][R_2 - E(R_2)]\}$$

i.e., the expected value of [(the deviation of R_1 from its mean) times (the deviation of R_2 from its mean)]. In general we define the covariance between R_i and R_j as

$$\sigma_{ij} = E\{[R_i - E(R_i)][R_j - E(R_j)]\}$$

σ_{ij} may be expressed in terms of the familiar correlation coefficient (p_{ij}). The covariance between R_i and R_j is equal to [(their correlation) times (the standard deviation of R_i) times (the standard deviation of R_j)]:

$$\sigma_{ij} = p_{ij} \sigma_i \sigma_j$$

[6] E.g., J.V. Uspensky, *Introduction to Mathematical Probability* (New York: McGraw-Hill, 1937), chapter 9, pp.161-81.

The variance of a weighted sum is

$$V(R) = \sum_{i=1}^{N} a_i^2 V(X_i) + 2 \sum_{i=1}^{N} \sum_{i>1}^{N} a_i a_j \sigma_{ij}$$

If we use the fact that the variance of R_i is σ_{ii} then

$$V(R) = \sum_{i=1}^{N} \sum_{j=1}^{N} a_i a_j \sigma_{ij}$$

Let R_i be the return on the ith security. Let μ_i be the expected value of R_i; σ_{ij} be the covariance between R_i and R_j (thus σ_{ii} is the variance of R_i). Let X_i be the percentage of the investor's assets which are allocated to the ith security. The yield (R) on the portfolio as a whole is

$$R = \sum R_i X_i$$

The R_i (and consequently R) are considered to be random variables.[7] The X_i are not random variables, but are fixed by the investor. Since the X_i are percentages we have $\Sigma X_i = 1$. In our analysis we will exclude negative values of the X_i (i.e., short sales); therefore $X_i \geq 0$ for all i.

The return (R) on the portfolio as a whole is a weighted sum of random variables (where the investor can choose the weights). From our discussion of such weighted sums we see that the expected return E from the portfolio as a whole is

$$E = \sum_{i=1}^{N} X_i \mu_i$$

[7] I.e., we assume that the investor does (and should) act as if he had probability beliefs concerning these variables. In general we would expect that the investor could tell us, for any two events (A and B), whether he personally considered A more likely than B, B more likely than A, or both equally likely. If the investor were consistent in his opinions on such matters, he would possess a system of probability beliefs. We cannot expect the investor to be consistent in every detail. We can, however, expect his probability beliefs to be roughly consistent on important matters that have been carefully considered. We should also expect that he will base his actions upon these probability beliefs – even though they be in part subjective. This paper does not consider the difficult question of how investors do (or should) form their probability beliefs.

and the variance is

$$V = \sum_{i=1}^{N} \sum_{j=1}^{N} \sigma_{ij} X_i X_j$$

For fixed probability beliefs (μ_i, σ_{ij}) the investor has a choice of various combinations of E and V depending on his choice of portfolio X_1, ..., X_N. Suppose that the set of all obtainable (E, V) combinations were as in Figure 1. The E–V rule states that the investor would (or should) want to select one of those portfolios which give rise to the (E, V) combinations indicated as efficient in the figure; i.e. those with minimum V for given E or more and maximum E for given V or less.

There are techniques by which we can compute the set of efficient portfolios and efficient (E, V) combinations associated with given μ_i and σ_{ij}. We will not present these techniques here. We will, however, illustrate geometrically the nature of the efficient surfaces for cases in which N (the number of available securities) is small.

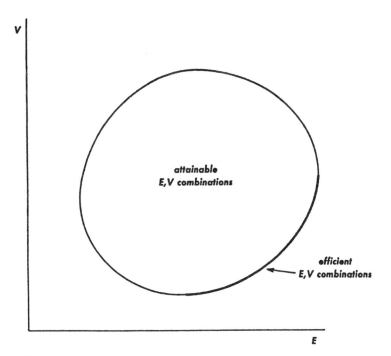

Figure 1

The calculation of efficient surfaces might possibly be of practical use. Perhaps there are ways, by combining statistical techniques and the judgement of experts, to form reasonable probability beliefs (μ_i, σ_{ij}). We could use these beliefs to compute the attainable efficient combinations of (E, V). The investor, being informed of what (E, V) combinations were attainable, could state which he desired. We could then find the portfolio which gave this desired combination.

Two conditions – at least – must be satisfied before it would be practical to use efficient surfaces in the manner described above. First, the investor must desire to act according to the E–V maxim. Second, we must be able to arrive at reasonable μ_i and σ_{ij}. We will return to these matters later.

Let us consider the case of three securities. In the three security case our model reduces to

(1)
$$E = \sum_{i=1}^{3} X_i \mu_i$$

(2)
$$V = \sum_{i=1}^{3} \sum_{j=1}^{3} X_i X_j \sigma_{ij}$$

(3)
$$\sum_{i=1}^{3} X_i = 1$$

(4)
$$X_i \geqslant 0 \quad \text{for} \quad i = 1, 2, 3.$$

From (3) we get

(3')
$$X_3 = 1 - X_1 - X_2$$

If we substitute (3') in equation (1) and (2) we get E and V as functions of X_1 and X_2. For example we find

(1')
$$E = \mu_3 + X_1 (\mu_1 - \mu_3) + X_2 (\mu_2 - \mu_3)$$

The exact formulas are not too important here (that of V is given below).[8] We can simply write

---

[8] $V = X_1^2(\sigma_{11} - 2\sigma_{13} + \sigma_{33}) + X_2^2(\sigma_{22} - 2\sigma_{23} + \sigma_{33}) + 2X_1 X_2(\sigma_{12} - \sigma_{13} - \sigma_{23} + \sigma_{33}) + 2X_1 (\sigma_{13} - \sigma_{33}) + 2X_2(\sigma_{23} - \sigma_{33}) + \sigma_{33}$

(a) $$E = E(X_1, X_2)$$

(b) $$V = V(X_1, X_2)$$

(c) $$X_1 \geqslant 0, X_2 \geqslant 0, 1 - X_1 - X_2 \geqslant 0$$

By using relations (a), (b), (c), we can work with two dimensional geometry.

The attainable set of portfolios consists of all portfolios which satisfy constraints (c) and (3') (or equivalently (3) and (4)). The attainable combinations of X_1, X_2 are represented by the triangle *abc* in Figure 2. Any point to the left of the X_2 axis is not attainable because it violates the condition that $X_1 \geqslant 0$. Any point below the X_1 axis is not attainable because it violates the condition that $X_2 \geqslant 0$. Any point above the line $(1 - X_1 - X_2 = 0)$ is not attainable because it violates the condition that $X_3 = 1 - X_1 - X_2 \geqslant 0$.

We define an *isomean* curve to be the set of all points (portfolios) with a given expected return. Similarly an *isovariance* line is defined to be the set of all points (portfolios) with a given variance of return.

An examination of the formulae for E and V tells us the shapes of the isomean and isovariance curves. Specifically they tell us that typically[9] the isomean curves are a system of parallel straight lines; the isovariance curves are a system of concentric ellipses (See Figure 2). For example, if $\mu_2 \neq \mu_3$ equation 1' can be written in the familiar form $X_2 = a + bX_1$; specifically (1)

$$X_2 = \frac{E - \mu_3}{\mu_2 - \mu_3} - \frac{\mu_1 - \mu_3}{\mu_2 - \mu_3} X_1.$$

Thus the slope of the isomean line associated with $E = E_0$ is $-(\mu_1 - \mu_3)/(\mu_2 - \mu_3)$ its intercept is $(E_0 - \mu_3)/(\mu_2 - \mu_3)$. If we change E we change the intercept but not the slope of the isomean line. This confirms the contention that the isomean lines form a system of parallel lines.

Similarly, by a somewhat less simple application of analytic geometry, we can confirm the contention that the isovariance lines form a family of concentric ellipses. The 'center' of the system is the point which minimizes V. We will label this point X. Its expected return and variance we will label E and V. Variance increases as you move away from X. More precisely, if one isovariance curve, C_1, lies closer to X than another, C_2, then C_1 is associated with a smaller variance than C_2.

---

[9] The isomean 'curves' are as described above except when $\mu_1 = \mu_2 = \mu_3$. In the latter case all portfolios have the same expected return and the investor chooses the one with minimum variance. As to the assumptions implicit in our description of the isovariance curves see footnote 12.

With the aid of the foregoing geometric apparatus let us seek the efficient sets.

X, the center of the system of isovariance ellipses, may fall either inside or outside the attainable set. Figure 4 illustrates a case in which *X* falls inside the attainable set. In this case: *X* is efficient. For no other portfolio has a *V* as low as *X*; therefore no portfolio can have either smaller *V* (with the same or greater *E*) or greater *E* with the same of smaller *V*. No point (portfolio) with expected return *E* less than **E** is efficient. For we have **E** > E and **V** < V.

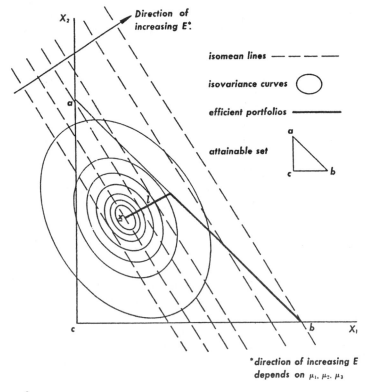

Figure 2

Consider all points with a given expected return *E*; i.e., all points on the isomean line associated with *E*. The point of the isomean line at which *V* takes on its least value is the point at which the isomean line is tangent to an isovariance curve. We call this point $\hat{X}(E)$. If we let *E* vary, $\hat{X}(E)$ traces out a curve.

Algebraic considerations (which we omit here) show us that this curve is a straight line. We will call it the critical line *l*. The critical line passes through

X for this point minimizes V for all points with $E(X_1, X_2) = E$. As we go along l in either direction from X, V increases. The segment of the critical line from X to the point where the critical line crosses the boundary of the attainable set is part of the efficient set. The rest of the efficient set is (in the case illustrated) the segment of the ab line from d to b. b is the point of maximum attainable E. In Figure 3, X lies outside the admissible area but the critical line cuts the admissible area. The efficient line begins at the attainable point with minimum variance (in this case on the ab line). It moves toward b until it intersects the critical line, moves along the critical line until it intersects a boundary and

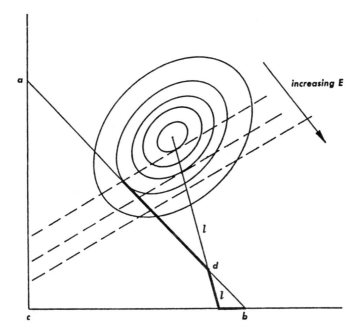

Figure 3

finally moves along the boundary to b. The reader may wish to construct and examine the following other cases: (1) X lies outside the attainable set and the critical line does not cut the attainable set. In this case there is a security which does not enter into any efficient portfolio. (2) Two securities have the same μ_i. In this case the isomean lines are parallel to a boundary line. It may happen that the efficient portfolio with maximum E is a diversified portfolio. (3) A case wherein only one portfolio is efficient.

The efficient set in the 4 security case is, as in the 3 security and also the N security case, a series of connected line segments. At one end of the efficient

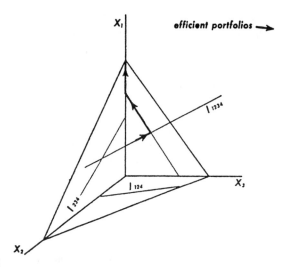

Figure 4

set is the point of minimum variance; at the other end is a point of maximum expected return[10] (see Figure 4).

Now that we have seen the nature of the set of efficient portfolios, it is not difficult to see the nature of the set of efficient (E, V) combinations. In the three security case $E = a_0 + a_1X_1 + a_2X_2$ is a plane; $V = b_0 + b_1X_1 + b_2X_2 +$

---

[10] Just as we used the equation

$$\sum_{i=1}^{4} X_i = 1$$

to reduce the dimensionality in the three security case, we can use it to represent the four security case in 3 dimensional space. Eliminating X_4 we get $E = E(X_1, X_2, X_3)$, $V = V(X_1, X_2, X_3)$. The attainable set is represented, in three-space, by the tetrahedron with vertices $(0,0,0)$, $(0,0,1)$, $(0,1,0)$, $(1,0,0)$, representing portfolios with, respectively, $X_4 = 1$, $X_3 = 1$, $X_2 = 1$, $X_1 = 1$.

Let s_{123} be the subspace consisting of all points with $X_4 = 0$. Similarly we can define s_{a1}, . . . , a_a to be the subspace consisting of all points with $X_i = 0$, $i \neq a_1$, . . . , a_a. For each subspace s_{a1}, . . . , a_a we can define a *critical line* l_{a1}, . . . a_a. This line is the locus of points P where P minimizes V for all points in s_{a1}, . . . a_a with the same E as P. If a point is in s_{a1}, . . . , a_a and is efficient it must be on la_1, . . . , a_a. The efficient set may be traced out by starting at the point of minimum available variance, moving continuously along various la_1, . . . , a_a according to definite rules, ending in a point which gives maximum E. As in the two dimensional case the point with minimum available variance may be in the interior of the available set or on one of its boundaries. Typically we proceed along a given critical line until either this line intersects one of a larger subspace or meets a boundary (and simultaneously the critical line of a lower dimensional subspace). In either of these cases the efficient line turns and continues along the new line. The efficient line terminates when a point with maximum E is reached.

$b_{12}X_1X_2 + b_{11}X_1^2 + b_{22}X_2^2$ is a paraboloid.[11] As shown in Figure 5, the section of the *E*-plane over the efficient portfolio set is a series of connected line segments. The section of the *V*-paraboloid over the efficient portfolio set is a series of connected parabola segments. If we plotted *V* against *E* for efficient portfolios we would again get a series of connected parabola segments (see Figure 6). This result obtains for any number of securities.

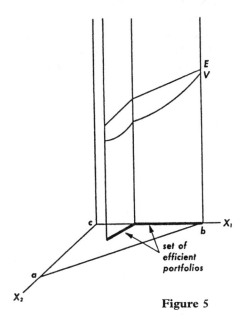

Figure 5

Various reasons recommend the use of the expected return-variance of return rule, both as a hypothesis to explain well-established investment behaviour and as a maxim to guide one's own action. The rule serves better, we will see, as an explanation of, and guide to, 'investment' as distinguished from 'speculative' behavior.

Earlier we rejected the expected returns rule on the grounds that it never implied the superiority of diversification. The expected return-variance of return rule, on the other hand, implies diversification for a wide range of μ_i, σ_{ij}. This does not mean that the *E–V* rule never implies the superiority of an undiversified portfolio. It is conceivable that one security might have an extremely higher yield and lower variance than all other securities; so much so that one particular undiversified portfolio would give maximum *E* and minimum *V*. But for a large, presumably representative range of μ_i, σ_{ij} the *E–V* rule leads to efficient portfolios almost all of which are diversified.

---

[11] See footnote 8.

Not only does the *E–V* hypothesis imply diversification, it implies the 'right kind' of diversification for the 'right reason'. The adequacy of diversification is not thought by investors to depend solely on the number of different securities held. A portfolio with sixty different railway securities, for example, would not be as well diversified as the same size portfolio with some railroad, some public utility, mining, various sort of manufacturing, etc. The reason is that it is generally more likely for firms within the same industry to do poorly at the same time than for firms in dissimilar industries.

Similarly in trying to make variance small it is not enough to invest in many securities. It is necessary to avoid investing in securities with high covariances among themselves. We should diversify across industries because firms in

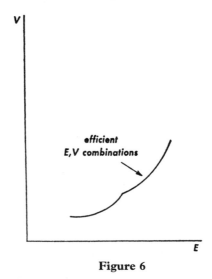

Figure 6

different industries, especially industries with different economic character-istics, have lower covariances than firms within an industry.

The concepts 'yield' and 'risk' appear frequently in financial writings. Usually if the term 'yield' were replaced by 'expected yield' or 'expected return', and 'risk' by 'variance of return', little change of apparent meaning would result.

Variance is a well-known measure of dispersion about the expected. If instead of variance the investor was concerned with standard error, $\sigma = \sqrt{V}$, or with the coefficient of dispersion, σ/E, his choice would still lie in the set of efficient portfolios.

Suppose an investor diversifies between two portfolios (i.e., if he puts some of his money in one portfolio, the rest of his money in the other. An example of diversifying among portfolios is the buying of the shares of two different investment companies). If the two original portfolios have *equal* variance then

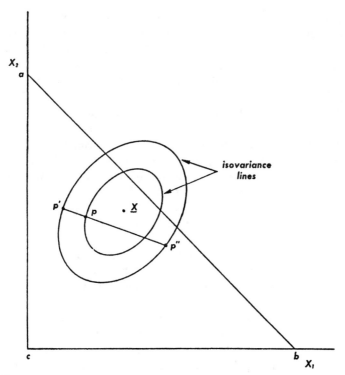

Figure 7

typically[12] the variance of the resulting (compound) portfolio will be less than the variance of either original portfolio. This is illustrated by Figure 7. To interpret Figure 7 we note that a portfolio (P) which is built out of two portfolios $P' = (X'_1, X'_2)$ and $P'' = (X''_1, X''_2)$ is of the form $P = \lambda P' + (1 - \lambda)P'' = (\lambda X'_1 + (1 - \lambda)X''_1, \lambda X'_2 + (1 - \lambda)X''_2)$. P is on the straight line connecting P' and P''.

The $E-V$ principle is more plausible as a rule for investment behaviour as distinguished from speculative behavior. The third moment[13] M_3 of the probability distribution of returns from the portfolio may be connected with a

[12] In no case will variance be increased. The only case in which variance will not be decreased is if the return from both portfolios are perfectly correlated. To draw the isovariance curves as ellipses it is both necessary and sufficient to assume that no two distinct portfolios have perfectly correlated returns.

[13] If R is a random variable that takes on a finite number of values $r_1, \ldots, r_n$ with probabilities $p_1, \ldots, p_n$ respectively, and expected value E, then

$$M_3 = \sum_{i=1}^{n} p_i(r_i - E)^3$$

propensity to gamble. For example if the investor maximizes utility (U) which depends on E and V $(U = U(E, V), \delta U/\delta E > 0, \delta U/\delta E < 0)$ he will never accept an actuarially fair[14] bet. But if $U = U(E, V, M_3)$ and if $\delta U/\delta M_3 \neq 0$ then there are some fair bets which would be accepted.

Perhaps – for a great variety of investing institutions which consider yield to be a good thing; risk, a bad thing; gambling, to be avoided – E, V efficiency is reasonable as a working hypothesis and a working maxim.

Two uses of the $E–V$ principle suggest themselves. We might use it in theoretical analyses or we might use it in the actual selection of portfolios.

In theoretical analyses we might inquire, for example, about the various effects of a change in the beliefs generally held about a firm, or a general change in preference as to expected return versus variance of return, or a change in the supply of a security. In our analyses the X_i might represent individual securities or they might represent aggregates such as, say, bonds, stocks and real estate.[15]

To use the $E–V$ rule in the selection of securities we must have procedures for finding reasonable μ_i and σ_{ij}. These procedures, I believe, should combine statistical techniques and the judgement of practical men. My feeling is that the statistical computations should be used to arrive at a tentative set of μ_i and σ_{ij}. Judgement should then be used in increasing or decreasing some of these μ_i and σ_{ij} on the basis of factors or nuances not taken into account by the formal computations. Using this revised set of μ_i and σ_{ij}, the set of efficient E, V combinations could be computed, the investor could select the combination he preferred, and the portfolio which gave rise to this E, V combination could be found.

One suggestion as to tentative μ_i, σ_{ij} is to use the observed μ_i, σ_{ij} for some period of the past. I believe that better methods, which take into account more information, can be found. I believe that what is needed is essentially a 'probabilistic' reformulation of security analysis. I will not pursue this subject here, for this is 'another story'. It is a story of which I have read only the first page of the first chapter.

In this paper we have considered the second stage in the process of selecting a portfolio. This stage starts with the relevant beliefs about the securities involved and ends with the selection of a portfolio. We have not considered the first stage: the formation of the relevant beliefs on the basis of observation.

Reproduced from Markowitz, H.M. (1952) Portfolio selection. *The Journal of Finance*, 7 (March), 77–91 by permission of the American Finance Association.

---

[14] One in which the amount gained by winning the bet times the probability of winning is equal to the amount lost by losing the bet, times the probability of losing.

[15] Care must be used in using and interpreting relations among aggregates. We cannot deal here with the problems and pitfalls of aggregation.

Part 3

Capital Asset Prices – Developing a Model of the Capital Market

4 Capital asset prices: a theory of market equilibrium under conditions of risk*

W. F. Sharpe

I Introduction

One of the problems which has plagued those attempting to predict the behavior of capital markets is the absence of a body of positive micro-economic theory dealing with conditions of risk. Although many useful insights can be obtained from the traditional models of investment under conditions of certainty, the pervasive influence of risk in financial transactions has forced those working in this area to adopt models of price behavior which are little more than assertions. A typical classroom explanation of the determination of capital asset prices, for example, usually begins with a careful and relatively rigorous description of the process through which individual preferences and physical relationships interact to determine an equilibrium pure interest rate. This is generally followed by the assertion that somehow a market risk-premium is also determined, with the prices of assets adjusting accordingly to account for differences in their risk.

A useful representation of the view of the capital market implied in such discussions is illustrated in Figure 1. In equilibrium, capital asset prices have adjusted so that the investor, if he follows rational procedures (primarily diversification), is able to attain any desired point along a *capital market line*.[1] He may obtain a higher expected rate of return on his holdings only by

* A great many people provided comments on early versions of this paper which led to major improvements in the exposition. In addition to the referees, who were most helpful, the author wishes to express his appreciation to Dr Harry Markowitz of the RAND Corporation, Professor Jack Hirshleifer of the University of California at Los Angeles, and to Professors Yoram Barzel, George Brabb, Bruce Johnson, Walter Oi and R. Haney Scott of the University of Washington.
[1] Although some discussions are also consistent with a non-linear (but monotonic) curve.

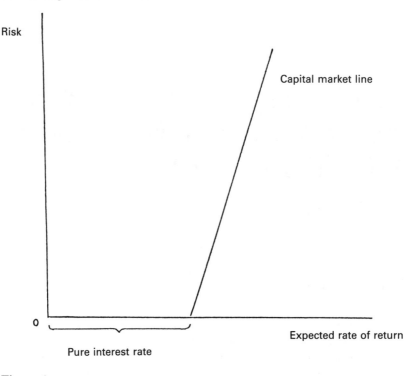

Figure 1

incurring additional risk. In effect, the market presents him with two prices: the *price of time*, or the pure interest rate (shown by the intersection of the line with the horizontal axis) and the *price of risk*, the additional expected return per unit of risk borne (the reciprocal of the slope of the line).

At present there is no theory describing the manner in which the price of risk results from the basic influences of investor preferences, the physical attributes of capital assets, etc. Moreover, lacking such a theory, it is difficult to give any real meaning to the relationship between the price of a single asset and its risk. Through diversification, some of the risk inherent in an asset can be avoided so that its total risk is obviously not the relevant influence on its price; unfortunately little has been said concerning the particular risk component which is relevant.

In the last ten years a number of economists have developed *normative* models dealing with asset choice under conditions of risk. Markowitz,[2]

[2] Harry M. Markowitz, *Portfolio Selection, Efficient Diversification of Investments* (New York: John Wiley and Sons, Inc., 1959). The major elements of the theory first appeared in his article 'Portfolio Selection', *The Journal of Finance*, XII (March 1952), 77–91.

following Von Neumann and Morgenstern, developed an analysis based on the expected utility maxim and proposed a general solution for the portfolio selection problem. Tobin[3] showed that under certain conditions Markowitz's model implies that the process of investment choice can be broken down into two phases: first, the choice of a unique optimum combination of risky assets; and second, a separate choice concerning the allocation of funds between such a combination and a single riskless asset. Recently, Hicks[4] has used a model similar to that proposed by Tobin to derive corresponding conclusions about individual investor behavior, dealing somewhat more explicitly with the nature of the conditions under which the process of investment choice can be dichotomized. An even more detailed discussion of this process, including a rigorous proof in the context of a choice among lotteries has been presented by Gordon and Gangolli.[5]

Although all the authors cited use virtually the same model of investor behavior,[6] none has yet attempted to extend it to construct a *market* equilibrium theory of asset prices under conditions of risk.[7] We will show that such an extension provides a theory with implications consistent with the assertions of traditional financial theory described above. Moreover, it sheds considerable light on the relationship between the price of an asset and the various components of its overall risk. For these reasons it warrants consideration as a model of the determination of capital asset prices.

Part II provides the model of individual investor behavior under conditions of risk. In Part III the equilibrium conditions for the capital market are considered and the capital market line derived. The implications for the relationship between the prices of individual capital assets and the various components of risk are described in Part IV.

---

[3] James Tobin, 'Liquidity Preference as Behavior Towards Risk', *The Review of Economic Studies*, XXV (February, 1958), 65–86.

[4] John R. Hicks, 'Liquidity', *The Economic Journal*, LXXII (December, 1962), 787–802.

[5] M.J. Gordon and Ramesh Gangolli, 'Choice Among and Scale of Play on Lottery Type Alternatives', College of Business Administration, University of Rochester, 1962. For another discussion of this relationship see W.F. Sharpe, 'A Simplified Model for Portfolio Analysis', *Management Science*, Vol. 9, No. 2 (January 1963), 277–293. A related discussion can be found in F. Modigliani and M.H. Miller, 'The Cost of Capital, Corporation Finance, and the Theory of Investment', *The American Economic Review*, XLVIII (June 1958), 261–297.

[6] Recently Hirshleifer has suggested that the mean-variance approach used in the articles cited is best regarded as a special case of a more general formulation due to Arrow. See Hirshleifer's 'Investment Decision Under Uncertainty', *Papers and Proceedings of the Seventy-Sixth Annual Meeting of the American Economic Association*, Dec. 1963, or Arrow's 'Le Role des Valeurs Boursieres pour la Repartition la Meilleure des Risques', *International Colloquium on Econometrics*, 1952.

[7] After preparing this paper the author learned that Mr Jack L. Treynor, of Arthur D. Little, Inc., had independently developed a model similar in many respects to the one described here. Unfortunately Mr Treynor's excellent work on this subject is, at present, unpublished.

II   Optimal investment policy for the individual

The investor's preference function

Assume that an individual views the outcome of any investment in probabilistic terms; that is, he thinks of the possible results in terms of some probability distribution. In assessing the desirability of a particular investment, however, he is willing to act on the basis of only two parameters of this distribution – its expected value and standard deviation.[8] This can be represented by a total utility function of the form:

$$U = f(E_w, \sigma_w)$$

where E_w indicates expected future wealth and σ_w the predicted standard deviation of the possible divergence of actual future wealth from E_w.

Investors are assumed to prefer a higher expected future wealth to a lower value, ceteris paribus ($dU/dE_w > 0$). Moreover, they exhibit risk-aversion, choosing an investment offering a lower value of σ_w to one with a greater level, given the level of E_w ($dU/d\sigma_w < 0$). These assumptions imply that indifference curves relating E_w and σ_w will be upward-sloping.[9]

To simplify the analysis, we assume that an investor has decided to commit a given amount (W_i) of his present wealth to investment. Letting W_t be his terminal wealth and R the rate of return on his investment:

$$R \equiv \frac{W_t - W_i}{W_i},$$

we have

$$W_t = R W_i + W_i.$$

This relationship makes it possible to express the investor's utility in terms of R, since terminal wealth is directly related to the rate of return:

$$U = g(E_R, \sigma_R).$$

---

[8] Under certain conditions the mean-variance approach can be shown to lead to unsatisfactory predictions of behavior. Markowitz suggests that a model based on the semi-variance (the average of the squared deviations below the mean) would be preferable; in light of the formidable computational problems, however, he bases his analysis on the variance and standard deviation.

[9] While only these characteristics are required for the analysis, it is generally assumed that the curves have the property of diminishing marginal rates of substitution between E_w and σ_w, as do those in our diagrams.

Figure 2 summarizes the model of investor preferences in a family of indifference curves; successive curves indicate higher levels of utility as one moves down and/or to the right.[10]

The investment opportunity curve

The model of investor behavior considers the investor as choosing from a set of investment opportunities that one which maximizes his utility. Every investment plan available to him may be represented by a point in the E_R, σ_R plane. If all such plans involve some risk, the area composed of such points will have an appearance similar to that shown in Figure 2. The investor will choose from among all possible plans the one placing him on the indifference curve representing the highest level of utility (point F). The decision can be made in two stages: first, find the set of efficient investment plans and, second choose one from among this set. A plan is said to be efficient if (and only if) there is no alternative with either (1) the same E_R and a lower σ_R, (2) the same σ_R and a higher E_R or (3) a higher E_R and a lower σ_R. Thus investment Z is inefficient since investments B, C, and D (among others) dominate it. The only plans which would be chosen must lie along the lower right-hand boundary (AFBDCX) – the *investment opportunity curve*.

To understand the nature of this curve, consider two investment plans – A and B, each including one or more assets. Their predicted expected values and

---

[10] Such indifference curves can also be derived by assuming that the investor wishes to maximize expected utility and that his total utility can be represented by a quadratic function of R with decreasing marginal utility. Both Markowitz and Tobin present such a derivation. A similar approach is used by Donald E. Farrar in *The Investment Decision Under Uncertainty* (Prentice-Hall, 1962). Unfortunately Farrar makes an error in his derivation; he appeals to the Von-Neumann-Morgenstern cardinal utility axioms to transform a function of the form:

$$E(U) = a + bE_R - cE_R^2 - c\sigma_R^2$$

into one of the form:

$$E(U) = k_1 E_R - k_2 \sigma_R^2$$

That such a transformation is not consistent with the axioms can readily be seen in this form, since the first equation implies non-linear indifference curves in the E_R, σ_R^2 plane while the second implies a linear relationship. Obviously no three (different) points can lie on both a line and a non-linear curve (with a monotonic derivative). Thus the two functions must imply different orderings among alternative choices in at least some instances.

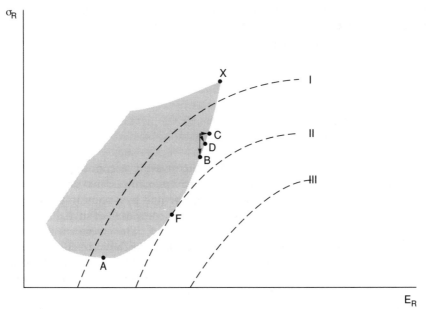

Figure 2

standard deviations of rate of return are shown in Figure 3. If the proportion α of the individual's wealth is placed in plan A and the remainder $(1-\alpha)$ in B, the expected rate of return of the combination will lie between the expected returns of the two plans:

$$E_{Rc} = \alpha E_{Ra} + (1 - \alpha) E_{Rb}$$

The predicted standard deviation of return of the combination is:

$$\sigma_{Rc} = \sqrt{\alpha^2 \sigma_{Ra}^2 + (1 - \alpha)^2 \sigma_{Rb}^2 + 2r_{ab}\, \alpha(1 - \alpha)\, \sigma_{Ra}\sigma_{Rb}}$$

Note that this relationship includes r_{ab}, the correlation coefficient between the predicted rates of return of the two investment plans. A value of $+1$ would indicate an investor's belief that there is a precise positive relationship between the outcomes of the two investments. A zero value would indicate a belief that the outcomes of the two investments are completely independent and -1 that the investor feels that there is a precise inverse relationship between them. In the usual case r_{ab} will have a value between 0 and $+1$.

Figure 3 shows the possible values of E_{Rc} and σ_{Rc} obtainable with different combinations of A and B under two different assumptions about the value of

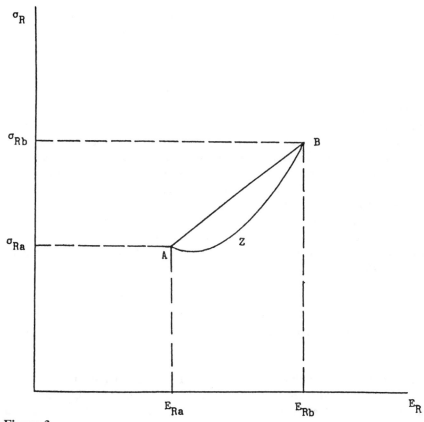

Figure 3

r_{ab}. If the two investments are perfectly correlated, the combinations will lie along a straight line between the two points, since in this case both E_{Rc} and σ_{Rc} will be linearly related to the proportions invested in the two plans.[11] If they are less than perfectly positively correlated, the standard deviation of any combination must be less than that obtained with perfect correlation (since r_{ab}

[11]

$$E_{Rc} = \alpha E_{Ra} + (1 - \alpha) E_{Rb} = E_{Rb} + (E_{Ra} - E_{Rb}) \alpha$$

$$\sigma_{Rc} = \sqrt{a^2 \sigma_{Ra}^2 + (1 - \alpha)^2 \sigma_{Rb}^2 \, \alpha(1 - \alpha) \, \sigma_{Ra} \, \sigma_{Rb}}$$

but $r_{ab} = 1$, therefore the expression under the square root sign can be factored:

$$\sigma_{Rc} = \sqrt{[\alpha \sigma_{Ra} + (1 - \alpha) \sigma_{Rb}]^2}$$

$$= \alpha \sigma_{Ra} + (1 - \alpha) \sigma_{Rb}$$

$$= \sigma_{Rb} + (\sigma_{Ra} - \sigma_{Rb}) \alpha$$

will be less); thus the combinations must lie along a curve below the line AB.[12] AZB shows such a curve for the case of complete independence ($r_{ab} = 0$); with negative correlation the locus is even more U-shaped.[13]

The manner in which the investment opportunity curve is formed is relatively simple conceptually, although exact solutions are usually quite difficult.[14] One first traces curves indicating E_R, σ_R values available with simple combinations of individual assets, then considers combinations of combinations of assets. The lower right-hand boundary must be either linear or increasing at an increasing rate ($d^2\sigma_R/dE^2_R > 0$). As suggested earlier, the complexity of the relationship between the characteristics of individual assets and the location of the investment opportunity curve makes it difficult to provide a simple rule for assessing the desirability of individual assets, since the effect of an asset on an investor's over-all investment opportunity curve depends not only on its expected rate of return (E_{Ri}) and risk (σ_{Ri}), but also on its correlations with the other available opportunities ($r_{i1}, r_{i2}, \ldots, r_{in}$). However, such a rule is implied by the equilibrium conditions for the model, as we will show in Part IV.

The pure rate of interest

We have not yet dealt with riskless assets. Let P be such an asset; its risk is zero ($\sigma_{Rp} = 0$) and its expected rate of return, E_{Rp}, is equal (by definition) to the pure interest rate. If an investor places α of his wealth in P and the remainder in some risky asset A, he would obtain an expected rate of return:

$$E_{Rc} = \alpha E_{Rp} + (1 - \alpha) E_{Ra}$$

The standard deviation of such a combination would be:

$$\sigma_{Rc} = \sqrt{\alpha^2\sigma_{Rp}^2 + (1 - \alpha)^2 \sigma_{Ra}^2 + 2r_{pa} \alpha(1 - \alpha) \sigma_{Rp}\sigma_{Ra}}$$

---

[12] This curvature is, in essence, the rationale for diversification.

[13] When $r_{ab} = 0$, the slope of the curve at point A is $-\dfrac{\sigma_{Ra}}{E_{Rb} - E_{Ra}}$, at point B it is $\dfrac{\sigma_{Rb}}{E_{Rb} - E_{Ra}}$.

When $r_{ab} = -1$, the curve degenerates to two straight lines to a point on the horizontal axis.

[14] Markowitz has shown that this is a problem in parametric quadratic programming. An efficient solution technique is described in his article, 'The Optimization of a Quadratic Function Subject to Linear Constraints', *Naval Research Logistics Quarterly*, Vol. 3 (March and June, 1956), 111–133. A solution method for a special case is given in the author's 'A Simplified Model for Portfolio Analysis', *op. cit.*

but since $\sigma_{Rp} = 0$, this reduces to:

$$\sigma_{Rc} = (1 - \alpha)\, \sigma_{Ra}.$$

This implies that all combinations involving any risky asset or combination of assets plus the riskless asset must have values of E_{Rc} and σ_{Rc} which lie along a straight line between the points representing the two components. Thus in Figure 4 all combinations of E_R and σ_R lying along the line PA are attainable if some money is loaned at the pure rate and some placed in A. Similarly, by lending at the pure rate and investing in B, combinations along PB can be attained. Of all such possibilities, however, one will dominate: that investment plan lying at the point of the original investment opportunity curve where a ray

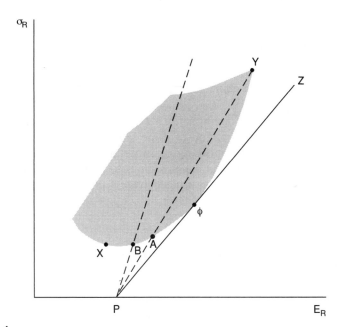

Figure 4

from point P is tangent to the curve. In Figure 4 all investments lying along the original curve from X to ϕ are dominated by some combination of investment in ϕ and lending at the pure interest rate.

Consider next the possibility of borrowing. If the investor can borrow at the pure rate of interest, this is equivalent to disinvesting in P. The effect of borrowing to purchase more of any given investment than is possible with the given amount of wealth can be found simply by letting α take on negative values in the equations derived for the case of lending. This will obviously give points lying along the extension of line PA if borrowing is used to purchase more of A; points lying along the extension of PB if the funds are used to purchase B, etc.

As in the case of lending, however, one investment plan will dominate all others when borrowing is possible. When the rate at which funds can be borrowed equals the lending rate, this plan will be the same one which is dominant if lending is to take place. Under these conditions, the investment opportunity curve becomes a line (PφZ in Figure 4). Moreover, if the original investment opportunity curve is not linear at point φ, the process of investment choice can be dichotomized as follows: first select the (unique) optimum combination of risky assets (point φ), and second borrow or lend to obtain the particular point on PZ at which an indifference curve is tangent to the line.[15]

Before proceeding with the analysis, it may be useful to consider alternative assumptions under which only a combination of assets lying at the point of tangency between the original investment opportunity curve and a ray from P can be efficient. Even if borrowing is impossible, the investor will choose φ (and lending) if his risk-aversion leads him to a point below φ on the line Pφ. Since a large number of investors choose to place some of their funds in relatively risk-free investments, this is not an unlikely possibility. Alternatively, if borrowing is possible but only up to some limit, the choice of φ would be made by all but those investors willing to undertake considerable risk. These alternative paths lead to the main conclusion, thus making the assumption of borrowing or lending at the pure interest rate less onerous than it might initially appear to be.

III   Equilibrium in the capital market

In order to derive conditions for equilibrium in the capital market we invoke two assumptions. First, we assume a common pure rate of interest, with all investors able to borrow or lend funds on equal terms. Second, we assume

---

[15] This proof was first presented by Tobin for the case in which the pure rate of interest is zero (cash). Hicks considers the lending situation under comparable conditions but does not allow borrowing. Both authors present their analysis using maximization subject to constraints expressed as equalities. Hicks' analysis assumes independence and thus insures that the solution will include no negative holdings of risky assets; Tobin's covers the general case, thus his solution would generally include negative holdings of some assets. The discussion in this paper is based on Markowitz' formulation, which includes non-negativity constraints on the holdings of all assets.

homogeneity of investor expectations:[16] investors are assumed to agree on the prospects of various investments – the expected values, standard deviations and correlation coefficients described in Part II. Needless to say, these are highly restrictive and undoubtedly unrealistic assumptions. However, since the proper test of a theory is not the realism of its assumptions but the acceptability of its implications, and since these assumptions imply equilibrium conditions which form a major part of classical financial doctrine, it is far from clear that this formulation should be rejected – especially in view of the dearth of alternative models leading to similar results.

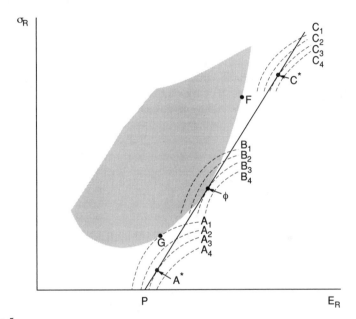

Figure 5

Under these assumptions, given some set of capital asset prices, each investor will view his alternatives in the same manner. For one set of prices the alternatives might appear as shown in Figure 5. In this situation, an investor with the preferences indicated by indifference curves A_1 through A_4 would seek to lend some of his funds at the pure interest rate and to invest the remainder in the combination of assets shown by point ϕ, since this would give him the preferred over-all position $A^\star$. An investor with the preferences

---

[16] A term suggested by one of the referees.

indicated by curves B_1 through B_4 would seek to invest all his funds in combination ϕ, while an investor with indifference curves C_1 through C_4 would invest all his funds plus additional (borrowed) funds in combination ϕ in order to reach his preferred position ($C^\star$). In any event, all would attempt to purchase only those risky assets which enter combination ϕ.

The attempts by investors to purchase the assets in combination ϕ and their lack of interest in holding assets not in combination ϕ would, of course, lead to a revision of prices. The prices of assets in ϕ will rise and, since an asset's expected return relates future income to present price, their expected returns will fall. This will reduce the attractiveness of combinations which include such assets; thus point ϕ (among others) will move to the left of its initial

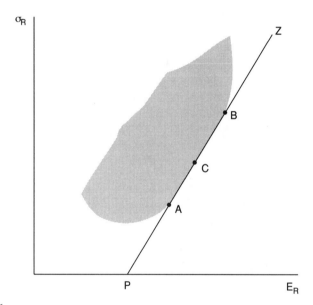

Figure 6

position.[17] On the other hand, the prices of assets not in ϕ will fall, causing an increase in their expected returns and a rightward movement of points representing combinations which include them. Such price changes will lead to a revision of investors' actions; some new combination or combinations will become attractive, leading to different demands and thus to further revisions

---

[17] If investors consider the variability of future dollar returns unrelated to present price, both E_R and σ_R will fall; under these conditions the point representing an asset would move along a ray through the origin as its price changes.

in prices. As the process continues, the investment opportunity curve will tend to become more linear, with points such as φ moving to the left and formerly inefficient points (such as F and G) moving to the right.

Capital asset prices must, of course, continue to change until a set of prices is attained for which every asset enters at least one combination lying on the capital market line. Figure 6 illustrates such an equilibrium condition.[18] All possibilities in the shaded area can be attained with combinations of risky assets, while points lying along the line PZ can be attained by borrowing or lending at the pure rate plus an investment in some combination of risky assets. Certain possibilities (those lying along PZ from point A to point B) can be obtained in either manner. For example, the E_R, σ_R values shown by point A can be obtained solely by some combination of risky assets; alternatively, the point can be reached by a combination of lending and investing in combination C of risky assets.

It is important to recognize that in the situation shown in Figure 6 many alternative combinations of risky assets are efficient (i.e., lie along line PZ), and thus the theory does not imply that all investors will hold the same combination.[19] On the other hand, all such combinations must be perfectly (positively) correlated, since they lie along a linear border of the E_R, σ_R region.[20] This provides a key to the relationship between the prices of capital assets and different types of risk.

IV   The prices of capital assets

We have argued that in equilibrium there will be a simple linear relationship between the expected return and standard deviation of return for efficient combinations of risky assets. Thus far nothing has been said about such a relationship for individual assets. Typically the E_R, σ_R values associated with

---

[18] The area in Figure 6 representing E_R, σ_R values attained with only risky assets has been drawn at some distance from the horizontal axis for emphasis. It is likely that a more accurate representation would place it very close to the axis.

[19] This statement contradicts Tobin's conclusion that there will be a unique optimal combination of risky assets. Tobin's proof of a unique optimum can be shown to be incorrect for the case of perfect correlation of efficient risky investment plans if the line connecting their E_R, σ_R points would pass through point P. In the graph on page 83 of this article (*op. cit.*) the constant-risk locus would, in this case, degenerate from a family of ellipses into one of straight lines parallel to the constant-return loci, thus giving multiple optima.

[20] E_R, σ_R values given by combinations of any two combinations must lie within the region and cannot plot above a straight line joining the points. In this case they cannot plot below such a straight line. But since only in the case of perfect correlation will they plot along a straight line, the two combinations must be perfectly correlated. As shown in Part IV, this does not necessarily imply that the individual securities they contain are perfectly correlated.

single assets will lie above the capital market line, reflecting the inefficiency of undiversified holdings. Moreover, such points may be scattered throughout the feasible region, with no consistent relationship between their expected return and total risk (σ_R). However, there will be a consistent relationship between their expected returns and what might best be called *systematic risk*, as we will now show.

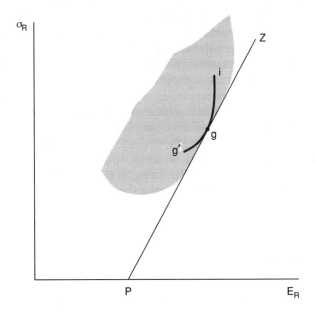

Figure 7

Figure 7 illustrates the typical relationship between a single capital asset (point i) and an efficient combination of assets (point g) of which it is a part. The curve igg' indicates all E_R, σ_R values which can be obtained with feasible combinations of asset i and combination g. As before, we denote such a combination in terms of a proportion α of asset i and $(1 - \alpha)$ of combination g. A value of $\alpha = 1$ would indicate pure investment in asset i while $\alpha = 0$ would imply investment in combination g. Note, however, that $\alpha = .5$ implies a total investment of more than half the funds in asset i, since half would be invested in i itself and the other half used to purchase combination g, which also includes some of asset i. This means that a combination in which asset i does not appear at all must be represented by some negative value of α. Point g' indicates such a combination.

In Figure 7 the curve igg' has been drawn tangent to the capital market line (PZ) at point g. This is no accident. All such curves must be tangent to the capital market line in equilibrium, since (1) they must touch it at the point representing the efficient combination and (2) they are continuous at that point.[21] Under these conditions a lack of tangency would imply that the curve intersects PZ. But then some feasible combination of assets would lie to the right of the capital market line, an obvious impossibility since the capital market line represents the efficient boundary of feasible values of E_R and σ_R.

The requirement that curves such as igg' be tangent to the capital market line can be shown to lead to a relatively simple formula which relates the expected rate of return to various elements of risk for all assets which are included in combination g.[22] Its economic meaning can best be seen if the relationship between the return of asset i and that of combination g is viewed in a manner

---

[21] Only if $r_{ig} = -1$ will the curve be discontinuous over the range in question.

[22] The standard deviation of a combination of g and i will be:

$$\sigma = \sqrt{\alpha^2 \sigma_{Ri}^2 + (1 - \alpha)^2 \sigma_{Rg}^2 + 2r_{ig}\,\alpha(1 - \alpha)\,\sigma_{Ri}\sigma_{Rg}}$$

at $\alpha = 0$:

$$\frac{d\sigma}{d\alpha} = -\frac{1}{\sigma}\,[\sigma_{Rg}^2 - r_{ig}\sigma_{Ri}\sigma_{Rg}]$$

but $\sigma = \sigma_{Rg}$ at $\alpha = 0$. Thus:

$$\frac{d\sigma}{d\alpha} = [\sigma_{Rg} - r_{ig}\sigma_{Ri}]$$

The expected return of a combination will be:

$$E = \alpha E_{Ri} + (1 - \alpha)\,E_{Rg}$$

Thus, at all values of α:

$$\frac{dE}{d\alpha} = -[E_{Rg} - E_{Ri}]$$

and, at $\alpha = 0$:

$$\frac{d\sigma}{dE} = \frac{\sigma_{Rg} - r_{ig}\sigma_{Ri}}{E_{Rg} - E_{Ri}}.$$

Let the equation of the capital market line be:

$$\sigma_R = s(E_R - P)$$

where P is the pure interest rate. Since igg' is tangent to the line when $\alpha = 0$, and since (E_{Rg}, σ_{Rg}) lies on the line:

$$\frac{\sigma_{Rg} - r_{ig}\sigma_{Ri}}{E_{Rg} - E_{Ri}} = \frac{\sigma_{Rg}}{E_{Rg} - P}$$

or

$$\frac{r_{ig}\sigma_{Ri}}{\sigma_{Rg}} = -\left[\frac{P}{E_{Rg} - P}\right] + \left[\frac{1}{E_{Rg} - P}\right]E_{Ri}.$$

Return on asset 1 (Ri)

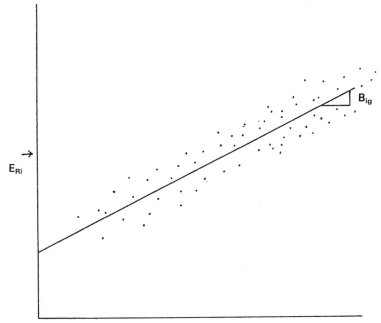

Figure 8

similar to that used in regression analysis.[23] Imagine that we were given a number of (ex post) observations of the return of the two investments. The points might plot as shown in Figure 8. The scatter of the R_i observations around their mean (which will approximate E_{Ri}) is, or course, evidence of the total risk of the asset – σ_{Ri}. But part of the scatter is due to an underlying relationship with the return on combination g, shown by B_{ig}, the slope of the regression line. The response of R_i to changes in R_g (and variations in R_g itself) account for much of the variation in R_i. It is this component of the asset's total risk which we term the *systematic risk*. The remainder,[24] being uncorrelated with R_g, is the unsystematic component. This formulation of the relationship between R_i and R_g can be employed *ex ante* as a predictive model. B_{ig} becomes the *predicted* response of R_i to changes in R_g. Then, given σ_{Rg} (the predicted risk of R_g), the systematic portion of the predicted risk of each asset can be determined.

[23] This model has been called the diagonal model since its portfolio analysis solution can be facilitated by re-arranging the data so that the variance-covariance matrix becomes diagonal. The method is described in the author's article, cited earlier.

[24] ex post, the standard error.

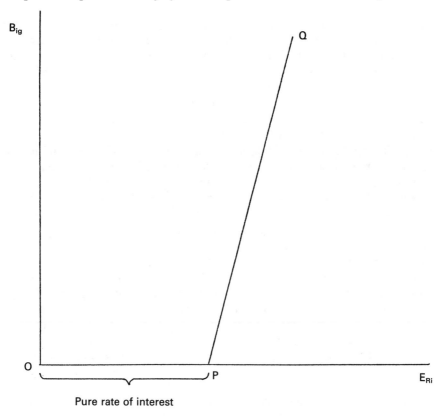

Figure 9

This interpretation allows us to state the relationship derived from the tangency of curves such as igg' with the capital market line in the form shown in Figure 9. All assets entering efficient combination g must have (predicted) B_{ig} and E_{Ri} values lying on the line PG.[25] Prices will adjust so that assets which are more responsive to changes in R_g will have higher expected returns than

<hr>

25

$$r_{ig} = \sqrt{\frac{Big^2 \sigma_{Rg}^2}{\sigma_{Ri}^2}} = \frac{B_{ig} \sigma_{Rg}}{\sigma_{Ri}}$$

and

$$B_{ig} = \frac{r_{ig} \sigma_{Ri}}{\sigma_{Rg}}.$$

The expression on the right is the expression on the left-hand side of the last equation in footnote 22. Thus:

$$B_{ig} = -\left[\frac{P}{E_{Rg} - P}\right] + \left[\frac{1}{E_{Rg} - P}\right] E_{Ri}.$$

those which are less responsive. This accords with common sense. Obviously the part of an asset's risk which is due to its correlation with the return on a combination cannot be diversified away when the asset is added to the combination. Since B_{ig} indicates the magnitude of this type of risk it should be directly related to expected return.

The relationship illustrated in Figure 9 provides a partial answer to the question posed earlier concerning the relationship between an asset's risk and its expected return. But thus far we have argued only that the relationship holds for the assets which enter some particular efficient combination (g). Had another combination been selected, a different linear relationship would have been derived. Fortunately this limitation is easily overcome. As shown in the footnote,[26] we may arbitrarily select *any* one of the efficient combinations, then measure the predicted responsiveness of *every* asset's rate of return to that of the combination selected; and these coefficients will be related to the expected rates of return of the assets in exactly the manner pictured in Figure 9.

The fact that rates of return from all efficient combinations will be perfectly correlated provides the justification for arbitrarily selecting any one of them. Alternatively we may choose instead any variable perfectly correlated with the rate of return of such combinations. The vertical axis in Figure 9 would then indicate alternative levels of a coefficient measuring the sensitivity of the rate of return of a capital asset to changes in the variable chosen.

---

[26] Consider the two assets i and i*, the former included in efficient combination g and the latter in combination g*. As shown above:

$$B_{ig} = - \left[\frac{P}{E_{Rg} - P} \right] + \left[\frac{1}{E_{Rg} - P} \right] E_{Ri}$$

and:

$$B_{i*g*} = - \left[\frac{P}{E_{Rg*} - P} \right] + \left[\frac{1}{E_{Rg*} - P} \right] E_{Ri*}$$

Since R_g and R_{g*} are perfectly correlated:

$$r_{i*g*} = r_{i*g}$$

Thus:

$$\frac{B_{i*g*}\sigma_{Rg*}}{\sigma_{Ri*}} = \frac{B_{i*g}\sigma_{Rg}}{\sigma_{Ri*}}$$

and:

$$B_{i*g*} = B_{i*g} \left[\frac{\sigma_{Rg}}{\sigma_{Rg*}} \right].$$

This possibility suggests both a plausible explanation for the implication that all efficient combinations will be perfectly correlated and a useful interpretation of the relationship between an individual asset's expected return and its risk. Although the theory itself implies only that rates of return from efficient combinations will be perfectly correlated, we might expect that this would be due to their common dependence on the over-all level of economic activity. If so, diversification enables the investor to escape all but the risk resulting from swings in economic activity – this type of risk remains even in efficient combinations. And, since all other types can be avoided by diversification, only the responsiveness of an asset's rate of return to the level of economic activity is relevant in assessing its risk. Prices will adjust until there is a linear relationship between the magnitude of such responsiveness and expected return. Assets which are unaffected by changes in economic activity will return the pure interest rate; those which move with economic activity will promise appropriately higher expected rates of return.

This discussion provides an answer to the second of the two questions posed in this paper. In Part III it was shown that with respect to equilibrium conditions in the capital market as a whole, the theory leads to results consistent with classical doctrine (i.e., the capital market line). We have now shown that with regard to capital assets considered individually, it also yields implications consistent with traditional concepts: it is common practice for investment counselors to accept a lower expected return from defensive

---

Since both g and g* lie on a line which intercepts the E-axis at P:

$$\frac{\sigma_{Rg}}{\sigma_{Rg^\star}} = \frac{E_{Rg} - P}{E_{Rg^\star} - P}$$

and:

$$B_{i^\star g^\star} = B_{i^\star g} \left[\frac{E_{Rg} - P}{E_{Rg^\star} - P} \right]$$

Thus:

$$-\left[\frac{P}{E_{Rg^\star} - P} \right] + \left[\frac{1}{E_{Rg^\star} - P} \right] E_{Ri^\star} = B_{i^\star g} \left[\frac{E_{Rg} - P}{E_{Rg^\star} - P} \right]$$

from which we have the desired relationship between $R_{i^\star}$ and g:

$$B_{i^\star g} = -\left[\frac{P}{E_{Rg} - P} \right] + \left[\frac{1}{E_{Rg} - P} \right] E_{Ri^\star}$$

$B_{i^\star g}$ must therefore plot on the same line as does B_{ig}

securities (those which respond little to changes in the economy) than they require from aggressive securities (which exhibit significant response). As suggested earlier, the familiarity of the implications need not be considered a drawback. The provision of a logical framework for producing some of the major elements of traditional financial theory should be a useful contribution in its own right.

Reproduced from Sharpe, W.F. (1964). Capital asset prices: a theory of market equilibrium under conditions of risk. *The Journal of Finance*, September, by permission of the American Finance Association.

5 Risk aversion in the stock market: some empirical evidence

W. F. Sharpe*

A recent article in this *Journal*[1] explored the conditions for equilibrium in the market for capital assets under the assumptions that investors are risk-averters, have similar (probabilistic) beliefs about the future performance of various assets, and can borrow or lend funds at a common (pure) interest rate. Briefly, the article showed that under such conditions market prices of capital assets will adjust so that the predicted risk of each efficient portfolio's rate of return is linearly related to its predicted expected rate of return. Letting σ_i stand for the standard deviation of the subjective probability distribution of the rate of return on an efficient portfolio, and E_i for the expected value of the distribution, the prices of capital assets will adjust until all efficient portfolios conform to the relationship:[2]

$$E_i = p + b\sigma_i$$

where p is the pure (riskless) interest rate and b (>0) is the risk-premium. An important corollary concerns the relationship among the predicted rates of return on efficient portfolios: under the assumed conditions they will be perfectly correlated.

Strictly speaking, the implications of this theory cannot be tested practically, since the relationships refer to predictions concerning expected returns from

---

* Associate Professor of Economics and Operations Research, University of Washington, and Consultant, The RAND Corporation. The views expressed in this paper are those of the author. They should not be interpreted as reflecting the views of The RAND Corporation or the official opinion or policy of any of its governmental or private research sponsors.

[1] W.F. Sharpe, 'Capital Asset Prices: A Theory of Market Equilibrium Under Conditions of Risk', *The Journal of Finance*, Vol. XIX, No. 3 (September 1964), pp.425–442.
[2] By definition, for an inefficient portfolio $E_i < p + b\sigma_1$.

assets and the associated risks. Clearly, actual results may diverge considerably from the predictions made by investors at the time they purchase assets. Moreover, investor preferences and investment opportunities presumably change over time. This poses a major problem: if the equilibrium value of p (the price of time) and b (the price of risk) change from year, it may be dangerous to use data from several years to estimate their average values. But if the results from several years are not used, how can predicted values of E_i and σ_i be estimated? In many respects the problem is similar to that of measuring demand curves. If any empirical tests are to be performed, rather stringent assumptions must be made.

The remainder of this paper shows the results obtained by using *ex post* values of the means and standard deviations of return as surrogates for the corresponding *ex ante* predictions of investors. Section I provides evidence concerning the relationship between E_i and σ_i for the portfolios held by a number of open-end mutual funds. With the additional assumption that such portfolios were efficient, the data can be used to test the assertion that for efficient portfolios, larger values of E_i are associated with larger values of σ_i – i.e., the risk-premium (b) is positive. The linearity of the relationship is discussed in Section II. Section III presents some results bearing on the corollary that the returns from efficient portfolios will be highly correlated with one another, and hence with some over-all index of performance. The results are summarized briefly in Section IV.

I

To provide some evidence concerning the behavior of the capital market, the annual returns from 34 open-end mutual funds[3] during the period from 1954 through 1963 were analyzed in the manner suggested by the theory. The average rate of return[4] for each fund over the ten-year period was used as an estimate of its expected rate of return (E_i). Similarly, the standard deviation[5] of the actual rate of return for each fund over the ten-year period was used as an estimate of its predicted risk (σ_i). Lacking any satisfactory test for reasonable diversification, all 34 funds were assumed to have chosen efficient

---

[3] The funds selected were those for which annual rates of return were given by Weisenberger for at least the last twenty years. All data are from Arthur Weisenberger and Co., *Investment Companies*, 1962 and 1964 editions.

[4] In all cases, rate of return is based on the sum of dividend payments, capital gains distributions, and changes in net asset value.

[5] Derived from an estimate of variance computed by dividing the sums of the squared deviations by (N–1).

combinations of securities.[6] Needless to say, the measures utilized cannot be expected to perfectly reflect investors' predictions and some mutual funds may hold rather inefficient portfolios; thus the relationship between the values of σ_i and E_i in the sample will be approximate at best. But if the theory is worth any consideration at all, there should be such a relationship, it should be significant, and funds experiencing greater variability should provide greater average returns.

Table 1 shows the results for the 34 funds in the sample; the E_i, σ_i, combination for each fund is plotted as a point in Figure 1. The predicted relationship is clearly present. The correlation coefficient between σ and E is +.836, highly significant[7] and consistent with the assumption of risk-aversion.

It is not a simple matter to select appropriate estimates for the pure interest rate and the risk-premium from the sample data. The market process by which E_i and σ_i values are made to follow a linear relationship involves changes in the prices of capital assets; the price changes in turn alter the values of both E_i and σ_i.[8]

Since neither can properly be considered an independent variable, the appropriate line for estimating their relationship presumably lies between the one obtained by regressing σ on E and that obtained by regressing E on σ. Figure 1 shows the two regression lines and an intermediate one. The latter is simply the line passing through the intersection of the two regression lines[9] with a risk-premium (b) equal to the average of the values for the regression lines. The estimates of the pure interest rate and the risk-premium corresponding to the three lines are:

	p	b
Regression line: σ on E	2.06	0.678
Regression line: E on σ	5.55	0.474
Intermediate line	3.81	0.576

The values obtained from the intermediate line can be interpreted as follows. During this period investors required (and got) an annual rate of

---

[6] The return on a fund is, of course, slightly less than the return on its portfolio, due to the expenses incurred by the fund's management. For the purposes of this analysis, the two are assumed to be equal.

[7] A coefficient of .45 is significant at $P = .01$; the t-value of the slope of the regression line is 8.61.

[8] Recall that E_i and σ_i refer to the mean and standard deviation of the rate of return.

[9] This point corresponds to the average values of E_i and σ_i for the funds in the sample. The values are:

$$\overline{E_i} = 13.64\% \text{ per annum}$$
$$\overline{\sigma_i} = 17.07\% \text{ per annum.}$$

return of approximately 3.8 per cent on riskless assets. To take on risk, they required (and got) an additional .58 per cent of expected return per annum for each 1 per cent of predicted standard deviation of annual return (risk). These values may or may not properly characterize the conditions in the capital

Table 1

Mutual fund	Average annual return 1954–1963 (E_1)	Standard deviation of annual return 1954–1963 (σ_i)
1 Affiliated Fund	14.6%	15.3%
2 American Business Shares	10.0	9.2
3 Axe-Houghton, Fund A	10.5	13.5
4 Axe-Houghton, Fund B	12.0	16.3
5 Axe-Houghton, Stock Fund	11.9	15.6
6 Boston Fund	12.4	12.1
7 Broad Street Investing	14.8	16.8
8 Bullock Fund	15.7	19.3
9 Commonwealth Investment Company	10.9	13.7
10 Delaware Fund	14.4	21.4
11 Dividend Shares	14.4	15.9
12 Eaton and Howard, Balanced Fund	11.0	11.9
13 Eaton and Howard, Stock Fund	15.2	19.2
14 Equity Fund	14.6	18.7
15 Fidelity Fund	16.4	23.5
16 Financial Industrial Fund	14.5	23.0
17 Fundamental Investors	16.0	21.7
18 Group Securities, Common Stock Fund	15.1	19.1
19 Group Securities, Fully Administered Fund	11.4	14.1
20 Incorporated Investors	14.0	25.5
21 Investment Company of America	17.4	21.8
22 Investors Mutual	11.3	12.5
23 Loomis-Sayles Mutual Fund	10.0	10.4
24 Massachusetts Investors Trust	16.2	20.8
25 Massachusetts Investors – Growth Stock	18.6	22.7
26 National Investors Corporation	18.3	19.9
27 National Securities – Income Series	12.4	17.8
28 New England Fund	10.4	10.2
29 Putnam Fund of Boston	13.1	16.0
30 Scudder, Stevens and Clark Balanced Fund	10.7	13.3
31 Selected American Shares	14.4	19.4
32 United Funds – Income Fund	16.1	20.9
33 Wellington Fund	11.3	12.0
34 Wisconsin Fund	13.8	16.9

market during the period covered by the sample. Even if they do, there is no *a priori* reason to assume that they will characterize any future period. However, for purposes of prediction these results may be as useful as any others presently available.

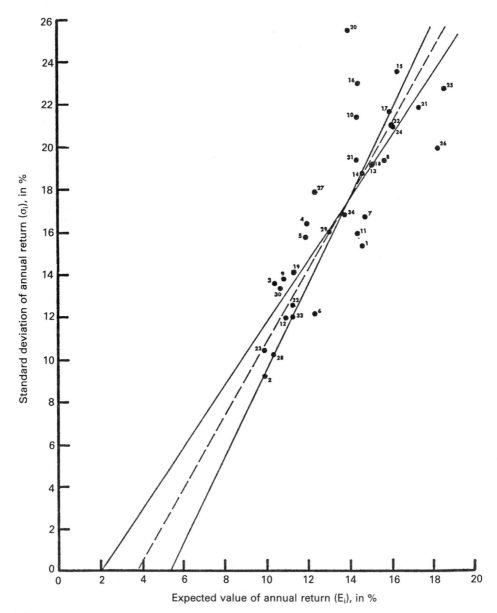

Figure 1

II

Thus far we have shown that higher values of σ_i are associated with higher values of E_i, but we have not tested directly the implication of the theory that the relationship is linear. This conclusion is a direct result of the assumption that investors can either borrow or lend at a common pure interest rate. If an investor's funds can be divided between a risky portfolio and an investment at the pure interest rate, he can obtain any combination of E and σ on the line connecting the point representing the E, σ combination of the risky portfolio and the point representing the E, σ combination obtained with the pure interest rate.[10] If the investor is able to borrow funds at the same rate of interest, any point on the extension of the line to higher values of E and σ is also attainable. Under these conditions all efficient portfolios must lie along a straight line passing through the point representing the pure interest rate. If the assumptions are violated, of course, this relationship need not hold. Since investors are probably unable to borrow extensively at the pure interest rate in order to purchase risky assets, we should not be too surprised to find that the relationship between σ and E turns upward from a straight line as higher values of E (and σ) are reached.

There is some evidence of such curvature in the sample data. A quadratic regression equation gave a slightly higher correlation coefficient than did the linear regression equation ($+.852$ instead of $+.836$)[11] and the curvature was of the type anticipated. This result could be due to the presence of one or more relatively inefficient portfolios in the region of high risk,[12] but no satisfactory method for testing the validity of this explanation is available. In any event, although the implication of linearity is violated to some extent, it seems reasonable to assert that for purposes of characterizing the general nature of the capital market the relationship between σ and E for efficient portfolios can be assumed to be linear.

---

[10] This relationship (and those in the remainder of the paragraph) can be found in Sharpe, *op. cit.*, pp.431–433.

[11] The regression equation was of the form: $E = a + b\sigma + c\sigma^2$. The t-values of the latter two coefficients were:

$$b: +2.87$$
$$c: -1.78$$

The relative magnitudes of the two correlation coefficients given in the text overstate slightly the advantage of the quadratic equation since one more degree of freedom was lost in its estimation. A χ^2 test of the normality of the distribution of the residuals from the regression of σ on E shows that the assumption of linearity is significant at $p = .30$.

[12] The fund with the highest standard deviation may well be guilty of this charge.

III

If all efficient portfolios lie along a straight line in the (E, σ) plane, their predicted rates of return will be perfectly correlated. Putting it another way, the predicted rate of return of any single portfolio should be linearly related to that of any other we might choose for the comparison. If each portfolio is compared with the same (standard) portfolio, the correlation coefficients should all equal $+1$. As before, we can only use actual results as surrogates for predicted performance, and thus cannot expect perfect correlations. However, if an appropriate standard is selected, relatively high values should be obtained.

To test this implication of the theory, a correlation coefficient was computed for each of the 34 funds – measuring the extent to which the values of the

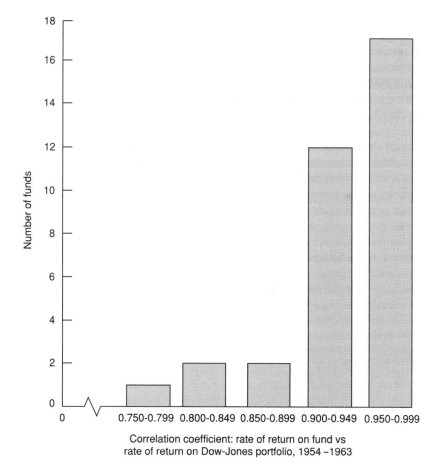

Correlation coefficient: rate of return on fund vs
rate of return on Dow-Jones portfolio, 1954–1963

Figure 2

fund's actual rate of return during the ten-year period were correlated with those of the 30-security portfolio used to compute the Dow-Jones Industrial Average. Figure 2 shows the distribution of the correlation coefficients for the 34 funds. Needless to say, none was +1, and the sample size used to compute each coefficient was only ten (since just ten values of annual rate of return were employed). However, although no satisfactory test for consistency can be employed, the results certainly appear to be in substantial agreement with the theory.

IV

This concludes the evidence. Although fragmentary, and not even particularly novel,[13] the data do lend considerable support to the theory tested. Mutual fund portfolios that show substantial variability in annual return provide larger returns on the average than do those with less variable returns, as predicted by the risk-aversion hypothesis. And though the relationship between average yield and standard deviation does not appear to be perfectly linear, the differences are slight and in the expected direction. Finally, the portfolios exhibit the high correlations with the over-all market predicted by the theory.

Although these results are comforting, the issues surrounding the behavior of the capital market are far from settled. It is entirely possible that data obtained from different segments of the market and different time periods may not conform to the relationships predicted by the theory and found here.[14] Hopefully more detailed and extensive investigations will be made in the future; the importance of the subject certainly warrants the effort.

Reproduced from Sharpe, W.F. (1965). Risk aversion in the stock market: some empirical evidence. *The Journal of Finance*, September, by permission of the American Finance Association.

---

[13] A similar analysis can be found in W.F. Sharpe, *Portfolio Analysis Based on a Simplified Model of the Relationships Among Securities*, PhD. Dissertation, UCLA, June 1961. A sample of 23 mutual funds showed similar relationships in two separate periods: 1940–1951 and 1951–1959. In the study leading to his recent article, 'How to Rate Management of Investment Funds', *The Harvard Business Review*, January/February 1965, Vol. 43, No. 1, pp.63–75, Jack L. Treynor apparently obtained results similar to those given here (although they are not stated explicitly in the article). The tests described here are sufficiently obvious that it seems reasonable to assume that they have been performed elsewhere as well, although no results appear to have been published.

[14] In particular, a sample of portfolios with larger standard deviations might exhibit even greater non-linearity due to the greater importance of the discrepancy between borrowing and lending rates.

6 The arbitrage theory of capital asset pricing

S. A. Ross *

The purpose of this paper is to examine rigorously the arbitrage model of capital asset pricing developed in Ross [13,14]. The arbitrage model was proposed as an alternative to the mean variance capital asset pricing model, introduced by Sharpe, Lintner, and Treynor, that has become the major analytic tool for explaining phenomena observed in capital markets for risky assets. The principal relation that emerges from the mean variance model holds that for any asset, i, its (ex ante) expected return

$$E_i = \rho + \lambda b_i, \tag{1}$$

where ρ is the riskless rate of interest, λ is the expected excess return on the market, $E_m - \rho$, and

$$b_i \equiv \sigma im^2/\sigma m^2,$$

is the beta coefficient on the market, where σm^2 is the variance of the market portfolio and σ_{im}^2 is the covariance between the returns on the ith asset and the market portfolio. (If a riskless asset does not exist, ρ is the zero-beta return, i.e., the return on all portfolios uncorrelated with the market portfolio.)[1]

The linear relation in (1) arises from the mean variance efficiency of the market portfolio, but on theoretical grounds it is difficult to justify either the assumption of normality in returns (or local normality in Weiner diffusion models) or of quadratic preferences to guarantee such efficiency, and on empirical grounds the conclusions as well as the assumptions of the theory

* This work was supported by a grant from the Rodney L. White Center for Financial Research at the University of Pennsylvania and by National Science Foundation Grant GS-35780.
[1] See Black [2] for an analysis of the mean variance model in the absence of a riskless asset.

have also come under attack.[2] The restrictiveness of the assumptions that underlie the mean variance model have, however, long been recognized, but its tractability and the evident appeal of the linear relation between return, E_i, and risk, b_i, embodied in (1) have ensured its popularity. An alternative theory of the pricing of risky assets that retains many of the intuitive results of the original theory was developed in Ross [13,14].

In its barest essentials the argument presented there is as follows. Suppose that the random returns on a subset of assets can be expressed by a simple factor model

$$\tilde{x}_i = E_i + \beta_i \tilde{\delta} + \tilde{\epsilon}_i, \tag{2}$$

where $\tilde{\delta}$ is a mean zero common factor, and $\tilde{\epsilon}_i$ is mean zero with the vector $\langle \tilde{\epsilon} \rangle$ sufficiently independent to permit the law of large numbers of hold. Neglecting the noise term, $\tilde{\epsilon}_i$, as discussed in Ross [14] (2) is a statement that the state space tableau of asset returns lies in a two-dimensional space that can be spanned by a vector with elements δ_θ, (where θ denotes the state of the world) and the constant vector, $e \equiv \langle 1, \ldots, 1 \rangle$.

Step 1 Form an arbitrage portfolio, η, of all the n assets, i.e., a portfolio which uses no wealth, $\eta e = 0$. We will also require η to be a well-diversified portfolio with each component, η_i, of order $1/n$ in (absolute) magnitude.

Step 2 By the law of large numbers, for large n the return on the arbitrage portfolio

$$\begin{aligned} \eta \tilde{x} &= \eta E + (\eta \beta)\, \tilde{\delta} + \eta \tilde{\epsilon} \\ &\approx \eta E + (\eta \beta)\, \tilde{\delta}. \end{aligned} \tag{3}$$

In other words the influence on the well-diversified portfolio of the independent noise terms becomes negligible.

Step 3 If we now also require that the arbitrage portfolio, η, be chosen so as to have no systematic risk, then

$$\eta \beta = 0,$$

and from (3)

$$\eta \tilde{x} \approx \eta E.$$

Step 4 Using no wealth, the random return $\eta \tilde{x}$ has now been engineered to be equivalent to a certain return, ηE, hence to prevent arbitrarily large

[2] See Blume and Friend [3] for a recent example of some of the empirical difficulties faced by the mean variance model. For a good review of the theoretical and empirical literature on the mean variance model see Jensen [6].

disequilibrium positions we must have $\eta E = 0$. Since this restriction must hold for all η such that $\eta e = \eta \beta = 0$, E is spanned by e and β or

$$E_i = \rho + \lambda \beta_i \qquad (4)$$

for constants ρ and λ. Clearly if there is a riskless asset, ρ must be its rate of return. Even if there is not such an asset, ρ is the rate of return on all zero-beta portfolios, α, i.e., all portfolios with $\alpha e = 1$ and $\alpha \beta = 0$. If α is a particular portfolio of interest, e.g., the market portfolio, α_m, with $E_m = \alpha_m E$, (4) becomes

$$E_i = \rho + (E_m - \rho) \beta_i. \qquad (5)$$

Condition (5) is the arbitrage theory equivalent of (1), and if $\tilde{\delta}$ is a market factor return then β_i will approximate b_i. The above approach, however, is substantially different from the usual mean-variance analysis and constitutes a related but quite distinct theory. For one thing, the argument suggests that (5) holds not only in equilibrium situations, but in all but the most profound sort of disequilibria. For another, the market portfolio plays no special role.

There are, however, some weak points in the heuristic argument. For example, as the number of assets, n, is increased, wealth will, in general, also increase. Increasing wealth, though, may increase the risk aversion of some economic agents. The law of large numbers implies, in Step 2, that the noise term, $\eta \tilde{\epsilon}$, becomes negligible for large n, but if the degree of risk aversion is increasing with n these two effects may cancel out and the presence of noise may persist as an influence on the pricing relation. In Section I we will present an example of a market where this occurs. Furthermore, even if the noise term can be eliminated, it is not at all obvious that (5) must hold, since the disequilibrium position of one agent might be offset by the disequilibrium position of another.[3]

In Ross [13], however, it was shown that if (5) holds then it represents an ϵ or quasi-equilibrium. The intent of this paper is to supply the rigorous analysis underlying the stronger stability arguments above. In Section II we will present some weak sufficient conditions to rule out the above exceptions (and the example of Section I) and we will prove a general version of the arbitrage result. Section II also includes a brief argument on the empirical practicality of the results. A mathematical appendix contains some supportive results of a somewhat technical and tangential nature. Section III will briefly summarize the paper and suggest further generalizations.

---

[3] Green has considered this point in a temporary equilibrium model. Essentially he argues that if subjective anticipations differ too much, then arbitrage possibilities will threaten the existence of equilibrium.

I   A counterexample

In this section we will present an example of a market where the sequence of equilibrium pricing relations does not approach the one predicted by the arbitrage theory as the number of assets is increased. The counterexample is valuable because it makes clear what sort of additional assumptions must be imposed to validate the theory.

Suppose that there is a riskless asset and that risky assets are independently and normally distributed as

$$\tilde{x}_i = E_i + \tilde{\epsilon}_i, \tag{6}$$

where

$$E\{\tilde{\epsilon}_i\} = 0,$$

and

$$E\{\tilde{\epsilon}_i^2\} = \sigma^2.$$

The arbitrage argument would imply that in equilibrium all of the independent risk would disappear and, therefore,

$$E_i \approx \rho. \tag{7}$$

Assume, however, that the market consists of a single agent with a von Neumann–Morgenstern utility function of the constant absolute risk aversion form,

$$U(z) = -\exp(-Az). \tag{8}$$

Letting w denote wealth with the riskless asset as the numeraire, and α the portfolio of risky assets (i.e. α_i is the proportion of wealth placed in the ith risky asset) and taking expectations we have

$$
\begin{aligned}
E\{U[w(\rho + \alpha[\tilde{x} - \rho \cdot e])]\} \\
&= -\exp(-Aw\rho) \, E\{\exp(-Aw\alpha[\tilde{x} - \rho \cdot e])\} \\
&= -\exp(-Aw\rho)\{\exp(-Aw\alpha[E - \rho \cdot e] + (\sigma^2/2)(Aw)^2(\alpha'\alpha))\}.
\end{aligned}
\tag{9}
$$

The first-order conditions at a maximum are given by

$$\sigma^2(Aw)\,\alpha_i = E_i - \rho. \tag{10}$$

If the riskless asset is in unit supply the budget constraint (Walras' Law for the market) becomes

$$w = \sum_{i=1}^{n} \alpha_i w + 1 = (1/A\sigma^2) \sum_{i=1}^{n} (E_i - \rho) + 1. \qquad (11)$$

The interpretation of the budget constraint (11) depends on the particular market situation we are describing. Suppose, first, that we are adding assets which will pay a random total numeraire amount, $\tilde{c}_i$. If p_i is the current numeraire price of the asset then

$$\tilde{x}_i = \tilde{c}_i/p_i.$$

Normalizing all risky assets to be in unit supply we must have

$$p_i = \alpha_i w,$$

and the budget constraint simply asserts that wealth is summed value,

$$w = \sum_{i=1}^{n} p_i + 1.$$

If we let $\bar{c}_i$ denote the mean of $\tilde{c}_i$ and c^2, its variance, then (10) can be solved for p_i as

$$p_i = (1/\rho)\{\bar{c}_i - Ac^2\}.$$

As a consequence, the expected returns,

$$E_i \equiv \bar{c}_i/p_i = \rho\{\bar{c}_i/(\bar{c}_i - Ac^2)\},$$

will be unaffected by changes in the number of assets, n, for $i < n$, and need bear no systematic relation to ρ as n increases. This is a violation of the arbitrage condition, (7). Notice, too, that as long as $\bar{c}_i$ is bounded above Ac^2, wealth and relative risk aversion, Aw, are unbounded in n.

An alternative interpretation of the market situation would be that as n increases the number of risky investment opportunities or activities is being increased, but *not* the number of assets. In this case wealth, w, would simply be the number of units of the riskless asset held and would remain constant as n increased. The quantities $\alpha_i w$ now represent the amount of the riskless holdings put into the ith investment opportunity and for the market as a whole we must have

$$\sum_{i=1}^{n} \alpha_i < 1.$$

Furthermore, if the random technological activities are irreversible, then each $\alpha_i \geq 0$. From (10) it follows that

$$E_i - \rho \geq 0$$

and

$$\sum_{i=1}^{n} E_i - \rho = \sum_{i=1}^{n} | E_i - \rho | = \sigma^2(Aw) \sum_{i=1}^{n} \alpha_i < \sigma^2 Aw.$$

Hence, as $n \rightarrow \infty$, the vector E approaches the constant vector with entries ρ in absolute sum (the l_1 norm) which is a very strong type of approximation. Under this second interpretation, then, the arbitrage condition (7) holds.

An easy way to understand the distinction between these two interpretations is to conceive of the riskless asset as silver dollars, and the risky assets as slot machines. In the first interpretation the slot machines come with a silver dollar in the slot and p_i is the relative price of the ith 'primed' machine in terms of silver dollars. In the alternative interpretation, the machines are 'unprimed' and we invest $\alpha_i w$ silver dollars in the ith machine. Which of these two senses of a market being 'large' is empirically more relevant is a debatable issue, and in the next section we will develop assumptions sufficient to verify the arbitrage result for both cases (and any intermediate ones as well).

II The arbitrage theory

The difficulty with the constant absolute risk aversion example arises because the coefficient of relative risk aversion increases with wealth. This suggests considering risk averse agents for whom the coefficient of relative risk aversion is uniformly bounded,

$$\sup_{x} \{-(U''(x) \, x/U'(x))\} \leq R < \infty. \tag{12}$$

We will refer to such agents as being of Type B (for bounded).

Pratt has shown that given a Type B utility function, U, there exists a monotone increasing convex function, $G(\cdot)$, such that

$$U(x) = G[U(x; R)], \tag{13}$$

where $U(x;R)$ is the utility function with constant relative risk aversion, R. It is well known that

$$U(x; R) = \begin{cases} x^{1-R}/(1 - R) & \text{if } R \neq 1, \\ \log x & \text{if } R = 1, \end{cases} \tag{14}$$

Essentially, then, Type B agents are uniformly less risk averse than some constant relative risk averse agents.

Assume that the returns on the particular subset of assets under consideration are subjectively viewed by agents in the market as being generated by a model of the form

$$\begin{aligned} \tilde{x}_i &= E_i + \beta_{i1}\tilde{\delta}_1 + \cdots + \beta_{ik}\tilde{\delta}_k + \tilde{\epsilon}_i, \\ &\equiv E_i + \beta_i\tilde{\delta} + \tilde{\epsilon}_i, \end{aligned} \tag{15}$$

where

$$E\{\tilde{\delta}_l\} = E\{\tilde{\epsilon}_i^2\} = 0,$$

and where the $\tilde{\epsilon}_i$'s are mutually stochastically uncorrelated. We will impose no further restrictions on the form of the multivariate distribution of $(\tilde{\delta}, \tilde{\epsilon})$ beyond the requirement that $(\exists\ \sigma < \infty)$

$$\sigma_i^2 \equiv E\{\tilde{\epsilon}_i^2\} \leq \sigma^2. \tag{16}$$

In particular, then, the $\tilde{\delta}_i$ need not be jointly independent or even independent of the $\tilde{\epsilon}_i$'s, they need not possess variances, and none of the random variables need be normally distributed.

A point on notation is also needed. In what follows, α^0 will denote an n-element optimal portfolio for the agent under consideration, i.e., α^0 maximizes $E\{U[w\alpha\tilde{x}]\}$, subject to $\alpha e = 1$. The vector β^l will be the column vector $\langle\beta_{1l} \ldots \beta_{nl}\rangle'$ and β_i, as above, denotes the row vector $\langle\beta_{i1}, \ldots, \beta_{ik}\rangle$. The single letter β will denote the matrix

$$[\beta^1\colon \cdots \cdots \colon\beta^k].$$

Assumption 1 (liability limitations)

There exists at least one asset with limited liability in the sense that there is some bound, t, (per unit invested) to the losses for which an agent is liable.

Assumption 1 is satisfied in the real world by a wide variety of assets. We can now prove a key result about Type B agents.

Theorem I

Consider a Type B agent who lives in a world that satisfies Assumption 1 and who believes that returns are generated by a model of the form of (15). If ($\exists m < \infty$) such that

$$\alpha^0 E \leq m, \tag{17}$$

then ($\exists \rho$ and a k vector, γ) such that

$$\sum_{i=1}^{\infty} [E_i - \rho - \beta_i \gamma]^2 < \infty. \tag{18}$$

Proof   The result is independent of the particular wealth sequence $\langle w^n \rangle$ and we must prove it for arbitrary sequences. Assume that $R \neq 1$. We will prove the theorem by constructing a portfolio that bests α^0 when (18) does not hold. First, from (17), concavity and monotonicity

$$E\{U[w^n \, \alpha^0 \tilde{x}]\}$$
$$\leq \; U[w^n \alpha^0 E]$$
$$\leq \; U[w^n m]$$
$$= \; G[(w^n)^{1-R} \, U(m; R)].$$

Now, consider the arbitrage portfolio sequence that solves the associated quadratic problem of minimizing unsystematic (ϵ) risk subject to the constraints of having no systematic (β) risk and attaining an expected return greater than $m + t$: minimize

$$\eta' V \eta,$$

subject to

$$\eta'e = 0,$$
$$\eta'\beta^l = 0; \quad l = 1, \ldots, k, \tag{19}$$

and

$$\eta'E = c > m + t,$$

where V is the covariance matrix of $\langle\tilde{\epsilon}\rangle$ and where t is the maximum liability loss associated with a unit investment in the limited liability asset. Assumption 1 guarantees that t is bounded. We will also assume, without loss of generality, that V is of full rank for all n.[4]

If the constraints are unsolvable for all n, then E must be linearly dependent on e and the columns of β and we are done. Suppose then, that the constraints are solvable for all n sufficiently large and, without loss of generality, let

$$X \equiv [E : \beta : e]$$

be of full rank.[5]

We will assume that if a sequence of random variables converges to a degenerate law (a constant) in quadratic mean, then the expected utility also converges, and defer a rigorous examination of this point to an appendix. It follows that there must not be any subsequence on which

$$\eta'V\eta \to 0.$$

If such a subsequence existed then

$$E\{U(\eta\tilde{x} - t; R)\} \to U(c - t; R) > U(m; R),$$

and by the convexity of $G(\bullet)$ there would exist an n such that putting all wealth in the limited liability asset and buying the arbitrage portfolio would yield

---

[4] Since the $\tilde{\epsilon}_i$ are uncorrelated, V is a diagonal matrix and will be of less than full rank only if some asset has no noise term. If there are two or more such assets the arbitrage argument holds exactly and we can eliminate such assets without loss of generality.

[5] If $[\beta]$ is not of full rank then we can simply eliminate dependent factors. If $[\beta]$ is of full rank, but $[\beta:e]$ is not, then all assets will have a common factor $\tilde{\xi}$ and we can write (15) as

$$\tilde{x}_i = E_i + \tilde{\xi} + \beta_i\delta + \tilde{\epsilon}_i.$$

Now the proof of Theorem I is essentially unaltered, with the common factor, ξ retained in all portfolios.

$$E\{U[w^n(\eta\tilde{x} - t)]\} = E\{G[(w^n)^{1-R} U((\eta\tilde{x} - t); R)]\}$$
$$\geq G[(w^n)^{1-R} E\{U((\eta\tilde{x} - t): R\}]$$
$$> G[(w^n)^{1-R} U(m; R)],$$

violating optimality. Hence ($\exists a > 0$) such that ($\forall n$)

$$\eta' V\eta \geq a > 0.$$

Solving (19) we have

$$V\eta = X\lambda,$$

where λ is a $(k + 2)$-vector of multipliers, and applying the constraints of (19) yields

$$[X'V^{-1} X]\,\lambda = \begin{bmatrix} c \\ 0 \end{bmatrix}.$$

It now follows that

$$\eta' V\eta = \lambda' \begin{bmatrix} c \\ 0 \end{bmatrix}$$
$$= [c, 0]\,[X'V^{-1}X]^{-1} \begin{bmatrix} c \\ 0 \end{bmatrix}$$
$$\geq a > 0.$$

Defining $b \equiv (c,0)$ we can apply Lemma I in the Appendix to obtain the existence of $a^\star$ and $A < \infty$ such that for all n

$$(Xa^\star)'(Xa^\star) \leq A < \infty, \tag{20}$$

where

$$a^\star b = ca_1^\star = 1$$

or

$$a_1^\star = 1/c.$$

Defining $(1, -\gamma, -\rho) = ca^\star$, (20) becomes the desired result (18).

If $R = 1$, wealth can be factored out of the utility function additively and the proof is nearly identical. QED

Theorem I asserts that for a Type B individual, if the optimal expected return is uniformly bounded, then it must be the case that the arbitrage condition

$$E_i \approx \rho + \beta_i \gamma$$
$$= \rho + \gamma_1 \beta_{i1} + \cdots + \gamma_k \beta_{ik},$$

holds in the approximate sense that the sum of squared deviations is uniformly bounded. This implies, among other things, that as n increases

$$| E_n - \rho - \beta_n \gamma | \to 0. \tag{21}$$

A number of simple corollaries of Theorem I are available. If we adopt the alternative interpretation, suggested in Section I, that $\tilde{x}_i$ is the return on the ith activity, then wealth will be confined to a compact interval if there are a limited number of actual assets. It is easy to see that if wealth is confined to a compact interval on which the utility function is bounded, then Theorem I will hold for any risk averse agent. We also have the following corollary.

Corollary I

Under the conditions of Theorem I if there is a riskless asset then ρ may be taken to be its rate of return.

Proof   The return per unit of wealth in the presence of a riskless asset is given by

$$\rho + \alpha(\tilde{x} - \rho),$$

where α is now the portfolio of risky assets. Deleting the constraint that $\eta e = 0$ we can simply repeat the proof of Theorem I with $(E - \rho e)$ in the place of the E vector.   QED

Corollary I, of course, also extends to the alternative interpretation.

To turn these results into a capital market theory we will assume that there is at least one Type B individual who does not become negligible as the number of assets, n, is increased. The following definition is helpful.

Definition   The agent, a^v, will be said to be asymptotically negligible if, as the number of assets increases,

$$\omega^v \equiv w^v/w \to 0,$$

where w^v is the agent's wealth and w is the total wealth, i.e.,

$$w \equiv \sum_v w^v.$$

For example, an agent will not be asymptotically negligible if the sequence of proportionate quantities of assets the agent is endowed with is bounded away from zero.

Assumption 2 (nonnegligibility of Type B agents)

There exists at least one Type B agent who believes that returns are generated by a model of the form of (15) and who is not asymptotically negligible.

To permit us to aggregate to a market relation we will make three more assumptions; essentially we must ensure that Theorem I will not be 'undone' by the rest of the economy. First we assume that agents hold compatible subjective beliefs.

Assumption 3 (homogeneity of expectations)

All agents hold the same expectations, E. Furthermore, all agents are risk averse.[6]

Assumption 4 (extent of disequilibria)

Let ξ_i denote the aggregate demand for the ith asset as a fraction of total wealth. We will assume that only situations with $\xi_i \geq 0$ are to be considered.

---

[6] The assumption of risk aversion is quite weak since if fair gambles are permitted, any bounded nonconcave portions of agents' utility functions would be irrelevant. See Raiffa [11] or Ross [12] for an elaboration of this point.

Notice that Assumption 4 does not rule out the possibility that an asset can be in excess supply; it only implies that the economy as a whole will wish to hold some of it. Assumptions 3 and 4 can be weakened considerably as will be shown below, but for purposes of demonstration we have chosen to leave them in a stronger than necessary form.

Lastly, we need to specify the generating model (15) a bit more.

Assumption 5 (boundedness of expectations)

The sequence, $\langle E_i \rangle$ is uniformly bounded, i.e.,

$$\| E \| \equiv \sup_i | E_i | < \infty. \tag{22}$$

Assumption 5 will be discussed in Section III.
We can now prove our central result.

Theorem II

Given Assumptions 1 through 5, $(\exists \rho, \gamma)$

$$\sum_{i=1}^{\infty} \{E_i - \rho - \beta_i \gamma\}^2 < \infty \tag{18}$$

Furthermore, if there is a riskless asset, then ρ is its rate of return.[7]
Proof From Theorem I we know that if the conclusion is false then for the Type B agent (on a subsequence)

$$\sum_i \alpha_i^0 E_i \to \infty \tag{23}$$

Let the total fraction of wealth held by the Type B agent be given by ω^0 and by the rest of the economy by $\hat\omega$. If $\hat\alpha_i$ denotes the fraction of $\hat\omega$ held in asset i by the rest of the economy then by Assumption 4

---

[7] Theorems I and II and Corollary I can be extended to the case where (15) holds for only a subset of the assets by generalizing the utility function to be a Lebesque dominated sequence of functions conditional on the other assets.

$$\xi_i \equiv \omega^0\alpha_i^0 + \hat{\omega}\hat{\alpha}_i \geqslant 0.$$

By definition,

$$\sum_i \xi_i = 1,$$

hence

$$\| E \| \geqslant \sum_i \xi_i E_i$$

$$= \sum_i (\omega^0\alpha_i^0 + \hat{\omega}\hat{\alpha}_i) \, E_i$$

$$= \omega^0 \sum_i \alpha_i^0 \, E_i + \hat{\alpha} \sum_i \hat{\omega}_i E_i.$$

From (23) and Assumption 2 the first sum in the last expression is divergent, which together with Assumption 5 (22) implies that

$$\hat{\omega} \sum_i \hat{\alpha}_i E_i \rightarrow \infty.$$

Since

$$\hat{\omega}\hat{\alpha}_i \equiv \sum_{v \neq 0} \omega^v\alpha_i^v,$$

where ω^v is the fraction of wealth held by a^v, it follows that

$$\hat{\omega} \sum_i \hat{\alpha}_i E_i = \sum_i \sum_{v \neq 0} \omega^v\alpha_i^v E_i$$

$$= \sum_{v \neq 0} \left\{ \sum_i \omega^v\alpha_i^v E_i \right\},$$

and for some agent, a^v,

$$\sum_i \omega^v \alpha_i^v E_i \to -\infty,$$

on a subsequence. By Assumptions 1 and 3 this contradicts optimality.

The identification of ρ with the riskless return follows from Corollary 1.

QED

Theorem II has a straightforward extension to the alternative interpretation of $\tilde{x}_i$ as the return on activity i. In the extension, though, we can, of course, drop Assumption 2 and obtain (18) from Assumptions 1, 3, 4 and 5 alone.

As was shown in Ross [14] the basic result of Theorem 2 can be written in a number of empirically interesting and intuitively appealing formats. For example, by appropriate normalization it can be shown that

$$E_i - \rho \approx \beta_{i1}(E^1 - \rho) + \cdots + \beta_{ik}(E^k - \rho), \tag{24}$$

where E^l is the return on all portfolios with $\alpha\beta^s = 0$ for $s \neq l$ and $\alpha\beta^l = 1$. The constant ρ is now the return on all $\alpha\beta = 0$, i.e., zero-beta portfolios. Thus, the risk premium on an asset is the β-weighted sum of the factor risk premiums.

While we have formally proven the main result that the sum of squared deviations from the basic pricing relation is bounded above as the number of assets increases, it is worthwhile spending some effort to obtain an empirical estimate of the size of this bound. To do this we will work with a more exact form of our results. Examining the proof of Theorem I and Lemma I in the Appendix, we have found a bound to

$$\sum_{i=1}^n [E_n - \rho - \beta_n \gamma]^2 \leq c^2 A$$

$$= (1/ha) \, c^2,$$

or, using the exact form of Lemma I, (obtained by leaving the H^n matrices in the sum) we have

$$\sum_{i=1}^n (1/\sigma_i^2)[E_i - \rho - \beta_i \gamma]^2 \leq c^2/a, \tag{25}$$

where c is the return premium on the arbitrage portfolio over a risk free rate ($-t$ in (19)) and a is the lower limit on the variance of an arbitrage portfolio.

If we assume that the market portfolio, as a well-diversified portfolio, cannot be grossly inefficient in a mean variance sense, and if we ignore ex ante-ex post distinctions, then we can use observed market data (see Friend [4] and Myers [9] for the data which follow) to obtain a rough estimate of the bound in (25). Over the period from January 1, 1962 to December 31, 1971 the yearly market return (Standard and Poor's Composite Index) averaged 7.4% and the risk free rate (prime corporates with 1 year to maturity) averaged 5.1% for a market risk premium of

$$c = 2.3\%.$$

The sample variance of the market portfolio in this period was $(0.123)^2$, and we will assume that no arbitrage portfolio earning the market risk premium could have had less than one-half the market variance. Hence,

$$a = \frac{1}{2}(0.123)^2,$$

and from (25),

$$\sum_{i=1}^{n} (1/\sigma_i^2)[E_i - \rho - \beta_i\gamma]^2 \leqslant 2(0.023)^2/(0.123)^2.$$

The average residual variance in this period from regressions of asset returns on the market portfolio was about $2(0.123)^2$ and using this as a proxy for σ_i^2, the average squared discrepancy is approximately

$$\text{average}(E_i - \rho - \beta_i\gamma)^2 \leqslant (1/n) \, 4(0.023)^2.$$

Taking the number of assets n to be the combined total of listed issues on the NYSE and the Amex on December 31, 1971, about 3000, the average absolute discrepancy is given by

$$\text{average} \mid E_i - \rho - \beta_i\gamma \mid \leqslant 2 \cdot 0.023/3000^{1/2} = 0.00084,$$

or about 1% of the market return of 7.4%.

Of course these estimates are very crude and are only intended to be indicative; assets with a high own variance will have a greater latitude for discrepancies than those with low own variances. Most importantly, though, to the extent that there is significant cross-sectional correlation across the $\tilde{\epsilon}_i$ terms, the addition of further factors should reduce the own variance terms, σ_i^2, and improve the estimates.

III Generalizations and conclusions

One of the strengths of Theorem II is that it does not require the stringent homogeneity of anticipations of the mean-variance theory. We are now obviously distinguishing between expectations, i.e., the E vector, and anticipations, the whole model (15). If other agents have the same ex ante expectations, but believe returns are generated in a different fashion, then (24) must still hold where β is that of the return generating model believed to hold by the Type B agent. Of course, this is a bit gratuitous since in this model, as in all others, it is necessary to translate the results into observable quantities and the usual ex ante-ex post identity becomes ambiguous with disparate anticipations. Even if all agents agree on (15), however, there is still considerable scope for disagreement on the underlying probability distributions. For example, if $\tilde{\delta}$ represents a market or 'GNP' factor, then as long as all agents agree on the impact of this factor on returns, through β_{i1}, they can hold a variety of views on the distribution of $\tilde{\delta}$ without violating the basic arbitrage condition, (24). Similarly, agents can also disagree on the distribution of the idiosyncratic noise terms, $\tilde{\epsilon}_i$, without altering (24). The primary difficulty with the analysis arises when agents differ in their expectations, E^v. Now the proof of Theorem II must be modified since, unless all E^v vectors are positive multiples of the same vector, we cannot be assured that the divergence of $\alpha^v E^\tau$ to $-\infty$ for $\tau \neq v$, implies that $\alpha^v E^v \to -\infty$. This is a fruitful area for generalizations.

It is also possible to weaken the condition that $\tilde{\epsilon}_i$ be mutually uncorrelated. For example, if the assets can be ordered so that $\tilde{\epsilon}_i$ and $\tilde{\epsilon}_j$ are uncorrelated if $|i - j|$ exceeds a given number, then the analysis is unchanged. In general, any weakening that permits a law of large numbers to hold should be sufficient, although weaker forms of the law would result in weaker approximation norms for the pricing relation (24).

Lastly, it should be emphasized that (24) is much more of an arbitrage relation than an equilibrium condition and may be expected to be quite robust. Assumptions 4 and 5 served only to guarantee that the market return,

$$E_m \equiv \sum_i \xi_i E_i, \qquad (26)$$

would be uniformly bounded and this will hold in a wide class of disequilibrium situations. Rather than simply assuming that E_m was bounded, we chose to make Assumptions 4 and 5 directly to see how sufficient conditions for a bounded E_m would appear in alternative economic situations. For example, Assumption 4 can be weakened if, instead of having required all $\xi_i \geq 0$, we had assumed that $\sum_i |\xi_i|$ was bounded, i.e., we had bounded the sum of the absolute proportions of wealth placed (or shorted) in all assets. This would also be sufficient to bound the market return. In practice, these are very weak conditions and easily satisfied.[8]

In conclusion, we have set forth a rigorous basis for the arbitrage relation and arguments analyzed in Ross [14] (and [13]), and the conditions which are sufficient to support the theory have some intuitive appeal. On a less optimistic note, though, while significantly weakening the assumption that investors have identical (or homogeneous) anticipations, the arbitrage theory still requires essentially identical expectations and agreement on the β coefficients, if the identification of ex ante beliefs with ex post realizations is to provide empirically fruitful results. If this assumption is to be fundamentally weakened, this theory (and all others) will require a closer examination of the dynamics by which ex ante beliefs are transformed into ex post observations. Such a study properly lies in the domain of general disequilibrium dynamics and, in particular, should focus on the impact of information on markets. It is one of the most difficult and important areas for future research.

Appendix 1

In this appendix we prove the lemma referred to in the proofs of the paper. Define a sequence of $n \times k$ matrices, $\langle X^n \rangle$, by taking the first row, the first two rows, and so on of an infinite matrix with k columns.

---

[8] A strong form of Theorem 2 can be obtained by assuming that the weighted sum of subjectively viewed expected portfolio returns

$$\sum_v \omega^v \sum_i \alpha_i^v E_i^v \tag{F1}$$

is uniformly bounded. This would permit us to delete Assumptions 4, 5 and even 3 and, formally at least, would allow heterogeneous expectations. Alternatively, we could replace Assumption 5 with $\|E^v\| < \infty$, retain Assumption 4 (or the weaker form described in Section III) and drop Assumption 3.

Furthermore, if agents agree on factors and if the actual ex post model generating returns is some convex combination (say wealth weighted, or, for that matter, any uniformly sup norm bounded linear operator) of the individual market ex ante models, then the basic arbitrage condition will be expressible in ex post observables and, as such, will be directly testable. See Ross [14] for a fuller discussion of these issues. None of this, however, is very satisfactory. For one thing, it is not clear what is the force of these boundedness conditions, particularly when the number of agents is typically much larger than the number of marketed assets. As an example, if we have two Type B agents with exactly divergent beliefs (in a sense, which can be made precise in special examples) then they can exactly offset each other. There is now no reason to expect (F1), unlike (26), to be bounded simply because observed ex post return is bounded. For another, we must translate the theory into a statement about observables and this requires relating divergent subjective ex ante expectations to ex post ones via the 'right' generating mechanism in a less ad hoc fashion. This is the problem posed in Section III and makes the 'strong' version of Theorem II inadequate to stand alone.

Lemma I

Let $\langle X^n \rangle$ be a sequence of $n \times k$ matrices and let $\langle H^n \rangle$ be a sequence of diagonal matrices with diagonal elements $\langle h_1 \rangle$, $\langle h_1, h_2 \rangle$, and so on where, for some h, $h_i \geq h > 0$ for all i. Assume ($\exists b$, a) ($\forall X^n$ of full rank)

$$b'[X^{n'}H^nX^n]^{-1}b \geq a > 0. \tag{A1}$$

It follows that ($\exists a^\star$ and A)

$$(X^n a^\star)'(X^n a^\star) \leq A < \infty$$

and

$$a^{\star'}b = 1.$$

Proof The result is trivial if X^n is of less than full rank for all n. In addition, if X^n is of full rank for some n ($\geq k$) then $X^{\tilde{n}}$ is of full rank, $\tilde{n} > n$, and we may assume that the sequence $\langle X^n \rangle$ ($n \geq k$) is of full rank for all n. By positive definiteness $X^{n'}H^nX^n$ is of full rank and (A1) holds.

Consider the problem:

$$\min(X^n z^n)' H^n (X^n z^n),$$

subject to

$$z^{n'}b = 1.$$

The solution is given by

$$z^n = \gamma[X^{n'}H^nX^n]^{-1}b,$$

where

$$\begin{aligned}
\gamma &= (X^n z^n)' H^n (X^n z^n) \\
&= (b'[X^{n'}H^nX^n]^{-1}b)^{-1} \\
&\leq 1/a < \infty,
\end{aligned}$$

by (A1). Consequently, from the lower bound on $\langle h_i \rangle$ we now obtain

$$(X^n z^n)'(X^n z^n) \leq A \equiv 1/ha < \infty.$$

Letting $y^n \equiv X^n z^n$ implies that $y^{n'} y^n \le A$. If X is a full rank submatrix of X^n then

$$Xz^n = y^n \mid X,$$

where $y^n \mid X$ is the corresponding subvector of y^n, and since $y^n \mid X$ is bounded in the norm it has a convergent subsequence. Letting $y^\star$ be its limit we must have $z^n \to a^\star \equiv X^{-1} y^\star$ on the subsequence. It remains to show that $(\forall n)(X^n a^\star)'(X^n a^\star) \le A$. Assume to the contrary that for some $\hat{n}$ (and, therefore, all $n > \hat{n}$)

$$(X^{\hat{n}} a^\star)'(X^{\hat{n}} a^\star) > A.$$

Since $z^n \to a^\star$ on a subsequence we would have the contradiction

$$(X^n z^n)'(X^n z^n) \ge (X^{\hat{n}} z^n)'(X^{\hat{n}} z^n) > A \qquad \text{for some } n.$$

It follows that $(\forall n)\ (X^n a^\star)'(X^n a^\star) \le A$. In addition, since $z^{n'} b = 1$ for all n we must also have $a^{\star'} b = 1$. QED

Appendix 2

In this appendix we discuss the relationship between convergence in quadratic mean (q.m.) and expected utility. The technical results can be found in Loeve [8] and Billingsley [1].

We can begin with a simple but powerful result. Let $\langle \tilde{X}_n \rangle$ be a sequence of random variables with $E\{\tilde{X}_n\} = 0$, and $\tilde{X}_n \to 0$ (q.m.), i.e., $\sigma^2(\tilde{X}_n) \to 0$.

Proposition

If $U(\cdot)$ is a concave and bounded below (which implies that the domain of $U(\cdot)$ is left bounded), then

$$E\{U[\rho + \tilde{X}_n]\} \to U(\rho).$$

Proof By Fatou's lemma

$$\liminf E\{U[\rho + \tilde{X}_n]\} \ge U(\rho).$$

But by concavity

$$E\{U[\rho + \tilde{X}_n]\} \leq U(\rho),$$

hence

$$\lim E\{U[\rho + \tilde{X}_n]\} = U(\rho),$$

QED

A problem arises when $U(\cdot)$ is unbounded from below. About the weakest condition which assures convergence is uniform integrability (UI):

$$\lim_{\alpha \to \infty} \sup_n \int_{\Omega_\alpha} |U(\rho + X_n)| \, d\eta_n = 0,$$

$$\Omega_\alpha \equiv \{|U(\rho + X_n)| \geq \alpha\},$$

where η_n is the distribution function of X_n.

A number of familiar conditions imply UI. If the sequence $U(\rho + \tilde{X}_n)$ is bounded below by an integrable function the Lebesque convergence theorem can be invoked or if ($\exists \delta > 0$)

$$\sup_n E\{|U(\rho + X_n)|^{1+\delta}\} < \infty,$$

then the sequence is UI.

In general, then, the convergence criterion will depend on both the utility function and the random variables. It is possible, however, to find weak sufficient conditions on the random variables alone, by taking advantage of the structure of $\tilde{X}_n$, but the condition that $\tilde{X}_n = (1/n)\Sigma_i \tilde{\epsilon}_i$; σ_i^2 uniformly bounded and $\tilde{\epsilon}_i$, $\tilde{\epsilon}_j$ independent is not sufficient.[9]

In the text, it is assumed that all sequences satisfy the UI condition, and therefore

$$\tilde{X}_n \to a \qquad \text{(q.m.)}$$

will imply that

$$E\{U(\tilde{X}_n)\} \to U(a).$$

---

[9] It is not difficult to construct counterexamples by having $U(\cdot)$ go to $-\infty$ rapidly enough as x approaches its lower bound.

References

1 P. Billingsley, 'Convergence of Probability Measures', Wiley, New York, 1968.
2 F. Black, Capital market equilibrium with restricted borrowing, *J. Business* **45** (1972), 444–455.
3 M. Blume and I. Friend, A new look at the capital asset pricing model, *J. Finance* (March 1973), 19–33.
4 I. Friend, Rates of return on bonds and stocks, the market price of risk, and the cost of capital, Working Paper No. 23–73, Rodney L. White Center for Financial Research, 1973.
5 J. Green, Preexisting contracts and temporary general equilibrium, *in* 'Essays on Economic Behavior under Uncertainty' (Balch, McFadden, and Wir, Eds.), North–Holland, Amsterdam, 1974.
6 M. Jensen, Capital markets: theory and evidence, *Bell. J. Econ. and Management Science* **3** (1972), 357–398.
7 J. Lintner, The valuation of risk assets and the selection of risky investments in stock portfolios and capital budgets, *Rev. Econ. Statist.* (February 1965), 30–55.
8 M. Loeve, 'Probability Theory', Van Nostrand, Princeton, N.J., 1963.
9 S. Myers, A reexamination of market and industry factors in stock price behavior, *J. Finance* (June 1973), 695–705.
10 J. Pratt, Risk aversion in the small and in the large, *Econometrica* **32** (1964), 122–137.
11 H. Raiffa, 'Decision Analysis', Addison-Wesley, Reading, Mass., 1968.
12 S. Ross, Comment on 'Consumption and Portfolio Choices with Transaction Costs', by E. Zabel and R. Multherjee, *in* 'Essays on Economic Behavior under Uncertainty' (Balch, McFadden, and Wir, Eds.), North–Holland, Amsterdam, 1974.
13 S. Ross, Portfolio and capital market theory with arbitrary preferences and distributions – The general validity of the mean-variance approach in large markets, Working Paper No. 12–72, Rodney L. White Center for Financial Research, 1971.
14 S. Ross, Return, risk and arbitrage, *in* 'Risk and Return in Finance' (Friend and Bicksler, Eds.), Ballinger, Cambridge, Mass., forthcoming.
15 W. Sharpe, Capital asset prices: A theory of market equilibrium under conditions of risk, *J. Finance* (September 1964), 425–442.
16 J. Treynor, Toward a theory of market value of risky assets, unpublished manuscript, 1961.

7 Does the capital asset pricing model work?

D. W. Mullins, Jr

Although its application continues to spark vigorous debate, modern financial theory is now applied as a matter of course to investment management. And increasingly, problems in corporate finance are also benefiting from the same techniques. The response promises to be no less heated. CAPM, the capital asset pricing model, embodies the theory. For financial executives, the proliferation of CAPM applications raises these questions: What is CAPM? How can they use the model? Most important, does it work?

CAPM, a theoretical representation of the behavior of financial markets, can be employed in estimating a company's cost of equity capital. Despite limitations, the model can be a useful addition to the financial manager's analytical tool kit.

The burgeoning work on the theory and application of CAPM has produced many sophisticated, often highly complex extensions of the simple model. But in addressing the above questions I shall focus exclusively on its simple version. Even so, finding answers to the questions requires an investment of time to understand the theory underlying CAPM.

What is CAPM?

Modern financial theory rests on two assumptions:

1 Securities markets are very competitive and efficient (that is, relevant information about the companies is quickly and universally distributed and absorbed);
2 these markets are dominated by rational, risk-averse investors, who seek to maximize satisfaction from returns on their investments.

The first assumption presumes a financial market populated by highly sophisticated, well-informed buyers and sellers. The second assumption describes investors who care about wealth and prefer more to less. In addition, the hypothetical investors of modern financial theory demand a premium in the form of higher expected returns for the risks they assume.

Although these two assumptions constitute the cornerstones of modern financial theory, the formal development of CAPM involves other, more specialized limiting assumptions. These include frictionless markets without imperfections like transaction costs, taxes, and restrictions on borrowing and short selling. The model also requires limiting assumptions concerning the statistical nature of securities returns and investors' preferences. Finally, investors are assumed to agree on the likely performance and risk of securities, based on a common time horizon.

The experienced financial executive may have difficulty recognizing the world postulated by this theory. Much research has focused on relaxing these restrictive assumptions. The result has been more complex versions of the model that, however, are quite consistent with the simple version of CAPM examined in this article.

Although CAPM's assumptions are obviously unrealistic, such simplification of reality is often necessary to develop useful models. The true test of a model lies not just in the reasonableness of its underlying assumptions but also in the validity and usefulness of the model's prescription. Tolerance of CAPM's assumptions, however fanciful, allows the derivation of a concrete, though idealized, model of the manner in which financial markets measure risk and transform it into expected return.

Portfolio diversification

CAPM deals with the risks and returns on financial securities and defines them precisely, if arbitrarily. The rate of return an investor receives from buying a common stock and holding it for a given period of time is equal to the cash dividends received plus the capital gain (or minus the capital loss) during the holding period divided by the purchase price of the security.

Although investors may expect a particular return when they buy a particular stock, they may be disappointed or pleasantly surprised, because fluctuations in stock prices result in fluctuating returns. Therefore common stocks are considered risky securities. (In contrast, because the returns on some securities, such as Treasury bills, do not differ from their expected returns, they are considered riskless securities.) Financial theory defines risk as the possibility that actual returns will deviate from expected returns, and the degree of potential fluctuation determines the degree of risk.

An underpinning of CAPM is the observation that risky stocks can be combined so that the combination (the portfolio) is less risky than any of its components. Although such diversification is a familiar notion, it may be worthwhile to review the manner in which diversification reduces risk.

Suppose there are two companies located on an isolated island whose chief industry is tourism. One company manufactures suntan lotion. Its stock predictably performs well in sunny years and poorly in rainy ones. The other company produces disposable umbrellas. Its stock performs equally poorly in sunny years and well in rainy ones. Each company earns a 12% average return.

In purchasing either stock, investors incur a great amount of risk because of variability in the stock price driven by fluctuations in weather conditions. Investing half the funds in the suntan lotion stock and half in the stock of the umbrella manufacturer, however, results in a return of 12% regardless of which weather condition prevails. Portfolio diversification thus transforms two risky stocks, each with an average return of 12%, into a riskless portfolio certain of earning the expected 12%.

Unfortunately, the perfect negative relationship between the returns on these two stocks is very rare in the real world. To some extent, corporate securities move together, so complete elimination of risk through simple portfolio diversification is impossible. However, as long as some lack of parallelism in the returns of securities exists, diversification will always reduce risk.

Two types of risk

Some of the risk investors assume is peculiar to the individual stocks in their portfolios – for example, a company's earnings may plummet because of a wildcat strike. On the other hand, because stock prices and returns move to some extent in tandem, even investors holding widely diversified portfolios are exposed to the risk inherent in the overall performance of the stock market.

So we can divide a security's total risk into *unsystematic risk*, the portion peculiar to the company that can be diversified away, and *systematic risk*, the nondiversifiable portion that is related to the movement of the stock market and is therefore unavoidable. Examples of systematic and unsystematic risk factors appear in Figure 1.

Figure 2 graphically illustrates the reduction of risk as securities are added to a portfolio. Empirical studies have demonstrated that unsystematic risk can be virtually eliminated in portfolios of 30 to 40 randomly selected stocks. Of course, if investments are made in closely related industries, more securities are required to eradicate unsystematic risk.

The investors inhabiting this hypothetical world are assumed to be risk averse. This notion, which agrees for once with the world most of us know, implies that investors demand compensation for taking on risk. In financial markets dominated by risk-averse investors, higher-risk securities are priced to yield higher expected returns than lower-risk securities.

Unsystematic risk factors

A company's technical wizard is killed in an auto accident.

Revolution in a foreign country halts shipments of an important product ingredient.

A lower-cost foreign competitor unexpectedly enters a company's product market.

Oil is discovered on a company's property.

Systematic risk factors

Oil-producing countries institute a boycott.

Congress votes a massive tax cut.

The Federal Reserve steps up its restrictive monetary policy.

Long-term interest rates rise precipitously.

Figure 1   *Some unsystematic and systematic risk factors*

A simple equation expresses the resulting positive relationship between risk and return. The risk-free rate (the return on a riskless investment such as a T-bill) anchors the risk/expected return relationship. The expected return on a risky security, R_s, can be thought of as the risk-free rate, R_f, plus a premium for risk:

$$R_s = R_f + \text{risk premium}$$

The reward for tolerating CAPM's unrealistic assumptions is in having a measure of this risk premium and a method of estimating the market's risk/

expected return curve. These assumptions and the risk-reducing efficacy of diversification lead to an idealized financial market in which, to minimize risk, CAPM investors hold highly diversified portfolios that are sensitive only to market-related risk.

Since investors can eliminate company-specific risk simply by properly diversifying portfolios, they are not compensated for bearing unsystematic risk. And because well-diversified investors are exposed only to systematic risk, with CAPM the relevant risk in the financial market's risk/expected return trade-off is systematic risk rather than total risk. Thus an investor is rewarded with higher expected returns for bearing only market-related risk.

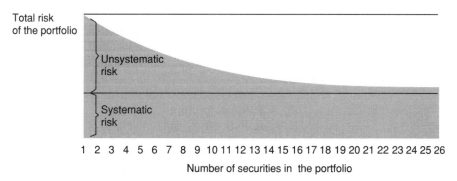

Figure 2 *Reduction of unsystematic risk through diversification*

This important result may seem inconsistent with empirical evidence that, despite low-cost diversification vehicles such as mutual funds, most investors do not hold adequately diversified portfolios.[1] Consistent with CAPM, however, large investors such as the institutions that dominate trading on the New York Stock Exchange do typically hold portfolios with many securities. These actively trading investors determine securities prices and expected returns. If their portfolios are well diversified, their actions may result in market pricing consistent with the CAPM prediction that only systematic risk matters.

Beta is the standard CAPM measure of systematic risk. It gauges the tendency of the return of a security to move in parallel with the return of the stock market as a whole. One way to think of beta is as a gauge of a security's volatility relative to the market's volatility. A stock with a beta of 1.00 – an

---

[1] See Marshall E. Blume, Jean Crockett, and Irwin Friend, 'Stock Ownership in the United States: Characteristics and Trends', *Survey of Current Business*, November 1974, p.16.

average level of systematic risk – rises and falls at the same percentage as a broad market index, such as Standard & Poor's 500-stock index.

Stocks with a beta greater than 1.00 tend to rise and fall by a greater percentage than the market – that is, they have a high level of systematic risk and are very sensitive to market changes. Conversely, a stock with a beta less than 1.00 has a low level of systematic risk and is less sensitive to market swings.

The security market line

The culmination of the sequence of conceptual building blocks is CAPM's risk/expected return relationship. This fundamental result follows from the proposition that only systematic risk, measured by beta (β), matters. Securities are priced such that:

$$R_s = R_f + \text{risk premium}$$
$$R_s = R_f + \beta_s (R_m - R_f)$$

where

R_s = the stock's expected return
    (and the company's cost of equity capital).
R_f = the risk-free rate.
R_m = the expected return on the stock market as a whole.
β_s = the stock's beta.

This risk/expected return relationship is called the security market line (SML). I have illustrated it graphically in Figure 3. As I indicated before, the expected return on a security generally equals the risk-free rate plus a risk premium. In CAPM the risk premium is measured as beta times the expected return on the market minus the risk-free rate. The risk premium of a security is a function of the risk premium on the market, $R_m - R_f$, and varies directly with the level of beta. (No measure of unsystematic risk appears in the risk premium, of course, for in the world of CAPM diversification has eliminated it.)

In the freely competitive financial markets described by CAPM, no security can sell for long at prices low enough to yield more than its appropriate return on the SML. The security would then be very attractive compared with other securities of similar risk, and investors would bid its price up until its expected return fell to the appropriate position on the SML. Conversely, investors would sell off any stock selling at a price high enough to put its expected return below its appropriate position. The resulting reduction in price would continue until the stock's expected return rose to the level justified by its systematic risk.

(An arbitrage pricing adjustment mechanism alone may be sufficient to justify the SML relationship with less restrictive assumptions than the traditional CAPM. The SML, therefore, can be derived from other models than CAPM.[2])

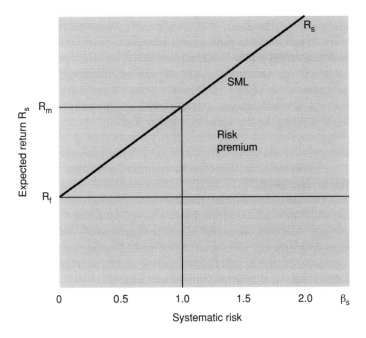

Figure 3 *The security market line*

One perhaps counterintuitive aspect of CAPM involves a stock exhibiting great total risk but very little systematic risk. An example might be a company in the very chancy business of exploring for precious metals. Viewed in isolation the company would appear very risky, but most of its total risk is unsystematic and can be diversified away. The well-diversified CAPM investor would view the stock as a low-risk security. In the SML the stock's low beta would lead to a low risk premium. Despite the stock's high level of total risk, the market would price it to yield a low expected return.

[2] See Stephen A. Ross, 'The Arbitrage Theory of Capital Asset Pricing', *Journal of Economic Theory*, December 1976, p.341.

In practice, such counterintuitive examples are rare; most companies with high total risk also have high betas and vice versa. Systematic risk as measured by beta usually coincides with intuitive judgments of risk for particular stocks. There is no total risk equivalent to the SML, however, for pricing securities and determining expected returns in financial markets where investors are free to diversify their holdings.

Let me summarize the conceptual components of CAPM. If the model correctly describes market behavior, the relevant measure of a security's risk is its market-related, or systematic, risk measured by beta. If a security's return bears a strong positive relationship with the return on the market and thus has a high beta, it will be priced to yield a high expected return; if it has a low beta, it will be priced to yield a low expected return.

Since unsystematic risk can be easily eliminated through diversification, it does not increase a security's expected return. According to the model, financial markets care only about systematic risk and price securities such that expected returns lie along the security market line.

How can it be used?

With its insight into the financial markets' pricing of securities and the determination of expected returns, CAPM has clear applications in investment management. Its use in this field has advanced to a level of sophistication far beyond the scope of this introductory exposition.

CAPM has an important application in corporate finance as well. The finance literature defines the cost of equity as the expected return on a company's stock. The stock's expected return is the shareholders' opportunity cost of the equity funds employed by the company.

In theory, the company must earn this cost on the equity-financed portion of its investments or its stock price will fall. If the company does not expect to earn at least the cost of equity, it should return the funds to the shareholders, who can earn this expected return on other securities at the same risk level in the financial marketplace. Since the cost of equity involves market expectations, it is very difficult to measure; few techniques are available.

Cost of equity

This difficulty is unfortunate in view of the role of equity costs in vital tasks such as capital budgeting evaluation and the valuation of possible acquisitions.

The cost of equity is one component of the weighted average cost of capital, which corporate executives often use as a hurdle rate in evaluating investments. Financial managers can employ CAPM to obtain an estimate of the cost of equity capital.

If CAPM correctly describes market behavior, the security market line gives the expected return on a stock. Because this expected return, R_s, is by definition the company's cost of equity, k_e, the SML provides estimates of equity costs as well. Thus:

$$k_e = R_s = R_f + \beta_s (R_m - R_f)$$

Arriving at a cost of equity for evaluating cash flows in the future requires estimates of the future values of the risk-free rate, R_f, the expected return on the market, R_m, and beta, β_s.

Over the past 50 years, the T-bill rate (the risk-free rate) has approximately equalled the annual inflation rate. In recent years, buffeted by short-term inflationary expectations, the T-bill rate has fluctuated widely. Although sophisticated techniques could be employed to estimate the future inflation and T-bill rates, for the purposes of this exposition let us make a rough estimate of 10%.

Estimating the expected return on the market is more difficult. A common approach is to assume that investors anticipate about the same risk premium $(R_m - R_f)$ in the future as in the past. From 1926 to 1978, the risk premium on the Standard & Poor's 500-stock index averaged 8.9%.[3] Benchmark estimates of 9% for the risk premium and 10% for the T-bill rate imply an estimated R_m of 19%.

This is substantially higher than the historical average of 11.2%. The difference reflects the long-term inflation rate of 10% incorporated in our estimated T-bill rate. The future inflation rate is assumed to be 7.5% higher than the 2.5% average rate over the 1926–1978 period. Expected returns (in nominal terms) should rise to compensate investors for the anticipated loss in purchasing power. As elsewhere, more sophisticated techniques exist, but an estimate of 19% for R_m is roughly consistent with historical spreads between stock returns and the returns on T-bills, long-term government bonds, and corporate bonds.

Statistical techniques that gauge the past variability of the stock relative to the market can estimate the stock's beta. Many brokerage firms and investment services also supply betas. If the company's past level of systematic

---

[3] See Roger G. Ibbotson and Rex A. Sinquefeld, *Stocks, Bonds, Bills and Inflation: Historical Returns (1926–1978)*, second edition (Charlottesville, Virginia: Financial Analysts Research Foundation, 1979). The rates I have used are arithmetic means. Arguments can be made that geometric mean rates are appropriate for discounting longer-term cash flows.

risk seems likely to continue, beta calculations from historical data can be used to estimate the cost of equity.

Plugging the assumed values of the risk-free rate, the expected return on the market, and beta into the security market line generates estimates of the cost of equity capital. In Figure 4 I give the cost of equity estimates of three hypothetical companies.

Security market line:

$K_e = R_s = R_f + \beta_s (R_m - R_f)$

$\quad = 10\% + \beta_s (19\% - 10\%)$

$\quad = 10\% + \beta_s (9\%)$

Electric utility	**Chemical company**
$\beta_u = 0.75$	$\beta_c = 1.10$
$R_u = 10\% + \beta_u (9\%)$	$R_c = 10\% + \beta_c (9\%)$
$\quad = 10\% + 0.75 (9\%)$	$\quad = 10\% + 1.10 (9\%)$
$\quad = 16.75\%$	$\quad = 19.9\%$
$k_e = 17\%$	$k_e = 20\%$

Airline

$\beta_A = 1.55$

$R_A = 10\% + \beta_A (9\%)$

$\quad = 10\% + 1.55 (9\%)$

$\quad = 23.95\%$

$k_e = 24\%$

Assumptions:
$R_f = 10\%, \quad R_m = 19\%$.

Figure 4 *Examples of estimating the cost of equity capital*

The betas in Figure 4 are consistent with those of companies in the three industries represented. Many electric utilities have low levels of systematic risk and low betas because of relatively modest swings in their earnings and stock returns. Airline revenues are closely tied to passenger miles flown, a yardstick very sensitive to changes in economic activity. Amplifying this systematic variability in revenues is high operating and financial leverage. The results are earnings and returns that vary widely and produce high betas in these stocks. Major chemical companies exhibit an intermediate degree of systematic risk.

I should stress that the methodology illustrated in Figure 4 yields only rough estimates of the cost of equity. Sophisticated refinements can help estimate each input. Sensitivity analyses employing various input values can produce a reasonably good range of estimates of the cost of equity. Nonetheless, the calculations in this exhibit demonstrate how the simple model can generate benchmark data.

Figure 5 shows the SML risk/expected return spectrum employing the average betas for companies in more than three dozen industries. The result is a pricing schedule for equity capital as a function of risk. The spectrum represents shareholders' risk/expected return opportunities in the financial markets and, therefore, shareholder opportunity costs to the particular company.

Employment of CAPM

Applications of these concepts are straightforward. For example, when a manager is calculating divisional costs of capital or hurdle rates, the cost of equity component should reflect the risk inherent in the division's operations rather than the parent company's risk. If the division is in one of the risky businesses listed in Figure 5, a cost of equity commensurate with this risk should be employed even though it may be much higher than the parent's cost of equity.

One approach to estimating a division's cost of equity is to calculate CAPM estimates of the cost of equity for similar, independent companies operating in the same industry. The betas of these companies reflect the risk level of the industry. Of course, refinements may be necessary to adjust for differences in financial leverage and other factors.

A second example concerns acquisitions. In discounted cash flow evaluations of acquisitions, the appropriate cost of equity should reflect the risks inherent in the cash flows that are discounted. Again, ignoring refinements required by changes in capital structure and the like, the cost of equity should reflect the risk level of the target company, not the acquiror.

Methodology and assumptions:
$(k_e = R_s = R_f + \beta_s(R_m - R_f) = 10\% + \beta_s(19\% - 10\%))$

Estimated cost of equity Percent	Beta	Industry	Spectrum (industries by beta)	Beta
26.20%	1.80	Air transport	Air transport	1.80
				1.75
			Real property	1.70
			Travel, outdoor recreation	1.65
24.40	1.60	Electronics	Miscellaneous, finance	1.60
				1.55
			Nondurables, entertainment	1.50
23.05	1.45	Consumer durables	Business machines / Retail, general	1.45
			Media	1.40
			Insurance / Trucking freight	1.35
21.70	1.30	Producer goods	Aerospace / Business services / Apparel / Construction / Motor vehicles	1.30
			Photographic, optical / Chemicals / Energy, raw materials / Tires, rubber goods	1.25
20.80	1.20	Railroads, shipping	Forest products, paper	1.20
20.35	1.15	Miscellaneous, conglomerate	Drugs, medicine / Domestic oil	1.15
			Soaps, cosmetics	1.10
			Steel / Containers	1.05

High-risk stocks

Figure 5 Risk/expected return spectrum

	Estimated cost of equity Percent	Beta	Industry	Methodology and assumptions: $(k_e = R_s = R_f + \beta_s (R_m - R_f) = 10\% + \beta_s (19\% - 10\%)$	Beta
Medium-risk stocks	19.00	1.00	Nonferrous metals	Agriculture, food	1.00
					0.95
				Liquor	0.90
	17.65	0.85	International oil	Banks	0.85
				Tobacco	0.80
Low-risk stocks	16.75	0.75	Telephone	Telephone	0.75
					0.70
					0.65
	15.40	0.60	Energy utilities	Energy utilities	0.60
					0.55
					0.50
					0.45
					0.40
	13.15	0.35	Gold	Gold	0.35

Source of betas:
Barr Rosenberg and James Guy, 'Prediction of Beta from Investment Fundamentals.' *Financial Analysts Journal*, July–August 1976, p.62.

Figure 5 *(continued)*

Does CAPM work?

As an idealized theory of financial markets, the model's assumptions are clearly unrealistic. But the true test of CAPM, naturally, is how well it works.

There have been numerous empirical tests of CAPM. Most of these have examined the past to determine the extent to which stock returns and betas have corresponded in the manner predicted by the security market line. With few exceptions the major empirical studies in this field have concluded that:

- As a measure of risk, beta appears to be related to past returns. Because of the close relationship between total and systematic risk, it is difficult to distinguish their effects empirically. Nonetheless, inclusion of a factor representing unsystematic risk appears to add little explanatory power to the risk/return relationship.
- The relationship between past returns and beta is linear – that is, reality conforms to what the model predicts. The relationship is also positively sloped – that is, there is a positive trade-off between the two (high risk equals high return, low risk equals low return).

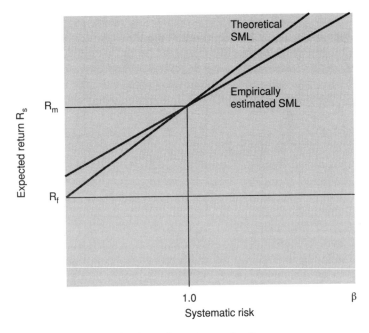

Figure 6 *Theoretical and estimated security market lines*

● The empirical SML appears less steeply sloped than the theoretical SML. As illustrated in Figure 6, low-beta securities earn a return somewhat higher than CAPM would predict, and high-beta stocks earn less than predicted. A variety of deficiencies in CAPM and/or in the statistical methodologies employed have been advanced to explain this phenomenon.

Although these empirical tests do not unequivocally validate CAPM, they do support its main implications. The systematic risk measure, beta, does appear to be related to past returns; a positive risk/return trade-off does exist; and this risk/return relationship does appear to be linear. The contradictory finding concerning the slope of the SML is a subject of continuing research. Some researchers suggest using a more gradually sloped 'empirical market line' based on these findings instead of the theoretical SML.

Recent work in the investment management field has challenged the proposition that only systematic risk matters. In a complex world it would be unlikely to find only one relevant type of risk – market risk.

Much progress has been made in the development of richer asset-pricing models. As of yet, however, none of these more sophisticated models has proved clearly superior to CAPM. This continues to be a fertile area of research, focused primarily on investment management applications.

Application problems

In corporate finance applications of CAPM, several potential sources of error exist. First, the simple model may be an inadequate description of the behavior of financial markets. (As I just noted, empirical work to date does not unequivocally support the validity of CAPM.) In attempts to improve its realism, researchers have developed a variety of extensions of the model.

A second problem is that betas are unstable through time. This fact creates difficulties when betas estimated from historical data are used to calculate costs of equity in evaluating future cash flows. Betas should change as both company fundamentals and capital structures change. In addition, betas estimated from past data are subject to statistical estimation error. Several techniques are available to help deal with these sources of instability.

The estimates of the future risk-free rate and the expected return on the market are also subject to error. Here too, research has focused on developing techniques to reduce the potential error associated with these inputs to the SML.

A final set of problems is unique to corporate finance applications of CAPM. There are practical and theoretical problems associated with employing CAPM, or any financial market model, in capital budgeting decisions involving real assets. These difficulties continue to be a fertile area of research.

Dividend growth model

The deficiencies of CAPM may seem severe. They must be judged, however, relative to other approaches for estimating the cost of equity capital. The most commonly used of these is a simple discounted cash flow (DCF) technique, which is known as the dividend growth model (or the Gordon-Shapiro model).

This approach is based on the proposition that the price of a company's stock equals the present value of future dividends per share discounted by the company's cost of equity capital. With the assumption that future dividends per share are expected to grow at a constant rate and that this growth rate will persist forever, the general present value formula collapses to a simple expression:

$$P = \frac{dps}{k_e - g}$$

where:

P = the current price of the stock.
dps = next year's dividends per share.
g = the perpetuity growth rate in dividends per share.
k_e = the company's cost of equity capital.

If the market is pricing the stock in this manner, we can infer the cost of equity impounded in the stock price. Solving for the cost of equity yields:

$$k_e = \frac{dps}{P} + g$$

The cost of equity implied by the current stock price and the assumptions of the model is simply the dividend yield plus the constant growth rate.

Like CAPM, two of the model's assumptions limit the dividend growth technique. One is the assumption of a constant, perpetual growth rate in dividends per share. Second, to permit the general present value formula to collapse to the simple stock price equation I gave, the perpetual constant growth rate must be less than the company's cost of equity. If this is not the case, the equation is not valid.

These two assumptions sharply limit the applicability of the dividend growth model. The model cannot be used in estimating costs of equity for companies with unstable dividend patterns or for rapidly growing companies where g is likely to be greater than k_e. (Obviously, the model also does not apply to companies paying no dividends.) Unlike CAPM, the model is limited mainly to companies enjoying slow, steady growth in dividends. More complex DCF techniques can, however, handle a wider range of companies.

Another problem with using the dividend growth model to estimate costs of equity is in gauging g. To derive a sound cost of equity figure, one must estimate the growth rate investors are using to value the stock. Thus it is the market's current estimate of g that matters, not the company's. This is a major source of error in the dividend growth model.

In contrast, the only company-specific input to the SML is the beta, which is derived by an objective statistical method. Even more sophisticated DCF techniques require as an input the market's estimate of the company's future dividends per share.

When compared with the dividend growth model and other DCF approaches, CAPM's deficiencies do not appear so severe. There is no reason, however, to consider CAPM and the dividend growth model as competitors. Very few techniques are available for the difficult task of measuring the cost of equity. Despite the shortcomings, investors should use both the DCF and CAPM models as well as sound judgment to estimate the cost of equity.[4]

Imperfect, but useful

Investment managers have widely applied the simple CAPM and its more sophisticated extensions. CAPM's application to corporate finance is a recent development. Although it has been employed in many utility rate-setting proceedings, it has yet to gain widespread use in corporate circles for estimating companies' costs of equity.

Because of its shortcomings, financial executives should not rely on CAPM as a precise algorithm for estimating the cost of equity capital. Nevertheless, tests of the model confirm that it has much to say about the way returns are determined in financial markets. In view of the inherent difficulty in measuring the cost of equity, CAPM's deficiencies appear no worse than those of other approaches. Its key advantage is that it quantifies risk and provides a

---

[4] For an exposition of the dividend growth model, see Thomas R. Piper and William E. Fruhan, Jr., 'Is Your Stock Worth Its Market Price?' *HBR* May-June 1981, p.124.

widely applicable, relatively objective routine for translating risk measures into estimates of expected return.

CAPM represents a new and different approach to an important task. Financial decision makers can use the model in conjunction with traditional techniques and sound judgement to develop realistic, useful estimates of the costs of equity capital.

Further reading

The development and testing of capital market theory have been fertile areas of research over the past 15 years. This work has produced an extensive body of literature exploring the issues raised in this introductory exposition.

Early development of the model

A number of researchers contributed to the development of CAPM. Harry M. Markowitz did the early work on diversification, summarized in his *Portfolio Selection: Efficient Diversification of Investment*, Cowles Foundation Monograph 16, Yale University Press, 1959. Jack L. Treynor ('Toward a Theory of the Market Value of Risky Assets', unpublished manuscript, 1961) conducted early work on equilibrium asset pricing. CAPM was developed independently in seminal papers by William F. Sharpe ('Capital Asset Prices: A Theory of Market Equilibrium under Conditions of Risk', *Journal of Finance*, September 1964, p.425); and John V. Lintner ('The Valuation of Risk Assets and the Selection of Risky Investments in Stock Portfolios and Capital Budgets', *Review of Economics and Statistics*, February 1965, p.13). Franco Modigliani and Gerald A. Pogue provide a useful introduction to CAPM in 'An Introduction to Risk and Return', *Financial Analysts Journal*, March-April 1974, p.68 and May-June 1974, p.69.

Assumptions and extensions

The assumed competitive efficiency of financial markets has been the subject of much empirical work. Classic references include two works by Eugene F. Fama, 'Efficient Capital Markets: A Review of the Theory and Empirical Work', *Journal of Finance*, May 1970, p.383 and *Foundations of Finance*, Basic Books, 1976; see chapter 5. The June-September 1978 issue of *Journal of Financial Economics* reviews recent evidence apparently contrary to the efficient markets hypothesis. Extensions of CAPM are examined in Michael C. Jensen, 'Capital Markets: Theory and Evidence', *Bell Journal of Economics and Management Science*, Autumn 1972, p.357, as well as in chapters 8 and 9 of Fama's book.

Empirical evidence

The risk-reducing efficacy of diversification is demonstrated in John L. Evans and Stephen H. Archer, 'Diversification and the Reduction of Dispersion: An Empirical Analysis', *Journal of Finance*, December 1968, p.761; and W.H. Wagner and S.C. Lau, 'The Effect of Diversification on Risk', *Financial Analysts Journal*, November-December 1971, p.48.

Researchers have extensively examined the stability of betas and have found past betas to be useful predictors of future betas. For discussion and references, see James C. Van Horne, *Financial Management and Policy*, fifth edition, Prentice-Hall, 1980, pp.61–62.

The major empirical studies of CAPM include Irwin Friend and Marshall E. Blume, 'Measurement of Portfolio Performance under Uncertainty', *American Economic Review*, September 1970, p.561; Merton H. Miller and Myron Scholes, 'Rates of Return in Relation to Risk: A Re-examination of Some Recent Finds'; and Fischer Black, Michael C. Jensen and Myron Scholes, 'The Capital Asset Pricing Model: Some Empirical Tests', both in Michael C. Jensen, editor, *Studies in the Theory of Capital Markets*, Praeger, 1972; Marshall E. Blume and Irwin Friend, 'A New Look at the Capital Asset Pricing Model', *Journal of Finance*, March 1973, p.19; Eugene F. Fama and James D. MacBeth, 'Risk, Return and Equilibrium: Empirical Test', *Journal of Political Economy*, May-June 1973, p.607. For an example of the recent evidence suggesting the relevance of unsystematic risk, see Irwin Friend, Randolph Westerfield, and Michael Granito, 'New Evidence on the Capital Asset Pricing Model', *Journal of Finance*, June 1978, p.903.

Richard Roll wrote an important article on the empirical tests of CAPM in 'A Critique of the Asset Pricing Theory's Tests', *Journal of Financial Economics*, March 1977, p.129. For a critique of Roll's critique see David Mayers and Edward M. Rice, 'Measuring Portfolio Performance and the Empirical Content of Asset Pricing Models', *Journal of Financial Economics*, March 1979, p.3.

Corporate finance applications

For a detailed analysis of the role of CAPM in estimating capital costs and in capital budgeting, see the discussion and references in Richard A. Brealey and Stewart C. Myers, *Principles of Corporate Finance*, McGraw-Hill, 1981, chapters 7–9; Thomas E. Copeland and J. Fred Weston, *Financial Theory and Corporate Policy*, Addison-Wesley, 1979, chapters 10–12; and James C. Van Horne's previously mentioned *Financial Management and Policy*, chapters 7–9.

Part 4
Dividends or Growth – the Continuing Puzzle

8 Dividends, dilution and delusion

J. T. S. Porterfield

As a stockholder, which of the following dividend announcements would have pleased you the most?

- In September 1958, the Commonwealth Edison Company announced a new dividend policy for its common stock. So long as this policy remains in effect, the company intends to pay a base cash dividend (current $2 per share) supplemented by an annual stock dividend approximately equal to the difference between earnings and the cash dividend. Thus, nearly all earnings will be distributed in a combination of cash and stock dividends.
- At a meeting of The New York Society of Security Analysts in September 1958, James R. Price, president of National Homes Corporation, stated that National Homes would pay no cash dividends on its common stock during his lifetime. (Mr Price was then 47 years old.)
- In December 1958, the directors of American Telephone and Telegraph Company recommended to stockholders a three-for-one split of the common stock and voted a 10% increase in the cash dividend to $3.30 per new common share.

If you share your taste in dividends with the financial public in general, your choice would probably be the last item in the list, namely the stock split plus a fat cash dividend. In fact, no dividend announcement of recent years has occasioned so much comment and approbation among analysts and investors. Predicting certain approval of the directors' recommendations by stockholders, one financial writer alluded to the impropriety of shooting Santa Claus so close to the Christmas season. In April 1959, stockholders of American Telephone and Telegraph Company overwhelmingly approved the split, and the company has subsequently paid dividends at the higher rate.

Public reaction to these and other dividend announcements suggests some fundamental misconceptions as to the nature of dividends. For, as I shall try to show (by the use of simple illustrations), from the stockholder's viewpoint no inherent difference exists among these three dividend plans. They may well have different effects, but that is because of other influences – one of which, indeed, is the very fact that investors expect the effects to be different because they do not understand the similarity.

This article is addressed primarily to executives who participate in making dividend decisions as officers or directors of their companies, but who are not financial specialists themselves. Even if they recognize the theoretical identity of the dividend plans, they must take into account that stockholders do not. The financial sophisticate may also find his thinking stimulated as he contemplates the gulf between theory and practice.

Single objective

A publicly owned company should have a single ultimate objective to guide its dividend decisions, or indeed any business decisions that it faces. This objective should *not* be, as is often variously stated, 'to make a profit', 'to make a fair profit', 'to maximize profits', or even, 'to maximize earnings per share'. The objective of a publicly owned company should be *to maximize the return on its owners' investment*.

Stockholders can realize a return in two ways – from dividends and from appreciation in the market value of their holdings. Hence, the company's ultimate objective in making its decisions should be to maximize the present value of future dividends and appreciation in the price of its stock. At the end of this article, the close and peculiar application of this objective to dividend policy will be discussed.

Stock dividends

Executives and investors frequently regard stock dividends as being unquestionably valuable – a form of largesse distributed to stockholders. They can often be sold for cash in the market, which reinforces belief in their value. Hence, many executives take pride in paying and many stockholders are delighted to receive stock dividends, especially if no accompanying reduction in the cash dividend is anticipated.

But let us remind ourselves that stock dividends per se are of no value to the investor. They represent simply a division of the corporate pie into a larger number of pieces. The individual stockholder's share in that pie is no greater than it was prior to the payment of the stock dividend. The pie itself is likewise no larger. True, the stock dividend can be sold for cash, but in theory this gain is offset by the decline in expected market value of the holder's remaining shares, resulting from the increase in the total number of shares outstanding. The stockholder who sells his stock dividend finds himself in a position no different than if he had never received it but merely had sold a part of his original holding.

An elementary example may help to make this concept clear. Assume that a new company, ABC Corporation, is formed with capital of $100 represented by one share of capital stock and $50 of capital surplus. The assets of the company are promptly deposited in a checking account at a commercial bank. The company's opening balance sheet would look like this:

Cash $100	Capital stock (1 share)	$50
	Capital surplus	50

Representing as it does a call on $100 in cash, the expected market value of the share of ABC stock would be $100 per share.

Now, assume that the directors decide to pay a stock dividend of 100%. After the payment, the balance sheet would look like this:

Cash $100	Capital stock (2 shares)	$100
	Capital surplus	–

The market value of ABC stock would now be expected to be $50 per share. The stockholder would thus be no better off and no worse off than before the stock dividend was paid.

One may object that this example is too unrealistic in that it employs a company without earnings and without cash dividend payments. Would the presence of these two factors lend value to the stock dividend? Assume that ABC Corporation, on founding, invests its assets not in a checking account but in a savings account, paying interest at the rate of 4% compounded annually. Further assume that it adopts a policy of paying $2 per year in cash dividends. At the end of a year, after the payment of this cash dividend, the balance sheet would run as follows:

Cash $102	Capital stock (1 share)	$50
	Capital surplus	50
	Earned surplus	2

The indicated market value per share would be $102.

Now, assume that a stock dividend of 100% is paid. The balance sheet would become:

Cash $102	Capital stock (2 shares)	$ 100
	Earned surplus	2

Thus, with no change in the aggregate amount of cash dividends, each holder of one original share still receives $2 (i.e. $1 for each of the two shares he has now). The equivalent amount of cash dividends becomes $1 per share, and the indicated market value of ABC stock is still $102 (i.e., $51 for each of his two shares). The stockholder, as in the case of the previous example, is no better off and no worse off than before he received the stock dividend.

Higher payout

The objection may be raised that in this example the cash dividend *per share* was cut in half from $2 to $1. What if it were maintained at the former level of $2 per share? Would this not give value to the stock dividend? In practice, with stock dividends of 1% to 10%, for example, this is the normal expectation of the investors.

Certainly, if the cash dividend is maintained at $2 per share after the stock dividend has been paid, ABC stock may well sell for $51, or probably more, even though earned surplus per share is $1 less than on the old dividend basis. But the price that investors will pay at a given time is another matter; it depends on the extent to which the stock sells in the market on a yield basis and the attractiveness of its yield compared with other stocks at that time. ABC's earning power, which underlies the yield, remains the same; and the stockholder's share of the earnings remains the same – he has $1 in cash instead of in increased value of earned surplus.

In discussions of theoretical aspects of stock dividends, this is frequently the point of maximum opacity. While some may concede that a stock dividend has no theoretical value when the cash dividend per share is proportionately reduced, the same persons will frequently insist that value does adhere to the stock dividend if the cash dividend per share is maintained.

It is quite possible that both the aggregate market value and the aggregate cash dividend income of a stockholding would increase if the cash dividend rate per share were maintained, after payment of a stock dividend. However, at bottom, these ostensibly favorable developments have nothing to do with the stock dividend. They are the result of a *de facto* increase in the cash dividend rate, which is simply the immediate distribution of a larger part of the same earnings. The ABC stockholder in the last example would be in exactly the same *final* position if the company, instead of paying a 100% stock dividend and maintaining the former cash dividend per share, had simply increased the cash dividend to $4 per share and had omitted the stock dividend entirely.

In practice, the use of stock dividends by a particular company or companies may have beneficial effects from the stockholder's viewpoint. For example, a policy of paying small stock dividends regularly may be interpreted by the market as signifying the company's intention to increase its aggregate cash dividend payments over the years. Stock dividends may also reduce share prices to a more popular trading range.

However, it is important for management and stockholders to realize that these and other possible benefits are not inherent in the nature of stock dividends and that the latter in themselves represent no net gain to the recipient. Stock dividends are customarily taxable only if sold, and then at the capital gains rate rather than at the ordinary personal income rate typically applied to cash dividends. This constitutes an advantage of stock over cash dividends but not an advantage over no dividends at all, which is the appropriate comparison.

Splits and rights

In the area of stock splits and stock rights misconceptions also exist to confuse the unwary. In theory, stock splits afford no problem: they are as valueless to the investor as stock dividends. Simply read 'two-for-one split' instead of '100% stock dividend' in each of the examples above, and the meaning is unchanged. (The accounting treatment differs, but this is not relevant to the principle involved.)

A more lengthy analysis, however, is required to reveal the exact nature of stock rights – the offering of new securities to existing security holders by means of rights, either as a matter of legal requirement, or financial policy, or both. The question of rights is intimately connected with that of dividends.

Companies frequently offer new stock (or securities convertible into stock) to existing stockholders at prices well below the current market value of the outstanding stock. In so doing, management may feel that it is giving something of value to its shareholders. Like stock dividends, stock rights are often highly prized by investors. And, like stock dividends, rights may typically be sold on the market for cash if the holder decides not to exercise them. Belief in the value of rights is, if anything, even more tenaciously held than belief in the value of stock dividends. Once again, however, it can be demonstrated that rights have no inherent value to the investor, no matter how large the discount at which the new shares are to be sold.

Return now to the example of ABC Corporation, and assume once more that its assets are invested in a 4% savings account and that it pays cash dividends aggregating $2 per year. If the initial capitalization were one share of stock, the balance sheet at the end of a year's operation would look like this:

Cash $102	Capital stock (1 share)	$100
	Earned surplus	2

The indicated market value for ABC stock would be $102.

Now, assume that the company decides to raise additional capital of $50 by a sale of stock. It offers one new share to the existing stockholder at a subscription price of $50. Hence, the stockholder is being offered a large and ostensibly attractive discount from the current market value of ABC stock. Assume further that the new stock is subscribed at $50 per share; the balance sheet then becomes:

Cash $152	Capital stock (2 shares)	$150
	Earned surplus	2

The indicated market value for the stock would be $76 per share.

The stockholder in this example is no better off and no worse off than before the rights issuance. He has invested $150 cash, and his stock is worth that plus $2 in retained earnings. Previously, he had invested $100 in cash, and his stock was worth that plus retained earnings. Hence, the right itself has no real value, no matter how large the spread between initial market price and offering price. Theoretically, as in the case of stock dividends, the market price should adjust to reflect the dilution resulting from the sale of new stock at below market value.

On the other hand, the sale of new shares by rights at discounts below current market prices (even very large discounts) does no harm to shareholders. Some financial mangers have a lurking fear that selling common stock at large discounts represents a 'giveaway'. This is not true if existing shareholders receive rights to subscribe to the new issues. The shareholder who subscribes is neither benefited nor injured, as the last example demonstrates. The shareholder who sells his rights in the market is theoretically recompensed for the drop in the value of his shares. The only loser would be the stockholder who failed either to exercise or sell his rights. As a result, a right represents not a valuable distribution to the stockholder but an obligation imposed on him. He must bestir himself and take some action simply to avoid loss.

As in the case of stock dividends, the question may be raised: What if the company, issuing additional stock at a discount via rights, were to maintain the former cash dividend per share on the increased number of shares; would this not tend to support the market price of the stock and result in larger aggregate dividends, thus giving value to the rights? The answer here is the same as in the stock dividend example. These benefits would not be the result of the rights but simply of a *de facto* increase in the cash paid out per share.

It is for this reason that it is correct only in a narrow sense to point to AT&T as an example of a company that has had a 'fixed' dividend rate. The frequent sale of new shares (and securities convertible into new shares) to existing stockholders at prices below market, and the maintenance until 1959 of the $9 dividend per share, have had the effect of a rising dividend rate for the stockholder who has exercised his rights or reinvested the proceeds of their sale in income producing assets.

Cash dividends

The recent AT&T dividend increase invites attention to cash dividends and their impact on investors. It may be very well to demonstrate that stock dividends, stock splits, and stock rights have no theoretical value to the investor. However, cash dividends surely must be something else again. They represent an actual dollar disbursement by the company. As such, it would appear that they should be welcomed by even the market sophisticate. Indeed, it is probably a truism that an increase in cash dividends on many stocks would in practice have a favorable effect on their market value.

Yet there is a paradox even here, and it is one that is not always recognized by management or by stockholders. It is important, moreover, that it be recognized. Both parties should be aware of what is really happening when dividends are paid. What many executives and stockholders forget is that cash dividends are merely a means of giving to the stockholder something that he already owns – the heretofore undistributed earnings of the corporation. They do not represent something extra – a windfall from a generous company. When it pays a dividend, a company puts into a stockholder's right pocket what it has taken out of his left.

Therefore, cash dividends, in simplest theory, should have no more value than stock dividends. The payment of cash dividends or their retention in the business should be a matter of indifference to the shareholder. True, they represent an inflow of cash to him. However, this is also true of stock dividends when sold. In each case, the immediate cash inflow is theoretically offset by a decline in share values. Critics of stock dividends sometimes denounce them as 'mere shuffling of paper'. Rarely do these critics acknowledge that, from the shareholder's viewpoint, the same charge applies in theory to cash dividends.

A final example using ABC Corporation will serve to demonstrate this. Assume again that the initial capital has been invested in a 4% savings account for a period of a year and that no dividends have yet been paid. The resulting balance sheet would look like this:

Cash $104	Capital stock (1 share)	$100
	Earned surplus	4

The indicated market value of the stock would be $104.

Now, assume that the company pays out all of its earnings as a cash dividend. The balance sheet would become:

Cash $100	Capital stock (1 share)	$100
	Earned surplus	—

The expected market value of the stock after payment of the dividend would be $100. Again the stockholder would be no better off and no worse off than if the dividend had not been paid.

At this point, the National Homes example is pertinent. For if the reasoning above is followed, this company's policy of no dividends becomes theoretically indistinguishable in the stockholders' eyes from Commonwealth Edison's policy of stock dividends to supplement cash distributions and AT&T's split and increase in the cash dividend.

Logic and paradox

What is the logical end of this line of reasoning? Are dividends a delusion? Would the ultimate absurdity be for no company to pay any dividends at all? Would companies simply split their stocks into shares of conveniently small value, so that each stockholder could in effect declare his own dividends by selling that portion of his holdings which he chose? It would not matter (except for tax and other legal considerations) if these 'dividends' exceeded accumulated earnings. For, in the last analysis, all dividends are liquidating dividends, serving as they do to reduce the assets of the corporation.

Such a policy would be particularly inviting to companies chronically in need of funds to take advantage of attractive investment opportunities. Paying no dividends would conserve cash for the company and reduce its demands for outside capital. At the same time, stockholders would not be injured, since the payment of dividends is theoretically irrelevant to them.

In practice, unfortunately, things do not work as ideally as this line of reasoning suggests. Indeed, it is highly probable that for many companies fairly regular and increasing cash dividend payments tend to have a favorable rather than an unfavorable effect on share prices over a period of time.

This may reflect a desire for income on the part of investors. It may reflect a discount applied to retained earnings because of the risks associated with retention. It may reflect more profitable investment opportunities available to the stockholder than those which are feasible for the corporation to undertake.

These are among the common explanations of the cash dividend paradox. However, I find none of them completely convincing. In each the stockholder could, in theory, realize income by selling a portion of his holding. I believe that, in part, the market's seemingly irrational reaction to cash dividend payments results from a lack of understanding of the nature of dividends among executives and investors.

Conclusion

What is the lesson here for businessmen who are concerned with dividend policy?

They should recognize that cash dividends (like stock dividends, splits, and rights) theoretically have no net value to the stockholder.

They must further recognize that in practice the market often does not act the way that it should. Irrational or not, the payment of dividends frequently tends to support share prices rather than to depress them. In cases like this management's goal of maximizing the present value of future dividends and appreciation may best be approached by a single stroke – to pay the former and realize the latter at the same time. Stockholders in such companies are in the happy position of eating their cake and having it too.

It behooves each company's management to study closely the market's reaction to changes in its dividend payments. In this way, the company may be able to determine whether its stock sells mainly on the basis of dividends paid or on the basis of earnings retained. This study should be a continuing one, since corporate images are not immutable. Today's 'growth stock' may be tomorrow's 'stable income producer', and vice versa.

One further thought is in order. When management considers such related financial devices as stock dividends, stock splits, rights to subscribe to new issues, and cash dividends, it is apparent that there frequently exists an impressive gulf between inherent value (theory) and market action (practice).

In some degree, this is traceable to a lack of sophistication among stockholders in general. If, then, the gap begins to close as a result of broader understanding, financial managers and investors may well be advised to look behind the folklore of dividends.

9 Capital equipment analysis: the required rate of profit

M. J. Gordon and E. Shapiro

The interest in capital equipment analysis that has been evident in the business literature of the past five years is the product of numerous social, economic, and business developments of the postwar period. No conclusive listing of these developments can be attempted here. However, four should be mentioned which are of particular importance in this search for a more systematic method for discovering, evaluating, and selecting investment opportunities. These are: (1) the high level of capital outlays (in absolute terms); (2) the growth in the size of business firms; (3) the delegation of responsibility for initiating recommendations from top management to the profit center, which has been part of the general movement toward decentralization; and (4) the growing use of 'scientific management' in the operations of the business firm.

These developments have motivated the current attempt to develop objective criteria whereby the executive committee in a decentralized firm can arrive at a capital budget. Since each of its profit centers submits capital proposals, the executive committee must screen these and establish an allocation and a level of capital outlays that is consistent with top management's criteria for rationing the firm's funds. Capital budgeting affords the promise that this screening process can be made amenable to some established criteria that are understandable to all the component parts of the firm. Consequently, capital budgeting appeals to top management, for, in the first place, each plant manager can see his proposal in the light of all competing proposals for the funds of the enterprise. This may not completely eliminate irritation among the various parts of the firm, but a rational capital budgeting program can go a long way toward maintaining initiative on the part of a plant manager, even though the executive committee may veto one or all of his proposals. In the second place, the use of a capital budgeting program serves to satisfy top management that each accepted proposal meets adequate predetermined standards and that the budget as a whole is part of a sound, long-run plan for the firm.

What specifically does a capital budgeting program entail? The focal points of capital budgeting are: (1) ascertaining the profit abilities of the array of capital outlay alternatives, and (2) determining the least profitability required to make an investment, i.e., a cut-off point. Capital budgeting also involves administrative procedures and organization designed to discover investment opportunities, process information, and carry out the budget; however, these latter aspects of the subject have been discussed in detail by means of cash studies that have appeared in publications of the American Management Association and the National Industrial Conference Board and in periodicals such as the *NACA Bulletin*.[1] Hence, we will not concern ourselves with them here.

There are at least four methods for establishing an order-preference array of the capital expenditure suggestions. They are: (1) the still popular 'payoff period'; (2) the average investment formula; (3) the present value formula with the rate of interest given; and (4) the present value formula used to find the rate of profit. It is not our intention in this paper to discuss these various methods specifically, since critical analyses of these alternatives are to be found in papers by Dean, by Lorie and Savage, and by Gordon in a recent issue of the *Journal of Business*,[2] which is devoted exclusively to the subject of capital budgeting.

However, it is of interest to note that in each of these methods the future revenue streams generated by the proposed outlays must be amenable to measurement if the method is to be operational. However, improvements in quality, more pleasant working conditions, strategic advantages of integration, and other types of benefits from a capital outlay are still recognized only in qualitative terms, and there is a considerable hiatus in the literature of capital budgeting with respect to the solution of this problem. Hence, in the absence of satisfactory methods for quantifying these types of benefits, the evaluation of alternative proposals is still characterized by intuitive judgments on the part of management, and a general quantitative solution to the capital budgeting problem is not now feasible. It appears to us that this problem affords one of the most promising opportunities for the application of the methods of management science. In fact, we anticipate that techniques for the quantification of the more important factors now treated qualitatively will soon be found.

---

[1] American Management Association, *Tested Approaches to Capital Equipment Replacement*, Special Report No. 1, 1954; American Management Association, *Capital Equipment Replacement; AMA Special Conference*, May 3–4, 1954 (New York, 1954, American Management Association, 105 pp.); J.H. Watson, III, National Industrial Conference Board, *Controlling Capital Expenditures*, Studies in Business Policy, No. 62, April, 1953; C.I. Fellers, 'Problems of Capital Expenditure Budgeting', *NACA Bulletin* 26 (May, 1955), 918–24; E.N. Martin, 'Equipment Replacement Policy and Application', *NACA Bulletin*, 35 (February, 1954), 715–30.

[2] *Journal of Business*, Vol. XXVIII, No. 3 (October, 1955).

Given the rate of profit on each capital outlay proposal, the size of the budget and its allocation are automatically determined with the establishment of the rate of profit required for the inclusion of a proposal in the budget. In the balance of this paper, a method for determining this quantity is proposed and its use in capital budgeting is analyzed.

II

We state that the objective of a firm is the maximization of the value of the stockholders' equity. While there may be legitimate differences of opinion as to whether this is the sole motivation of management, we certainly feel that there can be no quarrel with the statement that it is a dominant variable in management's decisions. It has been shown by Lutz and Lutz in their *Theory of the Investment of the Firm*[3] and by others[4] that this objective is realized in capital budgeting when the budget is set so as to equate the marginal return on investment with the rate of return at which the corporation's stock is selling in the market. The logic and operation of this criterion will be discussed later. Now, we only wish to note the role assigned in capital budgeting to the rate of profit that is required by the market.

At the present time, the dividend yield (the current dividend divided by the price) and the earnings yield (the current income per share divided by the price) are used to measure the rate of profit at which a share is selling. However, both these yields fail to recognize that a share's payments can be expected to grow, and the earnings yield fails to recognize that the corporation's earnings per share are not the payments made to the stockholder.

The practical significance of these failures is evidenced by the qualifications with which these two rate-of-profit measures are used by investment analysts. In the comparative analysis of common stocks for the purpose of arriving at buy or sell recommendations, the conclusions indicated by the dividend and/ or the earnings yield are invariably qualified by the presence or absence of the prospect of growth. If it is necessary to qualify a share's yield as a measure of the rate of profit one might expect to earn by buying the share, then it must follow that current yield, whether income or dividend, is inadequate for the purposes of capital budgeting, which is also concerned with the future. In

---

[3] Friedrich and Vera Lutz, *The Theory of Investment of the Firm* (Princeton, N.J., 1951, Princeton University Press, 253 pp.), 41–43.

[4] Joel Dean, *Capital Budgeting: Top Management Policy on Plant, Equipment, and Product Development* (New York, 1951, Columbia University Press, 174 pp.); Roland P. Soule, 'Trends in the Cost of Capital', *Harvard Business Review*, 31 (March, April, 1953), 33–47.

short, it appears to us that the prospective growth in a share's revenue stream should be reflected in a measure of the rate of profit at which the share is selling. Otherwise, its usefulness as the required rate of profit in capital budgeting is questionable.

In his *Theory of Investment Value*,[5] a classic on the subject, J.B. Williams tackled this problem of growth. However, the models he developed were arbitrary and complicated so that the problem of growth remained among the phenomena dealt with qualitatively. It is our belief that the following proposal for a definition of the rate of profit that takes cognizance of prospective growth has merit.

The accepted definition of the rate of profit on an asset is the rate of discount that equates the asset's expected future payments with its price. Let P_0 = a share's price at $t = 0$, let D_t = the dividend expected at time t, and let k = the rate of profit. Then, the rate of profit on a share of stock is the value of k that satisfies

$$P_0 = \sum_{t=1}^{\infty} \frac{D_t}{(1 + k)^t}. \tag{1}$$

It is mathematically convenient to assume that the dividend is paid and discounted continuously at the annual rates D_t and k, in which case

$$P_0 = \int_0^{\infty} D_t e^{-kt}\, dt. \tag{2}$$

Since P_0 is known, estimating the rate of profit at which a share of stock is selling requires the determination of D_t, $t = 1, 2, \ldots, \infty$.

At the outset it should be made clear that our objective is not to find the rate of profit that *will actually be earned* by buying a share of stock. This requires knowledge of the dividends that will be paid in the future, the price at which the share will be sold, and when it will be sold. Unfortunately, such information is not available to us. The rate of profit of interest here is a relation between the present known price and the *expected future dividends*. The latter will vary among individuals with the information they have on a host of variables and with their personality. Therefore, by expected future dividends we mean an estimate that (1) is derivable from known data in an objective manner, (2) is derived by methods that appear reasonable, i.e., not in conflict with common sense knowledge of corporation financial behavior, and (3) can

[5] J.B. Williams, *The Theory of Investment Value*, (Cambridge, Massachusetts, 1938, Harvard University Press), 87–96.

be used to arrive at a manageable measure of the rate of profit implicit in the expectation.

We arrive at D_t by means of two assumptions. One, a corporation is expected to retain a fraction b of its income after taxes; and two, a corporation is expected to earn a return of r on the book value of its common equity. Let Y_t equal a corporation's income per share of common after taxes at time t. Then the expected dividend at time t is

$$D_t = (1 - b) Y_t \tag{3}$$

The income per share at time t is the income at $(t - 1)$ plus r percent of the income at $(t - 1)$ retained, or

$$Y_t = Y_{t-1} + rbY_{t-1} \tag{4}$$

Equation (4) is simply a compound interest expression so that, if Y_t grows continuously at the rate $g = br$,

$$Y_t = Y_0 e^{gt}. \tag{5}$$

From Equations (3) and (5)

$$D_t = D_0 e^{gt}. \tag{6}$$

Substituting this expression for D_t in Equation (2) and integrating, yields

$$P_0 = \int_0^\infty D_0 e^{gt} e^{-kt} \, dt$$

$$= D_0 \int_0^\infty e^{-t(k-g)} \, dt \tag{7}$$

$$= \frac{D_0}{k - g}.$$

The condition for a solution is $k > g$, a condition that is easily satisfied, for otherwise, P_0 would be infinite or negative.

Solving Equation (7) for k we find that

$$k = \frac{D_0}{P_0} + g. \tag{8}$$

Translated, this means that the rate of profit at which a share of common stock is selling is equal to the current dividend, divided by the current price (the dividend yield), plus the rate at which the dividend is expected to grow. Since there are other possible empirical definitions of the market rate of profit on a share of stock, we will refer to k as the growth rate of profit.

III

Let us now review and evaluate the rationale of the model we have just established. Estimating the rate of profit on a share of stock involves estimating the future dividend stream that it provides, and the fundamental difference between this model and the dividend yield is the assumption of growth. The latter, as can be seen, assumes that the dividend will remain constant. Since growth is generally recognized as a factor in the value of a share and since it is used to explain differences in dividend yield among shares, its explicit recognition appears desirable. Future dividends are uncertain, but the problem cannot be avoided by ignoring it. To assume a constant rate of growth and estimate it to be equal to the current rate appears to be a better alternative.

Under this model the dividend will grow at the rate br, which is the product of the fraction of income retained and the rate of return earned on net worth. It is mathematically true that the dividend will grow at this rate if the corporation retains b and earns r. While we can be most certain that the dividend will not grow uniformly and continuously at some rate, unless we believe that an alternative method for estimating the future dividend stream is superior, the restriction of the model to the assumption that it will grow uniformly at some rate is no handicap. Furthermore, the future is discounted; hence, an error in the estimated dividend for a year in the distant future results in a considerably smaller error in k than an error in estimating the dividend in a near year.

It should be noted that this measure of the rate of profit is suspect, when *both* income and dividend are zero, and it may also be questioned when either falls to very low (or negative) values. In such cases, the model yields a lower rate of profit than one might believe that the market requires on a corporation in such difficulties. It is evident that the dividend and the income yields are even more suspect under these conditions and, hence, are subject to the same limitations.

There are other approaches to the estimation of future dividends than the extrapolation of the current dividend on the basis of the growth rate implicit in b and r. In particular, one can arrive at g directly by taking some average of the past rate of growth in a corporation's dividend. Whether or not this or some other measure of the expected future dividends is superior to the one presented earlier will depend on their relative usefulness in such purposes as the analysis of variation in prices among shares and the preferences of those who want an objective measure of a share's rate of profit.

So far, we have compared the growth rate of profit with the income and dividend yields on theoretical grounds. Let us now consider how they differ in practice, using the same measurement rules for the variables in each case. The numerical difference between the growth rate of profit and the dividend yield is simply the growth rate. However, the income yield, which is the measure of the rate of profit commonly recommended for capital budgeting, differs from the growth rate of profit in a more complex manner, and to establish this difference we first note that

$$b = \frac{Y - D}{Y} \text{ and } r = \frac{Y}{B} \tag{9}$$

where B = the net worth or book value per share. The growth rate of profit, therefore, may be written as

$$k = \frac{D}{P} + br = \frac{D}{P} + \frac{Y - D}{B}. \tag{10}$$

Next, the income yield can be decomposed as follows:

$$y = \frac{Y}{P} = \frac{D}{P} + \frac{Y - D}{P}. \tag{11}$$

We see then that y and k will be equal when book and market values are equal. It can be argued that the income yield overstates a share's payment stream by assuming that each payment is equal to the income per share and understates the payment stream by assuming that it will not grow. Hence, in this special case where book and market values are equal, the two errors exactly compensate each other.

Commonly market and book values differ, and y will be above k when market is below book, and it will be below k when market is above book. Hence, a share of IBM, for example, that is priced far above book had had an earnings yield of two to three percent in 1955. We know that the market requires a higher rate of profit on a common stock, even on IBM, and its growth rate of profit, k, is more in accord with the value suggested by common sense. Conversely, when US Steel was selling at one-half of book value in 1950, the high income yield grossly overstated the rate of profit that the market was, in fact, requiring on the stock.

Furthermore, the growth rate of profit will fluctuate in a narrower range than the earnings yield. For instance, during the last few years, income, dividends, and book value have gone up more or less together, but market price has gone up at a considerably higher rate. Consequently, the growth rate of profit, dependent in part on book value, has fallen less than the earnings yield. Conversely, in a declining market k would rise less rapidly than y.

There is a widespread feeling that many accounting figures, particularly book value per share, are insensitive to the realities of the world, and some may feel that the comparative stability of k is merely a consequence of the limitations of accounting data. This is not true! The behavior of k is not a consequence of the supposed lack of realism in accounting data. Rather, book value appears in the model because it, and not market value, is used to measure the rate of return the corporation earns on investment, which, we have seen, is the rate of return that enters into the determination of the rate at which the dividend will grow. The comparative stability of k follows from the simple fact that, when a revenue stream is expected to grow, a change in the required rate of profit will give rise to a more than proportional change in the asset's price. Conversely, a change in the price reflects a less than proportional change in the rate of profit.

IV

Given the rate of profit expected on each item in the schedule of available investment opportunities and given the rate of profit at which the corporation's stock is selling, what should the capital budget be? As stated earlier, the accepted theory is that the budget should be set so as to equate the marginal return on investment with the rate of profit at which the stock is selling. The reasoning is, if the market requires, let us say, a 10 percent return on investment in the corporation's stock, and if the corporation can earn 15 percent on additional investment, obtaining the funds and making the investment will increase the earnings per share. As the earnings and the dividend per share increase or as the market becomes persuaded that they will increase, the price of the stock will rise. The objective, it will be recalled, is the maximization of the value of the stockholder's equity.

The conclusion drawn implicitly assumes that the corporation can sell additional shares at or above the prevailing market, or if a new issue depresses the market, the fall will be slight, and the price will soon rise above the previous level. However, some other consideration may argue against a new stock issue; for example, the management may be concerned with dilution of control, or the costs of floating a new issue may be very high, or a new issue may be expected to depress the price severely and indefinitely for reasons not recognized in the theory. Hence, it does not automatically follow that a new issue should be floated when a firm's demand for funds exceeds, according to the above criterion, those that are internally available.

In determining whether the required rate of profit is above or below r', the marginal return on investment, one can use y, the earnings yield, or k, the growth rate of profit as the required rate of profit. If y and k differ and if the reasoning in support of k presented earlier is valid, using y to estimate the direction in which a new issue will change the price of the stock may result in a wrong conclusion.

In arriving at the optimum size of a stock issue, the objective is to equate r' and y or k, depending on which is used. Internal data may be used to estimate the marginal efficiency of capital schedule. If the required rate of profit is considered a constant, its definition, $y = Y/P$ or $k = D/P + br$, provides its value. However, the required rate of profit may vary with the size of the stock issue or with the variables that may change as a consequence of the issue. In this event, finding the optimum size of a stock issue requires a model that predicts the variation in the required rate of profit with the relevant variables.

Borrowing is an alternative source of funds for investment. However, an analysis of this alternative requires the measurement of both (1) the variation in risk with debt, and (2) the difference between the rate of profit and the rate of interest needed to cover a given increase in risk. This has not been done as yet, which may explain the widespread practice of arbitrarily establishing a 'satisfactory' financial structure and only borrowing to the extent allowed by it.

It has been stated by Dean[6] and Terborgh[7] that the long-term ceiling on a firm's capital outlays is the amount of its internally available funds. However, the share of its income a corporation retains is not beyond the control of its management; and, among the things we want from a capital budgeting model is guidance on whether the share of a corporation's income that is retained for investment should be raised or lowered.

Proceeding along traditional lines, the problem may be posed as follows. A firm estimates its earnings and depreciation allowances for the coming year and deducts the planned dividend to arrive at a preliminary figure for the capital budget. The marginal rate of return on investment in excess of this amount may be above or below the required rate of profit. We infer from theory that the two rates should be equated by (1) raising the budget and reducing the dividend when the marginal return on investment is above the required rate of return, and (2) raising the dividend and reducing the budget when the reverse holds. The conditions under which this process yields an equilibrium are illustrated in Figure 1. The marginal return on investment, r', should fall as the budget is increased, and the required rate of profit, y or k,

---

[6] Dean, *op. cit.*, 53–55.

[7] George Willard Terborgh, *Dynamic Equipment Policy* (New York, 1949, McGraw-Hill, 290 pp.), 228–29.

should increase or it should fall at a lower rate than r'. The latter case is illustrated by the line y_a or k_a.

Changing the dividend so as to equate r' and say y should maximize the price of the stock. For instance, if r' is above y, the company can earn a higher return on investment than stockholders require, and a dollar used this way is worth more to the stockholders than the dollar distributed in dividends. In other words, the price should go up by more than the income retained.

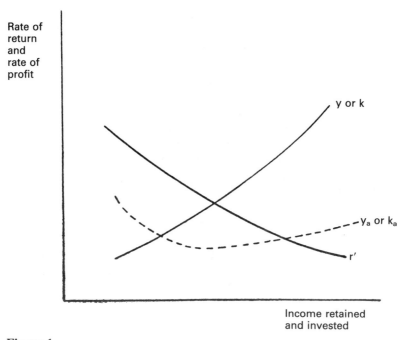

Figure 1

There are, of course, a number of problems connected with the use of this model for arriving at the optimum dividend rate. First, there is the question whether y or k should be used to measure the required rate of profit. Second, there is no question that the required rate of profit varies with the dividend rate. Hence, the current rate of profit given by the definition does not tell what profit rate will be required with a different dividend rate. This requires a model which predicts the variation in y or k with the dividend rate and other variables. Third, there is a very nasty problem of the short and the long run. It is widely believed, though the evidence has limitations, that the price of a share of stock varies with the dividend rate, in which case a corporation should distribute all of its income. However, it is quite possible that a change in the dividend gives rise to the expectation that earnings and future dividends are changing in the same direction. Further, in the short run, the market is not likely to be informed on a firm's marginal efficiency of capital schedule. For these and other reasons, it is likely that the dividend rate should not be made to vary with short-run changes in the marginal efficiency of capital, and more sophisticated methods than those now in use are needed to establish the variation in price or required rate of profit with the dividend rate.

V

The major points developed in this paper may be summarized as follows. We presented a definition of the rate of profit required by the market on a share of common stock, and we noted some of its advantages. It is theoretically superior to the income and dividend yields because it recognizes that the revenue stream provided by a share can be expected to grow. Furthermore, its empirical characteristics are also superior to those of the income and dividend yields since its value is generally in closer agreement with common sense notions concerning the prevailing rate of profit on a share of stock and since its value fluctuates in a narrower range over time. We next examined some of the problems involved in using this definition of the rate of profit and the earnings yield in capital budgeting models. Finally, we saw that, before capital budgeting theory can be made a reliable guide to action, we must improve our techniques for estimating the future revenue on a capital outlay proposal, and we must learn a good deal more about how the rate of profit the market requires on a share of stock varies with the dividend, the growth rate, and other variables that may influence it.

10 Dividends, earnings and stock prices

M. J. Gordon*

The three possible hypotheses with respect to what an investor pays for when he acquires a share of common stock are that he is buying (1) both the dividends and the earnings, (2) the dividends, and (3) the earnings. It may be argued that most commonly he is buying the price at some future date, but if the future price will be related to the expected dividends and/or earnings on that date, we need not go beyond the three hypotheses stated. This paper will critically evaluate the hypotheses by deriving the relation among the variables that follows from each hypothesis and then testing the theories with cross-section sample data. That is, price, dividend, and earnings data for a sample of corporations as of a point in time will be used to test the relation among the variables predicted by each hypothesis.

The variation in price among common stocks is of considerable interest for the discovery of profitable investment opportunities, for the guidance of corporate financial policy, and for the understanding of the psychology of investment behavior.[1] Although one would expect that this interest would find expression in cross-section statistical studies, a search of the literature is unrewarding.

Cross-section studies of a sort are used extensively by security analysts to arrive at buy and sell recommendations. The values of certain attributes such as the dividend yield, growth in sales, and management ability are obtained

* The research for this paper was supported by the Sloan Research Fund of the School of Industrial Management at Massachuesetts Institute of Technology. The author has benefited from the advice of Professors Edwin Kuh, Eli Shapiro, and Gregory Chow. The computations were done in part at the M.I.T. Computation Center.

[1] Assume that the hypothesis stock price, $P = f(x_1, x_2, \ldots)$, is stated so that it can be tested, and it is found to do a good job of explaining the variation in price among stocks. The model and its coefficients thereby shed light on what investors consider and the weight they give these variables in buying common stocks. This information is valuable to corporations insofar as the prices of their stocks influence their financial plans. It is also true that a stock selling at a price above or below that predicted by the model deserves special consideration by investors.

and compared for two or more stocks. Then, by some weighting process, a conclusion is reached from this information that a stock is or is not an attractive buy at its current price.[2] Graham and Dodd go so far as to state that stock prices should bear a specified relation to earnings and dividends, but they neither present nor cite data to support the generalization.[3] The distinguished theoretical book on investment value by J.B. Williams contains several chapters devoted to the application of the theory, but his empirical work is in the tradition of the investment analyst's approach.[4] The only study along the lines suggested here that is known to the writer is a recent one on bank stocks by David Durand.[5]

In contrast with the dearth of published studies the writer has encountered a number of unpublished cross-section regressions of stock prices on dividends, earnings, and sometimes other variables. In these the correlations were high, but the values of the regression coefficients and their variation among samples (different industries or different years) made the economic significance of the results so questionable that the investigators were persuaded to abandon their studies. There is reason to believe that the unsatisfactory nature of the findings is due in large measure to the inadequacy of the theory employed in interpreting the model, and it is hoped that this paper will contribute to a more effective use of cross-section stock price studies by presenting what might be called the elementary theory of the variation in stock prices with dividends and earnings.

Before proceeding, it may be noted that there have been some time series studies of the variation in stock prices with dividends and other variables. The focus of these studies has been the relation between the stock market and the business cycle[6] and the discovery of profitable investment opportunities.[7] They have not been concerned with explaining the variation in price among stocks, and it is questionable whether such data can be effectively used for this purpose. Auto-correlation in the time series would impair the significance of the regression coefficients for many of the variables. Possibly even more

---

[2] Illustrations of this method of analysis may be found in texts on investment analysis such as: Graham and Dodd, *Security Analysis*, 3rd Ed. (New York, 1951); and Dowrie and Fuller, *Investments* (New York, 1941).

[3] Graham and Dodd, op.cit., 454 ff.

[4] *The Theory of Investment Value* (Cambridge, 1938).

[5] *Bank Stock Prices and the Bank Capital Problem*, Occasional Paper 54, National Bureau of Economic Research (New York, 1957).

[6] J. Tinbergen, 'The Dynamics of Share-Price Formation', this Review, XXI (November 1939), 153–60; and Paul G. Darling, 'A Surrogative Measure of Business Confidence and its Relation to Stock Prices', *Journal of Finance*, X (December 1955), 442–58.

[7] The outstanding example of this is *The Value Line Investment Survey*. In addition, numerous articles in the *Analysts Journal* and the *Journal of Finance* analyze the change over time of price with other variables. A paper of some interest is D. Harkavy, 'The Relation Between Retained Earnings and Common Stock Prices for Large, Listed Corporations', *Journal of Finance*, VIII (September 1953), 183–97.

important, the use of time series assumes that the coefficient of a variable is constant over time but different among stocks. The exact opposite is assumed in any attempt to explain preference among investment opportunities.

The sample

To test each of the theories, price, dividend and earnings data were obtained for four industries and two years, so that there are eight samples in all. The years chosen were 1951 and 1954, and the industries and number of corporations for each industry are Chemicals, 32; Foods, 52; Steel, 34; and Machine Tools, 46.

Including only those corporations which conformed to a narrow definition of the industries mentioned did not provide samples of adequate size. Therefore, certain fringe classifications were included in each category. For instance, Chemicals includes pharmaceutical manufacturers, and Steel includes forging manufacturers and certain other fabricators of steel as well as the basic steel producers. In general, while the corporations included in each sample can be considered to come under the label, there is considerable variation among them in such attributes as size, profitability, structure of the markets in which they buy and sell, and investor status.[8]

The use of eight samples rather than one provides a more rigorous test of the hypotheses. The industry and year selection of the data has the further advantage of allowing the use of *a priori* economic knowledge in evaluating the regression statistics. For instance, if the dividend coefficient is considered an estimate of the rate of profit, we want to know whether the estimate is reasonable on grounds broader than statistical significance. Good preferred stocks sold in these years at dividend yields of four to five per cent, and companies acquired in mergers were purchased for about five times their earnings before income taxes. Therefore, we would expect the rate of profit on common stocks to fall between four and ten per cent and the coefficient in question to fall between ten and twenty-five. Further, we would expect a particular rank in the coefficients. Corporations in the chemical industry are considered to have the advantages of size, growth, and stability; foods represent an industry that is considered stable; steels represent an industry with large corporations which are considered vulnerable to cyclical fluctuations; and machine tools represent an industry of comparatively small corporations which are also vulnerable to the business cycle. Accordingly, one

---

[8] A list of the corporations and a description of how they were selected may be obtained from the writer on request.

might expect the rate of profit to vary among the industries in the order just given. Further, 1951 was a year of war profits with the outlook for the future somewhat uncertain. By contrast, while there was some talk of recession in 1954, there was little evidence that the high level of income extending back a number of years would fall sharply in the near future. Accordingly, one might expect that the coefficients would differ in a predictable manner between the two years.

Dividends and earnings

Given the task of explaining the variation in price among common stocks, the investigator may observe that stockholders are interested in both dividend and income per share and derive immediately from this observation the model:

$$P = a_0 + a_1 D + a_2 Y \tag{1}$$

where P = the year-end price, D = the year's dividend, and Y = the year's income. The equation may be considered of interest solely for the multiple correlation between the actual and predicted price, in which case no meaning can be given to the regression coefficients. Alternatively, the equation may be read to mean that the coefficients a_1 and a_2 represent the value the market places on dividends and earnings respectively, a possible objective being the measurement of the relative importance of the two variables. However, a share of stock like any other asset is purchased for the expected future income it provides. This income may be the dividend or it may be the earnings per share, but it cannot be both. The model is therefore conceptually weak.

The unfortunate consequence of this pragmatic approach to the measurement of the variation in stock prices with dividend and earnings is illustrated by the data of Table 1. The dividend coefficient for chemicals in 1951 is negative and machine tools has the highest coefficient. Between 1951 and 1954 the chemicals coefficient changes from approximately zero to 25. Many of the dividend coefficients are materially below ten, and in 1954 the highest coefficient is five times the lowest. The income coefficients, with the exception of chemicals in 1951, are extraordinarily low as measures of the price the market is willing to pay for earnings.

Machine tools in 1951 and chemicals in 1954 have income coefficients that are not significantly different from zero, and three of the other coefficients are materially below five. Armed only with the theory just stated, it would be most difficult to infer from the data the existence of a logical structure in the pricing of common stocks.

Table 1   Model I, regression of price on dividend and income

Sample		Constant term	Coefficient and standard error of		Multiple correlation
			D	Y	
1951 –	Chemicals	−7.0	−0.8 (5.2)	16.7 (3.1)	0.93
	Foods	0.1	7.0 (1.5)	5.5 (0.9)	0.90
	Steels	5.5	6.6 (1.8)	2.0 (0.6)	0.86
	Machine tools	2.4	12.0 (1.2)	0.8 (0.5)	0.90
1954 –	Chemicals	−3.0	25.7 (5.2)	0.3 (3.3)	0.92
	Foods	−0.4	10.4 (2.2)	5.6 (1.0)	0.91
	Steels	8.7	8.4 (1.7)	2.0 (0.8)	0.94
	Machine tools	6.3	5.5 (1.4)	4.1 (0.6)	0.89

The dividend hypothesis

The hypothesis that the investor buys the dividend when he acquires a share of stock seems intuitively plausible because the dividend is literally the payment stream that he expects to receive. In implementing the hypothesis it must be recognized that the stockholder is interested in the entire sequence of dividend payments that he may expect and not merely the current value. For the purpose of arriving at an operational model we may represent this infinite sequence by two quantities, one the current dividend and the other a measure of the expected growth in the dividend.

Among the events which will lead to an increase in a corporation's dividend are: successful trading on its equity, an increase in its return on investment, and selling additional common stock when the rate of profit the corporation can earn is above the rate at which its stock is selling. However, there is no doubt that the most important and predictable cause of growth in a corporation's dividend is retained earnings. For those interested in a more rigorous argument it has been shown that if a corporation is expected to earn a return r on investment and retain a fraction b of its income, the corporation's dividend can be expected to grow at the rate br.[9] If the investment or book value per share of common stock is B, then

$$br = \left(\frac{Y - D}{Y}\right)\left(\frac{Y}{B}\right) = \frac{Y - D}{B}. \tag{2}$$

Investors are interested in growth and not rate of growth, since a high rate of growth starting with a low initial value will pay off in the heavily discounted distant future, and it will not be as attractive as a lower rate of growth starting from a higher initial value. Therefore, in a model where price and dividend are absolute quantities, it is likely that retained earnings per share without deflation by book value is a better measure of growth than the rate of growth.

The previous discussion has provided the economic rationale for using the equation

$$P = a_0 + a_1 D + a_2 (Y - D) \tag{3}$$

to represent the hypothesis that the investor buys the dividend when he acquires a share of stock. The reciprocal of the dividend coefficient may be looked on as an estimate of the rate of profit the market requires on common stocks without growth, and the retained earnings coefficient is the estimate of what the market is willing to pay for growth.

Table 2 presents the eight sample estimates of the model's coefficients. The 1951 dividend coefficients are considerably superior to those of Model I under the criteria stated earlier for their absolute and relative values. Only the machine tools coefficient appears comparatively high. The 1954 coefficients vary among the industries as expected and they fall within the expected range. The spread in the coefficients is only one-half the range of those in Model I, but it still seems quite large. In particular one might wonder at the high chemicals-1954 coefficient, the low steels-1951 and machine tools-1954 values, and the strong inverse correlation between the coefficients and the constant terms.

Turning now to the retained earnings coefficients, what would we expect of them? Since they represent the price the market is willing to pay for growth in the dividend, with retained earnings serving as an index of growth, the only statement with respect to their values that follows from the theory is that they should be positive. It may be thought nonetheless that their values seem low, and the absence of statistical significance at the five per cent level for two coefficients, machine tools-1951 and chemicals-1954, is particularly disturb-

---

[9] The argument is developed more fully in M.J. Gordon and Eli Shapiro, 'Capital Equipment Analysis: The Required Rate of Profit', *Management Science*, III (October 1956), 102–10.

ing. The really surprising result is the negative chemicals coefficients for 1954. On the other hand there is some *a priori* credibility in the findings. Growth is most uncertain and it becomes quantitatively important by comparison with the current dividend in the distant future. Also, apart from the 1954 chemicals there is a rough correspondence between the rank of the coefficients and notions as to the comparative stability of earnings among the industries.

Table 2   Model II, regression of price on dividend and retained earnings

Sample	*Constant term*	*Coefficient and standard error of*		*Multiple correlation*
		D	*Y–D*	
1951 – Chemicals	–7.0	15.9 (2.7)	16.7 (3.1)	0.93
Foods	0.1	12.5 (1.1)	5.5 (0.9)	0.90
Steels	5.5	8.6 (1.5)	2.0 (0.6)	0.86
Machine tools	2.4	12.8 (1.0)	0.8 (0.5)	0.90
1954 – Chemicals	–3.0	30.0 (2.6)	0.3 (3.3)	0.92
Foods	–0.4	15.9 (1.5)	5.6 (1.0)	0.91
Steels	8.7	10.4 (1.4)	2.0 (0.8)	0.94
Machine tools	6.3	9.6 (1.2)	4.1 (0.6)	0.89

The reader may have noted (1) the multiple correlation coefficients in Tables 1 and 2 are the same for each industry year, (2) the earnings and retained earnings coefficients, a_2 and a_2 are the same, and (3) the dividend coefficient $a_1 = a_1 + a_2$. On the first point, in both equations price is a linear function of the same variables, so that they both yield the same correlation coefficients. The earnings and retained earnings coefficients are the same, since the change in earnings is the same as the change in retained earnings when the dividend is held constant. The difference in the dividend coefficients is due to the fact that in equation (1) the increase in dividend involves a corresponding reduction in retained earnings, whereas in equation (3) retained earnings is held constant.

The dividend hypothesis provides a more reasonable interpretation of equation (1) than the interpretation given in the previous section. If growth is valued highly, an increase in the dividend with a corresponding reduction in retained earnings will not increase the value of a share as much as when a low value is placed on growth. There is some tendency for the a_1 coefficients to vary among industries accordingly. Another point to be noted is that the standard error of a_1 is below that for a_1. This combined with the higher values of the former coefficients means that the change in price with the dividend can be predicted with much greater accuracy when retained earnings are held constant than when the increase comes out of retained earnings.

The earnings hypothesis

The third hypothesis is that the investor buys the income per share when he acquires a share of stock. The rationale is that regardless of whether they are distributed to him the stockholder has an ownership right in the earnings per share. He receives the dividend in cash and the retained earnings in a rise in the share's value, and if he wants additional cash he can always sell a fraction of his equity. In short, the corporate entity is a legal fiction that is not material with respect to his rights in the corporation or the value he places on them.[10] One can argue further that the different tax treatment of dividends and capital gains creates a stockholder preference for retained earnings.

The hypothesis may be tested by reference to the data of Table 2. If the investor is indifferent to the fraction of earnings distributed, the dividend and retained earnings coefficients of Model II should be the same. However, with the exception of chemicals-1951 the difference between the coefficients is statistically significant. Durand's bank stock study presents the same picture on this question.[11]

Since the proposition that the rate of profit at which a common stock sells is independent of the dividend rate has some intuitive merit, a theoretical explanation of the statistical findings presented above is of interest. The first point to be noted is that the dividend hypothesis is correct regardless of whether the earnings hypothesis is correct. The only point at issue is whether the dividend hypothesis is unnecessary. Can one study the pricing of common stocks and related questions without considering the fraction of income paid in dividends? It is therefore possible to investigate the problem by using a more

[10] This appears to be a widely held point of view in the economics literature. See for example Lutz and Lutz, *The Theory of Investment of the Firm* (Princeton, 1951). The question is nowhere considered explicitly, but it is implicit in the material treated on pages 155 ff.

[11] Durand, op. cit., 10–11.

rigorous formulation of the dividend hypothesis to establish the condition for the validity of the earnings hypothesis.

Let k be the rate of profit at which a stock is selling, Y_t the income expected in year t, b the fraction of income the corporation is expected to retain, and r the rate of profit it is expected to earn on investment. The corporation's dividend is expected to grow at the rate br, and the price of the stock at $t = 0$ is:

$$P_0 = \int_0^\infty (1 - b)\, Y_t\, e^{-kt}\, dt$$

$$= \int_0^\infty (1 - b)\, Y_0\, e^{brt}\, e^{-kt}\, dt. \tag{4}$$

The price of the share is finite and the integration may be carried out if $k > br$, in which case

$$P_0 = \frac{(1 - b)}{k - br}\, Y_0. \tag{5}$$

It may be noted that if $k = r$, equation (5) reduces to

$$P_0 = \frac{1}{k}\, Y_0, \tag{6}$$

but this is not relevant to the question at issue. For the earnings hypothesis to be valid, it is necessary that k be independent of b. That is, the rate of profit required by the market should be independent of the fraction of income retained.

We could reason as follows. A necessary condition for the price of a stock to be finite is $k > br$. This condition is most easily satisfied if k is an increasing function of br, and if this is true we would also expect that k will vary with b. Other things equal, the rate of profit required on a common stock will vary for a corporation and among corporations inversely with the dividend rate.

An argument with considerably more theoretical content can be derived from the two following assumptions, both of which appear reasonable. (1) The rate at which a future payment is discounted increases with its uncertainty; and (2) the uncertainty of a future payment increases with the time in the future at which it will be received. It follows that *the* rate of profit at which a stream of expected payments is discounted is really an average of rates, each weighted by the size of the payment. The larger the distant payments relative to the near payments, the higher the average rate that equates the stream of payments with the price, the latter obtained by discounting each future payment at its appropriate rate. The relative size of the distant payments will of course vary with the rate of growth. Therefore, given the current earnings, the rate of profit required on a share increases with the fraction of income retained. The same reasoning provides an explanation for the tendency of interest rates on bonds to increase, other things being the same, with the maturity of the bond.

Refinements in the model

Equation (3) is an extremely simple and crude expression of the dividend hypothesis, and insofar as the values of the coefficients are suspect, it may be due to limitations of the model. In this section we shall discuss the more important limitations, suggest how they may be dealt with, and then present data for a model that attempts to overcome some of these limitations.

1 Correlation between the variables and variation in the coefficients among industries is due in part to the scale factor. The problem may be stated as follows. Assume a sample of *n* corporations for all of which the dividend is the same, the price differs among the shares, and the average of the prices is higher than the dividend. There is no correlation between dividend and price. However, if *n* numbers are selected at random and the price and dividend of each share is multiplied by one of these numbers, correlation between the variables will be created. Further, if each of the *n* random numbers is first multiplied by a constant greater than one, the correlation and the regression coefficient will be larger the larger the value of this constant. The presence of so-called high-priced and low-priced stocks in a sample reflects in some part this scale factor. It is possible that by deflating the data, say by book value, and/or using logs we will moderate the influence of scale on the coefficients.

2 The independent variables in equation (3) are the current values of dividends and retained earnings. These quantities are of interest, however, only because they represent the latest available information for the prediction of future dividends. Insofar as these current values depart from averages over some prior period for extraordinary reasons, investment analysts maintain that the changes should be discounted to arrive at what might be considered normal values. This suggests that some combination of current values and averages over a prior period for dividends and retained earnings would provide a superior explanation of the variation in price among shares.

3 The value the market places on a dividend expectation derived from past dividends and retained earnings may be expected to vary among corporations with the confidence in the dividend stream. This would suggest that the price of a share varies with other variables such as the size of the corporation, the relation of debt to equity, and the stability of its earning record. Insofar as the values of these variables vary among industries, failure to include them introduces variation and error in the dividend and retained earnings coefficients.

4 In the present model the variation in price with growth in the dividend is estimated by using an index of growth, retained earnings, as the independent variable. A model in which it is possible to use the rate of growth itself might yield better results. More important, the definition of the rate of growth has considerable theoretical merit – to date nothing superior has been proposed – but there are empirical problems involved in using it. Variation in accounting practice among firms makes the use of book value as a measure of return on investment questionable. Also, the instability of corporate retained earnings and the possibility that they vary over time differently among industries may make the use of past values to predict the future an heroic assumption. This is particularly true if investors give considerable weight, rationally or otherwise, to other variables in predicting future earnings.

Table 3 presents the regression statistics for the following model

$$P = \beta_0 + \beta_1 \bar{d} + \beta_2 (d - \bar{d}) + \beta_3 \bar{g} + \beta_4 (g - \bar{g}). \qquad (7)$$

In this equation:

P = year-end price divided by book value,
$\bar{d}$ = average dividend for the prior five years divided by book value,
d = current year's dividend divided by book value,
$\bar{g}$ = average retained earnings for the prior five years divided by book value,
g = current year's retained earnings divided by book value.

The deflation by book value was undertaken to eliminate the scale effect discussed previously.[12] The objective was only partially accomplished, since correlation exists between the deflated and undeflated variables. For instance, correlation between P and p for the eight samples ranged from zero to .65 and was more than .4 for six of the samples.

[12] The use of deflated variables in regression analysis is a debatable question. See David Durand, op.cit., 56; and Edwin Kuh and John R. Meyer, 'Correlation and Regression Estimates when the Data are Ratios', *Econometrica* XXIII (October 1955), 400–16.

The use of $\bar{d}$ and $(d - \bar{d})$ assumes that the investor values a stock on the basis of the average dividend during the prior five years and the amount by which the current value differs from this average. The same reasoning applies to $\bar{g}$ and $(g - \bar{g})$, which by the way should be interpreted as deflated retained earnings and not as growth rates in the context of this model. The coefficients β_i may be interpreted as follows: $\beta_1 = \beta_2$ (or $\beta_3 = \beta_4$) implies that the investors

Table 3 Regression of price on dividend, retained earnings, change in dividend, change in retained earnings, all deflated by book value

Sample	*Constant term*	*Coefficient and standard error of*				*Multiple correlation*
		$\bar{d}$	$d-\bar{d}$	$\bar{g}$	$g-\bar{g}$	
1951 – Chemicals	−0.23	12.42	9.79	18.74	14.36	0.80
		(2.63)	(5.98)	(5.96)	(5.60)	
Foods	0.04	14.04	8.06	3.16	4.57	0.90
		(1.04)	(2.49)	(1.39)	(1.58)	
Steels	0.15	9.88	6.38	1.45	0.41	0.88
		(1.05)	(1.87)	(1.09)	(1.06)	
Machine tools	0.12	12.62	5.93	0.12	1.11	0.91
		(1.17)	(2.75)	(0.99)	(0.80)	
1954 – Chemicals	0.54	17.38	12.71	0.12	3.44	0.79
		(2.92)	(8.93)	(6.39)	(4.78)	
Foods	−0.03	15.51	8.74	5.15	5.96	0.92
		(1.04)	(2.82)	(1.66)	(1.67)	
Steels	0.18	9.69	3.85	2.02	2.85	0.91
		(0.99)	(1.13)	(0.68)	(0.67)	
Machine tools	0.05	11.65	6.06	3.70	1.92	0.87
		(1.16)	(1.74)	(1.12)	(1.04)	

ignore the average dividend for the prior five years and consider only the current dividend; $\beta_2 = 0$ implies that the current dividend is ignored; $\beta_1 > \beta_2$ implies that investors adjust to a change in the dividend with a lag,[13] i.e., the elasticity of expectations is less than one. The opposite is true if $\beta_1 < \beta_2$.

Turning to the data of Table 3 we see that five of the eight multiple correlation coefficients are lower than in Table 2, and for some the difference is large. This is due to the deflation by book value. For dividends, deflation

---

[13] We are talking about an unexpected change in the dividend, since d is the percentage that the dividend bears to book value. A rise in the dividend proportional to the rise in book value counts as no change in the dividend.

and/or the use of both the average value and the departure from average appears to have done some good. The range of the dividend coefficient has been reduced by comparison with Table 2, and the change in dividend coefficient is interesting. All but the chemicals coefficients are significant at the five per cent level, and they all are less than the $\bar{d}$ coefficients. Therefore, as expected, a rise in the dividend is discounted until the average has risen to the new level.

The growth coefficients, however, are disappointing. First, the values for $\bar{g}$ are if anything poorer than the values for $Y - D$ in Table 2. Second, three of the eight coefficients are not statistically significant at the five per cent level. Third, for some of the samples $\beta_4 = \beta_3$, which means that investors are either indifferent to past performance or prefer a share for which retained earnings has increased to one for which it has fallen.

The performance of the model just discussed in explaining the variation in price among stocks is far superior to the simple empirical approach presented earlier. However, considerable room for improvement remains. The lines along which it will be realized appear to be a more effective representation of growth and the recognition of variables which influence the valuation of a dividend expectation. Solution of the scale problem through a different structural relation among the variables may also be of value.

Reproduced from Gordon, M.J. (1959). Dividends, earnings and stock prices. *Review of Economics and Statistics*, May, by permission of Elsevier Science Publishers BV.

11 A note on dividend irrelevance and the Gordon Valuation Model

M. Brennan

The contributions of Modigliani and Miller to the theory of corporate finance are justly celebrated:[1] indeed many authorities would date the development of modern analytical financial theory to their path-breaking 1958 article. Yet, while the points of disagreement between the theory of capital structure expressed in their earlier articles and the traditional theory have been narrowed down to differing empirical assumptions, the same cannot be said of their later article on dividend policy: 'Dividend Policy, Growth, and the Valuation of Shares'.[2]

Nine years after the publication of this latter article there continue to co-exist among financial theorists two opposing views on the importance of dividend policy in perfect markets. The first and older view, originally articulated by Myron Gordon,[3] and still commanding widespread assent, can be paraphrased by the statement that even in perfect capital markets,[4] the existence of uncertainty about the future suffices to make the price of a share dependent upon the dividend policy which is followed: and that in particular, the more generous is the dividend policy, the higher will be the price of the share. Miller and Modigliani on the other hand, have argued that once the

---

[1] See Modigliani and Miller [8, 9, 10].
[2] Modigliani and Miller [8].
[3] Gordon [2, 3, 4].
[4] The perfection of capital markets in this sense is usually taken to exclude such factors as taxes and transactions costs. It is further assumed that all market participants have access to the same information, though of course the existence of uncertainty precludes the possession of perfect information about the future.

investment policy of a firm is given, the price of its shares is invariant with respect to the size of the dividend paid.[5]

The issue between these opposing views cannot be settled by resort to experience, for the fundamental reason that the above hypotheses relate to the effects of dividend policy in perfect capital markets, whereas of course actual securities markets suffer from several imperfections, the most important of which, from the point of view of dividend policy, are the existence of transactions costs and of differential taxes on income from dividends and capital gains.[6] Despite this, there is a paucity of articles on the theoretical differences between Gordon and M-M,[7] and the textbook treatment of the two conflicting theories is in most cases highly unsatisfactory.[8] The student of finance is thus left in a quandary: both authors develop plausible theories from reasonable assumptions, but mystifyingly reach opposing conclusions.

This paper does not aim to break new ground but rather to clarify the main points at issue between the two theories; first, by showing that the Gordon argument does in fact rest upon a confounding of the effects of dividend policy and investment policy; and secondly, by showing that the M-M dividend irrelevance theorem can be derived from a somewhat weaker assumption than that of symmetric market rationality.

Gordon's discussion of dividend policy develops directly from his stock price valuation model, which asserts that the price of a share is equal to the discounted value of expected future dividends.[9] If dividends are expected to grow at the constant rate, g, in perpetuity, and the discount rate is k, this principle leads to the familiar valuation formula:

$$P = \frac{D}{k - g} \qquad (1)$$

where P is the current stock price, and D is the current amount of dividends per share.

---

[5] Except insofar as current dividends may carry information about the future prospects of the firm.

[6] Both of these factors may cause investors to have specific preferences between the two income forms. For a summary of other difficulties in empirical tests of investor attitudes towards dividends see Friend and Puckett [1].

[7] However, see Walter [14].

[8] Weston and Brigham [15, P482] for example reach the rather surprising conclusion 'that all the approaches to dividends (including those of Gordon and M-M) result in the same policy implications as the Walter formulation'. Van Horne [13, P185] summarizes the arguments of Gordon and M-M, before passing on to questions of imperfections in capital markets, but offers the reader no guide as to how to choose between them. Mao [6, P484] leaves the question open stating that 'The cause of this conflict between the dividend (Gordon) and the earnings theorists (M-M) can be traced to their differing assumptions concerning the effect of dividend policy on the rate of return required by investors.'

[9] This presentation of Gordon's model relies mainly on Gordon [3].

If the firm retains a constant fraction, b, of its earnings per share, and earns a constant average rate of return, r, on its investment, employing no outside financing, then

$$g = br$$

and

$$D = (1 - b)Y$$

where Y is the current amount of earnings per share. Substitution for g and D in (1) yields

$$P = \frac{(1 - b)Y}{k - br}. \tag{2}$$

Equation (2) may then be used to evaluate the effect of alternative retention ratios (and therefore payout ratios) on the value of a share. In particular, if the discount rate, k, and the average rate of return on investment, r, are independent of the retention ratio, b, then the effect of alternative retention ratios may be examined by differentiating (2) partially with respect to b:

$$\frac{\partial P}{\partial b} = \frac{(r - k)Y}{(k - br)^2}. \tag{3}$$

It follows that the condition for the share price to be invariant with respect to the fraction of earnings retained and re-invested is just that the average rate of return, r, which is also the rate of return on the marginal investment of retained earnings, be equal to the discount rate, k. It should be observed that in this case the marginal investment has a zero net present value, so that Gordon has shown that if the effects of investment policy are neutralized by setting the net present value of marginal investment equal to zero, then dividend policy is irrelevant. The similarity of this result to that obtained by M-M may be noted.[10] M-M neutralized the effects of investment policy by holding the amount of investment constant under alternative dividend policies, whereas Gordon has achieved the same result by holding the net present value of investment constant.

However, Gordon goes on to argue that, contrary to what has been assumed so far, it is not in general the case that the discount rate, k, is independent of

---

[10] However, it should be observed that M-M's proof of dividend irrelevance under uncertainty proceeds in a much more general framework, which requires no assumptions about the way in which investors evaluate future dividends, whereas Gordon explicitly assumes that they are discounted.

the retention ratio, b. The rationale for this is that dividends expected at different dates in the future will be subject to different risks, and that therefore each expected future dividend should be discounted at a different rate to reflect this differential risk.[11] Thus the valuation formula for a share should be written explicitly as:

$$P = \frac{D(1)}{(1 + k_1)} + \frac{D(2)}{(1 + k_2)^2} + \cdots \frac{D(t)}{(1 + k_t)^t} + \cdots \qquad (4)$$

where:

$D(t)$ = the expected dividend per share t periods in the future,
k_t = the discount rate appropriate to the risk of a dividend expected t periods ahead.

As M-M point out,[12] since (4) gives the market value of a share, which is determined by the interactions of the supply and demand functions of all market participants, the k_t's should strictly be interpreted as market determined discount rates, rather than the subjective discount rates of any individual investor, although these will be equal in equilibrium.

Gordon admits that it is not possible a priori to determine whether k_t is an increasing or decreasing function of t. But, he observes, 'The important point to note, however, is that there is nothing to guarantee that k_t is a constant for all values of t.'[13]

Once it is admitted that k_t is a function of t, then it follows that k in the valuation formula (1) is a generalized average of the individual k_t, whose weights are not independent of the time path of expected dividends.[14] In the particular case of exponential dividend growth considered here, k is a function of the growth rate g. i.e.

$$\frac{\partial k}{\partial g} \neq 0.$$

Since the growth rate of dividends is given by g = br, it follows that if r is independent of b:

---

[11] Robichek and Myers [12] have argued for the use of certainty equivalents rather than adjustments to the discount rate to account for risk; however, when a different discount rate is assigned to each dividend payment, the two approaches are equivalent.

[12] M-M [8, P424] footnote 19.

[13] Gordon [3, P43].

[14] For a mathematical description of this dependence see the Appendix to Gordon [3] written by Gangolli.

$$\frac{\partial k}{\partial b} = \frac{\partial k}{\partial g} \cdot \frac{\partial g}{\partial b}$$

$$= \frac{\partial k}{\partial g} \cdot r \neq 0. \tag{5}$$

Thus, allowing for this dependence of k on b, the effect of a change in the retention ratio on share price is given by:

$$\frac{dP}{db} = \frac{Y \left[r - k - (1 - b) \dfrac{\partial k}{\partial b} \right]}{(k - br)^2}. \tag{6}$$

Then, if r = k

$$\frac{dP}{db} = \frac{- Y (1 - b) \dfrac{\partial k}{\partial b}}{(k - br)^2} \neq 0$$

So, even if the rate of return on the marginal investment, r, is set equal to the average discount rate, k, the price of a share is not independent of the retention ratio, unless

$$\frac{\partial k}{\partial b} = 0.$$

Gordon concludes from this that, in general, stock price and the cost of capital depend on dividend policy.[15]

M-M have asserted that Gordon's argument rests on a confounding of the effects of dividend and investment policy;[16] Gordon, however, has rejected this argument.[17] What does this confounding of the two effects mean? It means presumably that the change in the amount of investment which accompanies the change in dividend policy in Gordon's model would of itself

[15] 'Therefore the statement that a corporation's cost of capital is independent of its dividend rate, or that dividend policy has no influence on share price, implies that k is independent of br.' [6, P87]

[16] 'For all its ingenuity, however, and its seeming foundation in uncertainty, the argument clearly suffers fundamentally from the typical confounding of dividend policy with investment policy that so frequently accompanies use of the internal financing model.' [11, P425]

[17] 'It is well-known that when the rate of return on investment is set equal to the discount rate, changing the level of investment has no effect on share price. By this means I neutralized the profitability of investment. It seems to me perfectly clear that I did not confound investment and dividend policy: I changed the discount rate.' [5, P265]

have effected a change in share price, regardless of how it was financed, and that Gordon is mistakenly attributing to dividend policy the effect of the change in investment policy: in other words, M-M are disputing that the net present value of the marginal investment is zero, even when r is set equal to k. The validity of the M-M argument is readily examined by considering the net present value of the marginal investment implied by a change in the retention ratio in Gordon's model.

Observe first that a change in the retention ratio from b_1 to b_2 involves not just a single change in the amount invested and earned, but a change in earnings and investment in all subsequent periods, or a change in investment policy. It is the net present value of this change in investment policy which must be evaluated.

Denote by ΔI_t the change in period t investment implied by a change in the retention ratio from b_1 to b_2.[18] Then, given that the marginal investment earns a perpetual rate of return, r, and that cash flows expected t periods ahead are discounted at the rate k_t,[19] the net present value of the change in investment policy is given by:

$$
\text{NPV} = \sum_{t=1}^{\infty} \frac{\Delta I_t}{(1 + k_t)^t} \left(-1 + r \sum_{\tau=1}^{\infty} \frac{1}{(1 + k_{t+\tau})^\tau} \right) \tag{7}
$$

Now, in general, setting $r = k$ will not equate the expression in (7) to zero, unless all the k_t are equal, and equal to k – the only circumstance in which Gordon finds dividend policy to be irrelevant!

Thus it appears that Gordon has been misled by the fact that in the special case when all the k_t are equal, setting $r = k$ does neutralize the effect of the profitability of investment, into believing that this procedure neutralized the profitability of investment when the k_t are unequal.[20]

Therefore M-M's argument is upheld: Gordon's proof of the relevance of dividend policy does rest on a confounding of investment and dividend policy

---

[18] ΔI_t is given by:

$$
\Delta I_t = Y[b_2(1 + b_2 r)^t - b_1(1 + b_1 r)^t].
$$

[19] There is some awkwardness in assuming that cash outflows for investment, which are discretionary, should be discounted at the same rate as the resulting cash inflows, which are not. However, this assumption appears to be compatible with Gordon's practice, for he assumes that the discount rate applicable to a dividend depends only on its futurity and not on the magnitude of earnings and retentions in that period. This is one of the difficulties inherent in a discounted cash flow approach to valuation under uncertainty.

[20] It is worth noting that the k_t will be unequal even under conditions of certainty, if the term structure of interest rates is not flat. Thus Gordon's proof of dividend relevance, if it were valid, would apply even under conditions of certainty!

effects. It is true of course that changing the firm's dividend policy will change the average discount rate in the valuation formula (1). This is not to say, however, that it changes the corporation's cost of capital, for as should be clear by now, if the k_t are unequal, the corporation has no unique cost of capital: the average discount rate applicable to an investment project will depend upon the exact time path of the project's returns.[21] Thus k in the valuation formula (1), far from being the corporation's cost of capital, is but an algebraic artefact, and as such should be irrelevant for decision-making purposes.

M-M's proof of dividend irrelevance under uncertainty proceeds by way of the familiar arbitrage argument. Assuming that investment policy is held constant, M-M show that it follows from the firm's budget constraint that the total return to shareholders in firm i, $R_i(0)$,[22] from holding the shares of the firm for one period is:

$$\tilde{R}_1(0) = \tilde{X}_i(0) - \tilde{I}_i(0) + \tilde{V}_i(1) \tag{8}$$

where $X_i(0)$ and $I_i(0)$ are the firm's operating income stream and investment budget for the period, and $V_i(1)$ is its value at the end of the period. M-M posit two firms (i = 1,2) identical in all respects except their first period dividend, and argue that:

(1) $\tilde{R}_1(0) = \tilde{R}_2(0)$, and therefore,
(2) the initial values of the firms are identical.

(1) Since the two firms are assumed identical except for their first period dividend policies, it follows by assumption that $X_1(0) = X_2(0)$ and $I_1(0) = I_2(0)$. They argue moreover that all investors will expect that $V_1(1) = V_2(1)$.

This argument derives from their assumption of symmetric market rationality, which requires first that every market participant behaves rationally in the sense of preferring more wealth to less and being indifferent to the form in which his wealth increment is received; and secondly that, in forming his expectations, he believes that every other market participant both behaves rationally and believes that all others also behave rationally. Thus this assumption implies that all participants will believe that the two firms will be valued rationally at the end of the period so that $V_1(1)$ and $V_2(1)$ will depend only on the prospective future earnings, dividends and investment of the two firms from period 1. Since these are identical by assumption, it follows that all investors will expect $V_1(1) \equiv V_2(1)$, so that $R_1(0) \equiv R_2(0)$.

---

[21] For this reason it would appear preferable to employ the net present value approach to investment decisions, for this does not require specification of a single discount rate.

[22] Note that 'return' refers here, not to the rate of return, but to the total cash receipts of investors including their initial investment.

A more direct set of assumptions leading to the same conclusion might be called the 'independence of irrelevant information' which requires that:

(a) investors are rational in the above sense, and
(b) shares are valued only on the basis of their future prospects, and
(c) at least some investors know from experience that this is so.

It follows directly from this set of assumptions that since the prospects of the two firms are known to be identical as of the end of the period, at least some investors will expect $\tilde{V}_1(1) \equiv \tilde{V}_2(1)$. Assumption (a) is the standard assumption of rational behaviour; assumption (b), in addition to being plausible, has the advantage of familiarity, for it is an implicit assumption of all stock valuation models (including Gordon's), while assumption (c) would appear to be empirically valid.

(2) On the assumption of symmetric market rationality, all investors will perceive that $\tilde{R}_1(0) \equiv \tilde{R}_2(0)$, and therefore by the assumption of individual rationality will value the two firms equally, so that the value of the firm is independent of its first period dividend policy.

On the weaker assumption of the independence of irrelevant information, at least some traders who realize that $\tilde{R}_1(0) \equiv \tilde{R}_2(0)$ will arbitrage away any difference in the initial valuation of the two firms, leading to the same result.

Having shown that first period dividend policy is irrelevant, M-M proceed to show that $\tilde{V}_i(2)$ and hence $\tilde{V}_i(1)$ and $\tilde{V}_i(0)$ are independent of second period dividend policy, and thence by induction that the value of the firm is independent of its dividend policy in all subsequent periods, once investment policy is given.

Thus any denial of the irrelevance of dividend policy must rely upon a rejection of the principle of symmetric market rationality, and the assumption of the independence of irrelevant information. To reject the latter assumption requires one of the following three assertions: either that:

(a) investors are not rational, or
(b) stock prices depend on past events as well as on their expected future prospects, or
(c) there exist no investors who understand the security valuation process.

References

1 Irwin Friend and Marshall Puckett, 'Dividends and Stock Prices', *American Economic Review* Vol. 54, No. 5 (Sept., 1964), 656–682.
2 Myron Gordon, 'Dividends, Earnings and Stock Prices', *Review of Economics and Statistics* Vol. 41, No. 2, Part I (May, 1959), 99–105.

3 -- 'The Savings, Investment and Valuation of a Corporation', *Review of Economics and Statistics* Vol. 45, No. 1 (Feb., 1962), 37–51.

4 --*The Investment, Financing and Valuation of the Corporation.* Homewood, Illinois: Richard D. Irwin, 1962.

5 --'Optimal Investment and Financing Policy', *Journal of Finance* Vol. 18, No. 2 (May, 1963), 264–272.

6 --and Eugene F. Brigham. 'Leverage, Dividend Policy, and the Cost of Capital', *Journal of Finance* Vol. 23, No. 1 (Mar., 1968), 85–103.

7 James C.T. Mao. *Quantitative Analysis of Financial Decisions*, Toronto: MacMillan, 1969.

8 Merton H. Miller and Franco Modigliani. 'Dividend Policy, Growth and the Valuation of Shares', *Journal of Business* Vol. 34, No. 4 (Oct., 1961), 411–433.

9 Franco Modigliani and Merton H. Miller. 'The Cost of Capital, Corporation Finance and the Theory of Investment', *American Economic Review* Vol. 48, No. 3 (June, 1958), 261–297.

10 --'The Cost of Capital, Corporation Finance and the Theory of Investment: Reply', *American Economic Review* Vol. 49, No. 4 (Sept., 1959), 655–669.

11 --'Corporate Income Taxes and the Cost of Capital: A Correction', *American Economic Review* Vol. 53, No. 3 (June, 1963), 433–444.

12 Alexander A. Robichek and Stewart C. Meyers. *Optimal Financing Decisions*, Englewood Cliffs, N.J.: Prentice-Hall, 1965.

13 James C. van Horne. *Financial Management and Policy*, Englewood Cliffs, N.J.: Prentice-Hall, 1968.

14 James E. Walter. 'Dividend Policy: Its Influence on the Value of Enterprise', *Journal of Finance* Vol. 18, No. 2 (May, 1963), 280–291.

15 Fred Weston and Eugene F. Brigham. *Managerial Finance*, New York, Holt, Rinehart and Winston, 1966.

12 A survey of management views on dividend policy

H. Kent Baker, G. E. Farrelly and R. B. Edelman*

I Introduction

The effect of dividend policy on a corporation's market value is a subject of long-standing controversy. Black [2, p.5] epitomizes the lack of consensus by stating 'The harder we look at the dividend picture, the more it seems like a puzzle, with pieces that just don't fit together'.

Because the academic community has been unable to provide clear guidance about dividend policy, a shift in emphasis is proposed. In the spirit of Lintner's seminal work [11], we asked a sample of corporate financial managers what factors they considered most important in determining their firm's dividend policy. Our objectives were as follows:

(i)   to compare the determinants of dividend policy today with Lintner's behavioral model of corporate dividend policy and to assess management's agreement with Lintner's findings;
(ii) to examine management's perception of signalling and clientele effects; and
(iii) to determine whether managers in different industries share similar views about the determinants of dividend policy.[1]

* The authors wish to express their appreciation to Robert A. Taggart and the two anonymous referees for their helpful suggestions.

[1] Whether industry regulation influences dividend policy is a potentially rich issue, since it is quite conceivable that regulation creates incentives for management to adopt a different payout policy than nonregulated firms. Although briefly addressed in this article, this issue has been examined elsewhere by Edelman, Farrelly, and Baker [6].

Table 1 Major determinants of corporate dividend policy

Determinant	Level of importance					Mean	Rank	Standard deviation	χ² Probability	Industry
	None 0	Slight 1	Moderate 2	Great 3	Maximum 4					
1 Anticipated level of firm's future earnings	3.40%		6.80%	89.80%		3.20	1	0.74		Mfg
	1.75		14.04	84.21		3.12	1	0.71	0.4572*	W/R
	1.75		7.89	90.35		3.21	1	0.66		Util
9 Pattern of past dividends	6.12		29.25	64.63		2.73	2	0.89		Mfg
	1.75		29.82	68.42		2.86	2	0.74	0.4390*	W/R
	2.63		25.44	71.93		2.94	3	0.78		Util
8 Availability of cash	14.29		22.45	63.27		2.70	3	1.04		Mfg
	22.81		21.05	56.14		2.42	4	1.15	0.0273†	W/R
	21.24		34.51	44.25		2.35	4	1.02		Util
7 Concern about maintaining or increasing stock price	13.61		44.22	42.18		2.30	4	0.87		Mfg
	15.79		28.07	56.14		2.47	3	0.85	0.0001†	W/R
	3.51		22.81	73.68		2.96	2	0.79		Util

* An asterisk indicates inadequate cell size and the chi-square test may not be valid.
† Underlining indicates a significant relationship at the 0.05 level of significance.
Mfg = manufacturing; W/R = wholesale/retail; Util = utility.

The remaining portion of this paper consists of three sections. Section II sets forth the survey design. Section III presents the research findings and compares them with theory and other empirical evidence. Section IV discusses conclusions and limitations of the study. Because research on dividend policy is already well documented [3], a separate section on the dividend literature is not provided. Instead, relevant aspects of the literature are incorporated into Section III.

II Survey design

The firms surveyed were listed on the New York Stock Exchange (NYSE) and classified by four-digit Standard Industrial Classification (SIC) codes. A total of 562 NYSE firms were selected from three industry groups: utility (150), manufacturing (309), and wholesale/retail (103).

A mail questionnaire was used to obtain information about corporate dividend policy. The questionnaire consisted of three parts: (i) 15 closed-end statements about the importance of various factors that each firm used in determining its dividend policy; (ii) 18 closed-end statements about theoretical issues involving corporate dividend policy, and (iii) a respondent's profile including such items as the firm's dividends and earnings per share.

A pilot test of the preliminary questionnaire was conducted among 20 firms selected from the three industry groups but not included in the final sample of 562 firms. The final survey instrument was then sent to the chief financial officers (CFOs) of the 562 firms, followed by a second complete mailing to improve the response rate and reduce potential nonresponse bias. The survey, which was conducted during the period between February and April 1983, did not require firms to identify themselves.

The survey yielded 318 usable responses (a 56.6% response rate), which were divided among the three industry groups as follows: 114 utilities (76.0%), 147 manufacturing firms (47.6%), and 57 wholesale/retail (55.3%). Based on dividend and earnings per share data provided by the respondents, the 1981 average dividend payout ratios were computed. The payout ratio of the responding utilities (70.3%) was considerably higher than for manufacturing (36.6%) and wholesale/retail (36.1%).[2]

---

[2] In the electric utility segment, the dividend payout ratio can be distorted by non-cash items such as allowance for funds used during construction (AFUDC). *Moody's Public Utility Manual* reports that in 1981 (the year surveyed), AFUDC made a substantial contribution to electric utility net income. In that year, average earnings per share for the industry was $10.16 from which $7.16 was paid in dividends. This represents an average utility payout of 70.5% in contrast with 34% in the other segments. If AFUDC is excluded from net income, earnings are $4.79 per share. Earnings at this level would represent a utility payout ratio of nearly 150%.

III Results and discussion

A Determinants of dividend policy

Lintner's classic 1956 study [11] found that major changes in earnings 'out of line' with existing dividend rates were the most important determinant of the company's dividend decisions. However, because these managers believed that shareholders preferred a steady stream of dividends, firms tended to make periodic partial adjustments toward a target payout ratio rather than dramatic changes in payout. Thus, in the short run, dividends were smoothed in an effort to avoid frequent changes.

Fama and Babiak's [8] examination of several alternative models for explaining dividend behavior supports Lintner's position that managers increase dividends only after they are reasonably sure that they can permanently maintain them at the new level.

To examine how well Lintner's model describes current practice, the respondents were asked to indicate the importance of each of 15 factors in determining their firm's actual dividend policy. A five-point equal interval scale was used for this purpose: 0 = no importance, 1 = slight importance, 2 = moderate importance, 3 = great importance, and 4 = maximum importance. It should be noted that the questionnaire does not follow Lintner's model exactly.

Table 1 provides summary statistics on the major determinants of corporate dividend policy as reported by the three industry groups.[3] The results show that the same four determinants (identified later by 'D') are considered most important by the three industry groups when ranked by the mean response. The determinant numbers represent the order in which each factor was presented in the questionnaire.

The most highly ranked determinants are the anticipated level of a firm's future earnings (D1) and the pattern of past dividends (D9). The high ranking of these two factors is consistent with Lintner's findings.

A third factor cited as important in determining dividend policy is the availability of cash (D8). Although Lintner does not directly address this determinant, Van Horne [19, p.23] and Weston and Brigham [20, p.675] note that liquidity is an important managerial consideration.

Firms in the other industry segments surveyed also have non-cash items charged or added to their income figure. However, Compustat shows no equivalent items in those segments which are consistently used by all firms and have such a profound effect on reported income. It is our belief that with or without an adjustment in the utility payout ratio for AFUDC, utilities can be viewed as high payout firms relative to manufacturing and wholesale/retail firms.

[3] Summary statistics on all 15 determinants of corporate dividend policy are available from the authors.

A fourth major determinant is concern about maintaining or increasing stock price (D7). This concern is particularly strong among utilities who ranked this factor second in importance.

B   Issues involving dividend policy

The study's second objective was to investigate CFOs' perceptions of certain specific issues. The respondents were asked to indicate their general opinion about each of 18 closed-end statements based on a seven-point equal interval scale: -3 = strongly disagree, -2 = moderately disagree, -1 = slightly disagree, 0 = no opinion, $+1$ = slightly agree, $+2$ = moderately agree, and $+3$ = strongly agree. Table 2 provides summary statistics on the responses to each of the 18 statements (identified later by 'S') for the three industry groups. The statement numbers refer to the order in which the statements appeared in the questionnaire.

Attitudes on Lintner's findings

One issue was the level of agreement with statements supporting Lintner's research findings, namely, S2, S3, S9, S10, and S17. The results show that several such statements command the highest level of agreement. For example, two of the highest ranked statements were that a firm should avoid making changes in its dividend rates that might soon have to be reversed (S10) and should strive to maintain an uninterrupted record of dividend payments (S17). Respondents also generally agreed that a firm should have a target payout ratio and should periodically adjust the payout toward the target (S3).

Lintner's field work also suggests that managers focus on the change in the existing rate of dividend payout, not on the dollar amount of dividends (S9) so that investment requirements generally have little effect on modifying the pattern of dividend behavior (S2). On average, managers expressed no strong opinion on either of these statements.

Although management's perceptions could differ significantly from actual decisions, the results in Table 1 do not suggest this. That is, managers' views about continuity of dividend policy seem to be translated into factors (D1 and D9) that are in fact consistent with dividend continuity.

Attitudes on theoretical issues

A major controversy in the literature involves the relationship between dividends and value. Miller and Modigliani (MM) [15] suggest that dividend policy has no effect on the value of the corporation in a world without taxes, transaction costs, or other market imperfections. However, dividends may be relevant to the extent that market imperfections exist. Some of the explanations for dividend relevance include signaling and clientele effects.

Table 2 shows that respondents from all three industry groups agreed relatively strongly that dividend payout affects common stock prices (S1). The utilities showed the highest level of agreement with this statement. These results seem consistent with the finding reported in Table 1 that concern about maintaining or increasing stock price (D7) is a major determinant of corporate dividend policy, especially for utilities.

Management attitudes were also sought on several other theoretical issues. The first issue involves signaling effects. Managers have access to information about the firm's expected cash flows not possessed by outsiders and thus, changes in dividend payout may provide signals about the firm's future cash flows that cannot be communicated credibly by other means. With some exceptions, empirical studies indicate that dividend changes convey some unanticipated information to the market [1, 5, 9, 10, 16, 21].

Three statements involved signaling effects (S4, S5, and S14). The respondents from all three industry groups agreed, on average, that dividend payments provide a 'signaling device' of future company prospects (S14) and that the market uses dividend announcements as information for assessing security value (S5). The respondents also demonstrated a high level of agreement that the reasons for dividend policy changes should be adequately disclosed to investors (S4).

Another theoretical issue concerns the extent to which investors with different dividend preferences form clienteles. Two possible reasons for the formation of clienteles are different perceptions of the relative riskiness of dividends and retained earnings and different investor tax brackets. Although the research evidence is mixed, it does lean toward the existence of clientele effects [7, 12, 17].

Seven statements involved clientele effects (S6, S7, S11, S12, S15, S16, and S18) and these commanded mixed agreement. Respondents from all three industry groups thought that investors have different perceptions of the relative riskiness of dividends and retained earnings (S7) and hence are not indifferent between dividend and capital gains returns (S18). Yet, there was only slight agreement that a stockholder is attracted to firms with dividend policies appropriate to that stockholder's tax environment (S16) and that management should be responsive to its shareholders' dividend preferences (S6). However, the utilities differed from the other two groups, expressing significantly higher levels of agreement on S16 and S6.

C   Industry influence on dividend policy

The study's final objective was to investigate differences in managers' attitudes across three broad industry groups. Studies by Dhrymes and Kurz [4], McCabe [13], and Michel [14] have previously detected some effect of industry classification on corporate dividend policy. However, Rozeff [18]

Table 2 Issues involving corporate dividend policy

Statement	Disagreement −3 −2 −1	0	Agreement +1 +2 +3	Mean	Rank	Standard deviation	χ² Probability	Industry
10 A firm should avoid making changes in its dividend rates that might have to be reversed in a year or so.	1.37%	11.64%	86.99%	2.47	1	0.91		Mfg
	7.02	5.26	87.72	2.16	2	1.46	0.0155*†	W/R
	0.00	8.77	91.23	2.61	2	0.77		Util
4 Reasons for dividend policy changes should be adequately disclosed to investors.	2.05	20.55	77.40	2.09	2	1.28		Mfg
	0.00	19.30	80.70	2.14	3	1.04	0.3189*	W/R
	0.88	28.95	70.18	2.02	3	1.09		Util
17 A firm should strive to maintain an uninterrupted record of dividend payments.	1.36	25.85	72.79	1.97	3	1.05		Mfg
	3.51	10.53	85.96	2.28	1	1.25	0.0001*†	W/R
	0.00	6.14	93.86	2.63	1	0.72		Util
3 A firm should have a target payout ratio and periodically adjust the payout toward the target.	7.53	29.45	63.01	1.47	4	1.50		Mfg
	3.51	17.54	78.95	2.09	4	1.20	0.1715	W/R
	10.53	24.56	64.91	1.42	6	1.65		Util
1 Dividend payout affects the price of the common stock.	6.80	39.46	53.74	1.41	5	1.02		Mfg
	7.02	42.11	50.88	1.46	5	1.23	0.0059†	W/R
	3.51	21.93	74.56	1.99	4	1.22		Util
7 Investors have different perceptions of the relative riskiness of dividends and retained earnings.	0.69	45.83	53.47	1.38	6	1.04		Mfg
	3.57	42.86	53.57	1.34	6	1.28	0.3286*	W/R
	1.76	35.96	62.28	1.62	5	1.16		Util
14 Dividend payments provide a "signaling device" of future prospects.	6.80	38.10	55.10	1.37	7	1.35		Mfg
	7.02	49.12	43.86	1.18	7	1.26	0.6904	W/R
	7.02	42.11	50.88	1.19	10	1.38		Util
5 The market uses dividend announcements as information for assessing security value.	5.52	55.86	38.62	1.02	8	1.29		Mfg
	8.77	52.63	38.60	1.07	8	1.47	0.2040	W/R
	5.26	42.98	51.75	1.33	8	1.39		Util
9 A change in the existing dividend payout is more important than the actual amount of dividends.	10.27	49.32	40.41	0.86	9	1.60		Mfg
	21.05	50.88	28.07	0.40	12	1.67	0.0001†	W/R
	34.21	44.74	21.05	−0.21	16	1.85		Util

No.	Statement	Group					Rank		p-value
16	A stockholder is attracted to firms which have dividend policies appropriate to the stockholder's particular tax environment.	Mfg	6.85	58.22	34.93	0.80	10	1.32	
		W/R	10.53	45.61	43.86	0.88	10	1.48	0.0225†
		Util	6.14	39.47	54.39	1.37	7	1.29	
15	Capital gains expected to result from earnings retention are riskier than are dividend expectations.	Mfg	6.29	58.04	35.66	0.76	11	1.37	
		W/R	15.79	52.63	31.58	0.51	11	1.47	0.2816
		Util	9.65	51.75	38.60	0.85	12	1.44	
6	Management should be responsive to its shareholders' preferences regarding dividends.	Mfg	12.33	54.11	33.56	0.68	12	1.52	
		W/R	8.77	56.14	35.09	0.91	9	1.52	0.0240†
		Util	7.02	40.35	52.63	1.22	9	1.47	
12	Investors in low tax brackets are attracted to high-dividend stocks.	Mfg	10.96	63.01	26.03	0.50	13	1.41	
		W/R	15.79	56.14	28.07	0.39	13	1.57	0.1057
		Util	9.65	50.00	40.35	0.86	11	1.47	
2	New capital investment requirements of the firm generally have little effect on modifying the pattern of dividend behavior.	Mfg	21.92	38.36	39.73	0.38	14	1.88	
		W/R	31.58	31.58	36.84	0.09	15	1.97	0.0786
		Util	24.78	23.89	51.33	0.72	14	2.05	
11	Stockholders in high tax brackets are attracted to low-dividend stocks.	Mfg	19.31	57.93	22.76	0.24	15	1.56	
		W/R	17.86	55.36	26.79	0.29	14	1.59	0.0075†
		Util	14.91	41.23	43.86	0.83	13	1.61	
8	Dividend distributions should be viewed as a residual after financing desired investments from available earnings.	Mfg	28.08	36.30	35.62	0.13	16	1.97	
		W/R	38.60	26.32	35.09	−0.07	16	2.12	0.0001†
		Util	61.95	27.43	10.62	−1.35	17	1.78	
13	Financing decisions should be independent of a firm's dividend decisions.	Mfg	43.54	27.21	29.25	−0.36	17	2.12	
		W/R	49.12	22.81	28.07	−0.58	17	2.04	0.7495
		Util	38.60	28.07	33.33	−0.10	15	2.04	
18	Investors are basically indifferent between returns from dividends versus those from capital gains.	Mfg	55.48	38.36	6.16	−1.33	18	1.50	
		W/R	60.71	33.93	5.36	−1.46	18	1.54	0.0103†
		Util	76.32	18.42	5.26	−1.77	18	1.30	

* An asterisk indicates inadequate cell size and the chi-square test may not be valid.
† Underlining indicates a significant relationship at the 0.05 level of significance.
Mfg = manufacturing; W/R = wholesale/retail; Util = utility.

concluded that a company's industry does not help to explain its dividend payout ratio. Rozeff's conclusion is not applicable to utilities since he intentionally excluded regulated companies because their policies may be affected by their regulatory status.

Chi-square analysis was used to test for differences in the responses among the three industry groups. In order to perform these tests and to avoid inadequate cell sizes, both the five-interval importance scale and the seven-interval disagreement-agreement scale were collapsed into three classes as shown in Tables 1 and 2, respectively. Nevertheless, some warnings about low cell counts resulted because of the highly skewed nature of the responses. These tests showed that the responses of the three groups differed significantly at the .05 level among eight of the 15 determinants of dividend policy (partly shown in Table 1) and nine of the 18 issues (Table 2).

Further Chi-square tests were performed using pair-wise comparisons between the industry groups on all 15 determinants and 18 issues. The results revealed that the manufacturing and wholesale/retail firms had no significant differences in responses at the .05 level for those questions with adequate cell sizes. Hence, the differences occurred primarily as a result of the utilities' responses relative to either manufacturing or wholesale/retail.

The reported differences between the utilities and the other firms may be due to regulation. For example, since regulation gives utilities monopoly power over a product enjoying steady demand, their earnings are comparatively stable. Their risk of having to reduce dividends because of an unexpected decline in earnings is thus less than that for many other companies.

It is also plausible that regulation creates incentives for management to adopt a different payout policy than nonregulated firms. This incentive may stem from the fact that funds retained inside the firm are implicitly subject to expropriation by the regulators in future rate cases. Hence, managers of regulated firms may view the world differently than managers operating in a competitive environment.

On the other hand, the differences may have nothing to do with regulation *per se* but with other characteristics. For example, Rozeff [18] notes that the apparently significant industry effect found in past studies results from the fact that other variables are often similar within a given industry. These similarities are the fundamental reason why companies in the same industry have similar dividend payouts.

Utilities are high payout firms relative to the two other groups and this characteristic makes them different. To control for dividend payout, the responses by managers in the highest payout quartile for 1981 of nonregulated firms (51 firms) were compared with the utilities (114 firms).[4]

---

[4] Summary statistics of high payout regulated and nonregulated firms are available from the authors.

With a few exceptions, the results were strikingly similar to those in Table 2. Although the mean rankings changed little, the responses of the higher payout nonregulated firms more closely resembled the utilities on two statements – namely, dividend payout affects the price of the common stock (S1) and management should be responsive to its shareholders' dividend preferences (S6).

Overall, the findings suggest that the attitudes of even high-payout nonregulated firm managers are different from those of utility managers. Hence, regulation may be responsible for some of the relations observed.

IV Conclusions

Before drawing any conclusions, several limiting aspects of this research should be noted. Survey research typically involves some non-response bias and although steps were taken to ensure a high response rate, this study is no exception. The problem of non-response bias is potentially greatest among manufacturing firms which had the lowest response rate. Another limiting factor is that views about dividend policy were obtained only from chief financial officers. Although CFOs' views should reflect the attitudes of top management more generally, CFOs are not the only individuals involved in dividend policy decisions. Finally, coverage is restricted to three broad industry groups representing only New York Stock Exchange firms.

With these caveats in mind, several conclusions emerge from this survey. First, the results show that the major determinants of dividend payments today appear strikingly similar to Lintner's behavioral model developed during the mid-1950's. In particular, respondents were highly concerned with dividend continuity.

Second, the respondents seem to believe that dividend policy affects share value, as evidenced by the importance attached to dividend policy in maintaining or increasing stock price. Although the survey does not uncover the exact reasons for their belief in dividend relevance, it does provide evidence that the respondents are generally aware of signaling and clientele effects.

Finally, the opinions of the respondents from the utilities differ markedly from those of the other two industries. The results suggest that managers of regulated firms have a somewhat different view of the world than managers operating in a competitive environment. Thus, it may be worthwhile to segregate regulated from nonregulated firms when examining dividend policy.

References

1 P. Asquith and D. Mullins, Jr., 'The Impact of Initiating Dividend Payments on Shareholders' Wealth', *Journal of Business* (January 1983), pp.77–96.

2 F. Black, 'The Dividend Puzzle', *Journal of Portfolio Management* (Winter 1976), pp.5–8.

3 T.E. Copeland and J.F. Weston, *Financial Theory and Corporate Policy*, Reading, MA, Addison-Wesley, 1983.

4 P.J. Dhrymes and M. Kurz, 'Investment, Dividend, and External Finance Behavior of Firms', in R. Ferber (ed.), *Determinants of Investment Behavior*, New York, Columbia University Press, 1967, pp.427–467.

5 K.M. Eades, 'Empirical Evidence on Dividends as a Signal of Firm Value', *Journal of Financial and Quantitative Analysis* (November 1982), pp.471–500.

6 R.B. Edelman, G.E. Farrelly, and H.K. Baker, 'Public Utility Dividend Policy: Time for a Change?', *Public Utilities Fortnightly* (February 21, 1985), pp.26–31.

7 E.J. Elton and M.J. Gruber, 'Marginal Stockholder Tax Rates and the Clientele Effect', *Review of Economics and Statistics* (February 1970), pp.68–74.

8 E.F. Fama and H. Babiak, 'Dividend Policy: An Empirical Analysis', *Journal of the American Statistical Association* (December 1968), pp.1132–1161.

9 C. Kwan, 'Efficient Market Tests of the Informational Content of Dividend Announcements: Critique and Extension', *Journal of Financial and Quantitative Analysis* (June 1981), pp.193–206.

10 P.M. Laub, 'On the Informational Content of Dividends', *Journal of Business* (January 1976), pp.73–80.

11 J. Lintner, 'Distribution of Incomes of Corporations Among Dividends, Retained Earnings and Taxes', *American Economic Review* (May 1956), pp.97–113.

12 R.H. Litzenberger and K. Ramaswamy, 'The Effect of Personal Taxes and Dividends on Capital Asset Prices: Theory and Empirical Evidence', *Journal of Financial Economics* (June 1979), pp.163–196.

13 G.M. McCabe, 'The Empirical Relationship Between Investment and Financing: A New Look', *Journal of Financial and Quantitative Analysis* (March 1979), pp.119–135.

14 A. Michel, 'Industry Influence on Dividend Policy', *Financial Management* (Autumn 1979), pp.22–26.

15 M.H. Miller and F. Modigliani, 'Dividend Policy, Growth, and the Valuation of Shares', *Journal of Business* (October 1961), pp.411–433.

16 S.H. Penman, 'The Predictive Content of Earnings Forecasts and Dividends', *Journal of Finance* (September 1983), pp.1181–1199.

17 17 R.R. Pettit, 'Taxes, Transactions Costs and Clientele Effects of Dividends', *Journal of Financial Economics* (December 1977), pp.419–436.

18 M.S. Rozeff, 'Growth, Beta and Agency Costs as Determinants of Dividend Payout Ratios', *Journal of Financial Research* (Fall 1982), pp.249–259.

19 J.C. Van Horne, *Financial Management and Policy*, 6th ed., Englewood Cliffs, NJ, Prentice-Hall, 1983.

20 J.F. Weston and E.F. Brigham, *Managerial Finance*, 7th ed., Hinsdale, IL, Dryden Press, 1981.

21 J.R. Woolridge, 'The Information Content of Dividend Changes', *Journal of Financial Research* (Fall 1982), pp.237–247.

Reproduced from Kent Baker, H., Farrelly, G.E. and Edelman, R.B. (1985) A survey of management views on dividend policy. *Financial Management*, 14(3), 78–84, by permission of the Financial Management Association.

13 How much growth can a firm afford?

R. C. Higgins

For years growth has been second only to profits in the pantheon of corporate virtues. In recent years, however, there are increasing signs that some managements must finally face the fact that unrestrained growth may be inconsistent with established financial policies. The intent of this paper is to demonstrate that the financial policies and growth objectives established by some companies are mutually incompatible, and to explore the options open to firms for remedying this worsening problem.

To test the consistency of a company's growth objectives and its financial policies, a concept called sustainable growth is introduced. For those companies that want to maintain a target payout ratio and capital structure without issuing new equity, sustainable growth is defined as the annual percentage of increase in sales that is consistent with the firm's established financial policies. If sales expand at any greater rate, something in the company's constellation of financial objectives will have to give – usually to the detriment of financial soundness. Conversely, if sales grow at less than this rate, the firm will be able to increase its dividends, reduce its leverage or build up liquid assets.

A note of urgency is added to this discussion because, as will be demonstrated, the effect of inflation generally reduces *real* sustainable growth. If, for example, a company's sustainable growth rate in the absence of inflation is 8%, its *real* sustainable growth rate – measured as the annual percentage increase in physical volume – in the presence of a 10% inflation rate might fall to 3.5%. Inflationary growth therefore consumes limited financial resources almost as voraciously as does real growth, and neither the company nor the economy benefits. The inflation rate is no longer in double digits, but, inasmuch as the economy has been forced through the worst recession in decades to achieve this reduction, there is cause for concern that inflation will be on the rise again as the unemployment rate returns to politically acceptable levels.

Once a company's sustainable growth rate is known, an executive can see immediately whether the firm's growth objectives and financial policies are mutually feasible, and he or she can use the underlying model to search for a more appropriate mix of financial and growth objectives. The model presented is not intended as a replacement for more formal financial projection. For an initial overview of the growth problem, however, the model is much simpler to use and interpret than formal projections are, and it highlights potentially important interdependencies among key financial and operating variables.

Among the steps a company can take to balance its growth targets and its sustainable growth rate are the sale of new equity shares, a reduction in the firm's dividend payout ratio, an increase in its leverage, or an improvement in operating performance. After reviewing these alternatives, it will be suggested in closing that under present conditions the only viable options remaining for a number of companies are to make further cuts in the dividend payout ratio or to reduce the growth rate to a level which is consistent with the firm's financial targets. In this latter case, it is suggested that in certain instances managers must begin to look upon growth not as something to be maximized, but as a decision variable just as important as the firm's target payout ratio, capital structure, or any other policy parameter.

In more academic terms, the argument is that when new equity financing is impossible, the firm's investment, financing and dividend decisions are interdependent. Because investment capital beyond that provided by retained profits and accompanying borrowing is available only through a reduction of dividends or an increase in leverage, the marginal cost of capital increases with investment beyond a certain level. These increased costs are not limited to the usual 'issue cost' variety but also include the impact on share price of employing what management believes to be excessive debt, or distributing what is believed to be too little in dividends. The optimal growth rate, therefore, is not simply the outgrowth of accepting all average-risk investment opportunities yielding a return above the firm's cost of capital as convention-ally calculated. Instead, management must explicitly consider the tradeoffs between more growth and some combination of more leverage and less dividends.

The model

To explore the growth-financial policy nexus more closely, let us set aside the problem of inflation for the moment and concentrate on a company that wants to maintain a target payout ratio and capital structure without issuing new equity, and that also wants to increase sales at a rapid rate. We wish to demonstrate that under these conditions the firm's growth rate is not an independent variable, but rather is only one of several variables in an interdependent system. To keep the exposition simple and to concentrate on the important interdependencies, we will restrict the analysis here to a steady-state situation in which depreciation is just sufficient to maintain the value of existing assets. Also, we assume that the profit margin on new sales and the ratio of assets to sales on new sales equal the average of like quantities on existing sales. (Generalization of the model to more realistic conditions is considered in the appendix.)

To demonstrate the interdependencies between growth and financial policy, we need only equate annual sources of corporate capital to annual uses. Towards this end, let

p   = the profit margin on new and existing sales after taxes,
d   = the target dividend payout ratio [(1 − d) therefore is the target retention ratio],
L   = the target total debt to equity ratio,
t   = the ratio of total assets to net sales on new and existing sales,
s   = sales at the beginning of the year, and
Δs = increase in sales during the year.

Looking at Figure 1, and assuming that p and t are the same for new sales as for existing sales, the new assets required to support increased sales of Δs are

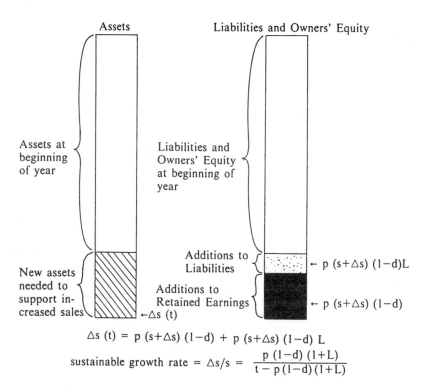

$$\Delta s \,(t) = p \,(s+\Delta s)\,(1-d) + p \,(s+\Delta s)\,(1-d)\,L$$

$$\text{sustainable growth rate} = \Delta s/s = \frac{p \,(1-d)\,(1+L)}{t - p\,(1-d)\,(1+L)}$$

Figure 1   *Calculating sustainable growth*

forecast to be $\Delta s(t)$, shown as the cross-hatched rectangle. On the other side of the balance sheet, total profits for the year are expected to be $(s + \Delta s)p$, and additions to retained earnings to be $(s + \Delta s)p(1 - d)$. This is shown in the figure by the shaded rectangle. Finally, because every \$1 added to retained earnings enables the company to borrow \$L without increasing its debt to equity ratio, new borrowings should equal $(s + \Delta s)p(1 - d)L$. This is shown in Figure 1 by the dotted rectangle.

To calculate the firm's sustainable growth rate, we need only observe that the addition to assets shown in Figure 1 must equal the addition to liabilities and owners' equity – in other words, the new assets must be financed by new debt and an increase in equity through retained earnings. Setting these two quantities equal and solving for the growth rate, $\Delta s/s$,

$$\text{sustainable growth rate in sales} = g^\star = \frac{p(1 - d)(1 + L)}{t - p(1 - d)(1 + L)}.$$

Unless actual growth in sales, g, equals $g^\star$, one or some combination of the variables p, d, L or t must change – or the firm must sell new shares.

Many people would argue that the problems posed by an actual growth rate in excess of the sustainable rate are not serious ones, because the firm can always sell new shares if need be. However, this ignores some important facts about new equities markets which we will discuss below. Let us note here that aggregate data on the significance of new equity capital for manufacturing firms suggest that many enterprises are either unable or unwilling to sell new equity [1,2]. For these companies, problems of sustainable growth are very real ones.

Sustainable growth in manufacturing

The most meaningful estimate of sustainable growth for a company would be based on management's estimates of the variables. To provide a feel for the numbers, however, and to calculate a representative $g^\star$, let us refer to the composite financial statements for all US manufacturing firms compiled quarterly by the Federal Trade Commission [6]. We can think of these figures as representative of the typical manufacturing firm, although individual companies can obviously have a higher or lower sustainable growth rate. Because 1975 was such a poor profit year, we will use figures for 1974 as more representative of typical performance. According to these figures, profit margin = 5.5%, payout ratio = 33%, debt to equity ratio = 88%, assets to sales ratio = 73%, and solving for sustainable growth,

$$g^\star = \frac{(0.055)(1 - 0.33)(1 + 0.88)}{0.73 - (0.055)(1 - 0.33)(1 + 0.88)} = 10.5\%.$$

For the typical manufacturing firm, therefore, the only growth rate in sales consistent with stable values of p, d, L, and t in the absence of new equity financing is 10.5%. We will compare this figure to recent growth rates in manufacturing after considering inflation.

Financing inflation

Inflation adversely affects corporations in several ways. One that is well known by now relates to the fact that depreciation in most countries must be based on the historical cost of assets rather than on their current replacement cost. Because historical depreciation is below replacement cost depreciation during inflationary periods, that portion of cash from operations represented by deprecation is insufficient to recover fully the economic value of the depreciating assets. In addition to asset erosion, historical depreciation also results in higher taxable earnings than does replacement cost depreciation, and naturally higher tax bills as well. Because taxable income is overstated, executives rightfully argue that they are taxed on capital as well as profits during inflation. Another manifestation of this excess tax is that the real rate of return on new corporate investment declines, making expansion less attractive.[1]

A second inflation effect is less well publicized but no less important. It relates to the fact that companies must finance inflation-induced increases in working capital just as if they were the result of real and not inflationary growth. This means that even if a company's goal is just to sell the same number of widgets annually, it must invest larger dollar amounts in accounts receivable and inventory to maintain the same physical volume. Part of this increased investment is offset by increasing accounts payable and possibly higher nominal profits, but these seldom cover the full amount. Because the rest must be financed from outside sources, inflation commonly creates financing problems of its own which add to those created by real growth.

The precise impact on a company of using historical cost depreciation during inflation depends in a complicated way on the capital intensity of the

---

[1] Taxation of fictitious profits may also affect the firm's target debt to equity ratio, but the direction and magnitude of the impact is difficult to predict. If the inflation is unanticipated by lenders, the real cost of debt will decline and the target should rise. If the inflation is anticipated, however, real borrowing costs will stay constant while real income declines due to excess taxes. In this instance, the firm's ability to service debt will fall, and the target debt to equity ratio may fall as well. The firm's payout ratio may also be affected. For example, if the firm recognizes fictitious profits as such, it may want to reduce its payout ratio to keep the proportion of 'true earnings' distributed constant.

firm's production process and on the longevity and vintage of its capital stock. For the sake of simplicity, let us make the admittedly artificial assumption that depreciation is sufficient to maintain the *replacement* value of existing assets. This will enable us to concentrate on the working capital effects of inflation.

As before, consider a company with an aversion to selling equity that wants to maintain a target payout ratio of d and a target debt to equity ratio of L. Assume a uniform inflation rate throughout the economy of j percent, and suppose that new investment in fixed assets varies only in proportion to real increases in sales. Then, total expected nominal profits are $(s + \Delta s)(1 + j)p$, and total sources of capital are expected to be

$$(s + \Delta s)(1 + j)p(1 - d)(1 + L).$$

Because current assets must increase in proportion to nominal sales, the expected increase in current assets is $[(s + \Delta s)(1 + j) - s]c$, where c is the ratio of nominal current assets to nominal sales. Total expected use of cash is therefore

$$[(s + \Delta s)(1 + j) - s]c + \Delta sf,$$

where f is the ratio of nominal fixed assets to real sales. Equating sources to uses and solving for $\Delta s/s$, the company's real sustainable growth rate under inflation is

$$g_r^\star = \frac{(1 + j)p(1 - d)(1 + L) - jc}{(1 + j)c + f - (1 + j)p(1 - d)(1 + L)}.$$

Inflation increases real sustainable growth by adding j percent to nominal retained profits and accompanying borrowing. For most companies, however, this is more than compensated for by the necessity to increase working capital by j percent more than would otherwise be necessary.

The above equation captures only one dimension of the inflation-financing problem; nonetheless, the impact is a significant one. Referring again to the composite figures for US manufacturing in 1974, Table 1 confirms that, although the nominal sustainable growth rate rises with inflation, the annual increments in physical volume the firm can finance without new equity decline. Roughly speaking, the real sustainable growth rate declines by 2.2% for every 5 percentage point increase in the inflation rate. With the approximate 10% inflation rate in 1974, real sustainable growth falls from an inflation-free 10.5% to 6.1%. For comparison, the actual real growth rate in manufacturing sales in 1974 was 3.8%, while the figures for the prior two years were 8.2% and 8.4%. Naturally if we were to allow the very real

Table 1 Relation between sustainable growth and inflation based on composite figures for US manufacturing 1974

Inflation rate (%)	Real sustainable growth rate (%)	Nominal sustainable growth rate* (%)
0	10.5	10.5
5	8.3	13.7
10	6.1	16.7
15	3.9	19.5

* Nominal rate = $(1 + j)(1 + \text{real rate}) - 1$.

likelihood that annual depreciation is insufficient to maintain the replacement value of existing assets, the impact of inflation on real sustainable growth would be even more damaging.[2]

Managing growth

An actual growth rate in sales different from $g^\star$ is inconsistent with a fixed financial policy, and, like it or not, companies will be unable to maintain financial targets under this condition. Executives therefore have two options: they can passively disregard the interdependencies inherent in the sustainable growth equation and continually fail to meet their financial objectives, or they can actively develop a set of growth objectives and financial targets which are mutually consistent. An actual growth rate below $g^\star$ implies that the company has more than enough capital to meet its investment needs, and calls for an increase in liquid assets, a reduction in leverage, or an increase in dividends. Because the financial problems posed in this case are far less demanding than those in the reverse situation, the following discussion will concentrate on the principal means by which management can cope with an actual growth rate in excess of sustainable levels.

---

[2] Assuming d and L stay constant, use of historical cost depreciation in the above model has two offsetting effects. First, p tends to rise due to fictitious profits; second, the investment required to replace expiring fixed assets rises above the cash flow from depreciation. The former is a source of cash and tends to increase $g^\star$, while the latter has the opposite effect. Principally because the fictitious profits are taxed, the increase in p is seldom sufficient to cover the added investment, and $g^\star$ generally declines.

Sell new equity

As already noted, the solution offered by many people to sustainable growth problems is simply to sell new equity capital. And indeed it appears that this recommendation will be heeded by an increasing number of firms in the near future. Based on Federal Reserve Board flow of funds data, Manufacturers Hanover Trust estimates that new equity issues by US nonfinancial corporations during 1976–1977 will average $11 billion annually, up more than 50% over the depressed levels of 1973–1975 [7].

While new equity is the obvious solution for a number of firms, particularly larger, well known companies and the healthier public utilities, it is equally apparent that this option is not open to many others. To put matters into perspective, it should first be noted that even in the land of Wall Street – by far the world's largest equity market – new common stock has never been a large source of capital for US corporations. Over the two decades, 1952–1972, new common stock provided *only* 4% of total funds required by US nonfinancial corporations. In fact, in 1963 and again in 1968, new equity was negative, indicating that the value of shares repurchased by companies exceeded the value of new shares issued in these years. This 4% figure compares with a projected 6.2% for 1976–1977; despite the increase, new common stock will continue to be a very modest source of corporate funds. Moreover, if in tabulating these percentages we remove public utilities with their traditional heavy reliance on new equity financing, we find that even these modest figures overstate the importance of new common stock to manufacturing firms. Thus, despite the fact that public utilities and manufacturing firms raised approximately the same total amount of external capital over the decade from 1965 to 1974, public utilities accounted for almost one-half of all new equity raised, while manufacturing firms accounted for less than 10%.

The numbers aside, it is still legitimate to ask why many companies will not break with tradition and issue new equity when their sustainable growth problems become severe. In addition to the obvious fact that common shares are still thought by many executives to be undervalued by recent historical standards, one reason companies do not raise more capital on the equity market is that executives are unwilling to make growth plans predicated on extensive use of such a fickle source of funds. The typical lag between the decision to issue new equity and knowledge of the precise terms on which the new shares can be sold is on the order of two to three months, and, with the stock market as volatile as it is, many companies think it wiser to make expansion plans that are feasible even in the absence of new equity. The stock market then becomes a distinctly secondary source of capital to be tapped only in unusual circumstances.

Other companies are deterred from using the new equities market by their prohibitive costs. These include the transactions costs of registering, underwriting, and selling the issue, as well as possible underpricing costs incurred when the new shares are issued at a price below the prevailing market. Although reliable data on underpricing costs are unavailable, studies indicate that registration, underwriting, and selling costs alone can exceed 20% of proceeds on smaller issues [8]. Moreover, many smaller firms and foreign companies without access to well-developed capital markets often have extreme difficulty selling new shares at any cost. Finally, there is the obvious fact that new equity issues in closely held companies can lead to loss of voting control.

We might also mention the 'hope springs eternal' school of financial management which holds that there is never a correct time to raise new equity. As one prominent investment banker puts it, 'In the view of corporate treasurers and financial vp's, there very rarely is a time when it is favorable to sell stock. When the price-earnings ratio is 15 to 1, they say "well, maybe at 20 to 1". And when it gets to 20 to 1 they say "well, let's wait until it gets to 30"'[3].

In sum, although breaking the financial policy-growth rate interdependency may be a feasible strategy for a number of companies, there are still many other firms that are unable or unwilling to turn to the equity market for relief. These companies must solve their sustainable growth problems in some other manner.

Relax the financial constraints

Often without complete understanding of the relationships involved, relaxation of financial constraints is the strategy adopted by many corporations in response to their sustainable growth problems. If actual growth, g, exceeds $g^\star$, at the current levels of payout ratio (d) and debt to equity ratio (L), management allows d to decline and L to rise until $g^\star = g$.

Figure 2 illustrates the effect of changes in d and L on sustainable growth for the typical manufacturing firm in 1974 when p and t stay constant. Ignoring inflation, it shows the values of d and L that are consistent with sustainable growth rates of 5, 10, and 15%.[3] To see how this figure can be used, suppose that, consistent with our prior calculations, the typical manufacturing firm's

---

[3] Figure 2 was constructed by fixing the values of $g^\star$, p, and t in the sustainable growth equation and finding the value of d consistent with an arbitrarily chosen value of L. This gives one point on a particular growth curve. Repeating this exercise at different values of L enables us to trace the curve. Note that we ignore the fact that increases in L will increase interest costs and reduce p as being of secondary importance. This interrelationship can be taken into account if desired by assuming a specific interest rate and calculating a new profit margin at each capital structure under consideration.

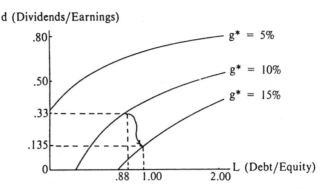

Figure 2   *Values of d and L consistent with sustainable growth rates of 5, 10 and 15% when p and t are constant. Composite US manufacturing firms, 1974*

sustainable growth rate is 10.5%, but that based on the market potential foreseen for its products, it wants to expand sales by 15% per annum. According to Figure 2, management can increase g^* to 15% by selecting any combination of d and L lying on the 15% growth line. As an example, one feasible combination would be to cut the payout ratio to 13.5% and increase the debt to equity ratio to 100%. Alternatively, if management is content with $g^* = 10.5\%$ but wishes to reduce its debt to equity ratio, Figure 2 shows the amount by which the payout ratio must decline to offset any reduction in the debt to equity ratio. For example, in order to reduce L from 88% to 75% without affecting g^*, Figure 2 reveals that d must fall from 33% to about 28%.

The obvious drawback of relaxing financial constraints to increase sustainable growth is that it either increases the risk borne by the firm or reduces the cash flowing to shareholders; an increase in g^* can be achieved only by increasing the firm's debt ratio or by reducing its payout ratio. Until recently, this drawback had not been a significant one for many companies. In the 1950s and 1960s ample reserve borrowing capacity enabled companies to increase L without undue concern for the added risks, and comparatively low yields on fixed income securities coupled with a growing investor preference for share price appreciation over dividend income allowed firms to reduce their payout ratios as well.

However, relaxation of financial constraints alone has not done the job. Even in 1974, with the payout ratio at an historic low and the debt to equity ratio at an historic high, actual growth still exceeded sustainable growth for many manufacturing firms. Moreover, there are indications that the continual relaxation of financial constraints has run its course for many enterprises. Looking first at corporate debt levels, Figure 3 illustrates the precipitous decline in the ratio of earnings before interest and taxes to interest expense

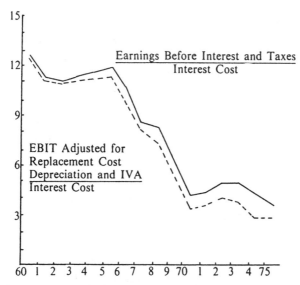

Figure 3   *Interest coverage by business 1960–75. Source:* 'Retreading the US Economy', Manufacturers Hanover Trust Economics Department, March 1976

(the interest coverage ratio) since 1960. From a high of over 12 times in 1960, interest coverage has fallen to less than 4 times by mid-1975. This means that if the average US firm's earnings before interest and taxes fell 75% or more in any year, its operating earnings would not be sufficient to meet even the interest obligations on its debt – to say nothing of principal repayments or dividends. Moreover, if we adjust earnings for replacement cost depreciation and inventory profits to get a more realistic measure of inflation-adjusted profits, Figure 3 shows that the coverage in 1975 further declines to below 3 times. There is ample reason to expect, therefore, that the rapid increase in corporate debt levels witnessed over the last decade or so will not continue, and that some other means of managing growth must be found.

Possibilities for further reducing corporate payout ratios are more promising – but still problematical. It is generally agreed that if equity shares are properly priced, a reduction in dividends to finance new investments offering a rate of return above the firm's cost of capital is not detrimental to shareholders. This is because the reduction in cash dividends should be more than compensated for by an increase in share price produced by the new investment [4,5].

Increasing the proportion of earnings retained is therefore one possible solution to sustainable growth problems; however, evidence indicates that a reduction in payout ratios of the magnitude required is apt to be a difficult undertaking for many companies. In 1974 the percentage of corporate profits distributed as dividends reached a post-war low of 38.5%, down from 63% in 1970, and a 1950–1974 average of 52%. Moreover, the sustainable growth equation reveals that, at least in the manufacturing sector, the dividends-sustainable growth tradeoff is not now a favorable one. Thus it is easy to show that holding all other determinants of $g^\star$ constant, a halving of the typical manufacturing firm's payout ratio from 33% to 16.5% adds only 2.9 percentage points to sustainable growth.[4] This is also apparent graphically in Figure 2. At low payout ratios we see that the sustainable growth lines become quite steep, indicating that large percentage changes in the payout ratio will have only minor effects on sustainable growth.

The fact that payout ratios are already low by historical standards and that significant further reductions will be required to generate only moderate increases in sustainable growth presents at least two problems. On a purely tactical level, most companies are loath to cut dividends directly unless long-run earnings are down as well. This means that reduction in the payout ratio can come only gradually as profits rise in the face of constant dividends, and it suggests that it is probably unrealistic to think that a reduction in payout ratios will solve sustainable growth problems in the short run.

On a more substantive level, the dividend yield on common stocks (dividends/stock price) in 1950 was 6.5%, well over twice the yield on corporate bonds; but by 1974, the situation had almost exactly reversed, and the 9% yield on corporate bonds was more than double the dividend yield on common stock. It therefore becomes legitimate to ask whether further cuts in corporate payout ratios in the face of the steep rise in yields on fixed income securities and renewed investor interest in safety and stability will really leave stock prices unchanged. Without contradicting the perceived long-run relation between dividends and stock price, we can say that significant further cuts in payout ratios will probably be greeted by at least temporary stock price declines, leaving firms open to corporate raids, and making it more difficult for those companies trying to sell new equity.

Improve operating performance

For completeness, Figure 4 shows a second approach to increasing sustainable growth. Referring again to the composite figures for US manufacturing firms in 1974 in the absence of inflation, it shows the values of the operating ratios

---

[4] Substituting into the equation for $g^\star$

$$g^\star = \frac{(0.055)\ (1 - 0.165)\ (1 + 0.88)}{0.73 - (0.055)\ (1 - 0.165)\ (1 + 0.88)} = 13.4\%$$

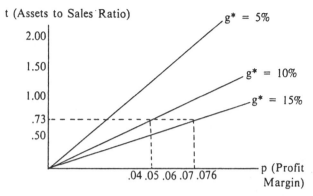

Figure 4 *Values of t and p consistent with sustainable growth rates of 5, 10 and 15% when d and L are constant. Composite US manufacturing firms, 1974*

t and p that are consistent with sustainable growth rates of 5, 10 and 15% when d and L are held constant. Consistent with prior calculations, we see that an assets to sales ratio (t) of .73 and a profit margin of 5.5% imply a sustainable growth rate of slightly more than 10%. If the typical manufacturing firm wants to increase its sustainable growth rate to 15%, Figure 4 shows the values of t and p that are consistent with this objective. Thus, one way to achieve the desired increase in g* would be to hold t constant and increase p from 5.5% to 7.6%.

It would be presumptuous in the space of this paper to attempt to catalogue the ways in which a company might improve the efficiency with which existing assets are employed and their profitability. So we will be content simply to observe that Figure 4 provides a convenient way to check on the internal consistency of a company's growth, financial, and operating objectives.

Make growth a decision variable

Our review of the standard techniques for managing growth suggests that sustainable growth problems are becoming more severe, and that the common solution of increasing firm indebtedness has about run its course. Many companies will be able to solve their growth problems by reducing their payout ratios and selling new equity. It is reasonable to presume, however, that there are a number of firms for which these standard techniques are no longer sufficient. Having exhausted the conventional means for managing growth, these firms must significantly reorient their thoughts about the subject. They must stop thinking about growth as uniformly beneficial and must begin to think about it as a decision variable to be managed and controlled in a manner analogous to the way executives manage their inventories, payout ratios, or capital structure. Rather than tinkering with d, L, p and t whenever g exceeds g^*, these firms must think about reducing g itself.

The crassest way to restrain growth is to raise prices. This lessens sustainable growth problems, first, by increasing the profit margin (p), and second, by reducing g. A subtler approach is to reduce or eliminate some of the services which accompany product sales. For example, fully one-half of the typical manufacturing firm's total assets is tied up in accounts receivable and inventory. By being less generous with credit terms and by reducing finished goods inventory, a company will increase g^* by reducing the ratio of assets to sales (t), and because its products are now less attractive to customers, it will also reduce g.

Increasing prices and reducing customer services can be dangerous strategies, for having sacrificed a competitive edge to other companies, it may be difficult to stem the resulting loss of market position. A possibly more effective strategy is the 'profitable pruning' technique employed by Cooper Industries, a leading producer of hand tools and compressors located in Houston, Texas. Faced in 1971 with unsatisfactory performance in its energy divisions, the company decided after much deliberation to pull out of the centrifugal compressor business rather than devote limited financial resources to improving performance in what was to Cooper a marginal operation. The business had growth and profit potential, and Cooper had an established reputation for quality, but the financial resources required were judged to be too large in view of the needs imposed by Cooper's other businesses. By marshalling resources in a few chosen businesses where it believed it could compete most effectively, Cooper sacrificed sales for financial strength and what it hoped would be added long-run profits.

In terms of the sustainable growth equation, effective corporate pruning should increase the profit margin (p) and reduce the ratio of assets to sales (t), and – at least in the year of sale – reduce g. Moreover, the cash generated from the sale of those businesses judged expendable provides another means of financing future growth in addition to retentions and accompanying borrowing. By carefully concentrating financial resources where they can be used most effectively, companies can bring g and g^* into balance without sacrificing their competitive edge. Cooper's almost five-fold increase in earnings per share since 1971 appears to show that profitable pruning has worked well for the company.

Yet another way to control g is to look for a cash cow – a mature product or business which because of its modest future growth potential generates more cash than can be profitably reinvested. By acquiring a cash cow (preferably in an exchange of shares merger), a company can ease its growth pains in several respects. First, if chosen carefully, the cash cow may increase g^* by increasing p and reducing t. Second, it may also increase g* by providing added borrowing capacity. Third, because it is in a mature industry the cash cow will probably reduce g.

In closing, we should note that while it is comparatively easy to list the ways a company can reduce its growth rate, limiting growth is not something many managers are used to thinking about, or even willing to think about. When generations of mangers have grown up in an environment which says that growth is good, it takes considerable strength to admit that in some cases excessive growth is bad. Moreover, an executive can anticipate significant morale problems when he attempts to enforce a growth rate which is below that attainable in the marketplace. In sum, the reader should recognize that enumeration of growth limiting strategies is likely to be easier than their implementation.

Concluding comments

How can an executive best use the information and techniques presented in this paper? The first step is to estimate the firm's sustainable growth rate. The example presented involving composite figures for all manufacturing firms is a particularly simple one. Done carefully for an individual company, estimation of g* requires 1) determining appropriate long-run targets for d and L, 2) estimating steady-state values of p and t, and 3) deciding exactly how inflation will affect the firm's sources and uses of funds.

If the resulting g* exceeds estimated g, the manager can turn to the pleasant tasks of deciding how to invest the excess cash and by how much to increase this quarter's dividend. If, as will occur for many firms, g* is less than g, the executive has three not necessarily mutually exclusive choices: 1) prepare to raise new equity, 2) adjust d, L, p and t until g* equals g, or 3) reduce g. As illustrated, the sustainable growth model is a useful device for evaluating alternatives and for guaranteeing that the financial, operating, and growth strategies adopted are internally consistent, but, as usual, the final policy choice and its implementation belong to the manager.

Appendix   A more general sustainable growth model

The purpose of this appendix is to generalize the sustainable growth model derived in the paper in three ways. In the model derived here, the level of investment and profits per dollar of new sales may differ from that of existing sales, depreciation need not be sufficient to maintain the value of existing assets, and the ratio of assets to existing sales may change.

Define the following variables, where in each case j = 1 refers to existing sales or assets and j = 2 refers to new sales or assets:

p_j = the profit margin on sales after tax,
t_j = the ratio of assets to sales,
Δt_1 = the change in t_1 over the forecast period,
k_j = the investment required per dollar of assets to maintain the value of existing assets,
n_j = the depreciation per dollar of total assets,
d = the target dividend payout ratio,
L = the target debt to equity ratio,
s = sales at beginning of period,
Δs = increase in sales during period.

Then, equating uses of cash for new investment and the maintenance of assets to sources of cash from retained profits, depreciation, new debt, and the improved utilization of existing assets,

$$t_2\Delta s + k_2 t_2 \Delta s + k_1 t_1 s = (p_1 s + p_2 \Delta s)(1 - d) + n_1 t_1 s + n_2 t_2 \Delta s + (p_1 s + p_2 \Delta s)(1 - d)L + \Delta t_1 s$$

$$\Delta s/s = g^\star = \frac{p_1(1 - d)(1 + L) - t_1(k_1 - n_1) + \Delta t_1}{t_2(1 + k_2 - n_2) - p_2(1 - d)(1 + L)}.$$

Comparing this expression for sustainable growth with that derived in the paper, the role of depreciation is more apparent. To the extent that depreciation is insufficient to maintain the value of assets (to the extent that $k_j > n_j$), sustainable growth is reduced. Also, it is apparent that if the newly acquired assets are more profitable than existing assets in the sense of producing sales with a higher profit margin, offering a more rapid depreciation rate, or generating more sales per dollar of assets (if $p_2 > p_1$, $n_2 > n_1$ or $t_2 < t_1$), sustainable growth will rise. Conversely, if new assets are less profitable in any of these senses, $g^\star$ will fall. Finally, the equation indicates that, other things being equal, $g^\star$ will rise if the firm can improve its asset utilization by reducing the assets required to support existing sales. This might be achieved by liquidating redundant fixed assets or, if possible, by reducing current assets while maintaining sales.

References

1 *Credit and Capital Markets*, New York, Bankers Trust Company, 1975.
2 *Flow of Funds Accounts 1945–72*, Washington, DC, Board of Governors of the Federal Reserve System (August 1973).

3 Henry Kaufman, *Business Week* (October 12, 1974), p.58.
4 Merton H. Miller and Franco Modigliani, 'Dividend Policy, Growth and the Valuation of Shares', *Journal of Business* (October 1961), pp.411–33.
5 James T.S. Porterfield, 'Dividends, Dilution and Delusion', *Harvard Business Review* (November–December, 1959), pp.156–61.
6 *Quarterly Financial Report for Manufacturing, Mining and Trade Corporations*, Washington, DC, Federal Trade Commission (1st Quarter, 1975).
7 'Retreading the U.S. Economy', New York, Manufacturers Hanover Trust Company Economics Department (March 1976).
8 Securities and Exchange Commission, *Cost of Flotation of Corporate Securities, 1951–1955*, Washington, DC, US Government Printing Office (June 1957).

Reproduced from Higgins, R.C. (1977). How much growth can a firm afford? *Financial Management*, **6**(3), 7–16, by permission of The Financial Management Association.

Part 5
Is There an Optimum Capital Structure?

14 The cost of capital, corporation finance and the theory of investment

F. Modigliani and M. H. Miller*

What is the 'cost of capital' to a firm in a world in which funds are used to acquire assets whose yields are uncertain; and in which capital can be obtained by many different media, ranging from pure debt instruments, representing money-fixed claims, to pure equity issues, giving holders only the right to a pro-rata share in the uncertain venture? This question has vexed at least three classes of economists: (1) the corporation finance specialist concerned with the techniques of financing firms so as to ensure their survival and growth; (2) the managerial economist concerned with capital budgeting; and (3) the economic theorist concerned with explaining investment behavior at both the micro and macro levels.[1]

In much of his formal analysis, the economic theorist at least has tended to side-step the essence of this cost-of-capital problem by proceeding as though physical assets – like bonds – could be regarded as yielding known, sure streams. Given this assumption, the theorist has concluded that the cost of capital to the owners of a firm is simply the rate of interest on bonds; and has

* This article is a revised version of a paper delivered at the annual meeting of the Econometric Society, December 1956. The authors express thanks for the comments and suggestions made at that time by the discussants of the paper, Evsey Domar, Robert Eisner and John Lintner, and subsequently by James Duesenberry. They are also greatly indebted to many of their present and former colleagues and students at Carnegie Tech who served so often and with such remarkable patience as a critical forum for the ideas here presented.

[1] The literature bearing on the cost-of-capital problem is far too extensive for listing here. Numerous references to it will be found throughout the paper though we make no claim to completeness. One phase of the problem which we do not consider explicitly, but which has a considerable literature of its own is the relation between the cost of capital and public utility rates. For a recent summary of the 'cost-of-capital theory' of rate regulation and a brief discussion of some of its implications, the reader may refer to H. M. Somers [20].

derived the familiar proposition that the firm, acting rationally, will tend to push investment to the point where the marginal yield on physical assets is equal to the market rate of interest.[2] This proposition can be shown to follow from either of two criteria of rational decision-making which are equivalent under certainty, namely (1) the maximization of profits and (2) the maximization of market value.

According to the first criterion, a physical asset is worth acquiring if it will increase the net profit of the owners of the firm. But net profit will increase only if the expected rate of return, or yield, of the asset exceeds the rate of interest. According to the second criterion, an asset is worth acquiring if it increases the value of the owners' equity, *i.e.*, if it adds more to the market value of the firm than the costs of acquisition. But what the asset adds is given by capitalizing the stream it generates at the market rate of interest, and this capitalized value will exceed its cost if and only if the yield of the asset exceeds the rate of interest. Note that, under either formulation, the cost of capital is equal to the rate of interest on bonds, regardless of whether the funds are acquired through debt instruments or through new issues of common stock. Indeed, in a world of sure returns, the distinction between debt and equity funds reduces largely to one of terminology.

It must be acknowledged that some attempt is usually made in this type of analysis to allow for the existence of uncertainty. This attempt typically takes the form of superimposing on the results of the certainty analysis the notion of a "risk discount" to be subtracted from the expected yield (or a "risk premium" to be added to the market rate of interest). Investment decisions are then supposed to be based on a comparison of this "risk adjusted" or "certainty equivalent" yield with the market rate of interest.[3] No satisfactory explanation has yet been provided, however, as to what determines the size of the risk discount and how it varies in response to changes in other variables.

Considered as a convenient approximation, the model of the firm constructed via this certainty – or certainty-equivalent – approach has admittedly been useful in dealing with some of the grosser aspects of the processes of capital accumulation and economic fluctuations. Such a model underlies, for example, the familiar Keynesian aggregate investment function in which aggregate investment is written as a function of the rate of interest – the same riskless rate of interest which appears later in the system in the liquidity-preference equation. Yet few would maintain that this approximation is adequate. At the macroeconomic level there are ample grounds for doubting

---

[2] Or, more accurately, to the marginal cost of borrowed funds since it is customary, at least in advanced analysis, to draw, the supply curve of borrowed funds to the firm as a rising one. For an advanced treatment of the certainty case, see F. and V. Lutz [13].

[3] The classic examples of the certainty-equivalent approach are found in J. R. Hicks [8] and O. Lange [11].

that the rate of interest has as large and as direct an influence on the rate of investment as this analysis would lead us to believe. At the microeconomic level the certainty model has little descriptive value and provides no real guidance to the finance specialist or managerial economist whose main problems cannot be treated in a framework which deals so cavalierly with uncertainty and ignores all forms of financing other than debt issues.[4]

Only recently have economists begun to face up seriously to the problem of the cost of capital *cum* risk. In the process they have found their interests and endeavors merging with those of the finance specialist and the managerial economist who have lived with the problem longer and more intimately. In this joint search to establish the principles which govern rational investment and financial policy in a world of uncertainty two main lines of attack can be discerned. These lines represent, in effect, attempts to extrapolate to the world of uncertainty each of the two criteria – profit maximization and market value maximization – which were seen to have equivalent implications in the special case of certainty. With the recognition of uncertainty this equivalence vanishes. In fact, the profit maximization criterion is no longer even well defined. Under uncertainty there corresponds to each decision of the firm not a unique profit outcome, but a plurality of mutually exclusive outcomes which can at best be described by a subjective probability distribution. The profit outcome, in short, has become a random variable and as such its maximization no longer has an operational meaning. Nor can this difficulty generally be disposed of by using the mathematical expectation of profits as the variable to be maximized. For decisions which affect the expected value will also tend to affect the dispersion and other characteristics of the distribution of outcomes. In particular, the use of debt rather than equity funds to finance a given venture may well increase the expected return to the owners, but only at the cost of increased dispersion of the outcomes.

Under these conditions the profit outcomes of alternative investment and financing decisions can be compared and ranked only in terms of a *subjective* 'utility function' of the owners which weighs the expected yield against other characteristics of the distribution. Accordingly, the extrapolation of the profit maximization criterion of the certainty model has tended to evolve into utility maximization, sometimes explicitly, more frequently in a qualitative and heuristic form.[5]

The utility approach undoubtedly represents an advance over the certainty or certainty-equivalent approach. It does at least permit us to explore (within

---

[4] Those who have taken a 'case-method' course in finance in recent years will recall in this connection the famous Liquigas case of Hunt and Williams, [9, pp.193–96] a case which is often used to introduce the student to the cost-of-capital problem and to poke a bit of fun at the economist's certainty-model.

[5] For an attempt at a rigorous explicit development of this line of attack, see F. Modigliani and M. Zeman [14].

limits) some of the implications of different financing arrangements, and it does give some meaning to the 'cost' of different types of funds. However, because the cost of capital has become an essentially subjective concept, the utility approach has serious drawbacks for normative as well as analytical purposes. How, for example, is management to ascertain the risk preferences of its stockholders and to compromise among their tastes? And how can the economist build a meaningful investment function in the face of the fact that any given investment opportunity might or might not be worth exploiting depending on precisely who happens to be the owners of the firm at the moment?

Fortunately, these questions do not have to be answered; for the alternative approach, based on market value maximization, can provide the basis for an operational definition of the cost of capital and a workable theory of investment. Under this approach any investment project and its concomitant financing plan must pass only the following test: Will the project, as financed, raise the market value of the firm's shares? If so, it is worth undertaking; if not, its return is less than the marginal cost of capital to the firm. Note that such a test is entirely independent of the tastes of the current owners, since market prices will reflect not only their preferences but those of all potential owners as well. If any current stockholder disagrees with management and the market over the valuation of the project, he is free to sell out and reinvest elsewhere, but will still benefit from the capital appreciation resulting from management's decision.

The potential advantages of the market-value approach have long been appreciated; yet analytical results have been meager. What appears to be keeping this line of development from achieving its promise is largely the lack of an adequate theory of the effect of financial structure on market valuations, and of how these effects can be inferred from objective market data. It is with the development of such a theory and of its implications for the cost-of-capital problem that we shall be concerned in this paper.

Our procedure will be to develop in Section I the basic theory itself and to give some brief account of its empirical relevance. In Section II, we show how the theory can be used to answer the cost-of-capital question and how it permits us to develop a theory of investment of the firm under conditions of uncertainty. Throughout these sections the approach is essentially a partial-equilibrium one focusing on the firm and 'industry'. Accordingly, the 'prices' of certain income streams will be treated as constant and given from outside the model, just as in the standard Marshallian analysis of the firm and industry the prices of all inputs and of all other products are taken as given. We have chosen to focus at this level rather than on the economy as a whole because it is at the level of the firm and the industry that the interests of the various specialists concerned with the cost-of-capital problem come most closely together. Although the emphasis has thus been placed on partial-equilibrium analysis, the results obtained also provide the essential building blocks for a general equilibrium model which shows how those prices which are here taken as given, are themselves determined. For reasons of space, however, and because the material is of interest in its own right, the presentation of the general equilibrium model which rounds out the analysis must be deferred to a subsequent paper.

I The valuation of securities, leverage and the cost of capital

A The capitalization rate for uncertain streams

As a starting point, consider an economy in which all physical assets are owned by corporations. For the moment, assume that these corporations can finance their assets by issuing common stock only; the introduction of bond issues, or their equivalent, as a source of corporate funds is postponed until the next part of this section.

The physical assets held by each firm will yield to the owners of the firm – its stockholders – a stream of 'profits' over time; but the elements of this series need not be constant and in any event are uncertain. This stream of income, and hence the stream accruing to any share of common stock, will be regarded as extended indefinitely into the future. We assume, however, that the mean value of the stream over time, or average profit per unit of time, is finite and represents a random variable subject to a (subjective) probability distribution. We shall refer to the average value over time of the stream accruing to a given share as the return of that share; and to the mathematical expectation of this average as the expected return of the share.[6] Although individual investors

---

[6] These propositions can be restated analytically as follows: The assets of the ith firm generate a stream:

$$X_i(1), X_i(2) \cdots X_i(T)$$

whose elements are random variables subject to the joint probability distribution:

$$x_i[X_i(1), X_i(2) \cdots X_i(t)].$$

The return to the ith firm is defined as:

$$X_i = \lim_{T \to \infty} \frac{1}{T} \sum_{t=1}^{T} X_i(t).$$

X_i is itself a random variable with a probability distribution $\Phi_i(X_i)$ whose form is determined uniquely by x_i. The expected return $\overline{X}_i$ is defined as $\overline{X}_i = E(X_i) = \int x_i X_i \Phi_i(X_i) dX_i$. If N_i is the number of shares outstanding, the return of the ith share is $x_i = (1/N) X_i$ with probability distribution $\phi_i(x_i) dx_i = \Phi_i(Nx_i) d(Nx_i)$ and expected value $\overline{x}_i = (1/N) \overline{X}_i$.

may have different views as to the shape of the probability distribution of the return of any share, we shall assume for simplicity that they are at least in agreement as to the expected return.[7]

This way of characterizing uncertain streams merits brief comment. Notice first that the stream is a stream of profits, not dividends. As will become clear later, as long as management is presumed to be acting in the best interests of the stockholders, retained earnings can be regarded as equivalent to a fully subscribed, pre-emptive issue of common stock. Hence, for present purposes, the division of the stream between cash dividends and retained earnings in any period is a mere detail. Notice also that the uncertainty attaches to the mean value over time of the stream of profits and should not be confused with variability over time of the successive elements of the stream. That variability and uncertainty are two totally different concepts should be clear from the fact that the elements of a stream can be variable even though known with certainty. It can be shown, furthermore, that whether the elements of a stream are sure or uncertain, the effect of variability per se on the valuation of the stream is at best a second-order one which can safely be neglected for our purposes (and indeed most others too).[8]

The next assumption plays a strategic role in the rest of the analysis. We shall assume that firms can be divided into 'equivalent return' classes such that the return on the shares issued by any firm in any given class is proportional to (and hence perfectly correlated with) the return on the shares issued by any other firm in the same class. This assumption implies that the various shares within the same class differ, at most, by a 'scale factor'. Accordingly, if we adjust for the difference in scale, by taking the *ratio* of the return to the expected return, the probability distribution of that ratio is identical for all shares in the class. It follows that all relevant properties of a share are uniquely characterized by specifying (1) the class to which it belongs and (2) its expected return.

The significance of this assumption is that it permits us to classify firms into groups within which the shares of different firms are 'homogeneous', that is, perfect substitutes for one another. We have, thus, an analogue to the familiar concept of the industry in which it is the commodity produced by the firms that is taken as homogeneous. To complete this analogy with Marshallian price theory, we shall assume in the analysis to follow that the shares

---

[7] To deal adequately with refinements such as differences among investors in estimates of expected returns would require extensive discussion of the theory of portfolio selection. Brief references to these and related topics will be made in the succeeding article on the general equilibrium model.

[8] The reader may convince himself of this by asking how much he would be willing to rebate to his employer for the privilege of receiving his annual salary in equal monthly instalments rather than in irregular amounts over the year. See also J. M. Keynes [10, esp. pp.53–54].

concerned are traded in perfect markets under conditions of atomistic competition.[9]

From our definition of homogeneous classes of stock it follows that in equilibrium in a perfect capital market the price per dollar's worth of expected return must be the same for all shares of any given class. Or, equivalently, in any given class the price of every share must be proportional to its expected return. Let us denote this factor of proportionality for any class, say the kth class, by $1/\rho_k$. Then if p_j denotes the price and $\bar{x}_j$ is the expected return per share of the jth firm in class k, we must have:

$$p_j = \frac{1}{\rho_k} \bar{x}_j; \tag{1}$$

or, equivalently,

$$\frac{\bar{x}_j}{p_j} = \rho_k \text{ a constant for all firms } j \text{ in class } k. \tag{2}$$

The constants ρ_k (one for each of the k classes) can be given several economic interpretations: (a) From (2) we see that each ρ_k is the expected rate of return of any share in class k. (b) From (1) $1/\rho_k$ is the price which an investor has to pay for a dollar's worth of expected return in the class k. (c) Again from (1), by analogy with the terminology for perpetual bonds, ρ_k can be regarded as the market rate of capitalization for the expected value of the uncertain streams of the kind generated by the kth class of firms.[10]

B   Debt financing and its effects on security prices

Having developed an apparatus for dealing with uncertain streams we can now approach the heart of the cost-of-capital problem by dropping the assumption that firms cannot issue bonds. The introduction of debt-financing changes the

[9] Just what our classes of stocks contain and how the different classes can be identified by outside observers are empirical questions to which we shall return later. For the present, it is sufficient to observe: (1) Our concept of a class, while not identical to that of the industry is at least closely related to it. Certainly the basic characteristics of the probability distributions of the returns on assets will depend to a significant extent on the product sold and the technology used. (2) What are the appropriate class boundaries will depend on the particular problem being studied. An economist concerned with general tendencies in the market, for example, might well be prepared to work with far wider classes than would be appropriate for an investor planning his portfolio, or a firm planning its financial strategy.

[10] We cannot, on the basis of the assumptions so far, make any statements about the relationship or spread between the various ρ's or capitalization rates. Before we could do so we would have to make further specific assumptions about the way investors believe the probability distributions vary from class to class, as well as assumptions about investors' preferences as between the characteristics of different distributions.

market for shares in a very fundamental way. Because firms may have different proportions of debt in their capital structure, shares of different companies, even in the same class, can give rise to different probability distributions of returns. In the language of finance, the shares will be subject to different degrees of financial risk or 'leverage' and hence they will no longer be perfect substitutes for one another.

To exhibit the mechanism determining the relative prices of shares under these conditions, we make the following two assumptions about the nature of bonds and the bond market, though they are actually stronger than is necessary and will be relaxed later: (1) All bonds (including any debts issued by households for the purpose of carrying shares) are assumed to yield a constant income per unit of time, and this income is regarded as certain by all traders regardless of the issuer. (2) Bonds, like stocks, are traded in a perfect market, where the term perfect is to be taken in its usual sense as implying that any two commodities which are perfect substitutes for each other must sell, in equilibrium, at the same price. It follows from assumption (1) that all bonds are in fact perfect substitutes up to a scale factor. It follows from assumption (2) that they must all sell at the same price per dollar's worth of return, or what amounts to the same thing must yield the same rate of return. This rate of return will be denoted by r and referred to as the rate of interest or, equivalently, as the capitalization rate for sure streams. We now can derive the following two basic propositions with respect to the valuation of securities in companies with different capital structures:

Proposition I

Consider any company j and let $\overline{X}_j$ stand as before for the expected return on the assets owned by the company (that is, its expected profit before deduction of interest). Denote by D_j the market value of the debts of the company; by S_j the market value of its common shares; and by $V_j \equiv S_j + D_j$ the market value of all its securities or, as we shall say, the market value of the firm. Then, our Proposition I asserts that we must have in equilibrium:

$$V_j \equiv (S_j + D_j) = \overline{X}_j / \rho_k, \text{ for any firm } j \text{ in class } k. \tag{3}$$

That is, the *market value of any firm is independent of its capital structure and is given by capitalizing its expected return at the rate ρ_k appropriate to its class.*

This proposition can be stated in an equivalent way in terms of the firm's 'average cost of capital', $\overline{X}_j / V_j$, which is the ratio of its expected return to the market value of all its securities. Our proposition then is:

$$\frac{\overline{X}_j}{(S_j + D_j)} \equiv \frac{\overline{X}_j}{V_j} = \rho_k, \text{ for any firm } j \text{ in class } k. \tag{4}$$

That is, *the average cost of capital to any firm is completely independent of its capital structure and is equal to the capitalization rate of a pure equity stream of its class.*

To establish Proposition I we will show that as long as the relations (3) or (4) do not hold between any pair of firms in a class, arbitrage will take place and restore the stated equalities. We use the term arbitrage advisedly. For if Proposition I did not hold, an investor could buy and sell stocks and bonds in such a way as to exchange one income stream for another stream, identical in all relevant respects but selling at a lower price. The exchange would therefore be advantageous to the investor quite independently of his attitudes toward risk.[11] As investors exploit these arbitrage opportunities, the value of the overpriced shares will fall and that of the underpriced shares will rise, thereby tending to eliminate the discrepancy between the market values of the firms.

By way of proof, consider two firms in the same class and assume for simplicity only, that the expected return, $\overline{X}$, is the same for both firms. Let company 1 be financed entirely with common stock while company 2 has some debt in its capital structure. Suppose first the value of the levered firm, V_2, to be larger than that of the unlevered one, V_1. Consider an investor holding s_2 dollars' worth of the shares of company 2, representing a fraction α of the total outstanding stock, S_2. The return from this portfolio, denoted by Y_2, will be a fraction α of the income available for the stockholders of company 2, which is equal to the total return X_2 less the interest charge, rD_2. Since under our assumption of homogeneity, the anticipated total return of company 2, X_2, is, under all circumstances, the same as the anticipated total return to company 1, X_1, we can hereafter replace X_2 and X_1 by a common symbol X. Hence, the return from the initial portfolio can be written as:

$$Y_2 = a(X - rD_2). \tag{5}$$

Now suppose the investor sold his αS_2 worth of company 2 shares and acquired instead an amount $s_1 = \alpha(S_2 + D_2)$ of the shares of company 1. He could do so by utilizing the amount αS_2 realized from the sale of his initial holding and borrowing an additional amount αD_2 on his own credit, pledging his new holdings in company 1 as a collateral. He would thus secure for himself a fraction $s_1/S_1 = \alpha(S_2 + D_2)/S_1$ of the shares and earnings of company 1. Making proper allowance for the interest payments on his personal debt αD_2, the return from the new portfolio, Y_1, is given by:

---

[11] In the language of the theory of choice, the exchanges are movements from inefficient points in the interior to efficient points on the boundary of the investor's opportunity set; and not movements between efficient points along the boundary. Hence for this part of the analysis nothing is involved in the way of specific assumptions about investor attitudes or behaviour other than that investors behave consistently and prefer more income to less income, *ceteris paribus.*

$$Y_1 = \frac{\alpha(S_2 + D_2)}{S_1} X - r\alpha D_2 = \alpha \frac{V_2}{V_1} X - r\alpha D_2. \tag{6}$$

Comparing (5) with (6) we see that as long as $V_2 > V_1$ we must have $Y_1 > Y_2$, so that it pays owners of company 2's shares to sell their holdings, thereby depressing S_2 and hence V_2; and to acquire shares of company 1, thereby raising S_1 and thus V_1. We conclude therefore that levered companies cannot command a premium over unlevered companies because investors have the opportunity of putting the equivalent leverage into their portfolio directly by borrowing on personal account.

Consider now the other possibility, namely that the market value of the levered company V_2 is less than V_1. Suppose an investor holds initially an amount s_1 of shares in company 1, representing a fraction α of that total outstanding stock, S_1. His return from this holding is:

$$Y_1 = \frac{s_1}{S_1} X = \alpha X.$$

Suppose he were to exchange this initial holding for another portfolio, also worth s_1, but consisting of s_2 dollars of stock of company 2 and of d dollars of bonds, where s_2 and d are given by:

$$s_2 = \frac{S_2}{V_2} s_1, \qquad d = \frac{D_2}{V_2} s_1. \tag{7}$$

In other words the new portfolio is to consist of stock of company 2 and of bonds in the proportions S_2/V_2 and D_2/V_2, respectively. The return from the stock in the new portfolio will be a fraction s_2/S_2 of the total return to stockholders of company 2, which is $(X-rD_2)$, and the return from the bonds will be rd. Making use of (7), the total return from the portfolio, Y_2, can be expressed as follows:

$$Y_2 = \frac{s_2}{S_2} (X - rD_2) + rd = \frac{s_1}{V_2} (X - rD_2) + r\frac{D_2}{V_2} s_1 =$$

$$\frac{s_1}{V_2} X = \alpha \frac{S_1}{V_2} X$$

(since $s_1 = \alpha S_1$). Comparing Y_2 with Y_1 we see that, if $V_2 < S_1 \equiv V_1$, then Y_2 will exceed Y_1. Hence it pays the holders of company 1's shares to sell these holdings and replace them with a mixed portfolio containing an appropriate fraction of the shares of company 2.

The acquisition of a mixed portfolio of stock of a levered company j and of bonds in the proportion S_j/V_j and D_j/V_j respectively, may be regarded as an operation which 'undoes' the leverage, giving access to an appropriate fraction of the unlevered return X_j. It is this possibility of undoing leverage which prevents the value of levered firms from being consistently less than those of unlevered firms, or more generally prevents the average cost of capital $\overline{X}_j/V_j$ from being systematically higher for levered than for nonlevered companies in the same class. Since we have already shown that arbitrage will also prevent V_2 from being larger than V_1, we can conclude that in equilibrium we must have $V_2 = V_1$, as stated in Proposition I.

Proposition II

From Proposition I we can derive the following proposition concerning the rate of return on common stock in companies whose capital structure includes some debt: the expected rate of return or yield, i, on the stock of any company j belonging to the kth class is a linear function of leverage as follows:

$$i_j = \rho_k + (\rho_k - r)D_j/S_j. \tag{8}$$

That is, *the expected yield of a share of stock is equal to the appropriate capitalization rate p_k for a pure equity stream in the class, plus a premium related to financial risk equal to the debt-to-equity ratio times the spread between ρ_k and $_k$.* Or equivalently, the market price of any share of stock is given by capitalizing its expected return at the continuously variable rate i_j of (8).[12]

A number of writers have stated close equivalents of our Proposition I although by appealing to intuition rather than by attempting a proof and only to insist immediately that the results were not applicable to the actual capital markets.[13] Proposition II, however, so far as we have been able to discover is

---

[12] To illustrate, suppose $\overline{X} = 1000$, $D = 4000$, $r = 5$ per cent and $\rho_k = 10$ per cent. These values imply that $V = 10,000$ and $S = 6000$ by virtue of Proposition I. The expected yield or rate of return per share is then:

$$i = \frac{1000 - 200}{6000} = 0.1 + (0.1 - 0.05)\frac{4000}{6000} = 13\tfrac{1}{3} \text{ per cent.}$$

[13] See, for example, J. B. Williams [21, esp. pp.72–73]; David Durand [3]; and W. A. Morton [15]. None of these writers describe in any detail the mechanism which is supposed to keep the average cost of capital constant under changes in capital structure. They seem, however, to be visualizing the equilibrating mechanism in terms of switches by investors between stocks and bonds as the yields of each get out of line with their 'riskiness'. This is an argument quite different from the pure arbitrage mechanism underlying our proof, and the difference is crucial. Regarding Proposition I as resting on investors' attitudes toward risk leads inevitably to a misunderstanding of many factors influencing relative yields such as, for example, limitations on the portfolio composition of financial institutions. See below, esp. Section I.D.

new.[14] To establish it we first note that, by definition, the expected rate of return, i, is given by:

$$i_j \equiv \frac{\overline{X}_j - rD_j}{S_j}. \tag{9}$$

From Proposition I, equation (3), we know that:

$$\overline{X}_j = \rho_k(S_j + D_j).$$

Substituting in (9) and simplifying, we obtain equation (8).

C   Some qualifications and extensions of the basic propositions

The methods and results developed so far can be extended in a number of useful directions, of which we shall consider here only three: (1) allowing for a corporate profits tax under which interest payments are deductible; (2) recognizing the existence of a multiplicity of bonds and interest rates; and (3) acknowledging the presence of market imperfections which might interfere with the process of arbitrage. The first two will be examined briefly in this section with some further attention given to the tax problem in Section II. Market imperfections will be discussed in Part D of this section in the course of a comparison of our results with those of received doctrines in the field of finance.

Effects of the present method of taxing corporations

The deduction of interest in computing taxable corporate profits will prevent the arbitrage process from making the value of all firms in a given class proportional to the expected returns generated by their physical assets. Instead, it can be shown (by the same type of proof used for the original version of Proposition I) that the market values of firms in each class must be proportional in equilibrium to their expected return net of taxes (that is, to the sum of the interest paid and expected net stockholder income). This means we must replace each $\overline{X}_j$ in the original versions of Propositions I and II with a new variable $\overline{X}_j^\tau$ representing the total income net of taxes generated by the firm:

---

[14] Morton does make reference to a linear yield function but only ' . . . for the sake of simplicity and because the particular function used makes no essential difference in my conclusions' [15, p.443, note 2].

$$\overline{X}_j^\tau \equiv (\overline{X}_j - rD_j)(1 - \tau) + rD_j \equiv \overline{\pi}_j^\tau + rD_j, \tag{10}$$

where $\overline{\pi}_j^\tau$ represents the expected net income accruing to the common stockholders and τ stands for the average rate of corporate income tax.[15]

After making these substitutions, the propositions, when adjusted for taxes, continue to have the same form as their originals. That is, Proposition I becomes:

$$\frac{\overline{X}_j^\tau}{V_j} = \rho k^\tau, \text{ for any firm in class } k, \tag{11}$$

and Proposition II becomes

$$i_j \equiv \frac{\overline{\pi}_j^r}{S_j} = \rho j^r + (\rho k^r - r)D_j/S_j \tag{12}$$

where ρ_k^τ is the capitalization rate for income net of taxes in class k.

Although the form of the propositions in unaffected, certain interpretations must be changed. In particular, the after-tax capitalization rate ρ_k^τ can no longer be identified with the 'average cost of capital' which is $\rho_k = \overline{X}_j/V_j$. The difference between ρ_k^τ and the 'true' average cost of capital, as we shall see, is a matter of some relevance in connection with investment planning within the firm (Section II). For the description of market behavior, however, which is our immediate concern here, the distinction is not essential. To simplify presentation, therefore, and to preserve continuity with the terminology in the standard literature we shall continue in this section to refer to ρ_k^τ as the average cost of capital, though strictly speaking this identification is correct only in the absence of taxes.

Effects of a plurality of bonds and interest rates

In existing capital markets we find not one, but a whole family of interest rates varying with maturity, with the technical provisions of the loan and, what is most relevant for present purposes, with the financial condition of the borrower.[16] Economic theory and market experience both suggest that the yields demanded by lenders tend to increase with the debt-equity ratio of the borrowing firm (or individual). If so, and if we can assume as a first

---

[15] For simplicity, we shall ignore throughout the tiny element of progression in our present corporate tax and treat τ as a constant independent of $(X_i - rD_i)$.

[16] We shall not consider here the extension of the analysis to encompass the time structure of interest rates. Although some of the problems posed by the time structure can be handled within our comparative statics framework, an adequate discussion would require a separate paper.

approximation that this yield curve, $r = r(D/S)$, whatever its precise form, is the same for all borrowers, then we can readily extend our propositions to the case of a rising supply curve for borrowed funds.[17]

Proposition I is actually unaffected in form and interpretation by the fact that the rate of interest may rise with leverage; while the average cost of *borrowed* funds will tend to increase as debt rises, the average cost of funds from *all* sources will still be independent of leverage (apart from the tax effect). This conclusion follows directly from the ability of those who engage in arbitrage to undo the leverage in any financial structure by acquiring an appropriately mixed portfolio of bonds and stocks. Because of this ability, the ratio of earnings (*before* interest charges) to market value – i.e., the average cost of capital from all sources – must be the same for all firms in a given class.[18] In other words, the increased cost of borrowed funds as leverage increases will tend to be offset by a corresponding reduction in the yield of common stock. This seemingly paradoxical result will be examined more closely below in connection with Proposition II.

A significant modification of Proposition I would be required only if the yield curve $r = r(D/S)$ were different for different borrowers, as might happen if creditors had marked preferences for the securities of a particular class of debtors. If, for example, corporations as a class were able to borrow at lower rates than individuals having equivalent personal leverage, then the average cost of capital to corporations might fall slightly, as leverage increased over some range, in reflection of this differential. In evaluating this possibility,

---

[17] We can also develop a theory of bond valuation along lines essentially parallel to those followed for the case of shares. We conjecture that the curve of bond yields as a function of leverage will turn out to be a nonlinear one in contrast to the linear function of leverage developed for common shares. However, we would also expect that the rate of increase in the yield on new issues would not be substantial in practice. This relatively slow rise would reflect the fact that interest rate increases by themselves can never be completely satisfactory to creditors as compensation for their increased risk. Such increases may simply serve to raise r so high relative to ρ that they become self-defeating by giving rise to a situation in which even normal fluctuations in earnings may force the company into bankruptcy. The difficulty of borrowing more, therefore, tends to show up in the usual case not so much in higher rates as in the form of increasingly stringent restrictions imposed on the company's management and finances by the creditors; and ultimately in a complete inability to obtain new borrowed funds, at least from the institutional investors who normally set the standards in the market for bonds.

[18] One normally minor qualification might be noted. Once we relax the assumptions that all bonds have certain yields, our arbitrage operator faces the danger of something comparable to 'gambler's ruin'. That is, there is always the possibility that an otherwise sound concern – one whose long-run expected income is greater than its interest liability – might be forced into liquidation as a result of a run of temporary losses. Since reorganization generally involves costs, and because the operation of the firm may be hampered during the period of reorganization with lasting unfavorable effects on earnings prospects, we might perhaps expect heavily levered companies to sell at a slight discount relative to less heavily indebted companies of the same class.

however, remember that the relevant interest rate for our arbitrage operators is the rate on brokers' loans and, historically, that rate has not been noticeably higher than representative corporate rates.[19] The operations of holding companies and investment trusts which can borrow on terms comparable to operating companies represent still another force which could be expected to wipe out any marked or prolonged advantages from holding levered stocks.[20]

Although Proposition I remains unaffected as long as the yield curve is the same for all borrowers, the relation between common stock yields and leverage will no longer be the strictly linear one given by the original Proposition II. If r increases with leverage, the yield i will still tend to rise as D/S increases, but at a decreasing rather than a constant rate. Beyond some high level of leverage, depending on the exact form of the interest function, the yield may even start to fall.[21] The relation between i and D/S could conceivably take the form indicated by the curve MD in Figure 2, although in practice the curvature would be much less pronounced. By contrast, with a constant rate of interest, the relation would be linear throughout as shown by line MM', Figure 2.

The downward sloping part of the curve MD perhaps requires some comment since it may be hard to imagine why investors, other than those who like lotteries, would purchase stocks in this range. Remember, however, that the yield curve of Proposition II is a consequence of the more fundamental Proposition I. Should the demand by the risk-lovers prove insufficient to keep the market to the peculiar yield-curve MD, this demand would be reinforced by the action of arbitrage operators. The latter would find it profitable to own a pro-rata share of the firm as a whole by holding its stock *and* bonds, the lower yield of the shares being thus offset by the higher return on bonds.

---

[19] Under normal conditions, moreover, a substantial part of the arbitrage process could be expected to take the form, not of having the arbitrage operators go into debt on personal account to put the required leverage into their portfolios, but simply of having them reduce the amount of corporate bonds they already hold when they acquire underpriced unlevered stock. Margin requirements are also somewhat less of an obstacle to maintaining any desired degree of leverage in a portfolio than might be thought at first glance. Leverage could be largely restored in the face of higher margin requirements by switching to stocks having more leverage at the corporate level.

[20] An extreme form of inequality between borrowing and lending rates occurs, of course, in the case of preferred stocks, which cannot be directly issued by individuals on personal account. Here again, however, we would expect that the operations of investment corporations plus the ability of arbitrage operators to sell off their holdings of preferred stocks would act to prevent the emergence of any substantial premiums (for this reason) on capital structures containing preferred stocks. Nor are preferred stocks so far removed from bonds as to make it impossible for arbitrage operators to approximate closely the risk and leverage of a corporate preferred stock by incurring a somewhat smaller debt on personal account.

[21] Since new lenders are unlikely to permit this much leverage (cf. note 17), this range of the curve is likely to be occupied by companies whose earnings prospects have fallen substantially since the time when their debts were issued.

D   The relation of Propositions I and II to current doctrines

The propositions we have developed with respect to the valuation of firms and shares appear to be substantially at variance with current doctrines in the field of finance. The main differences between our view and the current view are summarized graphically in Figures 1 and 2. Our Proposition I [equation (4)] asserts that the average cost of capital, $\overline{X}_j^\tau / V_j$, is a constant for all firms j in class k, independently of their financial structure. This implies that, if we were to take a sample of firms in a given class, and if for each firm we were to plot the ratio of expected return to market value against some measure of leverage or financial structure, the points would tend to fall on a horizontal straight line

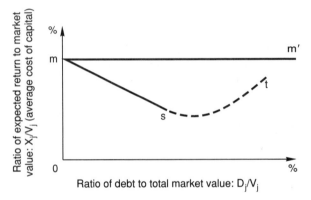

Figure 1

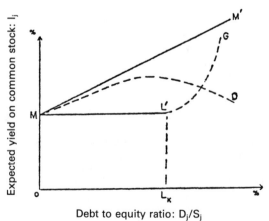

Figure 2

with intercept ρ_k^τ, like the solid line mm' in Figure 1.[22] From Proposition I we derived Proposition II [equation (8)] which, taking the simplest version with r constant, asserts that, for all firms in a class, the relation between the yield on common stock and financial structure, measured by D_j/S_j, will approximate a straight line with slope $(\rho_k^\tau-\tau)$ and intercept ρ_k^τ. This relationship is shown as the solid line MM' in Figure 2, to which reference has been made earlier.[23]

By contrast, the conventional view among finance specialists appears to start from the proposition that, other things equal, the earnings-price ratio (or its reciprocal, the times-earnings multiplier) of a firm's common stock will normally be only slightly affected by 'moderate' amounts of debt in the firm's capital structure.[24] Translated into our notation, it asserts that for any firm j in the class k,

$$\frac{\overline{X}_j^r - rD_j}{S_j} \equiv \frac{\overline{\pi}_j^r}{S_j} = i_k^\star, \text{ a constant for } \frac{D_j}{S_j} \leq L_k \tag{13}$$

or, equivalently,

$$S_j = \overline{\pi}_j^r/i_k^\star. \tag{14}$$

Here $i_k^\star$ represents the capitalization rate or earnings-price ratio on the common stock and L_k denotes some amount of leverage regarded as the maximum 'reasonable' amount for firms of the class k. This assumed relationship between yield and leverage is the horizontal solid line ML' of Figure 2. Beyond L', the yield will presumably rise sharply as the market discounts 'excessive' trading on the equity. This possibility of a rising range for high leverages is indicated by the broken-line segment $L'G$ in the figure.[25]

---

[22] In Figure 1 the measure of leverage used is D_j/V_j (the ratio of debt to market value, rather than D_j/S_j (the ratio of debt to equity), the concept used in the analytical development. The D_j/V_j measure is introduced at this point because it simplifies comparison and contrast of our view with the traditional position.

[23] The line MM' in Figure 2 has been drawn with a positive slope on the assumption that $\rho_k^\tau > r$, a condition which will normally obtain. Our Proposition II as given in equation (8) would continue to be valid, of course, even in the unlikely event that $\rho_k^\tau < r$, but the slope of MM' would be negative.

[24] See, e.g., Graham and Dodd [6, pp.461–66]. Without doing violence to this position, we can bring out its implications more sharply by ignoring the qualification and treating the yield as a virtual constant over the relevant range. See in this connection the discussion in Durand [3, esp. pp.225–37] of what he calls the 'net income method' of valuation.

[25] To make it easier to see some of the implications of this hypothesis as well as to prepare the ground for later statistical testing, it will be helpful to assume that the notion of a critical limit on leverage beyond which yields rise rapidly, can be epitomized by a quadratic relation of the form:

$$\overline{\pi}_j^r/S_j = i_k^\star + \beta(D_j/S_j) + \alpha\,(D_j/S_j)^2, \qquad \alpha > 0. \tag{15}$$

If the value of shares were really given by (14) then the over-all market value of the firm must be:

$$V_j \equiv S_j + D_j = \frac{\overline{X}_j^r - rD_j}{i_k^\star} + D_j = \frac{\overline{X}_j^r}{i_k^\star} + \frac{(i_k^\star - r)D_j}{I_k^\star}. \tag{16}$$

That is, for any given level of expected total returns after taxes $(\overline{X}_j^r)$ *and assuming, as seems natural, that* $i_k^\star > r$, the value of the firm must tend to *rise* with debt;[26] whereas our Proposition I asserts that the value of the firm is completely independent of the capital structure. Another way of contrasting our position with the traditional one is in terms of the cost of capital. Solving (16) for $\overline{X}_j^r/V_j$ yields:

$$\overline{X}_j^r/V_j = i_k^\star - (i_k^\star - r)D_j/V_j. \tag{17}$$

According to this equation, the average cost of capital is not independent of capital structure as we have argued, but should tend to *fall* with increasing leverage, at least within the relevant range of moderate debt ratios, as shown by the line *ms* in Figure 1. Or to put it in more familiar terms, debt-financing should be 'cheaper' than equity-financing if not carried too far.

When we also allow for the possibility of a rising range of stock yields for large values of leverage, we obtain a U-shaped curve like *mst* in Figure 1.[27] That a yield-curve for stocks of the form $ML'G$ in Figure 2 implies a U-shaped cost-of-capital curve has, of course, been recognized by many writers. A natural further step has been to suggest that the capital structure corresponding to the trough of the U is an 'optimal capital structure' towards which management ought to strive in the best interests of the stockholders.[28] According to our model, by contrast, no such optimal structure exists – all structures being equivalent from the point of view of the cost of capital.

---

[26] For a typical discussion of how a promoter can, supposedly, increase the market value of a firm by recourse to debt issues, see W. J. Eiteman [4, esp. pp.11–13].

[27] The U-shaped nature of the cost-of-capital curve can be exhibited explicitly if the yield curve for shares as a function of leverage can be approximated by equation (15) of footnote 25. From that equation, multiplying both sides by S_i we obtain: $\pi_j^r = \overline{X}_j^r - rD_j = i_k^\star S_j + \beta D_j + \alpha D_j^2/S_j$ or, adding and subtracting $i_k^\star D_k$ from the right-hand side and collecting terms,

$$\overline{X}_j^r = i_k^\star(S_i + D_i) + (\beta + r - i_k^\star)D_i + \alpha D_j^2/S_j. \tag{18}$$

Dividing (18) by V_j gives an expression for the cost of capital:

$$\overline{X}_j^r/V_i = i_k^\star - (i_k^\star - r - \beta)D_i/V_i + \alpha D_j^2/S_j V_j = i_k^\star - (i_k^\star - r - \beta)D_j/V_j + \alpha\,(D_i/V_i)^2/(1 - D_i/V_i) \tag{19}$$

which is clearly U-shaped since α is supposed to be positive.

[28] For a typical statement see S. M. Robbins [16, p.307]. See also Graham and Dodd [6, pp.468–74].

Although the falling, or at least U-shaped, cost-of-capital function is in one form or another the dominant view in the literature, the ultimate rationale of that view is by no means clear. The crucial element in the position – that the expected earnings-price ratio of the stock is largely unaffected by leverage up to some conventional limit – is rarely even regarded as something which requires explanation. It is usually simply taken for granted or it is merely asserted that this is the way the market behaves.[29] To the extent that the constant earnings-price ratio has a rationale at all we suspect that it reflects in most cases the feeling that moderate amounts of debt in 'sound' corporations do not really add very much to the 'riskiness' of the stock. Since the extra risk is slight, it seems natural to suppose that firms will not have to pay noticeably higher yields in order to induce investors to hold the stock.[30]

A more sophisticated line of argument has been advanced by David Durand [3, pp.231–33]. He suggests that because insurance companies and certain other important institutional investors are restricted to debt securities, nonfinancial corporations are able to borrow from them at interest rates which are lower than would be required to compensate creditors in a free market. Thus, while he would presumably agree with our conclusions that stock-holders could not gain from leverage in an unconstrained market, he concludes that they can gain under present institutional arrangements. This gain would arise by virtue of the 'safety superpremium' which lenders are willing to pay corporations for the privilege of lending.[31]

The defective link in both the traditional and the Durand version of the argument lies in the confusion between investors' subjective risk preferences and their objective market opportunities. Our Propositions I and II, as noted earlier, do not depend for their validity on any assumption about individual risk preferences. Nor do they involve any assertion as to what is an adequate compensation to investors for assuming a given degree of risk. They rely merely on the fact that a given commodity cannot consistently sell at more than one price in the market; or more precisely that the price of a commodity representing

---

[29] See e.g., Graham and Dodd [6, p.466].

[30] A typical statement is the following by Guthmann and Dougall [7, p.245]: 'Theoretically it might be argued that the increased hazard from using bonds and preferred stocks would counterbalance this additional income and so prevent the common stock from being more attractive than when it had a lower return but fewer prior obligations. In practice, the extra earnings from 'trading on the equity' are often regarded by investors as more than sufficient to serve as a 'premium for risk' when the proportions of the several securities are judiciously mixed.'

[31] Like Durand, Morton [15] contends 'that the actual market deviates from [Proposition I] by giving α changing over-all cost of money at different points of the [leverage] scale' (p. 443, note 2, inserts ours), but the basis for this contention is nowhere clearly stated. Judging by the great emphasis given to the lack of mobility of investment funds between stocks and bonds and to the psychological and institutional pressures toward debt portfolios (see pp.444–51 and especially his discussion of the optimal capital structure on p.453) he would seem to be taking a position very similar to that of Durand above.

a 'bundle' of two other commodities cannot be consistently different from the weighted average of the prices of the two components (the weights being equal to the proportion of the two commodities in the bundle).

An analogy may be helpful at this point. The relations between $1/\rho_k$, the price per dollar of an unlevered stream in class k; $1/r$, the price per dollar of a sure stream, and $1/i_j$, the price per dollar of a levered stream j, in the kth class, are essentially the same as those between, respectively, the price of whole milk, the price of butter fat, and the price of milk which has been thinned out by skimming off some of the butter fat. Our Proposition I states that a firm cannot reduce the cost of capital – *i.e.*, increase the market value of the stream it generates – by securing part of its capital through the sale of bonds, even though debt money appears to be cheaper. This assertion is equivalent to the proposition that, under perfect markets, a dairy farmer cannot in general earn more for the milk he produces by skimming some of the butter fat and selling it separately, even though butter fat per unit weight, sells for more than whole milk. The advantage from skimming the milk rather than selling whole milk would be purely illusory; for what would be gained from selling the high-priced butter fat would be lost in selling the low-priced residue of thinned milk. Similarly our Proposition II – that the price per dollar of a levered stream falls as leverage increases – is an exact analogue of the statement that the price per gallon of thinned milk falls continuously as more butter fat is skimmed off.[32]

It is clear that this last assertion is true as long as butter fat is worth more per unit weight than whole milk, and it holds even if, for many consumers, taking a little cream out of the milk (adding a little leverage to the stock) does not detract noticeably from the taste (does not add noticeably to the risk). Furthermore the argument remains valid even in the face of institutional

---

[32] Let M denote the quantity of whole milk, B/M the proportion of butter fat in the whole milk, and let p_M, p_B and p_α denote, respectively, the price per unit weight of whole milk, butter fat and thinned milk from which a fraction α of the butter fat has been skimmed off. We then have the fundamental perfect market relation:

$$P_\alpha(M - \alpha B) + p_{B\alpha}B = p_M M, \qquad 0 \leq \alpha \leq 1, \qquad \text{(a)}$$

stating that total receipts will be the same amount $p_M M$, independently of the amount αB of butter fat that may have been sold separately. Since p_M corresponds to $1/\rho$, p_B to $1/r$, p_α to $1/i$, M to $\overline{X}$ and αB to rD, (a) is equivalent to Proposition I, $S + D = \overline{X}/\rho$. From (a) we derive:

$$p_\alpha = p_M \frac{M}{M - \alpha B} - p_B \frac{\alpha B}{M - \alpha B} \qquad \text{(b)}$$

which gives the price of thinned milk as an explicit function of the proportion of butter fat skimmed off; the function decreasing as long as $p_B > p_M$. From (a) also follows:

$$1/p_\alpha = 1/p_M + (1/p_M - 1/p_B) \frac{p_B \alpha B}{p_\alpha(M - \alpha B)} \qquad \text{(c)}$$

which is the exact analogue of Proposition II, as given by (8).

limitations of the type envisaged by Durand. For suppose that a large fraction of the population habitually dines in restaurants which are required by law to serve only cream in lieu of milk (entrust their savings to institutional investors who can only buy bonds). To be sure the price of butter fat will then tend to be higher in relation to that of skimmed milk than in the absence of such restrictions (the rate of interest will tend to be lower), and this will benefit people who eat at home and who like skim milk (who manage their own portfolio and are able and willing to take risk). But it will still be the case that a farmer cannot gain by skimming some of the butter fat and selling it separately (firm cannot reduce the cost of capital by recourse to borrowed funds).[33]

Our propositions can be regarded as the extension of the classical theory of markets to the particular case of the capital markets. Those who hold the current view – whether they realize it or not – must assume not merely that there are lags and frictions in the equilibrating process – a feeling we certainly share,[34] claiming for our propositions only that they describe the central tendency around which observations will scatter – but also that there are large and *systematic* imperfections in the market which permanently bias the outcome. This is an assumption that economists, at any rate, will instinctively eye with some skepticism.

In any event, whether such prolonged, systematic departures from equilibrium really exist or whether our propositions are better descriptions of long-run market behavior can be settled only by empirical research. Before going on to the theory of investment it may be helpful, therefore, to look at the evidence.

E Some preliminary evidence on the basic propositions

Unfortunately the evidence which has been assembled so far is amazingly skimpy. Indeed, we have been able to locate only two recent studies – and these of rather limited scope – which were designed to throw light on the issue. Pending the results of more comprehensive tests which we hope will soon be

---

[33] The reader who likes parables will find that the analogy with interrelated commodity markets can be pushed a good deal farther than we have done in the text. For instance, the effect of changes in the market rate of interest on the over-all cost of capital is the same as the effect of a change in the price of butter on the price of whole milk. Similarly, just as the relation between the prices of skim milk and butter fat influences the kind of cows that will be reared, so the relation between i and r influences the kind of ventures that will be undertaken. If people like butter we shall have Guernseys; if they are willing to pay a high price for safety, this will encourage ventures which promise smaller but less uncertain streams per dollar of physical assets.

[34] Several specific examples of the failure of the arbitrage mechanism can be found in Graham and Dodd [6, e.g., pp.646–48]. The price discrepancy described on pp.646–47 is particularly curious since it persists even today despite the fact that a whole generation of security analysts has been brought up on this book!

available, we shall review briefly such evidence as is provided by the two studies in question: (1) an analysis of the relation between security yields and financial structure for some 43 large electric utilities by F. B. Allen [1], and (2) a parallel (unpublished) study by Robert Smith [19], for 42 oil companies designed to test whether Allen's rather striking results would be found in an industry with very different characteristics.[35] The Allen study is based on average figures for the years 1947 and 1948, while the Smith study relates to the single year 1953.

The effect of leverage on the cost of capital

According to the received view, as shown in equation (17) the average cost of capital, $\overline{X}^{\tau}/V$, should decline linearly with leverage as measured by the ratio D/V, at least through most of the relevant range.[36] According to Proposition I, the average cost of capital within a given class k should tend to have the same value ρ_k^{τ} independently of the degree of leverage. A simple test of the merits of the two alternative hypotheses can thus be carried out by correlating $\overline{X}^{\tau}/V$ with D/V. If the traditional view is correct, the correlation should be significantly negative; if our view represents a better approximation to reality, then the correlation should not be significantly different from zero.

Both studies provide information about the average value of D – the market value of bonds and preferred stock – and of V – the market value of all securities.[37] From these data we can readily compute the ratio D/V and this ratio (expressed as a percentage) is represented by the symbol d in the regression equations below. The measurement of the variable $\overline{X}^{\tau}/V$, however, presents serious difficulties. Strictly speaking, the numerator should measure the expected returns net of taxes, but this is a variable on which no direct information is available. As an approximation, we have followed both authors and used (1) the average value of actual net returns in 1947 and 1948 for

---

[35] We wish to express our thanks to both writers for making available to us some of their original worksheets. In addition to these recent studies there is a frequently cited (but apparently seldom read) study by the Federal Communications Commission in 1938 [22] which purports to show the existence of an optimal capital structure or range of structures (in the sense defined above) for public utilities in the 1930s. By current standards for statistical investigations, however, this study cannot be regarded as having any real evidential value for the problem at hand.

[36] We shall simplify our notation in this section by dropping the subscript j used to denote a particular firm wherever this will not lead to confusion.

[37] Note that for purposes of this test preferred stocks, since they represent an *expected* fixed obligation, are properly classified with bonds even though the tax status of preferred dividends is different from that of interest payments and even though preferred dividends are really fixed only as to their maximum in any year. Some difficulty of classification does arise in the case of convertible preferred stocks (and convertible bonds) selling at a substantial premium, but fortunately very few such issues were involved for the companies included in the two studies. Smith included bank loans and certain other short-term obligations (at book values) in his data on oil company debts and this treatment is perhaps open to some question. However, the amounts involved were relatively small and check computations showed that their elimination would lead to only minor differences in the test results.

Allen's utilities; and (2) actual net returns in 1953 for Smith's oil companies. Net return is defined in both cases as the sum of interest, preferred dividends and stockholders' income net of corporate income taxes. Although this approximation to expected returns is undoubtedly very crude, there is no reason to believe that it will systematically bias the test in so far as the sign of the regression coefficient is concerned. The roughness of the approximation, however, will tend to make for a wide scatter. Also contributing to the scatter is the crudeness of the industrial classification, since especially within the sample of oil companies, the assumption that all the firms belong to the same class in our sense, is at best only approximately valid.

Denoting by x our approximation to $\overline{X}^{\tau}/V$ (expressed, like d, as a percentage), the results of the tests are as follows:

$$\text{Electric Utilities } x = 5.3 + 0.006d \qquad r = 0.12$$
$$(\pm 0.008)$$

$$\text{Oil Companies } x = 8.5 + 0.006d \qquad r = 0.04.$$
$$(\pm 0.024)$$

The data underlying these equations are also shown in scatter diagram form in Figures 3 and 4.

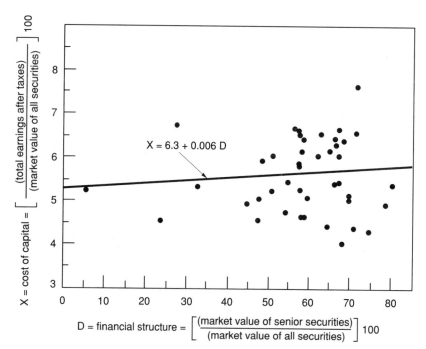

Figure 3 *Cost of capital in relation to financial structure for 43 electric utilities, 1947–48*

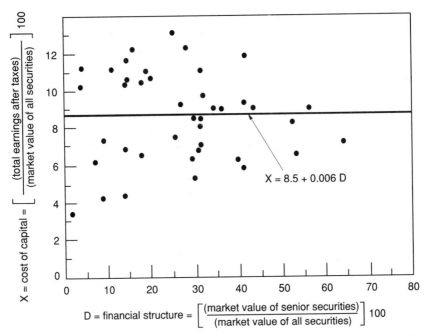

Figure 4   *Cost of capital in relation to financial structure for 42 oil companies, 1953*

The results of these tests are clearly favorable to our hypothesis. Both correlation coefficients are very close to zero and not statistically significant. Furthermore, the implications of the traditional view fail to be supported even with respect to the sign of the correlation. The data in short provide no evidence of any tendency for the cost of capital to fall as the debt ratio increases.[38]

[38] It may be argued that a test of the kind used is biased against the traditional view. The fact that both sides of the regression equation are divided by the variable V which may be subject to random variation might tend to impart a positive bias to the correlation. As a check on the results presented in the text, we have, therefore, carried out a supplementary test based on equation (16). This equation shows that, if the traditional view is correct, the market value of a company should, for given $\overline{X}^\tau$, increase with debt through most of the relevant range; according to our model the market value should be uncorrelated with D, given $\overline{X}^\tau$. Because of wide variations in the size of the firms included in our samples, all variables must be divided by a suitable scale factor in order to avoid spurious results in carrying out a test of equation (16). The factor we have used is the book value of the firm denoted by A. The hypothesis tested thus takes the specific form:

$$V/A = a + b(\overline{X}^\tau/A) + c(D/A)$$

and the numerator of the ratio X^τ/A is again approximated by actual net returns. The partial correlation between V/A and D/A should now be positive according to the traditional view and zero according to our model. Although division by A should, if anything, bias the results in favor of the traditional hypothesis, the partial correlation turns out to be only 0.03 for the oil companies and −0.28 for the electric utilities. Neither of these coefficients is significantly different from zero and the larger one even has the wrong sign.

It should also be apparent from the scatter diagrams that there is no hint of a curvilinear, U-shaped, relation of the kind which is widely believed to hold between the cost of capital and leverage. This graphical impression was confirmed by statistical tests which showed that for both industries the curvature was not significantly different from zero, its sign actually being opposite to that hypothesized.[39]

Note also that according to our model, the constant terms of the regression equations are measures of $\rho_k{}^\tau$, the capitalization rates for unlevered streams and hence the average cost of capital in the classes in question. The estimates of 8.5 per cent for the oil companies as against 5.3 per cent for electric utilities appear to accord well with a priori expectations, both in absolute value and relative spread.

The effect of leverage on common stock yields

According to our Proposition II – see equation 12 and Figure 2 – the expected yield on common stock, $\bar{\pi}^\tau/S$, in any given class, should tend to increase with leverage as measured by the ratio D/S. The relation should tend to be linear and with positive slope through most of the relevant range (as in the curve MM' of Figure 2), though it might tend to flatten out if we move far enough to the right (as in the curve MD'), to the extent that high leverage tends to drive up the cost of senior capital. According to the conventional view, the yield curve as a function of leverage should be a horizontal straight line (like ML') through most of the relevant range; far enough to the right, the yield may tend to rise at an increasing rate. Here again, a straight-forward correlation – in this case between $\bar{\pi}^\tau/S$ and D/S – can provide a test of the two positions. If our view is correct, the correlation should be significantly positive; if the traditional view is correct, the correlation should be negligible.

Subject to the same qualifications noted above in connection with $\bar{X}^\tau$, we can approximate $\bar{\pi}^\tau$ by actual stockholder net income.[40] Letting s denote in

---

[39] The tests consisted of fitting to the data the equation (19) of footnote 27. As shown there, it follows from the U-shaped hypothesis that the coefficient α of the variable $(D/V)^2/(1-D/V)$, denoted hereafter by $d^\star$, should be significant and positive. The following regression equations and partials were obtained:

Electric Utilities $x = 5.0 + 0.017d - 0.003d^\star; r_{xd^\star \cdot d} = -0.15$

Oil Companies $x = 8.0 + 0.05d - 0.03d^\star; r_{xd^\star \cdot d} = -0.14.$

[40] As indicated earlier, Smith's data were for the single year 1953. Since the use of a single year's profits as a measure of expected profits might be open to objection we collected profit data for 1952 for the same companies and based the computation of $\bar{\pi}^\tau/S$ on the average of the two years. The value of $\bar{\pi}^\tau/S$ was obtained from the formula:

$$\left(\text{net earnings in 1952} \cdot \frac{\text{assets in '53}}{\text{assets in '52}} + \text{net earnings in '53} \right) \frac{1}{2} \div$$
(average market value of common stock in '53).

The asset adjustment was introduced as rough allowance for the effects of possible growth in the size of the firm. It might be added that the correlation computed with $\bar{\pi}^\tau/S$ based on net profits in 1953 alone was found to be only slightly smaller, namely 0.50.

each case the approximation to $\bar{\pi}^\tau/S$ (expressed as a percentage) and letting h denote the ratio D/S (also in percentage terms) the following results are obtained:

$$\text{Electric Utilities } z = 6.6 + 0.017h \qquad r = 0.53$$
$$(\pm 0.004)$$

$$\text{Oil Companies } z = 8.9 + 0.051h \qquad r = 0.53.$$
$$(\pm 0.012)$$

These results are shown in scatter diagram form in Figures 5 and 6.

Here again the implications of our analysis seem to be borne out by the data. Both correlation coefficients are positive and highly significant when account is taken of the substantial sample size. Furthermore, the estimates of the coefficients of the equations seem to accord reasonably well with our hypothesis. According to equation (12) the constant term should be the value of ρ_k^τ for the given class while the slope should be $(\rho_k^\tau - r)$. From the test of Proposition I we have seen that for the oil companies the mean value of ρ_k^τ could be estimated at around 8.7. Since the average yield of senior capital during the period covered

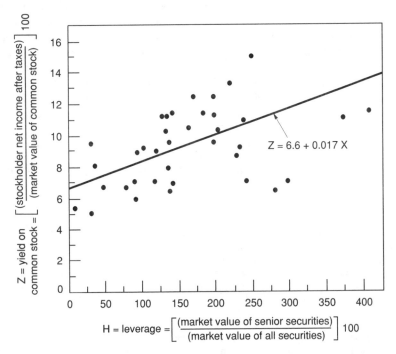

Figure 5   *Yield on common stock in relation to leverage for 43 electric utilities, 1947–48*

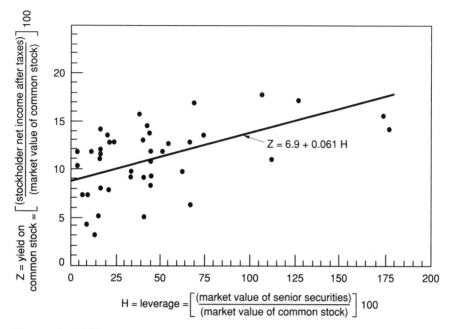

Figure 6 *Yield on common stock in relation to leverage for 42 oil companies, 1952–53*

was in the order of 3½ per cent, we should expect a constant term of about 8.7 per cent and a slope of just over 5 per cent. These values closely approximate the regression estimates of 8.9 per cent and 5.1 per cent respectively. For the electric utilities, the yield of senior capital was also on the order of 3½ per cent during the test years, but since the estimate of the mean value of ρ_k^τ from the test of Proposition I was 5.6 per cent, the slope should be just above 2 per cent. The actual regression estimate for the slope of 1.7 per cent is thus somewhat low, but still within one standard error of its theoretical value. Because of this underestimate of the slope and because of the large mean value of leverage (h = 160 per cent) the regression estimate of the constant term, 6.6 per cent, is somewhat high, although not significantly different from the value of 5.6 per cent obtained in the test of Proposition I.

When we add a square term to the above equations to test for the presence and direction of curvature we obtain the following estimates:

Electric Utilities $z = 4.6 + 0.004h - 0.007h^2$

Oil Companies $z = 8.5 + 0.072h - 0.016h^2$.

For both cases the curvature is negative. In fact, for the electric utilities, where the observations cover a wider range of leverage ratios, the negative coefficient of the square term is actually significant at the 5 per cent level. Negative curvature, as we have seen, runs directly counter to the traditional hypothesis, whereas it can be readily accounted for by our model in terms of rising cost of borrowed funds.[41]

In summary, the empirical evidence we have reviewed seems to be broadly consistent with our model and largely inconsistent with traditional views. Needless to say much more extensive testing will be required before we can firmly conclude that our theory describes market behavior. Caution is indicated especially with regard to our test of Proposition II, partly because of possible statistical pitfalls[42] and partly because not all the factors that might have a systematic effect on stock yields have been considered. In particular, no attempt was made to test the possible influence of the dividend pay-out ratio whose role has tended to receive a great deal of attention in current research and thinking. There are two reasons for this omission. First, our main objective has been to assess the prima facie tenability of *our* model, and in this model, based as it is on rational behavior by investors, dividends per se play no role. Second, in a world in which the policy of dividend stabilization is widespread, there is no simple way of disentangling the true effect of dividend payments on stock prices from their apparent effect, the latter reflecting only the role of dividends as a proxy measure of long-term earning anticipations.[43] The difficulties just mentioned are further compounded by possible inter-relations between dividend policy and leverage.[44]

---

[41] That the yield of senior capital tended to rise for utilities as leverage increased is clearly shown in several of the scatter diagrams presented in the published version of Allen's study. This significant negative curvature between stock yields and leverage for utilities may be partly responsible for the fact, previously noted, that the constant in the linear regression is somewhat higher and the slope somewhat lower than implied by equation (12). Note also in connection with the estimate of ρ_k^τ that the introduction of the quadratic term reduced the constant considerably, pushing it in fact below the a priori expectation of 5.6, though the difference is again not statistically significant.

[42] In our test, e.g., the two variables z and h are both ratios with S appearing in the denominator, which may tend to impart a positive bias to the correlation (cf. note 36). Attempts were made to develop alternative tests, but although various possibilities were explored, we have so far been unable to find satisfactory alternatives.

[43] We suggest that failure to appreciate this difficulty is responsible for many fallacious, or at least unwarranted, conclusions about the role of dividends.

[44] In the sample of electric utilities, there is a substantial negative correlation between yields and pay-out ratios, but also between pay-out ratios and leverage, suggesting that either the association of yields and leverage or of yields and pay-out ratios may be (at least partly) spurious. These difficulties however do not arise in the case of the oil industry sample. A preliminary analysis indicates that there is here no significant relation between leverage and pay-out ratios and also no significant correlation (either gross or partial) between yields and pay-out ratios.

II Implications of the analysis for the theory of investment

A Capital structure and investment policy

On the basis of our propositions with respect to cost of capital and financial structure (and for the moment neglecting taxes), we can derive the following simple rule for optimal investment policy by the firm:

Proposition III

If a firm in class k is acting in the best interest of the stockholders at the time of the decision, it will exploit an investment opportunity if and only if the rate of return on the investment, say $\rho^\star$, is as large as or larger than ρ_k. That is, *the cut-off point for investment in the firm will in all cases be ρ_k and will be completely unaffected by the type of security used to finance the investment.* Equivalently, we may say that regardless of the financing used, the marginal cost of capital to a firm is equal to the average cost of capital, which is in turn equal to the capitalization rate for an unlevered stream in the class to which the firm belongs.[45]

To establish this result we will consider the three major financing alternatives open to the firm – bonds, retained earnings, and common stock issues – and show that in each case an investment is worth undertaking if, and only if, $\rho^\star \geqq \rho_k$.[46]

Consider first the case of an investment financed by the sale of bonds. We know from Proposition I that the market value of the firm before the investment was undertaken was:[47]

$$V_0 = \overline{X}_0/\rho_k \tag{20}$$

and that the value of the common stock was:

$$S_0 = V_0 - D_0. \tag{21}$$

---

[45] The analysis developed in this paper is essentially a comparative-statics, not a dynamic analysis. This note of caution applies with special force to Proposition III. Such problems as those posed by expected changes in r and in ρ_k over time will not be treated here. Although they are in principle amenable to analysis within the general framework we have laid out, such an undertaking is sufficiently complex to deserve separate treatment. *Cf.* note 17.

[46] The extension of the proof to other types of financing, such as the sale of preferred stock or the issuance of stock rights is straightforward.

[47] Since no confusion is likely to arise, we have again, for simplicity, eliminated the subscripts identifying the firm in the equation to follow. Except for ρ_k, the subscripts now refer to time periods.

If now the firm borrows I dollars to finance an investment yielding $\rho^\star$ its market value will become:

$$V_1 = \frac{\overline{X}_0 + \rho^\star I}{\rho_k} = V_0 + \frac{\rho^\star I}{\rho_k} \tag{22}$$

and the value of its common stock will be:

$$S_1 = V_1 - (D_0 + I) = V_0 + \frac{\rho^\star I}{\rho_k} - D_0 - I \tag{23}$$

or using equation 21,

$$S_1 = S_0 + \frac{\rho^\star I}{\rho_k} - I. \tag{24}$$

Hence $S_i \gtreqless S_0$ as $\rho^\star \gtreqless \rho_k$.[48]

To illustrate, suppose the capitalization rate for uncertain streams in the kth class is 10 per cent and the rate of interest is 4 per cent. Then if a given company had an expected income of 1,000 and if it were financed entirely by common stock we know from Proposition I that the market value of its stock would be 10,000. Assume now that the managers of the firm discover an investment opportunity which will require an outlay of 100 and which is expected to yield 8 per cent. At first sight this might appear to be a profitable opportunity since the expected return is double the interest cost. If, however, the management borrows the necessary 100 at 4 per cent, the total expected income of the company rises to 1,008 and the market value of the firm to 10,080. But the firm now will have 100 of bonds in its capital structure so that, paradoxically, the market value of the stock must actually be reduced from 10,000 to 9,980 as a consequence of this apparently profitable investment. Or, to put it another way, the gains from being able to tap cheap, borrowed funds are more than offset for the stockholders by the market's discounting of the stock for the added leverage assumed.

Consider next the case of retained earnings. Suppose that in the course of its operations the firm acquired I dollars of cash (without impairing the

---

[48] In the case of bond-financing the rate of interest on bonds does not enter explicitly into the decision (assuming the firm borrows at the market rate of interest). This is true, moreover, given the conditions outlined in Section I.C, even though interest rates may be an increasing function of debt outstanding. To the extent that the firm borrowed at a rate other than the market rate the two I's in equation (24) would no longer be identical and an additional gain or loss, as the case might be, would accrue to the shareholders. It might also be noted in passing that permitting the two I's in (24) to take on different values provides a simple method for introducing underwriting expenses into the analysis.

earning power of its assets). If the cash is distributed as a dividend to the stockholders, their wealth, W_0, after the distribution will be:

$$W_0 = S_0 + I = \frac{\overline{X}_0}{\rho_k} - D_0 + I \qquad (25)$$

where $\overline{X}_0$ represents the expected return from the assets exclusive of the amount I in question. If however the funds are retained by the company and used to finance new assets whose expected rate of return is ρ^*, then the stockholders' wealth would become:

$$W_1 = S_1 = \frac{\overline{X}_0 + \rho^* I}{\rho_k} - D_0 = S_0 + \frac{\rho^* I}{\rho_k}. \qquad (26)$$

Clearly $W_1 \gtreqless W_0$ as $\rho^* \gtreqless \rho_k$ so that an investment financed by retained earnings raises the net worth of the owners if and only if $\rho^* > \rho_k$.[49]

Consider finally, the case of common-stock financing. Let P_0 denote the current market price per share of stock and assume, for simplicity, that this price reflects currently expected earnings only, that is, it does not reflect any future increase in earnings as a result of the investment under consideration.[50] Then if N is the original number of shares, the price per share is:

$$P_0 = S_0 N \qquad (27)$$

and the number of new shares, M, needed to finance an investment of I dollars is given by:

$$M = \frac{I}{P_0}. \qquad (28)$$

As a result of the investment the market value of the stock becomes:

$$S_1 = \frac{\overline{X}_0 + \rho^* I}{\rho_k} - D_0 = S_0 + \frac{\rho^* I}{\rho_k} = N P_0 + \frac{\rho^* I}{\rho_k}$$

and the price per share:

[49] The conclusion that ρ_k is the cut-off point for investments financed from internal funds applies not only to undistributed net profits, but to depreciation allowances (and even to the funds represented by the current sale value of any asset or collection of assets). Since the owners can earn ρ_k by investing funds elsewhere in the class, partial or total liquidating distributions should be made whenever the firm cannot achieve a marginal internal rate of return equal to ρ_k.

[50] If we assumed that the market price of the stock did reflect the expected higher future earnings (as would be the case if our original set of assumptions above were strictly followed) the analysis would differ slightly in detail but not in essentials. The cut-off point for new investment would still be ρ_k, but where $\rho^* > \rho_k$ the gain to the original owners would be larger than if the stock price were based on the pre-investment expectations only.

$$P_1 = \frac{S_1}{N + M} = \frac{1}{N + M}\left[NP_0 + \frac{\rho^\star I}{\rho_k}\right]. \tag{29}$$

Since by equation (28), $I = MP_0$, we can add MP_0 and subtract I from the quantity in bracket, obtaining:

$$P_1 = \frac{1}{N + M}\left[(N + M)P_0 + \frac{\rho^\star - \rho_k}{\rho_k}I\right]$$

$$= P_0 + \frac{1}{N + M}\frac{\rho^\star - \rho_k}{\rho_k}I > P_0 \text{ if,} \tag{30}$$

and only if, $\rho^\star > \rho_k$.

Thus an investment financed by common stock is advantageous to the current stockholders if and only if its yield exceeds the capitalization rate ρ_k.

Once again a numerical example may help to illustrate the result and make it clear why the relevant cut-off rate is ρ_k and not the current yield on common stock, i. Suppose that ρ_k is 10 per cent, r is 4 per cent, that the original expected income of our company is 1,000 and that management has the opportunity of investing 100 having an expected yield of 12 per cent. If the original capital structure is 50 per cent debt and 50 per cent equity, and 1,000 shares of stock are initially outstanding, then, by Proposition I, the market value of the common stock must be 5,000 or 5 per share. Furthermore, since the interest bill is $0.04 \times 5,000 = 200$, the yield on common stock is $800/5,000 = 16$ per cent. It may then appear that financing the additional investment of 100 by issuing 20 shares to outsiders at 5 per share would dilute the equity of the original owners since the 100 promises to yield 12 per cent whereas the common stock is currently yielding 16 per cent. Actually, however, the income of the company would rise to 1,012; the value of the firm to 10,120; and the value of the common stock to 5,120. Since there are now 1,020 shares, each would be worth 5.02 and the wealth of the original stockholders would thus have been increased. What has happened is that the dilution in expected earnings per share (from 0.80 to 0.796) has been more than offset, in its effect upon the market price of the shares, by the decrease in leverage.

Our conclusion is, once again, at variance with conventional views,[51] so much so as to be easily misinterpreted. Read hastily, Proposition III seems to imply that the capital structure of a firm is a matter of indifference; and that, consequently, one of the core problems of corporate finance – the problem of the optimal capital structure for a firm – is no problem at all. It may be helpful, therefore, to clear up such possible misunderstandings.

[51] In the matter of investment policy under uncertainty there is no single position which represents 'accepted' doctrine. For a sample of current formulations, all very different from ours, see M. Gordon and E. Shapiro [5], and Harry Roberts [17].

B Proposition III and financial planning by firms

Misinterpretation of the scope of Proposition III can be avoided by remembering that this Proposition tells us only that the type of instrument used to finance an investment is irrelevant to the question of whether or not the investment is worthwhile. This does not mean that the owners (or the managers) have no grounds whatever for preferring one financing plan to another; or that there are no other policy or technical issues in finance at the level of the firm.

That grounds for preferring one type of financial structure to another will still exist within the framework of our model can readily be seen for the case of common-stock financing. In general, except for something like a widely publicized oil-strike, we would expect the market to place very heavy weight on current and recent past earnings in forming expectations as to future returns. Hence, if the owners of a firm discovered a major investment opportunity which they felt would yield much more than ρ_k, they might well prefer not to finance it via common stock at the then ruling price, because this price may fail to capitalize the new venture. A better course would be a pre-emptive issue of stock (and in this connection it should be remembered that stockholders are free to borrow and buy). Another possibility would be to finance the project initially with debt. Once the project had reflected itself in increased actual earnings, the debt could be retired either with an equity issue at much better prices or through retained earnings. Still another possibility along the same lines might be to combine the two steps by means of a convertible debenture or preferred stock, perhaps with a progressively declining conversion rate. Even such a double-stage financing plan may possibly be regarded as yielding too large a share to outsiders since the new stockholders are, in effect, being given an interest in any similar opportunities the firm may discover in the future. If there is a reasonable prospect that even larger opportunities may arise in the near future and if there is some danger that borrowing now would preclude more borrowing later, the owners might find their interests best protected by splitting off the current opportunity into a separate subsidiary with independent financing. Clearly the problems involved in making the crucial estimates and in planning the optimal financial strategy are by no means trivial, even though they should have no bearing on the basic decision to invest (as long as $\rho^* = \rho_k$.)[52]

Another reason why the alternatives in financial plans may not be a matter of indifference arises from the fact that managers are concerned with more

---

[52] Nor can we rule out the possibility that the existing owners, if unable to use a financing plan which protects their interest, may actually prefer to pass up an otherwise profitable venture rather than give outsiders an 'excessive' share of the business. It is presumably in situations of this kind that we could justifiably speak of a shortage of 'equity capital', though the kind of market imperfection is likely to be of significance only for small or new firms.

than simply furthering the interest of the owners. Such other objectives of the management – which need not be necessarily in conflict with those of the owners – are much more likely to be served by some types of financing arrangements than others. In many forms of borrowing agreements, for example, creditors are able to stipulate terms which the current management may regard as infringing on its prerogatives or restricting its freedom to maneuver. The creditors might even be able to insist on having a direct voice in the formation of policy.[53] To the extent, therefore, that financial policies have these implications for the management of the firm, something like the utility approach described in the introductory section becomes relevant to financial (as opposed to investment) decision-making. It is, however, the utility functions of the managers per se and not of the owners that are now involved.[54]

In summary, many of the specific considerations which bulk so large in traditional discussions of corporate finance can readily be superimposed on our simple framework without forcing any drastic (and certainly no systematic) alteration of the conclusion which is our principal concern, namely that for investment decisions, the marginal cost of capital is ρ_k.

C   The effect of the corporate income tax on investment decisions

In Section I it was shown that when an unintegrated corporate income tax is introduced, the original version of our Proposition I,

$$\overline{X}/V = \rho_k = \text{a constant}$$

must be rewritten as:

$$\frac{(\overline{X} - rD)(1 - r) + rD}{V} \equiv \frac{\overline{X}^{\tau}}{V} = \rho_k^r = \text{a constant.} \qquad (11)$$

[53] Similar considerations are involved in the matter of dividend policy. Even though the stockholders may be indifferent as to payout policy as long as investment policy is optimal, the management need not be so. Retained earnings involve far fewer threats to control than any of the alternative sources of funds and, of course, involve no underwriting expense or risk. But against these advantages management must balance the fact that sharp changes in dividend rates, which heavy reliance on retained earnings might imply, may give the impression that a firm's finances are being poorly managed, with consequent threats to the control and professional standing of the management.

[54] In principle, at least, this introduction of management's risk preferences with respect to financing methods would do much to reconcile the apparent conflict between Proposition III and such empirical findings as those of Modigliani and Zeman [14] on the close relation between interest rates and the ratio of new debt to new equity issues; or of John Lintner [12] on the considerable stability in target and actual dividend-payout ratios.

Throughout Section I we found it convenient to refer to $\overline{X}^\tau/V$ as the cost of capital. The appropriate measure of the cost of capital relevant to investment decisions, however, is the ratio of the expected return *before* taxes to the market value, *i.e.*, $\overline{X}/V$. From (11) above we find:

$$\frac{\overline{X}}{V} = \frac{\rho_k^\tau - \tau_r(D/V)}{1 - \tau} = \frac{\rho_k^\tau}{1 - \tau}\left[1 - \frac{\rho r D}{\rho_k^\tau V}\right], \tag{31}$$

which shows that the cost of capital now depends on the debt ratio, decreasing, as D/V rises, at the constant rate $_{\tau r}/(1-_\tau)$.[55] Thus, with a corporate income tax under which interest is a deductible expense, gains can accrue to stockholders from having debt in the capital structure, even when capital markets are perfect. The gains however are small, as can be seen from (31), and as will be shown more explicitly below.

From (31) we can develop the tax-adjusted counterpart of Proposition III by interpreting the term D/V in that equation as the proportion of debt used in any additional financing of V dollars. For example, in the case where the financing is entirely by new common stock, $D = 0$ and the required rate of return ρ_k^s on a venture so financed becomes:

$$\rho_k^S = \frac{\rho_k^\tau}{1 - \tau}. \tag{32}$$

For the other extreme of pure debt financing $D = V$ and the required rate of return, ρ_k^D, becomes:

$$\rho_k^D = \frac{\rho_k^\tau}{1 - \tau}\left[1 - \tau\frac{r}{\rho_k^\tau}\right] = \rho_k^S\left[1 - \tau\frac{r}{\rho_k^\tau}\right] = \rho_k^S - \frac{\tau}{1 - \tau}r.^{56} \tag{33}$$

For investments financed out of retained earnings, the problem of defining the required rate of return is more difficult since it involves a comparison of the tax consequences to the individual stockholder of receiving a dividend versus having a capital gain. Depending on the time of realization, a capital gain

---

[55] Equation (31) is amenable, in principle, to statistical tests similar to those described in Section I.E. However we have not made any systematic attempt to carry out such tests so far, because neither the Allen nor the Smith study provides the required information. Actually, Smith's data included a very crude estimate of tax liability and, using this estimate, we did in fact obtain a negative relation between $\overline{X}/V$ and D/V. However, the correlation (-0.28) turned out to be significant only at about the 10 per cent level. While this result is not conclusive, it should be remembered that, according to our theory, the slope of the regression equation should be in any event quite small. In fact, with a value of τ in the order of 0.5, and values of ρk^τ and τ in the order of 8.5 and 3.5 per cent respectively (*cf.* Section I.E.) an increase in D/V from 0 to 60 per cent (which is, approximately, the range of variation of this variable in the sample) should tend to reduce the average cost of capital only from about 17 to about 15 per cent.

[56] This conclusion does not extend to preferred stocks even though they have been classed with debt issues previously. Since preferred dividends except for a portion of those of public utilities are not in general deductible from the corporate tax, the cut-off point for new financing via preferred stock is exactly the same as that for common stock.

produced by retained earnings may be taxed either at ordinary income tax rates, 50 per cent of these rates, 25 per cent, or zero, if held till death. The rate on any dividends received in the event of a distribution will also be a variable depending on the amount of other income received by the stockholder, and with the added complications introduced by the current dividend-credit provisions. If we assume that the managers proceed on the basis of reasonable estimates as to the average values of the relevant tax rates for the owners, then the required return for retained earnings $\rho_k{}^R$ can be shown to be:

$$\rho_k{}^R = \rho_k{}^\tau \frac{1}{1 - \tau} \frac{1 - \tau_d}{1 - \tau_g} = \frac{1 - \tau_d}{1 - \tau_g} \rho_k{}^s \qquad (34)$$

where τ_d is the assumed rate of personal income tax on dividends and τ_g is the assumed rate of tax on capital gains.

A numerical illustration may perhaps be helpful in clarifying the relationship between these required rates of return. If we take the following round numbers as representative order-of-magnitude values under present conditions: an after-tax capitalization rate $\rho_k{}^\tau$ of 10 per cent, a rate of interest on bonds of 4 per cent, a corporate tax rate of 50 per cent, a marginal personal income tax rate on dividends of 40 per cent (corresponding to an income of about $25,000 on a joint return), and a capital gains rate of 20 per cent (one-half the marginal rate on dividends), then the required rates of return would be: (1) 20 per cent for investments financed entirely by issuance of new common shares; (2) 16 per cent for investments financed entirely by new debt; and (3) 15 per cent for investments financed wholly from internal funds.

These results would seem to have considerable significance for current discussions of the effect of the corporate income tax on financial policy and on investment. Although we cannot explore the implications of the results in any detail here, we should at least like to call attention to the remarkably small difference between the 'cost' of equity funds and debt funds. With the numerical values assumed, equity money turned out to be only 25 per cent more expensive than debt money, rather than something on the order of 5 times as expensive as is commonly supposed to be the case.[57] The reason for

---

[57] See *e.g.*, D. T. Smith [18]. It should also be pointed out that our tax system acts in other ways to reduce the gains from debt financing. Heavy reliance on debt in the capital structure, for example, commits a company to paying out a substantial proportion of its income in the form of interest payments taxable to the owners under the personal income tax. A debt-free company, by contrast, can reinvest in the business all of its (smaller) net income and to this extent subject the owners only to the low capital gains rate (or possibly no tax at all by virtue of the loophole at death). Thus, we should expect a high degree of leverage to be of value to the owners, even in the case of closely held corporations, primarily in cases where their firm was not expected to have much need for additional funds to expand assets and earnings in the future. To the extent that opportunities for growth were available, as they presumably would be for most successful corporations, the interest of the stockholders would tend to be better served by a structure which permitted maximum use of retained earnings.

the wide difference is that the traditional view starts from the position that debt funds are several times cheaper than equity funds even in the absence of taxes, with taxes serving simply to magnify the cost ratio in proportion to the corporate rate. By contrast, in our model in which the repercussions of debt financing on the value of shares are taken into account, the *only* difference in cost is that due to the tax effect, and its magnitude is simply the tax on the 'grossed up' interest payment. Not only is this magnitude likely to be small but our analysis yields the further paradoxical implication that the stockholders' gain from, and hence incentive to use, debt financing is actually smaller the lower the rate of interest. In the extreme case where the firm could borrow for practically nothing, the advantage of debt financing would also be practically nothing.

III Conclusion

With the development of Proposition III the main objectives we outlined in our introductory discussion have been reached. We have in our Propositions I and II at least the foundations of a theory of the valuation of firms and shares in a world of uncertainty. We have shown, moreover, how this theory can lead to an operational definition of the cost of capital and how that concept can be used in turn as a basis for rational investment decision-making within the firm. Needless to say, however, much remains to be done before the cost of capital can be put away on the shelf among the solved problems. Our approach has been that of static, partial equilibrium analysis. It has assumed among other things a state of atomistic competition in the capital markets and an ease of access to those markets which only a relatively small (though important) group of firms even come close to possessing. These and other drastic simplifications have been necessary in order to come to grips with the problem at all. Having served their purpose they can now be relaxed in the direction of greater realism and relevance, a task in which we hope others interested in this area will wish to share.

References

1 F.B. Allen, 'Does Going into Debt Lower the "Cost of Capital"?', *Analysts Jour.*, Aug. 1954, 10, 57–61.
2 J. Dean, *Capital Budgeting*, New York 1951.
3 D. Durand, 'Costs of Debt and Equity Funds for Business: Trends and Problems of Measurement' in Nat. Bur. Econ. Research, *Conference on Research in Business Finance*, New York 1952, pp.215–47.
4 W.J. Eiteman, 'Financial Aspects of Promotion', in *Essays on Business Finance* by M.W. Waterford and W.J. Eiteman. Ann Arbor, Mich. 1952, pp.1–17.

5 M.J. Gordon and E. Shapiro, 'Capital Equipment Analysis: The Required Rate of Profit', *Manag. Sci.*, Oct. 1956, 3, 102–10.

6 B. Graham and L. Dodd, *Security Analysis*, 3rd ed. New York 1951.

7 G. Guthmann and H.E. Dougall, *Corporate Financial Policy*, 3rd ed. New York 1955.

8 J.R. Hicks, *Value and Capital*, 2nd ed. Oxford 1946.

9 P. Hunt and M. Williams, *Case Problems in Finance*, rev. ed. Homewood, Ill. 1954.

10 J.M. Keynes, *The General Theory of Employment, Interest and Money*. New York 1936.

11 O. Lange, *Price Flexibility and Employment*. Bloomington, Ind. 1944.

12 J. Lintner, 'Distribution of Incomes of Corporations among Dividends, Retained Earnings and Taxes', *Am. Econ. Rev.*, May 1956, 46, 97–113.

13 F. Lutz and V. Lutz, *The Theory of Investment of the Firm*. Princeton 1951.

14 F. Modigliani and M. Zeman, 'The Effect of the Availability of Funds, and the Terms Thereof, on Business Investment' in Nat. Bur. Econ. Research, *Conference on Research in Business Finance*. New York 1952, pp.263–309.

15 W.A. Morton, 'The Structure of the Capital Market and the Price of Money', *Am. Econ. Rev.*, May 1954, 44, 440–54.

16 S.M. Robbins, *Managing Securities*. Boston 1954.

17 H.V. Roberts, 'Current Problems in the Economics of Capital Budgeting', *Jour. Bus.*, 1957, 30(1), 12–16.

18 D.T. Smith, *Effects of Taxation on Corporate Financial Policy*. Boston 1952.

19 R. Smith, 'Cost of Capital in the Oil Industry', (hectograph). Pittsburgh: Carnegie Inst. Tech. 1955.

20 H.M. Somers, '"Cost of Money" as the Determinant of Public Utility Rates', *Buffalo Law Rev.*, Spring 1955, 4, 1–28.

21 J.B. Williams, *The Theory of Investment Value*, Cambridge, Mass. 1938.

22 US Federal Communications Commission, *The Problem of the 'Rate of Return' in Public Utility Regulation*. Washington 1938.

Reproduced from Modigliani, F. and Miller, M.H. (1958). The cost of capital, corporation finance and the theory of investment. *The American Economic Review*, **XLVII** (3), 261–297, by permission of the American Economic Association.

15 Corporate income taxes and the cost of capital: a correction

F. Modigliani and M. H. Miller

The purpose of this communication is to correct an error in our paper 'The Cost of Capital, Corporation Finance and the Theory of Investment' (this *Review*, June 1958). In our discussion of the effects of the present method of taxing corporations on the valuation of firms, we said (p.272):

> The deduction of interest in computing taxable corporate profits will prevent the arbitrage process from making the value of all firms in a given class proportional to the expected returns generated by their physical assets. Instead, it can be shown (by the same type of proof used for the original version of Proposition I) that *the market values of firms in each class must be proportional in equilibrium to their expected returns net of taxes (that is, to the sum of the interest paid and expected net stockholder income)*. (Italics added.)

The statement in italics, unfortunately, is wrong. For even though one firm may have an *expected* return after taxes (our $\overline{X}^{\tau}$) twice that of another firm in the same risk-equivalent class, it will not be the case that the *actual* return after taxes (our X^{τ}) of the first firm will always be twice that of the second, if the two firms have different *degrees* of leverage.[1] And since the distribution of returns after taxes of the two firms will not be proportional, there can be no 'arbitrage' process which forces their values to be proportional to their expected after-tax returns.[2] In fact, it can be shown – and this time it really will be shown – that

---

[1] With some exceptions, which will be noted when they occur, we shall preserve here both the notation and the terminology of the original paper. A working knowledge of both on the part of the reader will be presumed.

[2] Barring, of course, the trivial case of universal linear utility functions. Note that in deference to Professor Durand (see his Comment on our paper and our reply, this *Review*, Sept. 1959, *49*, 639–69) we here and throughout use quotation marks when referring to arbitrage.

'arbitrage' will make values within any class a function not only of expected after-tax returns, but of the tax rate and the degree of leverage. This means, among other things, that the tax advantages of debt financing are somewhat greater than we originally suggested and, to this extent, the quantitative difference between the valuations implied by our position and by the traditional view is narrowed. It still remains true, however, that under our analysis the tax advantages of debt are the *only* permanent advantages so that the gulf between the two views in matters of interpretation and policy is as wide as ever.

I   Taxes, leverage and the probability distribution of after-tax returns

To see how the distribution of after-tax earnings is affected by leverage, let us again denote by the random variable X the (long-run average) earnings before interest and taxes generated by the currently owned assets of a given firm in some stated risk class, k.[3] From our definition of a risk class it follows that X can be expressed in the form $\overline{X}Z$, where $\overline{X}$ is the expected value of X, and the random variable $Z = X/\overline{X}$, having the same value for all firms in class k, is a drawing from a distribution, say $f_k(Z)$. Hence the random variable X^τ, measuring the after-tax return, can be expressed as:

$$X^\tau = (1 - \tau)(X - R) + R = (1 - \tau)X + \tau R = (1 - \tau)\overline{X}Z + \tau R \quad (1)$$

where τ is the marginal corporate income tax rate (assumed equal to the average), and R is the interest bill. Since $E(X^\tau) \equiv \overline{X}^\tau = (1 - \tau)\overline{X} + \tau R$ we can substitute $\overline{X}^\tau - \tau R$ for $(1 - \tau)\overline{X}$ in (1) to obtain:

$$X^\tau = (\overline{X}^\tau - \tau R)Z + \tau R = \overline{X}^\tau \left(1 - \frac{\tau R}{\overline{X}^\tau}\right)Z + \tau R. \quad (2)$$

---

[3] Thus our X corresponds essentially to the familiar EBIT concept of the finance literature. The use of EBIT and related 'income' concepts as the basis of valuation is strictly valid only when the underlying real assets are assumed to have perpetual lives. In such a case, of course, EBIT and 'cash flow' are one and the same. This was, in effect, the interpretation of X we used in the original paper and we shall retain it here both to preserve continuity and for the considerable simplification it permits in the exposition. We should point out, however, that the perpetuity interpretation is much less restrictive than might appear at first glance. Before-tax cash flow and EBIT can also safely be equated even where assets have finite lives as soon as these assets attain a steady state age distribution in which annual replacements equal annual depreciation. The subject of finite lives of assets will be further discussed in connection with the problem of the cut-off rate for investment decisions.

Thus, if the tax rate is other than zero, the shape of the distribution of X^τ will depend not only on the 'scale' of the stream $\overline{X}^\tau$ and on the distribution of Z, but also on the tax rate and the degree of leverage (one measure of which is $R/\overline{X}^\tau$). For example, if Var $(Z) = \sigma^2$, we have:

$$\text{Var } (X^\tau) = \sigma^2(\overline{X}^\tau)^2 \left(1 - \tau \frac{R}{\overline{X}^\tau}\right)^2$$

implying that for given $\overline{X}^\tau$ the variance of after-tax returns is smaller, the higher τ and the degree of leverage.[4]

II The valuation of after-tax returns

Note from equation (1) that, from the investor's point of view, the long-run average stream of after-tax returns appears as a sum of two components: (1) an uncertain stream $(1 - \tau)\overline{X}Z$; and (2) a sure stream τR.[5] This suggests that the equilibrium market value of the combined stream can be found by capitalizing each component separately. More precisely, let ρ^τ be the rate at which the market capitalizes the expected returns net of tax of an unlevered company of size $\overline{X}$ in class k, i.e.,

$$\rho^\tau = \frac{(1 - \tau)\overline{X}}{V_U} \qquad \text{or} \qquad V_U = \frac{(1 - \tau)\overline{X}}{\rho^\tau};^6$$

---

[4] It may seem paradoxical at first to say that leverage *reduces* the variability of outcomes, but remember we are here discussing the variability of total returns, interest plus net profits. The variability of stockholder net profits will, of course, be greater in the presence than in the absence of leverage, though relatively less so than in an otherwise comparable world of no taxes. The reasons for this will become clearer after the discussion in the next section.

[5] The statement that τR – the tax saving per period on the interest payments – is a sure stream is subject to two qualifications. First, it must be the case that firms can always obtain the tax benefit of their interest deductions either by offsetting them directly against other taxable income in the year incurred; or, in the event no such income is available in any given year, by carrying them backward or forward against past or future taxable earnings; or, in the extreme case, by merger of the firm with (or its sale to) another firm that can utilize the deduction. Second, it must be assumed that the tax rate will remain the same. To the extent that neither of these conditions holds exactly then some uncertainty attaches even to the tax savings, though, of course, it is of a different kind and order from that attaching to the stream generated by the assets. For simplicity, however, we shall here ignore these possible elements of delay or of uncertainty in the tax saving; but it should be kept in mind that this neglect means that the subsequent valuation formulas overstate, if anything, the value of the tax saving for any given permanent level of debt.

[6] Note that here, as in our original paper, we neglect dividend policy and 'growth' in the sense of opportunities to invest at a rate of return greater than the market rate of return. These subjects are treated extensively in our paper, 'Dividend Policy, Growth and the Valuation of Shares', *Jour. Bus.*, Univ. Chicago, Oct. 1961, 411–33.

and let r be the rate at which the market capitalizes the sure streams generated by debts. For simplicity, assume this rate of interest is a constant independent of the size of the debt so that

$$r = \frac{R}{D} \quad \text{or} \quad D = \frac{R}{r}.[7]$$

Then we would expect the value of a levered firm of size $\overline{X}$, with a permanent level of debt D_L in its capital structure, to be given by:

$$V_L = \frac{(1 - \tau)\overline{X}}{\rho^{\tau}} + \frac{\tau R}{r} = V_U + \tau D_L.[8] \tag{3}$$

In our original paper we asserted instead that, within a risk class, market value would be proportional to expected after-tax return $\overline{X}^{\tau}$ (cf. our original equation [11]), which would imply:

$$V_L = \frac{\overline{X}^{\tau}}{\rho^{\tau}} = \frac{(1 - \tau)\overline{X}}{\rho^{\tau}} + \frac{\tau R}{\rho^{\tau}} = V_U + \frac{r}{\rho^{\tau}} \tau D_L. \tag{4}$$

We will now show that if (3) does not hold, investors can secure a more efficient portfolio by switching from relatively overvalued to relatively undervalued firms. Suppose first that unlevered firms are overvalued or that

$$V_L - \tau D_L < V_U.$$

An investor holding m dollars of stock in the unlevered company has a right to the fraction m/V_U of the eventual outcome, i.e., has the uncertain income

$$Y_U = \left(\frac{m}{V_U}\right)(1 - \tau)\overline{X}Z.$$

Consider now an alternative portfolio obtained by investing m dollars as follows: (1) the portion,

$$m\left(\frac{S_L}{S_L + (1 - \tau)D_L}\right),$$

---

[7] Here and throughout, the corresponding formulas when the rate of interest rises with leverage can be obtained merely by substituting $r(L)$ for r, where L is some suitable measure of leverage.

[8] The assumption that the debt is permanent is not necessary for the analysis. It is employed here both to maintain continuity with the original model and because it gives an upper bound on the value of the tax saving. See in this connection footnote 5 and footnote 9.

is invested in the stock of the levered firm, S_L; and (2) the remaining portion,

$$m\left(\frac{(1 - \tau)D_L}{S_L + (1 - \tau)D_L}\right),$$

is invested in its bonds. The stock component entitles the holder to a fraction,

$$\frac{m}{S_L + (1 - \tau)D_L},$$

of the net profits of the levered company or

$$\left(\frac{m}{S_L + (1 - \tau)D_L}\right)[(1 - \tau)(\overline{X}Z - R_L)].$$

The holding of bonds yields

$$\left(\frac{m}{S_L + (1 - \tau)D_L}\right)[(1 - \tau)R_L].$$

Hence the total outcome is

$$Y_L = \left(\frac{m}{S_L + (1 - \tau)D_L}\right)[(1 - \tau)\overline{X}Z]$$

and this will dominate the uncertain income Y_U if (and only if)

$$S_L + (1 - \tau)D_L \equiv S_L + D_L - \tau D_L \equiv V_L - \tau D_L < V_U.$$

Thus, in equilibrium, V_U cannot exceed $V_L - \tau D_L$, for if it did investors would have an incentive to sell shares in the unlevered company and purchase the shares (and bonds) of the levered company.

Suppose now that $V_L - \tau D_L > V_U$. An investment of m dollars in the stock of the levered firm entitles the holder to the outcome

$$Y_L = (m/S_L)[(1 - \tau)(\overline{X}Z - R_L)]$$
$$= (m/S_L)(1 - \tau)\overline{X}Z - (m/S_L)(1 - \tau)R_L.$$

Consider the following alternative portfolio: (1) borrow an amount (m/S_L) $(1 - \tau)D_L$ for which the interest cost will be $(m/S_L)(1 - \tau)R_L$ (assuming, of course, that individuals and corporations can borrow at the same rate, r); and (2) invest m plus the amount borrowed, i.e.,

$$m + \frac{m(1 - \tau)D_L}{S_L} = m\,\frac{S_L + (1 - \tau)D_L}{S_L} = (m/S_L)[V_L - \tau D_L]$$

in the stock of the unlevered firm. The outcome so secured will be

$$(m/S_L)\left(\frac{V_L - \tau D_L}{V_U}\right)(1 - \tau)\overline{X}Z.$$

Subtracting the interest charges on the borrowed funds leaves an income of

$$Y_U = (m/S_L)\left(\frac{V_L - \tau D_L}{V_U}\right)(1 - \tau)\overline{X}Z - (m/S_L)(1 - \tau)R_L$$

which will dominate Y_L if (and only if) $V_L - \tau D_L > V_U$. Thus, in equilibrium, both $V_L - \tau D_L > V_U$ and $V_L - \tau D_L < V_U$ are ruled out and (3) must hold.

III   Some implications of formula (3)

To see what is involved in replacing (4) with (3) as the rule of valuation, note first that both expressions make the value of the firm a function of leverage and the tax rate. The difference between them is a matter of the size and source of the tax advantages of debt financing. Under our original formulation, values within a class were strictly proportional to expected earnings after taxes. Hence the tax advantage of debt was due solely to the fact that the deductibility of interest payments implied a higher level of after-tax income for any given level of before-tax earnings (i.e., higher by the amount τR since $\overline{X}^\tau = (1 - \tau)\overline{X} + \tau R$). Under the corrected rule (3), however, there is an additional gain due to the fact that the extra after-tax earnings, τR, represent a sure income in contrast to the uncertain outcome $(1 - \tau)\overline{X}$. Hence τR is capitalized at the more favorable certainty rate, $1/r$, rather than at the rate for uncertain streams, $1/\rho^\tau$.[9]

---

[9] Remember, however, that in one sense formula (3) gives only an upper bound on the value of the firm since $\tau R/r = \tau D$ is an exact measure of the value of the tax saving only where both the tax rate and the level of debt are assumed to be fixed forever (and where the firm is certain to be able to use its interest deduction to reduce taxable income either directly or via transfer of the loss to another firm). Alternative versions of (3) can readily be developed for cases in which the debt is not assumed to be permanent, but rather to be outstanding only for some specified finite length of time. For reasons of space, we shall not pursue this line of inquiry here beyond observing that the shorter the debt period considered, the closer does the valuation formula approach our original (4). Hence, the latter is perhaps still of some interest if only as a lower bound.

Since the difference between (3) and (4) is solely a matter of the rate at which the tax savings on interest payments are capitalized, the required changes in all formulas and expressions derived from (4) are reasonably straightforward. Consider, first, the before-tax earnings yield, i.e., the ratio of expected earnings before interest and taxes to the value of the firm.[10] Dividing both sides of (3) by V and by $(1 - \tau)$ and simplifying we obtain:

$$\frac{\overline{X}}{V} = \frac{\rho^\tau}{1 - \tau}\left[1 - \tau\frac{D}{V}\right] \tag{31.c}$$

which replaces our original equation (31) (p.294). The new relation differs from the old in that the coefficient of D/V in the original (31) was smaller by a factor of r/ρ^τ.

Consider next the after-tax earnings yield, i.e., the ratio of interest payments plus profits after taxes to total market value.[11] This concept was discussed extensively in our paper because it helps to bring out more clearly the differences between our position and the traditional view, and because it facilitates the construction of empirical tests of the two hypotheses about the valuation process. To see what the new equation (3) implies for this yield we need merely substitute $\overline{X}^\tau - \tau R$ for $(1 - \tau)\overline{X}$ in (3) obtaining:

$$V = \frac{\overline{X}^\tau - \tau R}{\rho^\tau} + \tau D = \frac{\overline{X}^\tau}{\rho^\tau} + \tau\frac{\rho^\tau - r}{\rho^\tau}D, \tag{5}$$

from which it follows that the after-tax earnings yield must be:

$$\frac{\overline{X}^\tau}{V} = \rho^\tau - \tau(\rho^\tau - r)D/V. \tag{11.c}$$

This replaces our original equation (11)(p.272) in which we had simply $\overline{X}^\tau/V = \rho^\tau$. Thus, in contrast to our earlier result, the corrected version (11.c) implies that even the after-tax yield is affected by leverage. The predicted rate of decrease of $\overline{X}^\tau/V$ with D/V, however, is still considerably smaller than under the naive traditional view, which, as we showed, implied essentially $\overline{X}^\tau/V = \rho^\tau - (\rho^\tau - r)D/V$. See our equation (17) and the discussion immediately preceding

---

[10] Following usage common in the field of finance we referred to this yield as the 'average cost of capital'. We feel now, however, that the term 'before-tax earnings yield' would be preferable both because it is more immediately descriptive and because it releases the term 'cost of capital' for use in discussions of optimal investment policy (in accord with standard usage in the capital budgeting literature).

[11] We referred to this yield as the 'after-tax cost of capital'. Cf. the previous footnote.

it (p.277).[12] And, of course, (11.c) implies that the effect of leverage on $\overline{X}^\tau/V$ is *solely* a matter of the deductibility of interest payments whereas, under the traditional view, going into debt would lower the cost of capital regardless of the method of taxing corporate earnings.

Finally, we have the matter of the after-tax yield on *equity* capital, i.e., the ratio of net profits after taxes to the value of the shares.[13] By subtracting D from both sides of (5) and breaking $\overline{X}^\tau$ into its two components – expected net profits after taxes, $\overline{\pi}^\tau$, and interest payments, $R = rD$ – we obtain after simplifying:

$$S = V - D = \frac{\overline{\pi}^\tau}{\rho^\tau} - (1 - \tau)\left(\frac{\rho^\tau - r}{\rho^\tau}\right)D. \tag{6}$$

From (6) it follows that the after-tax yield on equity capital must be:

$$\frac{\overline{\pi}^\tau}{S} = \rho^\tau + (1 - \tau)[\rho^\tau - r]D/S \tag{12.c}$$

which replaces our original equation (12), $\overline{\pi}^\tau/S = \rho^\tau + (\rho^\tau - r)D/S$ (p.272). The new (12.c) implies an increase in the after-tax yield on equity capital as leverage increases which is smaller than that of our original (12) by a factor of $(1 - \tau)$. But again, the linear increasing relation of the corrected (12.c) is still fundamentally different from the naive traditional view which asserts the cost of equity capital to be completely independent of leverage (at least as long as leverage remains within 'conventional' industry limits).

IV   Taxes and the cost of capital

From these corrected valuation formulas we can readily derive corrected measures of the cost of capital in the capital budgeting sense of the minimum prospective yield an investment project must offer to be just worth undertaking from the standpoint of the present stockholders. If we interpret earnings streams as perpetuities, as we did in the original paper, then we actually have two equally good ways of defining this minimum yield: either by the required increase in before-tax earnings, $d\overline{X}$, or by the required increase in

---

[12] The $i_k{}^\star$ of (17) is the same as ρ^τ in the present context, each measuring the ratio of net profits to the value of the shares (and hence of the whole firm) in an unlevered company of the class.

[13] We referred to this yield as the 'after-tax cost of equity capital'. Cf. footnote 9.

earnings net of taxes, $d\overline{X}(1 - \tau)$.[14] To conserve space, however, as well as to maintain continuity with the original paper, we shall concentrate here on the before-tax case with only brief footnote references to the net-of-tax concept.

Analytically, the derivation of the cost of capital in the above sense amounts to finding the minimum value of $d\overline{X}/dI$ for which $dV = dI$, where I denotes the level of new investment.[15] By differentiating (3) we see that:

$$\frac{dV}{dI} = \frac{1 - \tau}{\rho^\tau} \frac{d\overline{X}}{dI} + \tau \frac{dD}{dI} \geq 1 \qquad \text{if } \frac{d\overline{X}}{dI} \geq \frac{1 - \tau \dfrac{dD}{dI}}{1 - \tau} \rho^\tau. \qquad (7)$$

Hence the before tax required rate of return cannot be defined without reference to financial policy. In particular, for an investment considered as being financed entirely by new equity capital $dD/dI = 0$ and the required rate of return or marginal cost of equity financing (neglecting flotation costs) would be:

$$\rho^S = \frac{\rho^\tau}{1 - \tau}.$$

This result is the same as that in the original paper (see equation [32], p.294) and is applicable to any other sources of financing where the remuneration to the suppliers of capital is not deductible for tax purposes. It applies, therefore, to preferred stock (except for certain partially deductible issues of public utilities) and would apply also to retained earnings were it not for the favorable tax treatment of capital gains under the personal income tax.

For investments considered as being financed entirely by new debt capital $dI = dD$ and we find from (7) that:

$$\rho^D = \rho^\tau \qquad (33.c)$$

---

[14] Note that we use the term 'earnings net of taxes' rather than 'earnings after taxes'. We feel that to avoid confusion the latter term should be reserved to describe what will actually appear in the firm's accounting statements, namely the net cash flow including the tax savings on the interest (our $\overline{X}^\tau$). Since financing sources cannot in general be allocated to particular investments (see below), the after-tax or accounting concept is not useful for capital budgeting purposes, although it can be extremely useful for valuation equations as we saw in the previous section.

[15] Remember that when we speak of the minimum required yield on an investment we are referring in principle only to investments which increase the *scale* of the firm. That is, the new assets must be in the same 'class' as the old. See in this connection, J. Hirshleifer, 'Risk, the Discount Rate and Investment Decisions', *Am. Econ. Rev.*, May 1961, *51*, 112–20 (especially pp.119–20). See also footnote 16.

which replaces our original equation (33) in which we had:

$$\rho^D = \rho^S - \frac{\tau}{1 - \tau} r. \tag{33}$$

Thus for borrowed funds (or any other tax-deductible source of capital) the marginal cost or before-tax required rate of return is simply the market rate of capitalization for net of tax unlevered streams and is thus independent of both the tax rate and the interest rate. This required rate is lower than that implied by our original (33), but still considerably higher than that implied by the traditional view (see esp. pp.276–77 of our paper) under which the before-tax cost of borrowed funds is simply the interest rate, r.

Having derived the above expressions for the marginal costs of debt and equity financing it may be well to warn readers at this point that these expressions represent at best only the hypothetical extremes insofar as costs are concerned and that neither is directly usable as a cut-off criterion for investment planning. In particular, care must be taken to avoid falling into the famous 'Liquigas' fallacy of concluding that if a firm intends to float a bond issue in some given year then its cut-off rate should be set that year at ρ^D; while, if the next issue is to be an equity one, the cut-off is ρ^S. The point is, or course, that no investment can meaningfully be regarded as 100 per cent equity financed if the firm makes any use of debt capital – and most firms do, not only for the tax savings, but for many other reasons having nothing to do with 'cost' in the present static sense (cf. our original paper pp.292–93). And no investment can meaningfully be regarded as 100 per cent debt financed when lenders impose strict limitations on the maximum amount a firm can borrow relative to its equity (and when most firms actually plan on normally borrowing less than this external maximum so as to leave themselves with an emergency reserve of unused borrowing power). Since the firm's long-run capital structure will thus contain both debt and equity capital, investment planning must recognize that, over the long pull, *all* of the firm's assets are really financed by a mixture of debt and equity capital even though only one kind of capital may be raised in any particular year. More precisely, if $L^\star$ denotes the firm's long-run 'target' debt ratio (around which its actual debt ratio will fluctuate as it 'alternately' floats debt issues and retires them with internal or external equity) then the firm can assume, to a first approximation at least, that for any particular investment $dD/dI = L^\star$. Hence, the relevant marginal cost of capital for investment planning, which we shall here denote by $\rho^\star$, is:

$$\rho^\star = \frac{1 - \tau_L^\star}{1 - \tau} \rho^\tau = \rho^S - \frac{\tau}{1 - \tau} \rho^D L^\star = \rho^S(1 - L^\star) + \rho^D L^\star.$$

That is, the appropriate cost of capital for (repetitive) investment decisions over time is, to a first approximation, a weighted average of the costs of debt and equity financing, the weights being the proportions of each in the 'target' capital structure.[16]

V   Some concluding observations

Such, then, are the major corrections that must be made to the various formulas and valuation expressions in our earlier paper. In general, we can say that the force of these corrections has been to increase somewhat the estimate of the tax advantages of debt financing under our model and consequently to reduce somewhat the quantitative difference between the estimates of the effects of leverage under our model and under the naive traditional view. It may be useful to remind readers once again that the existence of a tax advantage for debt financing – even the larger advantage of the corrected version – does not necessarily mean that corporations should at all times seek to use the maximum possible amount of debt in their capital structures. For

---

[16] From the formulas in the text one can readily derive corresponding expressions for the required net-of-tax yield, or net-of-tax cost of capital for any given financing policy. Specifically, let $\tilde{\rho}(L)$ denote the required net-of-tax yield for investment financed with a proportion of debt $L = dD/dI$. (More generally L denotes the proportion financed with tax deductible sources of capital.) Then from (7) we find:

$$\tilde{\rho}(L) = (1-r)\,\frac{d\overline{X}}{dI} = (1 - L\tau)\rho^\tau \tag{8}$$

and the various costs can be found by substituting the appropriate value for L. In particular, if we substitute in this formula the 'target' leverage ratio, $L^\star$, we obtain:

$$\tilde{\rho}^\star \equiv \tilde{\rho}(L^\star) = (1 - \tau L^\star)\rho^\tau$$

and $\tilde{\rho}^\star$ measures the average net-of-tax cost of capital in the sense described above.

   Although the before-tax and the net-of-tax approaches to the cost of capital provide equally good criteria for investment decisions when assets are assumed to generate perpetual (i.e., non-depreciating) streams, such is not the case when assets are assumed to have finite lives (even when it is also assumed that the firm's assets are in a steady state age distribution so that our X or EBIT is approximately the same as the net cash flow before taxes). See footnote 3 above. In the latter event, the correct method for determining the desirability of an investment would be, in principle, to discount the net-of-tax stream at the net-of-tax cost of capital. Only under this net-of-tax approach would it be possible to take into account the deductibility of depreciation (and also to choose the most advantageous depreciation policy for tax purposes). Note that we say that the net-of-tax approach is correct 'in principle' because, strictly speaking, nothing in our analysis (or anyone else's, for that matter) has yet established that it is indeed legitimate to 'discount' an uncertain stream. One can hope that subsequent research will show the analogy to discounting under the certainty case is a valid one; but, at the moment, this is still only a hope.

one thing, other forms of financing, notably retained earnings, may in some circumstances be cheaper still when the tax status of investors under the personal income tax is taken into account. More important, there are, as we pointed out, limitations imposed by lenders (see pp.292–93), as well as many other dimensions (and kinds of costs) in real world problems of financial strategy which are not fully comprehended within the framework of static equilibrium models, either our own or those of the traditional variety. These additional considerations, which are typically grouped under the rubric of 'the need for preserving flexibility', will normally imply the maintenance by the corporation of a substantial reserve of untapped borrowing power. The tax advantage of debt may well tend to lower the optimal size of that reserve, but it is hard to believe that advantages of the size contemplated under our model could justify any substantial reduction, let alone their complete elimination. Nor do the data indicate that there has in fact been a substantial increase in the use of debt (except relative to preferred stock) by the corporate sector during the recent high tax years.[17]

As to the differences between our modified model and the traditional one, we feel that they are still large in quantitative terms and still very much worth trying to detect. It is not only a matter of the two views having different implications for corporate financial policy (or even for national tax policy). But since the two positions rest on fundamentally different views about investor behavior and the functioning of the capital markets, the results of tests between them may have an important bearing on issues ranging far beyond the immediate one of the effects of leverage on the cost of capital.

Reproduced from Modigliani, F. and Miller, M.H. (1963). Corporate income taxes and the cost of capital: a correction. *The American Economic Review,* June, by permission of The American Economic Association.

---

[17] See, e.g., Merton H. Miller, 'The Corporate Income Tax and Corporate Financial Policies', in *Staff Reports to the Commission on Money and Credit* (forthcoming).

16 The capital structure puzzle

S. C. Myers

This paper's title is intended to remind you of Fischer Black's well-known note on 'The Dividend Puzzle', which he closed by saying, "What should the corporation do about dividend policy? We don't know". [6, p.8] I will start by asking, 'How do firms choose their capital structures?' Again, the answer is, 'We don't know'.

The capital structure puzzle is tougher than the dividend one. We know quite a bit about dividend policy. John Lintner's model of how firms set dividends [20] dates back to 1956, and it still seems to work. We know stock prices respond to unanticipated dividend changes, so it is clear that dividends have information content – this observation dates back at least to Miller and Modigliani (MM) in 1961 [28]. We do not know whether high dividend yield increases the expected rate of return demanded by investors, as adding taxes to the MM proof of dividend irrelevance suggests, but financial economists are at least hammering away at this issue.

By contrast, we know very little about capital structure. We do not know how firms choose the debt, equity or hybrid securities they issue. We have only recently discovered that capital structure changes convey information to investors. There has been little if any research testing whether the relationship between financial leverage and investors' required return is as the pure MM theory predicts. In general, we have inadequate understanding of corporate financing behavior, and of how that behavior affects security returns.

I do not want to sound too pessimistic or discouraged. We have accumulated many helpful insights into capital structure choice, starting with the most important one, MM's No Magic in Leverage Theorem (Proposition I) [31]. We have thought long and hard about what these insights imply for optimal capital structure. Many of us have translated these theories, or stories, of optimal capital structure into more or less definite advice to managers. But our theories don't seem to explain actual financing behavior, and it seems presumptuous to advise firms on optimal capital structure when we are so far from explaining actual decisions. I have done more than my share of writing on optimal capital structure, so I take this opportunity to make amends, and to try to push research in some new directions.

I will contrast two ways of thinking about capital structure.

1 A *static tradeoff* framework, in which the firm is viewed as setting a target debt-to-value ratio and gradually moving towards it, in much the same way that a firm adjusts dividends to move towards a target payout ratio.
2 An old-fashioned *pecking order* framework, in which the firm prefers internal to external financing, and debt to equity if it issues securities. In the pure pecking order theory, the firm has no well-defined target debt-to-value ratio.

Recent theoretical work has breathed new life into the pecking order framework. I will argue that this theory performs at least as well as the static tradeoff theory in explaining what we know about actual financing choices and their average impacts on stock prices.

Managerial and neutral mutation hypotheses

I have arbitrarily, and probably unfairly, excluded 'managerial' theories which might explain firms' capital structure choices.[1] I have chosen not to consider models which cut the umbilical cord that ties managers' acts to stockholders' interests.

I am also sidestepping Miller's idea of 'neutral mutation'.[2] He suggests that firms fall into some financing patterns or habits which have no material effect on firm value. The habits may make managers feel better, and since they do no harm, no one cares to stop or change them. Thus someone who identifies these habits and uses them to predict financing behavior would not be explaining anything important.

The neutral mutations idea is important as a warning. Given time and imagination, economists can usually invent some model that assigns apparent

---

[1] The finance and economics literature has at least three 'managerial' strands: (1) descriptions of managerial capitalism, in which the separation of ownership and control is taken as a central fact of life, for example Berle and Means [5]; (2) agency theory, pioneered for finance by Jensen and Meckling [18]; and (3) the detailed analysis of the personal risks and rewards facing managers and how their responses affect firms' financing or investment choices. For examples of Strand (3), see Ross's articles on financial signalling [36,37].

[2] Put forward in 'Debt and Taxes', [27], esp. pp.272–273. Note that Miller did not claim that all of firms' financing habits are neutral mutations, only that some of them may be. I doubt that Miller intended this idea as a strict null hypothesis (see below).

economic rationality to any random event. But taking neutral mutation as a strict null hypothesis makes the game of research too tough to play. If an economist identifies costs of various financing strategies, obtains independent evidence that the costs are really there, and then builds a model based on these costs which explains firms' financing behavior, then some progress has been made, even it if proves difficult to demonstrate that, say, a type *A* financing strategy gives higher firm value than a type *B*. (In fact, we would never see type *B* if all firms follow value-maximizing strategies.)

There is another reason for not immediately embracing neutral mutations: we know investors are interested in the firm's financing choices, because stock prices change when the choices are announced. The change might be explained as an 'information effect' having nothing to do with financing per se – but again, it is a bit too easy to wait until the results of an event study are in, and then to think of an information story to explain them. On the other hand, if one starts by assuming that managers have special information, builds a model of how that information changes financing choices, and predicts which choices will be interpreted by investors as good or bad news, then some progress has been made.

So this paper is designed as a one-on-one competition of the static tradeoff and pecking-order stories. If neither story explains actual behavior, the neutral mutations story will be there faithfully waiting.

The static tradeoff hypothesis

A firm's optimal debt ratio is usually viewed as determined by a tradeoff of the costs and benefits of borrowing, holding the firm's assets and investment plans constant. The firm is portrayed as balancing the value of interest tax shields against various costs of bankruptcy or financial embarrassment. Of course, there is controversy about how valuable the tax shields are, and which, if any, of the costs of financial embarrassment are material, but these disagreements give only variations on a theme. The firm is supposed to substitute debt for equity, or equity for debt, until the value of the firm is maximized. Thus the debt-equity tradeoff is as illustrated in Figure 1.

Costs of adjustment

If there were no costs of adjustment, and the static tradeoff theory is correct, then each firm's observed debt-to-value ratio should be its optimal ratio. However, there must be costs, and therefore lags, in adjusting to the optimum. Firms cannot immediately offset the random events that bump them away

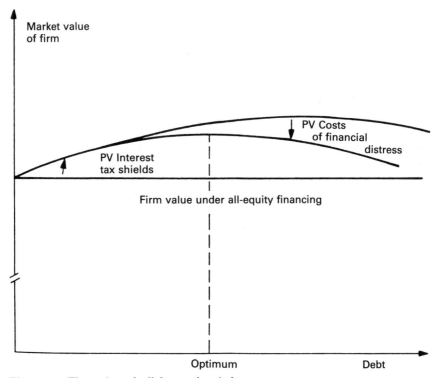

Figure 1   *The static tradeoff theory of capital structure*

from the optimum, so there should be some cross-sectional dispersion of actual debt ratios across a sample of firms having the same target ratio.

Large adjustment costs could possibly explain the observed wide variation in actual debt ratios, since firms would be forced into long excursions away from their optimal ratios. But there is nothing in the usual static tradeoff stories suggesting that adjustment costs are a first-order concern – in fact, they are rarely mentioned. Invoking them without modelling them is a cop-out.

Any cross-sectional test of financing behavior should specify whether firms' debt ratios differ because they have different optimal ratios or because their actual ratios diverge from optimal ones. It is easy to get the two cases mixed up. For example, think of the early cross-sectional studies which attempted to test MM's Proposition I. These studies tried to find out whether differences in leverage affected the market value of the firm (or the market capitalization rate for its operating income). With hindsight, we can quickly see the problem: if adjustment costs are small, and each firm in the sample is at, or close to its optimum, then the in-sample dispersion of debt ratios must reflect differences in risk or in other variables affecting optimal capital structure. But then MM's Proposition I cannot be tested unless the effects of risk and other variables on firm value can be adjusted for. By now we have learned from experience how hard it is to hold 'other things constant' in cross-sectional regressions.

Of course, one way to make sense of these tests is to assume that adjustment costs are small, but managers don't know, or don't care, what the optimal debt ratio is, and thus do not stay close to it. The researcher then assumes some (usually unspecified) 'managerial' theory of capital structure choice. This may be a convenient assumption for a cross-sectional test of MM's Proposition I, but not very helpful if the object is to understand financing behavior.[3]

But suppose we don't take this 'managerial' fork. Then if adjustment costs are small, and firms stay near their target debt ratios, I find it hard to understand the observed diversity of capital structures across firms that seem similar in a static tradeoff framework. If adjustment costs are large, so that some firms take extended excursions away from their targets, then we ought to give less attention to refining our static tradeoff stories and relatively more to understanding what the adjustment costs are, why they are so important, and how rational managers would respond to them.

But I am getting ahead of my story. On to debt and taxes.

Debt and taxes

Miller's famous 'Debt and Taxes' paper [27] cut us loose from the extreme implications of the original MM theory, which made interest tax shields so valuable that we could not explain why all firms were not awash in debt. Miller described an equilibrium of *aggregate* supply and demand for corporate debt,

---

[3] The only early cross-sectional study I know of which sidesteps these issues is MM's 1966 paper on the cost of capital for the electric utility industry [28]. Their 'corrected' theory says that firm value is independent of capital structure except for the value added by the present value of interest tax shields. Thus tax-paying firms would be expected to substitute debt for equity, at least up to the point where the probability of financial distress starts to be important. However, the regulated firms MM examined had little tax incentive to use debt, because their interest tax shields were passed through to consumers. If a regulated firm pays an extra one dollar of interest, and thus saves T_c in corporate income taxes, regulators are supposed to reduce the firm's pre-tax operating income by $T_c/(1 - T_c)$, the grossed-up value of the tax saving. This roughly cancels out any tax advantage of borrowing. Thus regulated firms should have little incentive to borrow enough to flirt with financial distress, and their debt ratios could be dispersed across a conservative range.

Moreover, MM's test could pick up the present value of interest tax shields *provided* they adjusted for differences in operating income. Remember, interest tax shields are not eliminated by regulation, just offset by reductions in allowed operating income.

Thus regulated firms are relatively good subjects for cross-sectional tests of static tradeoff theories. MM's theory seemed to work fairly well for three years in the mid-1950s. Unfortunately, MM's equations didn't give sensible coefficients when fitted on later data (see for example, Robicheck, McDonald and Higgins [35]). There has been little further work attempting to extend or adapt MM's 1966 model. In the meantime, theory has moved on.

in which personal income taxes paid by the marginal investor in corporate debt just offset the corporate tax saving. However, since the equilibrium only determines aggregates, debt policy should not matter for any single tax-paying firm. Thus Miller's model allows us to explain the dispersion of actual debt policies without having to introduce non-value-maximizing managers.[4]

Trouble is, this explanation works only if we assume that all firms face approximately the same marginal tax rate, and *that* is an assumption we can immediately reject. The extensive trading of depreciation tax shields and investment tax credits, through financial leases and other devices, proves that plenty of firms face low marginal rates.[5]

Given significant differences in effective marginal tax rates, and given that the static tradeoff theory works, we would expect to find a strong tax effect in any cross-sectional test, regardless of whose theory of debt and taxes you believe.

Figure 2 plots the net tax gain from corporate borrowing against the expected realizable tax shield from a future deduction of one dollar of interest paid. For some firms this number is 46 cents, or close to it. At the other extreme, there are firms with large unused loss carryforwards which pay no immediate taxes. An extra dollar of interest paid by these firms would create only a potential future deduction, usable when and if the firm earns enough to work off prior carryforwards. The expected realizable tax shield is positive but small. Also, there are firms paying taxes today which cannot be sure they will do so in the future. Such a firm values expected future interest tax shields at somewhere between zero and the full statutory rate.

In the 'corrected' MM theory [28] any tax-paying corporation gains by borrowing; the greater the marginal tax rate, the greater the gain. This gives the top line in the figure. In Miller's theory, the personal income taxes on interest payments would exactly offset the corporate interest tax shield, provided that the firm pays the full statutory tax rate. However, any firm paying a lower rate would see a net loss to corporate borrowing and a net gain to lending. This gives the bottom line.

There are also compromise theories, advanced by D'Angelo and Masulis [12], Modigliani [30] and others, indicated by the middle dashed line in the figure. The compromise theories are appealing because they seem less extreme than either the MM or Miller theories. But regardless of which theory holds, the *slope* of the line is always positive. The *difference* between (1) the tax advantage of borrowing to firms facing the full statutory rate, and (2) the tax

---

[4] Although Miller's 'Debt and Taxes' model [27] was a major conceptual step forward, I do not consider it an adequate description of how taxes affect optimum capital structure or expected rates of return on debt and equity securities. See Gordon and Malkiel [16] for a recent review of the evidence.

[5] Cordes and Scheffrin [8] present evidence on the cross-sectional dispersion of effective corporate tax rates.

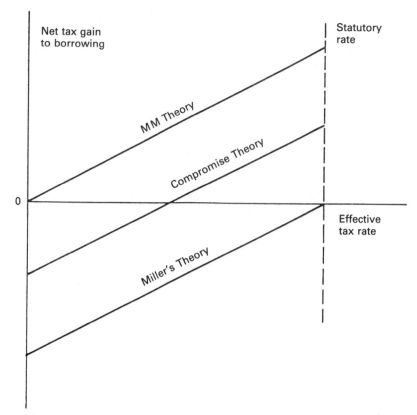

Figure 2 *The net tax gain to corporate borrowing*

advantage of lending (or at least *not* borrowing) to firms with large tax loss carryforwards, is exactly the same as in the 'extreme' theories. Thus, although the theories tell different stories about aggregate supply and demand of corporate debt, they make essentially the same predictions about which firms borrow more or less than average.

So the tax side of the static tradeoff theory predicts that IBM should borrow more than Bethlehem Steel, other things equal, and that General Motors' debt-to-value ratio should be more than Chrysler's.

Costs of financial distress

Costs of financial distress include the legal and administrative costs of bankruptcy, as well as the subtler agency, moral hazard, monitoring and contracting costs which can erode firm value even if formal default is avoided. We know these costs exist, although we may debate their magnitude. For example, there is no satisfactory explanation of debt covenants unless agency costs and moral hazard problems are recognized.

The literature on costs of financial distress supports two qualitative statements about financing behavior.[6]

1 Risky firms ought to borrow less, other things equal. Here 'risk' would be defined as the variance rate of the market value of the firm's assets. The higher the variance rate, the greater the probability of default on any given package of debt claims. Since costs of financial distress are caused by threatened or actual default, safe firms ought to be able to borrow more before expected costs of financial distress offset the tax advantages of borrowing.

2 Firms holding tangible assets in-place having active second-hand markets will borrow less than firms holding specialized, intangible assets or valuable growth opportunities. The expected cost of financial distress depends not just on the probability of trouble, but the value lost if trouble comes. Specialized, intangible assets or growth opportunities are more likely to lose value in financial distress.

The pecking order theory

Contrast the static tradeoff theory with a competing popular story based on a financing pecking order:

1 Firms prefer internal finance.

2 They adapt their target dividend payout ratios to their investment opportunities, although dividends are sticky and target payout ratios are only gradually adjusted to shifts in the extent of valuable investment opportunities.

3 Sticky dividend policies, plus unpredictable fluctuations in profitability and investment opportunities, mean that internally-generated cash flow may be more or less than investment outlays. If it is less, the firm first draws down its cash balance or marketable securities portfolio.[7]

---

[6] I have discussed these two points in more detail in [32 and 33].

[7] If it is more, the firm first pays off debt or invests in cash or marketable securities. If the surplus persists, it may gradually increase its target payout ratio.

4 If external finance is required, firms issue the safest security first. That is, they start with debt, then possibly hybrid securities such as convertible bonds, then perhaps equity as a last resort. In this story, there is no well-defined target debt-equity mix, because there are two kinds of equity, internal and external, one at the top of the pecking order and one at the bottom. Each firm's observed debt ratio reflects its cumulative requirements for external finance.

The pecking order literature

The pecking order hypothesis is hardly new.[8] For example, it comes through loud and clear in Donaldson's 1961 study of the financing practices of a sample of large corporations. He observed [13, p.67] that 'Management strongly favored internal generation as a source of new funds even to the exclusion of external funds except for occasional unavoidable "bulges" in the need for funds.' These bulges were not generally met by cutting dividends: Reducing the 'customary cash dividend payment . . . was unthinkable to most managements except as a defensive measure in a period of extreme financial distress' (p.70). Given that external finance was needed, managers rarely thought of issuing stock:

> Though few companies would go so far as to rule out a sale of common under any circumstances, the large majority had not had such a sale in the past 20 years and did not anticipate one in the foreseeable future. This was particularly remarkable in view of the very high Price-Earnings ratios of recent years. Several financial officers showed that they were well aware that this had been a good time to sell common, but the reluctance still persisted (pp.57–58).

Of course, the pecking order hypothesis can be quickly rejected if we require it to explain everything. There are plenty of examples of firms issuing stock when they could issue investment-grade debt. But when one looks at aggregates, the heavy reliance on internal finance and debt is clear. For all non-financial corporations over the decade 1973–1982, internally generated cash covered, on average, 62 percent of capital expenditures, including investment in inventory and other current assets. The bulk of required external financing came from borrowing. Net new stock issues were never more than 6 percent of external financing.[9] Anyone innocent of modern finance who looked at these statistics would find the pecking order idea entirely plausible, at least as a description of typical behavior.

---

[8] Although I have not seen the term 'pecking order' used before.
[9] These figures were computed from Brealey and Myers [7], Table 14–3, p.291.

Writers on 'managerial capitalism' have interpreted firms' reliance on internal finance as a byproduct of the separation of ownership and control: professional managers avoid relying on external finance because it would subject them to the discipline of the capital market.[10] Donaldson's 1969 book was not primarily about managerial capitalism, but he nevertheless observed that the financing decisions of the firms he studied were *not* directed towards maximizing shareholder wealth, and that scholars attempting to explain those decisions would have to start by recognizing the 'managerial view' of corporate finance. [14. Ch.2]

This conclusion is natural given the state of finance theory in the 1960s. Today it is not so obvious that financing by a pecking order goes against shareholders' interests.

External financing with asymmetric information

I used to ignore the pecking order story because I could think of no theoretical foundation for it that would fit in with the theory of modern finance. An argument could be made for internal financing to avoid issue costs, and if external finance is needed, for debt to avoid the still higher costs of equity. But issue costs in themselves do not seem large enough to override the costs and benefits of leverage emphasized in the static tradeoff story. However, recent work based on asymmetric information gives predictions roughly in line with the pecking order theory. The following brief exposition is based on a forthcoming joint paper by me and Nicholas Majluf [34], although I will here boil down that paper's argument to absolute essentials.

Suppose the firm has to raise N dollars in order to undertake some potentially valuable investment opportunity. Let y be this opportunity's net present value (NPV) and x be what the firm will be worth if the opportunity is passed by. The firm's manager knows what x and y are, but investors in capital markets do not: they see only a joint distribution of possible values ($\tilde{x}$, $\tilde{y}$). The information asymmetry is taken as given. Aside from the information asymmetry, capital markets are perfect and semi-strong form efficient. MM's Proposition I holds in the sense that the stock of debt relative to real assets is irrelevant if information available to investors is held constant.

The *benefit* to raising N dollars by a security issue is y, the NPV of the firm's investment opportunity. There is also a possible cost: the firm may have to sell the securities for less than they are really worth. Suppose the firm issues *stock* with an aggregate market value, when issued, of N. (I will consider debt issues in a moment.) However, the manager knows the shares are really worth N_1. That is, N_1 is what the new shares will be worth, other things equal, when investors acquire the manager's special knowledge.

---

[10] For example, see Berle [4], or Berle and Means [5].

Majluf and I discuss several possible objectives managers might pursue in this situation. The one we think makes the most sense is maximizing the 'true', or 'intrinsic' value of the firm's *existing* shares. That is, the manager worries about the value of the 'old' shareholders' stake in the firm. Moreover, investors know the manager will do this. In particular, the 'new' investors who purchase any stock issue will assume that the manager is *not* on their side, and will rationally adjust the price they are willing to pay.

Define ΔN as the amount by which the shares are over- or undervalued: $\Delta N \equiv N_1 - N$. Then the manager will issue and invest when

$$y \geq \Delta N. \tag{1}$$

If the manager's inside information is unfavorable, ΔN is negative and the firm will always issue, even if the only good use for the funds raised is to put them in the bank – a zero-NPV investment.[11] If the inside information is favorable, however, the firm may pass up a positive-NPV investment opportunity rather than issue undervalued shares.

But if management acts this way, its decision to issue will signal bad news to both old and new shareholders. Let V be the market value of the firm (price per share times number of shares) if it does *not* issue, and V' be market value if it does issue; V' includes the value of the newly-issued shares. Thus, if everyone knows that managers will act according to Inequality (1), the conditions for a rational expectations equilibrium are:[12]

$$V = E(\tilde{x} \mid \text{no issue}) = E(\tilde{x} \mid y < \Delta N) \tag{2a}$$

$$V' = E(\tilde{x} + \tilde{y} + N \mid \text{issue}) = E(\tilde{x} + \tilde{y} + N \mid y \geq \Delta N). \tag{2b}$$

The total dollar amount raised is fixed by assumption, but the number of new shares needed to raise that amount is not. Thus ΔN is endogenous: it

---

[11] If the firm always has a zero-NPV opportunity available to it, the distribution of $\tilde{y}$ is truncated at $\tilde{y} = 0$. I also assume that $\tilde{x}$ is non-negative.

[12] The simple model embodied in (1) and (2) is a direct descendant of Akerlof's work [1]. He investigated how markets can fail when buyers cannot verify the quality of what they are offered. Faced with the risk of buying a lemon, the buyer will demand a discount, which in turn discourages the potential sellers who do *not* have lemons. However, in Majluf's and my model, the seller is offering not a single good, but a partial claim on two, the investment project (worth y) and the firm without the project (worth x). The information asymmetry applies to both goods – for example, the manager may receive inside information that amounts to good news about x and bad news about y, or vice versa, or good or bad news about both.

Moreover, the firm may suffer by not selling stock, because the investment opportunity is lost. Management will sometimes issue even when the stock is undervalued by investors. Consequently, investors on the other side of the transaction do not automatically interpret every stock issue as an attempted ripoff – if they did, stock would never be issued in a rational expectations equilibrium.

depends on V'. For example, if the firm issues, the fraction of all shares held by 'new' stockholders is N/V'. The manager sees the true value of their claim as:

$$N_1 = \frac{N}{V'}(x + y + N) \tag{3}$$

Thus, given N, x and y, and given that stock is issued, the greater the price per share, the less value is given up to new stockholders, and the less ΔN is.

Majluf and I have discussed the assumptions and implications of this model in considerable detail. But here are the two key points:

1 *The cost of relying on external financing.* We usually think of the cost of external finance as administrative and underwriting costs, and in some cases underpricing of the new securities. Asymmetric information creates the possibility of a different sort of cost: the possibility that the firm will choose *not* to issue, and will therefore pass up a positive-NPV investment. This cost is avoided if the firm can retain enough internally-generated cash to cover its positive-NPV opportunities.

2 *The advantages of debt over equity issues.* If the firm does seek external funds, it is better off issuing debt than equity securities. The general rule is, 'Issue safe securities before risky ones'.

This second point is worth explaining further. Remember that the firm issues and invests if y, the NPV of its investment opportunity, is greater than or equal to ΔN, the amount by which the new shares are undervalued (if $\Delta N > 0$) or overvalued (if $\Delta N < 0$). For example, suppose the investment requires $N = \$10$ million, but in order to raise that amount the firm must issue shares that are really worth \$12 million. It will go ahead only if project NPV is at least \$2 million. If it is worth only \$1.5 million, the firm refuses to raise the money for it; the intrinsic overall value of the firm is reduced by \$1.5 million, but the old shareholders are \$0.5 million better off.

The manager could have avoided this problem by building up the firm's cash reserves – but that is hindsight. The only thing he can do now is to redesign the security issue to reduce ΔN. For example, if ΔN could be cut to \$0.5 million, the investment project could be financed without diluting the true value of existing shares. The way to reduce ΔN is to issue the safest possible securities – strictly speaking, securities whose future value changes least when the manager's inside information is revealed to the market.

Of course, ΔN is endogenous, so it is loose talk to speak of the manager controlling it. However, there are reasonable cases in which the absolute value of ΔN is always less for debt than for equity. For example, if the firm can issue default-risk free debt, ΔN is zero, and the firm never passes up a valuable investment opportunity. Thus, the ability to issue default-risk free debt is as good as cash in the bank. Even if default risk is introduced, the absolute value of ΔN will be less for debt than for equity if we make the customary assumptions of option pricing models.[13] Thus, if the manager has favorable information ($\Delta N > 0$), it is better to issue debt than equity.

This example assumes that new shares or risky debt would be underpriced. What if the managers' inside information is *unfavorable*, so that any risky security issue would be *over*priced? In this case, wouldn't the firm want to make ΔN as *large* as possible, to take maximum advantage of new investors? If so, stock would seem better than debt (and warrants better still). The decision rule seems to be, 'Issue debt when investors undervalue the firm, and equity, or some other risky security, when they overvalue it'.

The trouble with this strategy is obvious once you put yourself in investors' shoes. If you know the firm will issue equity only when it is overpriced, and debt otherwise, you will refuse to buy equity unless the firm has already exhausted its 'debt capacity' – that is, unless the firm has issued so much debt already that it would face substantial additional costs in issuing more. Thus investors would effectively force the firm to follow a pecking order.

Now this is clearly too extreme. The model just presented would need lots of fleshing out before it could fully capture actual behavior. I have presented it just to show how models based on asymmetric information can predict the two central ideas of the pecking order story: first, the preference for internal finance, and, second, the preference for debt over equity if external financing is sought.

What we know about corporate financing behavior

I will now list what we know about financing behavior and try to make sense of this knowledge in terms of the two hypotheses sketched above. I begin with five facts about financing behavior, and then offer a few generalizations from weaker statistical evidence or personal observation. Of course even 'facts' based on apparently good statistics have been known to melt away under further examination, so read with caution.

---

[13] This amounts to assuming that changes in firm value are lognormally distributed, that managers and investors agree on the variance rate, and that managers know the current value of $\tilde{x} + \tilde{y}$ but investors do not. If there is asymmetric information about the variance rate, but not about firm value at the time of issue, the pecking order could be reversed. See Giammarino and Neave [15].

Internal vs external equity

Aggregate investment outlays are predominantly financed by debt issues and internally-generated funds. New stock issues play a relatively small part. Moreover, as Donaldson has observed, this is what many managers say they are trying to do.

This fact is what suggested the pecking order hypothesis in the first place. However, it might also be explained in a static tradeoff theory by adding significant transaction costs of equity issues and noting the favorable tax treatment of capital gains relative to dividends. This would make external equity relatively expensive. It would explain why companies keep target dividend payouts low enough to avoid having to make regular stock issues.[14] It would also explain why a firm whose debt ratio soars above target does not immediately issue stock, buy back debt, and re-establish a more moderate debt-to-value ratio. Thus firms might take extended excursions *above* their debt targets. (Note, however, that the static tradeoff hypothesis as usually presented rarely mentions this kind of adjustment cost.)

But the out-of-pocket costs of *repurchasing* shares seems fairly small. It is thus hard to explain extended excursions *below* a firm's debt target by an augmented static tradeoff theory – the firm could quickly issue debt and buy back shares. Moreover, if personal income taxes are important in explaining firms' apparent preferences for internal equity, then it's difficult to explain why *external* equity is not strongly *negative* – that is, why most firms haven't gradually moved to materially lower target payout ratios and used the released cash to repurchase shares.

Timing of security issues

Firms apparently try to 'time' stock issues when security prices are 'high'. *Given that they seek external finance*, they are more likely to issue stock (rather than debt) after stock prices have risen than after they have fallen. For example, past stock price movements were one of the best-performing variables in Marsh's study [22] of British firms' choices between new debt and new equity issues. Taggart [39] and others[15] have found similar behavior in the United States.

---

[14] Regulated firms, particularly electric utilities, typically pay dividends generous enough to force regular trips to the equity market. They have a special reason for this policy: it improves their bargaining position vs. consumers and regulators. It turns the opportunity cost of capital into cash requirements.

[15] Jalilvand and Harris [16], for example.

This fact is embarrassing to static tradeoff advocates. If firm value rises, the debt-to-value ratio falls, and firms ought to issue *debt*, not equity, to rebalance their capital structures.

The fact is equally embarrassing to the pecking order hypothesis. There is no reason to believe that the manager's inside information is systematically more favorable when stock prices are 'high'. Even if there were such a tendency, investors would have learned it by now, and would interpret the firm's issue decision accordingly. There is no way firms can *systematically* take advantage of purchasers of new equity in a rational expectations equilibrium.

Borrowing against intangibles and growth opportunities

Firms holding valuable intangible assets or growth opportunities tend to borrow less than firms holding mostly tangible assets. For example, Long and Malitz [21] found a significant negative relationship between rates of investment in advertising and research and development (R & D) and the level of borrowing. They also found a significant *positive* relationship between the rate of capital expenditure (in fixed plant and equipment) and the level of borrowing.

Williamson [41] reached the same conclusion by a different route. His proxy for a firm's intangibles and growth opportunities was the difference between the market value of its debt and equity securities and the replacement cost of its tangible assets. The higher this proxy, he found, the less the firm's debt-to-value ratio.

There is plenty of indirect evidence indicating that the level of borrowing is determined not just by the value and risk of the firm's assets, but also by the type of assets it holds. For example, without this distinction, the static tradeoff theory would specify all target debt ratios in terms of market, not book values. Since many firms have market values far in excess of book values (even if those book values are restated in current dollars), we ought to see at least a few such firms operating comfortably at *very* high book debt ratios – and of course we do not. This fact begins to make sense, however, as soon as we realize that book values reflect assets-in-place (tangible assets and working capital). Market values reflect intangibles and growth opportunities as well as assets-in-place. Thus, firms do not set target book debt ratios because accountants certify the books. Book asset values are proxies for the values of assets in place.[16]

---

[16] The problem is not that intangibles and growth opportunities are risky. The *securities* of growth firms may be excellent collateral. But the firm which borrows against intangibles or growth opportunities may end up reducing their value.

Exchange offers

Masulis [23,24] has shown that stock prices rise, on average, when a firm offers to exchange debt for equity, and fall when they offer to exchange equity for debt. This fact could be explained in various ways. For example, it might be a tax effect. If most firms' debt ratios are below their optimal ratios (i.e., to the left of the optimum in Figure 1), and if corporate interest tax shields have significant positive value, the debt-for-equity exchanges would tend to move firms closer to optimum capital structure. Equity-for-debt swaps would tend to move them farther away.

The evidence on exchanges hardly builds confidence in the static tradeoff theory as a description of financing behavior. If the theory were right, firms would be sometimes above, and sometimes below, their optimum ratios. Those above would offer to exchange equity for debt. Those below would offer debt for equity. In both cases, the firm would move closer to the optimum. Why should an exchange offer be good news if in one direction and bad news if in the other?

As Masulis points out, the firm's willingness to exchange debt for equity might signal that the firm's debt capacity had, in management's opinion, increased. That is, it would signal an increase in firm value or a reduction in firm risk. Thus, a debt-for-equity exchange would be good news, and the opposite exchange bad news.

This 'information effect' explanation for exchange offers is surely right in one sense. Any time an announcement affects stock price, we can infer that the announcement conveyed information. That is not much help except to prove that managers have some information investors do not have.

The idea that an exchange offer reveals a change in the firm's target debt ratio, and thereby signals changes in firm value or risk, sounds plausible. But an equally plausible story can be told without saying anything about a target debt ratio. If the manager with superior information acts to maximize the intrinsic value of existing shares, then the announcement of a stock issue should be bad news, other things equal, because stock issues will be more likely when the *manager* receives bad news.[17] On the other hand, stock retirements should be good news. The news in both cases has no evident necessary connection with shifts in target debt ratios.

It may be possible to build a model combining asymmetric information with the costs and benefits of borrowing emphasized in static tradeoff stories. My guess, however, is that it will prove difficult to do this without also introducing some elements of the pecking order story.

---

[17] This follows from the simple model presented above. See Myers and Majluf [34] for a formal proof.

Issue or repurchase of shares

The fifth fact is no surprise given the fourth. On average, stock price falls when firms announce a stock issue. Stock prices rise, on average, when a stock repurchase is announced. This fact has been confirmed in several studies, including those by Korwar [19], Asquith and Mullins [2], Dann and Mikkleson [10], and Vermaelen [40], and DeAngelo, DeAngelo and Rice [11].

This fact is again hard to explain by a static tradeoff model, except as an information effect in which stock issues or retirements signal changes in the firm's target debt ratio. I've already commented on that.

The simple asymmetric information model I used to motivate the pecking order hypothesis does predict that the announcement of a stock issue will cause stock price to fall. It also predicts that stock price should *not* fall, other things equal, if default-risk debt is issued. Of course, no private company can issue debt that is absolutely protected from default, but it seems reasonable to predict that the average stock price impact of high-grade debt issues will be small relative to the average impact of stock issues. This is what Dann and Mikkleson [10] find.

These results may make one a bit more comfortable with asymmetric information models of the kind sketched above, and thus a bit more comfortable with the pecking order story.

That's the five facts. Here now are three items that do not qualify for that list – just call them 'observations'.

Existence of target ratios

Marsh [22] and Taggart [39] have found some evidence that firms adjust towards a target debt-to-value ratio. However, a model based solely on this partial adjustment process would have a very low R^2. Apparently the static tradeoff model captures only a small part of actual behavior.[18]

Risk

Risky firms tend to borrow less, other things equal. For example, both Long and Malitz [21] and Williamson [41] found significant negative relationships between unlevered betas and the level of borrowing. However, the evidence on risk and debt policy is not extensive enough to be totally convincing.

---

[18] Of course, we could give each firm its own target, and leave that target free to wander over time. But then we would explain everything and know nothing. We want a theory which predicts how debt ratios vary across firms and time.

Taxes

I know of no study clearly demonstrating that a firm's tax status has predictable, material effects on its debt policy.[19] I think the wait for such a study will be protracted.

Admittedly it's hard to classify firms by tax status without implicitly classifying them on other dimensions as well. For example, firms with large tax loss carryforwards may also be firms in financial distress, which have high debt ratios almost by definition. Firms with high operating profitability, and therefore plenty of unshielded income, may also have valuable intangible assets and growth opportunities. Do they end up with a higher or lower than average debt-to-value ratio? Hard to say.

Conclusion

People feel comfortable with the static tradeoff story because it sounds plausible and yields an interior optimum debt ratio. It rationalizes 'moderate' borrowing.

Well, the story may be moderate and plausible, but that does not make it right. We have to ask whether it explains firms' financing behavior. If it does, fine. If it does not, then we need a better theory before offering advice to managers.

The static tradeoff story works to some extent, but it seems to have an unacceptably low R^2. Actual debt ratios vary widely across apparently similar firms. Either firms take extended excursions from their targets, or the targets themselves depend on factors not yet recognized or understood.

At this point we face a tactical choice between two research strategies. First, we could try to expand the static tradeoff story by introducing adjustment costs, possibly including those stemming from asymmetric information and agency problems. Second, we could *start* with a story based on asymmetric information and expand it by adding only those elements of the static tradeoff which have clear empirical support. I think we will progress farther faster by the latter route.

Here is what I really think is going on. I warn you that the following 'modified pecking order' story is grossly oversimplified and underqualified. But I think it is generally consistent with the empirical evidence.

---

[19] For example, both Williamson [41] and Long and Malitz [21] introduced proxies for firms' tax status, but failed to find any significant, independent effect on debt ratios.

1 Firms have good reasons to avoid having to finance real investment by issuing common stock or other risky securities. They do not want to run the risk of falling into the dilemma of either passing by positive-NPV projects or issuing stock at a price they think is too low.

2 They set target dividend payout ratios so that normal rates of equity investment can be met by internally generated funds.

3 The firm may also plan to cover part of normal investment outlays with new borrowing, but it tries to restrain itself enough to keep the debt safe – that is, reasonably close to default-risk free. It restrains itself for two reasons: first, to avoid any material costs of financial distress; and second, to maintain financial slack in the form of reserve borrowing power. 'Reserve borrowing power' means that it can issue safe debt if it needs to.

4 Since target dividend payout ratios are sticky, and investment opportunities fluctuate relative to internal cash flow, the firm will from time to time exhaust its ability to issue safe debt. When this happens, the firm turns to less risky securities first – for example, risky debt or convertibles before common stock.

The crucial difference between this and the static tradeoff story is that, in the modified pecking order story, observed debt ratios will reflect the cumulative requirement for external financing – a requirement cumulated over an extended period.[20] For example, think of an unusually profitable firm in an industry generating relatively slow growth. That firm will end up with an unusually low debt ratio compared to its industry's average, *and it won't do much of anything about it*. It won't go out of its way to issue debt and retire equity to achieve a more normal debt ratio.

An unprofitable firm in the same industry will end up with a relatively high debt ratio. If it is high enough to create significant costs of financial distress, the firm *may* rebalance its capital structure by issuing equity. On the other hand, it may not. The same asymmetric information problems which sometimes prevent a firm from issuing stock to finance real investment will sometimes also block issuing stock to retire debt.[21]

If this story is right, average debt ratios will vary from industry to industry, because asset risk, asset type, and requirements for external funds also vary by industry. But a long-run industry average will not be a meaningful target for individual firms in that industry.

---

[20] The length of that period reflects the time required to make a significant shift in a target dividend payout ratio.

[21] The factors that make financial distress costly also make it difficult to escape. The gain in firm value from rebalancing is highest when the firm has gotten into deep trouble and lenders have absorbed a significant capital loss. In that case, rebalancing gives lenders a windfall gain. This is why firms in financial distress often do not rebalance their capital structures.

Let me wrap this up by noting the two clear gaps in my description of 'what is really going on'. First, the modified pecking order story depends on sticky dividends, but does not explain why they are sticky. Second, it leaves us with at best a fuzzy understanding of when and why firms issue common equity. Unfortunately I have nothing to say on the first weakness, and only the following brief comments on the second.

The modified pecking order story recognizes both asymmetric information and costs of financial distress. Thus the firm faces two increasing costs as it climbs up the pecking order: it faces higher odds of incurring costs of financial distress and also higher odds that future positive-NPV projects will be passed by because the firm will be unwilling to finance them by issuing common stock or other risky securities. The firm may choose to reduce these costs by issuing stock now even if new equity is not needed immediately to finance real investment, just to move the firm *down* the pecking order. In other words, financial slack (liquid assets or reserve borrowing power) is valuable, and the firm may rationally issue stock to acquire it. (I say 'may' because the firm which issues equity to buy financial slack faces the same asymmetric information problems as a firm issuing equity to finance real investment.) The optimal *dynamic* issue strategy for the firm under asymmetric information is, as far as I know, totally unexplored territory.[22]

References

1 Akerlof, G.A., 'The Market for "Lemons": Quality and the Market Mechanism', *Quarterly Journal of Economics*, 84 (August 1970), 488–500.
2 Asquith, P. and D.W. Mullins, 'Equity Issues and Stock Price Dilution', Working Paper, Harvard Business School, May 1983.
3 Barges, A., *The Effect of Capital Structure on the Cost of Capital*, Prentice-Hall, Inc., Englewood Cliffs, N.J., 1963.
4 Berle, A., *The 20th Century Capitalist Revolution*, Harcourt, Brace and World, Inc., 1954.
5 Berle, A. and G. Means, *The Modern Corporation and Private Property*, Macmillan, New York, 1932.
6 Black, F., 'The Dividend Puzzle', *Journal of Portfolio Management*, 2 (Winter 1976), 5–8.
7 Brealey, R.A. and S.C. Myers, *Principles of Corporate Finance*, 2nd Ed., McGraw-Hill Book Co., New York, 1984.
8 Cordes, J.J. and S.M. Sheffrin, 'Estimating the Tax Advantage of Corporate Debt'. *Journal of Finance*, 38 (March 1983), 95–105.
9 Dann, L.Y., 'Common Stock Repurchases: An Analysis of Returns to Bondholders and Stockholders,' *Journal of Financial Economics*, 9 (June 1981), 113–138.

[22] If the information asymmetry disappears from time to time, then the firm clearly should stock up with equity before it reappears. This observation is probably not much practical help, however, because we lack an objective proxy for changes in the degree of asymmetry.

10 Dann, L.Y. and W.H. Mikkleson, 'Convertible Debt Issuance, Capital Structure Change and Financing-Related Information: Some New Evidence', Working Paper, Amos Tuck School of Business Administration, 1983.

11 DeAngelo, H., L. DeAngelo, and E.M. Rice, 'Minority Freezeouts and Stockholder Wealth', Working Paper, Graduate School of Business Administration, University of Washington, 1982.

12 DeAngelo, H., and R. Masulis, 'Optimal Capital Structure Under Corporate and Personal Taxation', *Journal of Financial Economics*, 8 (March 1980), 3–29.

13 Donaldson, G., *Corporate Debt Capacity: A Study of Corporate Debt Policy and the Determination of Corporate Debt Capacity*, Boston, Division of Research, Harvard Graduate School of Business Administration, 1961.

14 Donaldson, G., *Strategy for Financial Mobility*, Boston, Division of Research, Harvard Graduate School of Business Administration, 1969.

15 Giammarino, R.M. and E.H. Neave, 'The Failure of Financial Contracts and the Relevance of Financial Policy', Working Paper, Queens University, 1982.

16 Gordon, R.H. and G.B. Malkiel, 'Corporation Finance', in H.J. Aaron and J.A. Pechman, *How Taxes Affect Economic Behavior*, Brookings Institution, Washington, DC, 1981.

17 Jalilvand, A. and R.S. Harris, 'Corporate Behavior in Adjusting Capital Structure and Dividend Policy: An Econometric Study', *Journal of Finance*, 39 (March 1984), 127–145.

18 Jensen, M.C. and W. Meckling, 'Theory of the Firm: Managerial Behavior, Agency Costs and Capital Structure', *Journal of Financial Economics*, 3 (October 1976), 11–25.

19 Korwar, A.N., 'The Effect of New Issues of Equity: An Empirical Examination', Working Paper, University of California, Los Angeles, 1981.

20 Lintner, J., 'Distribution of Incomes of Corporations Among Dividends, Retained Earnings and Taxes', *American Economic Review*, 46 (May 1956), 97–113.

21 Long, M.S., and E.B. Malitz, 'Investment Patterns and Financial Leverage', Working Paper, National Bureau of Economic Research, 1983.

22 Marsh, P.R., 'The Choice Between Equity and Debt: An Empirical Study', *Journal of Finance*, 37 (March 1982), 121–144.

23 Masulis, R.W., 'The Effects of Capital Structure Change on Security prices: A Study of Exchange Offers', *Journal of Financial Economics*, 8 (June 1980), 139–177.

24 Masulis, R.W., 'The Impact of Capital Structure Change on Firm Value', *Journal of Finance*, 38 (March 1983), 107–126.

25 Mikkelson, W.H., 'Capital Structure Change and Decreases in Stockholders' Wealth: A Cross-Sectional Study of Convertible Security Calls', Forthcoming in B. Friedman, Ed., *Corporate Capital Structures in the United States*, (National Bureau of Economic Research Conference Volume).

26 Mikkelson, W.H., 'Convertible Calls and Security Returns', *Journal of Financial Economics*, 9 (June 1981), 113–138.

27 Miller, M., 'Debt and Taxes', *Journal of Finance*, 32 (May 1977), 261–275.

28 Miller, M., and F. Modigliani, 'Dividend Policy, Growth and the Valuation of Shares', *Journal of Business*, 34 (October 1961), 411–433. 'Some Estimates of the Cost of Capital to the Electric Utility Industry, 1954–1957', *American Economic Review*, 56 (June 1966), 333–391.

29 Miller, M.H., and K. Rock, 'Dividend Policy Under Information Asymmetry', Working Paper, Graduate School of Business, University of Chicago, November 1982.

30 Modigliani, F., 'Debt, Dividend Policy, Taxes, Inflation and Market Valuation', *Journal of Finance*, 37 (May 1982), 255–273.

31 Modigliani, F. and M. Miller, 'The Cost of Capital, Corporation Finance and the Theory of Investment', *American Economic Review*, 53 (June 1958), 261–297.

32 Myers, S., 'Determinants of Corporate Borrowing', *Journal of Financial Economics*, 5 (November 1977), 147–176.

33 Myers, S., 'The Search for Optimal Capital Structure', *Midland Corporate Finance Journal*, 1 (Spring 1984), 6–16.

34 Myers, S., and N. Majluf, 'Corporate Financing and Investment Decisions When Firms Have Information Investors Do Not Have', *Journal of Financial Economics*, forthcoming.

35 Robicheck, A.A., J. MacDonald and R. Higgins, 'Some Estimates of the Cost of Capital to the Electric Utility Industry, 1954–1957: Comment', *American Economic Review*, 57 (December 1967), 1278–1288.

36 Ross, S.A., 'Some Notes on Financial-Incentive Signalling Models, Activity Choice and Risk Preferences', *Journal of Finance*, 33 (June 1978), 777–792.

37 Ross, S.A., 'The Determination of Financial Structure: The Incentive-Signalling Approach', *Bell Journal of Economics*, 8 (Spring 1977), 23–40.

38 Smith, C. and Warner, J., 'On Financial Contracting: An Analysis of Bond Covenants', *Journal of Financial Economics*, 7 (June 1979), 117–161.

39 Taggart, R., 'A Model of Corporate Financing Decisions', *Journal of Finance*, 32 (December 1977), 1467–1484.

40 Vermaelen, T., 'Common Stock Repurchases and Market Signalling: An Empirical Study', *Journal of Financial Economics*, 9 (June 1981), 139–183.

41 Williamson, S., 'The Moral Hazard Theory of Corporate Financial Structure: An Empirical Test,' Unpublished Ph.D. Dissertation, MIT, 1981.

Reproduced from Myers, S.C. (1984). The capital structure puzzle. *The Journal of Finance*, **XXXIX** (3), 575–592, by permission of the American Finance Association.

Part 6

More Complex and Sophisticated Financial Products

17 The pricing of options and corporate liabilities

F. Black and M. Scholes

If options are correctly priced in the market, it should not be possible to make sure profits by creating portfolios of long and short positions in options and their underlying stocks. Using this principle, a theoretical valuation formula for options is derived. Since almost all corporate liabilities can be viewed as combinations of options, the formula and the analysis that led to it are also applicable to corporate liabilities such as common stock, corporate bonds, and warrants. In particular, the formula can be used to derive the discount that should be applied to a corporate bond because of the possibility of default.

Introduction

An option is a security giving the right to buy or sell an asset, subject to certain conditions, within a specified period of time. An 'American option' is one that can be exercised at any time up to the date the option expires. A 'European option' is one that can be exercised only on a specified future date. The price that is paid for the asset when the option is exercised is called the 'exercise price' or 'striking price'. The last day on which the option may be exercised is called the 'expiration date' or 'maturity date'.

The simplest kind of option is one that gives the right to buy a single share of common stock. Throughout most of the paper, we will be discussing this kind of option, which is often referred to as a 'call option'.

In general, it seems clear that the higher the price of the stock, the greater the value of the option. When the stock price is much greater than the exercise price, the option is almost sure to be exercised. The current value of the option will thus be approximately equal to the price of the stock minus the price of a

The inspiration for this work was provided by Jack L. Treynor (1961a, 1961b). We are grateful for extensive comments on earlier drafts by Eugene F. Fama, Robert C. Merton, and Merton H. Miller. This work was supported in part by the Ford Foundation.

pure discount bond that matures on the same date as the option, with a face value equal to the striking price of the option.

On the other hand, if the price of the stock is much less than the exercise price, the option is almost sure to expire without being exercised, so its value will be near zero.

If the expiration date of the option is very far in the future, then the price of a bond that pays the exercise price on the maturity date will be very low, and the value of the option will be approximately equal to the price of the stock.

On the other hand, if the expiration date is very near, the value of the option will be approximately equal to the stock price minus the exercise price, or zero, if the stock price is less than the exercise price. Normally, the value of an option declines as its maturity date approaches, if the value of the stock does not change.

These general properties of the relation between the option value and the stock price are often illustrated in a diagram like Figure 1. Line *A* represents

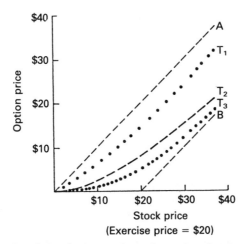

Figure 1   *The relation between option value and stock price*

the maximum value of the option, since it cannot be worth more than the stock. Line *B* represents the minimum value of the option, since its value cannot be negative and cannot be less than the stock price minus the exercise price. Lines T_1, T_2, and T_3 represent the value of the option for successively shorter maturities.

Normally, the curve representing the value of an option will be concave upward. Since it also lies below the 45° line, *A*, we can see that the option will be more volatile than the stock. A given percentage change in the stock price, holding maturity constant, will result in a larger percentage change in the option value. The relative volatility of the option is not constant, however. It depends on both the stock price and maturity.

Most of the previous work on the valuation of options has been expressed in terms of warrants. For example, Sprenkle (1961), Ayres (1963), Boness (1964), Samuelson (1965), Baumol, Malkiel, and Quandt (1966), and Chen (1970) all produced valuation formulas of the same general form. Their formulas, however, were not complete, since they all involved one or more arbitrary parameters.

For example, Sprenkle's formula for the value of an option can be written as follows:

$$kxN\ (b_1) - K^*cN\ (b_2)$$

$$b_1 = \frac{\ln\ kx/c + \dfrac{1}{2}\ v^2(t^* - t)}{v\sqrt{(t^* - t)}}$$

$$b_2 = \frac{\ln\ kx/c - \dfrac{1}{2}\ v^2(t^* - t)}{v\sqrt{(t^* - t)}}$$

In this expression, x is the stock price, c is the exercise price, t^* is the maturity date, t is the current date, v^2 is the variance rate of the return on the stock,[1] ln is the natural logarithm, and $N(b)$ is the cumulative normal density function. But k and k^* are unknown parameters. Sprenkle (1961) defines k as the ratio of the expected value of the stock price at the time the warrant matures to the current stock price, and k^* as a discount factor that depends on the risk of the stock. He tries to estimate the values of k and k^* empirically, but finds that he is unable to do so.

More typically, Samuelson (1965) has unknown parameters α and β, where α is the rate of expected return on the stock, and β is the rate of expected return on the warrant or the discount rate to be applied to the warrant.[2] He assumes that the distribution of possible values of the stock when the warrant matures is log-normal and takes the expected value of this distribution, cutting it off at the exercise price. He then discounts this expected value to the present at the rate β. Unfortunately, there seems to be no model of the pricing of

---

[1] The variance rate of the return on a security is the limit, as the size of the interval of measurement goes to zero, of the variance of the return over that interval divided by the length of the interval.

[2] The rate of expected return on a security is the limit, as the size of the interval of measurement goes to zero, of the expected return over that interval divided by the length of the interval.

securities under conditions of capital market equilibrium that would make this an appropriate procedure for determining the value of a warrant.

In a subsequent paper, Samuelson and Merton (1969) recognize the fact that discounting the expected value of the distribution of possible values of the warrant when it is exercised is not an appropriate procedure. They advance the theory by treating the option price as a function of the stock price. They also recognize that the discount rates are determined in part by the requirement that investors be willing to hold all of the outstanding amounts of both the stock and the option. But they do not make use of the fact that investors must hold other assets as well, so that the risk of an option or stock that affects its discount rate is only that part of the risk that cannot be diversified away. Their final formula depends on the shape of the utility function that they assume for the typical investor.

One of the concepts that we use in developing our model is expressed by Thorp and Kassouf (1967). They obtain an empirical valuation formula for warrants by fitting a curve to actual warrant prices. Then they use this formula to calculate the ratio of shares of stock to options needed to create a hedged position by going long in one security and short in the other. What they fail to pursue is the fact that in equilibrium, the expected return on such a hedged position must be equal to the return on a riskless asset. What we show below is that this equilibrium condition can be used to derive a theoretical valuation formula.

The valuation formula

In deriving our formula for the value of an option in terms of the price of the stock, we will assume 'ideal conditions' in the market for the stock and for the option:

(a) The short-term interest rate is known and is constant through time.
(b) The stock price follows a random walk in continuous time with a variance rate proportional to the square of the stock price. Thus the distribution of possible stock prices at the end of any finite interval is log-normal. The variance rate of the return on the stock is constant.
(c) The stock pays no dividends or other distributions.
(d) The option is 'European', that is, it can only be exercised at maturity.
(e) There are no transaction costs in buying or selling the stock or the option.
(f) It is possible to borrow any fraction of the price of a security to buy it or to hold it, at the short-term interest rate.

(g) There are no penalties to short selling. A seller who does not own a security will simply accept the price of the security from a buyer, and will agree to settle with the buyer on some future date by paying him an amount equal to the price of the security on that date.

Under these assumptions, the value of the option will depend only on the price of the stock and time and on variables that are taken to be known constants. Thus, it is possible to create a hedged position, consisting of a long position in the stock and a short position in the option, whose value will not depend on the price of the stock, but will depend only on time and the values of known constants. Writing $w(x,t)$ for the value of the option as a function of the stock price x and time t, the number of options that must be sold short against one share of stock long is:

$$1/w_1(x,t). \tag{1}$$

In expression (1), the subscript refers to the partial derivative of $w(x,t)$ with respect to its first argument.

To see that the value of such a hedged position does not depend on the price of the stock, note that the ratio of the change in the option value to the change in the stock price, when the change in the stock price is small, is $w_1(x,t)$. To a first approximation, if the stock price changes by an amount Δx, the option price will change by an amount $w_1(x,t)\,\Delta x$, and the number of options given by expression (1) will change by an amount Δx. Thus, the change in the value of a long position in the stock will be approximately offset by the change in value of a short position in $1/w_1$ options.

As the variables x and t change, the number of options to be sold short to create a hedged position with one share of stock changes. If the hedge is maintained continuously, then the approximations mentioned above become exact, and the return on the hedged position is completely independent of the change in the value of the stock. In fact, the return on the hedged position becomes certain.[3]

To illustrate the formation of the hedged position, let us refer to the solid line (T_2) in Figure 1 and assume that the price of the stock starts at $15.00, so that the value of the option starts at $5.00. Assume also that the slope of the line at that point is 1/2. This means that the hedged position is created by buying one share of stock and selling two options short. One share of stock costs $15.00, and the sale of two options brings in $10.00, so the equity in this position is $5.00.

If the hedged position is not changed as the price of the stock changes, then there is some uncertainty in the value of the equity at the end of a finite

---

[3] This was pointed out to us by Robert Merton.

interval. Suppose that two options go from $10.00 to $15.75 when the stock goes from $15.00 to $20.00, and that they go from $10.00 to $5.75 when the stock goes from $15.00 to $10.00. Thus, the equity goes from $5.00 to $4.25 when the stock changes by $5.00 in either direction. This is a $.75 decline in the equity for a $5.00 change in the stock in either direction.[4]

In addition, the curve shifts (say from T_2 to T_3 in Figure 1) as the maturity of the options changes. The resulting decline in value of the options means an increase in the equity in the hedged position and tends to offset the possible losses due to a large change in the stock price.

Note that the decline in the equity value due to a large change in the stock price is small. The ratio of the decline in the equity value to the magnitude of the change in the stock price becomes smaller as the magnitude of the change in the stock price becomes smaller.

Note also that the direction of the change in the equity value is independent of the direction of the change in the stock price. This means that under our assumption the stock price follows a continuous random walk and the return has a constant variance rate, the covariance between the return on the equity and the return on the stock will be zero. If the stock price and the value of the 'market portfolio' follow a joint continuous random walk with constant covariance rate, it means that the covariance between the return on the equity and the return on the market will be zero.

Thus the risk in the hedged position is zero if the short position in the option is adjusted continuously. If the position is not adjusted continuously, the risk is small, and consists entirely of risk that can be diversified away by forming a portfolio of a large number of such hedged positions.

In general, since the hedged position contains one share of stock long and $1/w_1$ options short, the value of the equity in the position is:

$$x - w/w_1. \tag{2}$$

The change in the value of the equity in a short interval Δt is:

$$\Delta x - \Delta w/w_1. \tag{3}$$

Assuming that the short position is changed continuously, we can use stochastic calculus[5] to expand Δw, which is $w(x + \Delta x, t + \Delta t) - w(x,t)$, as follows:

$$\Delta w = w_1 \Delta x + \frac{1}{2} w_{11} v^2 x^2 \Delta t + w_2 \Delta t. \tag{4}$$

---

[4] These figures are purely for illustrative purposes. They correspond roughly to the way Figure 1 was drawn, but not to an option on any actual security.

[5] For an exposition of stochastic calculus, see McKean (1969).

In equation (4), the subscripts on w refer to partial derivatives, and v^2 is the variance rate of the return on the stock.[6] Substituting from equation (4) into expression (3), we find that the change in the value of the equity in the hedged position is:

$$-\left(\frac{1}{2} w_{11} v^2 x^2 + w_2\right) \Delta t / w_1. \qquad (5)$$

Since the return on the equity in the hedged position is certain, the return must be equal to $r\Delta t$. Even if the hedged position is not changed continuously, its risk is small and is entirely risk that can be diversified away, so the expected return on the hedged position must be at the short term interest rate.[7] If this were not true, speculators would try to profit by borrowing large amounts of money to create such hedged positions, and would in the process force the returns down to the short term interest rate.

Thus the change in the equity (5) must equal the value of the equity (2) times $r\Delta t$.

$$-\left(\frac{1}{2} w_{11} v^2 x^2 + w_2\right) \Delta t / w_1 = (x - w/w_1) r\Delta t. \qquad (6)$$

Dropping the Δt from both sides, and rearranging, we have a differential equation for the value of the option.

$$w_2 = rw - rxw_1 - \frac{1}{2} v^2 x^2 w_{11}. \qquad (7)$$

Writing $t^\star$ for the maturity date of the option, and c for the exercise price, we known that:

$$\begin{aligned} w(x,t^\star) &= x - c, & x \geq c, \\ &= 0, & x < c. \end{aligned} \qquad (8)$$

---

[6] See footnote 1.

[7] For a thorough discussion of the relation between risk and expected return, see Fama and Miller (1972) or Sharpe (1970). To see that the risk in the hedged position can be diversified away, note that if we don't adjust the hedge continuously, expression (5) becomes:

$$-\left(\frac{1}{2} w_{11} \Delta x^2 + w_2 \Delta t\right) \bigg/ w_1. \qquad (5')$$

Writing Δm for the change in the value of the market portfolio between t and $t + \Delta t$, the 'market risk' in the hedged position is proportional to the covariance between the change in the value of the hedged portfolio, as given by expression (5'), and Δm: $-\frac{1}{2} w_{11}$ cov $(\Delta x^2, \Delta m)$. But if Δx and Δm follow a joint normal distribution for small intervals Δt, this covariance will be zero. Since there is no market risk in the hedged position, all of the risk due to the fact that the hedge is not continuously adjusted must be risk that can be diversified away.

There is only one formula $w(x,t)$ that satisfies the differential equation (7) subject to the boundary condition (8). This formula must be the option valuation formula.

To solve this differential equation, we make the following substitution:

$$w(x,t) = e^{r(t-t^*)}y\left[(2/v^2)\left(r - \frac{1}{2}v^2\right)\right.$$

$$\left[\ln x/c - \left(r - \frac{1}{2}v^2\right)(t - t^*)\right],$$

$$\left. - (2/v^2)\left(r - \frac{1}{2}v^2\right)^2(t - t^*)\right]. \qquad (9)$$

With this substitution, the differential equation becomes:

$$y_2 = y_{11}, \qquad (10)$$

and the boundary condition becomes:

$$y(u,0) = 0, \qquad\qquad u < 0$$

$$= c\left[e^{u\left(\frac{1}{2}v^2\right)/\left(r - \frac{1}{2}v^2\right)} - 1\right], \qquad u \geqslant 0. \qquad (11)$$

The differential equation (10) is the heat-transfer equation of physics, and its solution is given by Churchill (1963, p.155). In our notation, the solution is:

$$y(u,s) = 1/\sqrt{2\pi}\int_{-u/\sqrt{2s}}^{\infty} c\left[e^{(u + q\sqrt{2s})\left(\frac{1}{2}v^2\right)/\left(r - \frac{1}{2}v^2\right)} - 1\right]e^{-q^2/2} \, dq. \qquad (12)$$

Substituting from equation (12) into equation (9), and simplifying, we find:

$$w(x,t) = xN(d_1) - ce^{r(t - r^*)}N(d_2)$$

$$d_1 = \frac{\ln x/c + (r + \frac{1}{2}v^2)(t^* - t)}{v\sqrt{t^* - t}} \qquad (13)$$

$$d_2 = \frac{\ln x/c + (r - \frac{1}{2}v^2)(t^* - t)}{v\sqrt{t^* - t}}$$

In equation (13), $N(d)$ is the cumulative normal density function.

Note that the expected return on the stock does not appear in equation (13). The option value as a function of the stock price is independent of the expected return on the stock. The expected return on the option, however, will depend on the expected return on the stock. The faster the stock price rises, the faster the option price will rise through the functional relationship (13).

Note that the maturity $(t^* - t)$ appears in the formula only multiplied by the interest rate r or the variance rate v^2. Thus, an increase in maturity has the same effect on the value of the option as an equal percentage increase in both r and v^2.

Merton (1973) has shown that the option value as given by equation (13) increases continuously as any one of t^*, r, or v^2 increases. In each case, it approaches a maximum value equal to the stock price.

The partial derivative w_1 of the valuation formula is of interest, because it determines the ratio of shares of stock to options in the hedged position as in expression (1). Taking the partial derivative of equation (13), and simplifying, we find that:

$$w_1(x,t) = N(d_1). \tag{14}$$

In equation (14), d_1 is as defined in equation (13).

From equations (13) and (14), it is clear that xw_1/w is always greater than one. This shows that the option is always more volatile than the stock.

An alternative derivation

It is also possible to derive the differential equation (7) using the 'capital asset pricing model'. This derivation is given because it gives more understanding of the way in which one can discount the value of an option to the present, using a discount rate that depends on both time and the price of the stock.

The capital asset pricing model describes the relation between risk and expected return for a capital asset under conditions of market equilibrium.[8] The expected return on an asset gives the discount that must be applied to the

---

[8] The model was developed by Treynor (1961*b*), Sharpe (1964), Lintner (1965), and Mossin (1966). It is summarized by Sharpe (1970), and Fama and Miller (1972). The model was originally stated as a single-period model. Extending it to a multi-period model is, in general, difficult. Fama (1970), however, has shown that if we make an assumption that implies that the short-term interest rate is constant through time, then the model must apply to each successive period in time. His proof also goes through under somewhat more general assumptions.

end-of-period value of the asset to give its present value. Thus, the capital-asset pricing model gives a general method for discounting under uncertainty.

The capital-asset pricing model says that the expected return on an asset is a linear function of its β, which is defined as the covariance of the return on the asset with the return on the market, divided by the variance of the return on the market. From equation (4) we see that the covariance of the return on the option $\Delta w/w$ with the return on the market is equal to xw_1/w times the covariance of the return on the stock $\Delta x/x$ with the return on the market. Thus, we have the following relation between the option's β and the stock's β:

$$\beta_w = (xw_1/w)\beta_x. \tag{15}$$

The expression xw_1/w may also be interpreted as the 'elasticity' of the option price with respect to the stock price. It is the ratio of the percentage change in the option price to the percentage change in the stock price, for small percentage changes, holding maturity constant.

To apply the capital-asset pricing model to an option and the underlying stock, let us first define a as the rate of expected return on the market minus the interest rate.[9] Then the expected return on the option and the stock are:

$$E(\Delta x/x) = r\Delta t + a\beta_x\Delta t, \tag{16}$$

$$E(\Delta w/w) = r\Delta t + a\beta_w\Delta t. \tag{17}$$

Multiplying equation (17) by w, and substituting for βw from equation (15), we find:

$$E(\Delta w) = rw\Delta t + axw_1\beta_x\Delta t. \tag{18}$$

Using stochastic calculus,[10] we can expand Δw, which is $w(x + \Delta x, t + \Delta t) - w(x,t)$, as follows:

$$\Delta w = w_1\Delta x + \frac{1}{2} w_1 v^2 x^2 \Delta t + w_2\Delta t. \tag{19}$$

Taking the expected value of equation (19), and substituting for $E(\Delta x)$ from equation (16), we have:

---

[9] See footnote 2.

[10] For an exposition of stochastic calculus, see McKean (1969).

$$E(\Delta w) = rxw_1 \Delta t + axw_1 \beta_x \Delta t + \frac{1}{2} v^2 x^2 w_{11} \Delta t + w_2 \Delta t. \tag{20}$$

Combining equations (18) and (20), we find that the terms involving a and β_x cancel, giving:

$$w_2 = rw - rxw_1 - \frac{1}{2} v^2 x^2 w_{11}. \tag{21}$$

Equation (21) is the same as equation (7).

More complicated options

The valuation formula (13) was derived under the assumption that the option can only be exercised at time $t^\star$. Merton (1973) has shown, however, that the value of the option is always greater than the value it would have if it were exercised immediately $(x - c)$. Thus, a rational investor will not exercise a call option before maturity, and the value of an American call option is the same as the value of a European call option.

There is a simple modification of the formula that will make it applicable to European put options (options to sell) as well as call options (options to buy). Writing $u(x,t)$ for the value of a put option, we see that the differential equation remains unchanged.

$$u_2 = ru - rxu_1 - \frac{1}{2} v^2 x^2 u_{11}. \tag{22}$$

The boundary condition, however, becomes:

$$\begin{aligned} u(x,t^\star) &= 0, &x \geq c \\ &= c - x, &x < c. \end{aligned} \tag{23}$$

To get the solution to this equation with the new boundary condition, we can simply note that the difference between the value of a call and the value of a put on the same stock, if both can be exercised only at maturity, must obey the same differential equation, but with the following boundary condition:

$$w(x,t^\star) - u(x,t^\star) = x - c. \tag{24}$$

The solution to the differential equation with this boundary condition is:

$$w(x,t) - u(x,t) = x - ce^{r(t-t^*)}. \tag{25}$$

Thus the value of the European put option is:

$$u(x,t) = w(x,t) - x + ce^{r(t-t^*)}. \tag{26}$$

Putting in the value of $w(x,t)$ from (13), and noting that $1 - N(d)$ is equal to $N(-d)$, we have:

$$u(x,t) = -xN(-d_1) + ce^{-rt^*}N(-d_2). \tag{27}$$

In equation (27), d_1 and d_2 are defined as in equation (13).

Equation (25) also gives us a relation between the value of a European call and the value of a European put.[11] We see that if an investor were to buy a call and sell a put, his returns would be exactly the same as if he bought the stock on margin, borrowing $ce^{r(t-t^*)}$ toward the price of the stock.

Merton (1973) has also shown that the value of an American put option will be greater than the value of a European put option. This is true because it is sometimes advantageous to exercise a put option before maturity, if it is possible to do so. For example, suppose the stock price falls almost to zero and that the probability that the price will exceed the exercise price before the option expires is negligible. Then it will pay to exercise the option immediately, so that the exercise price will be received sooner rather than later. The investor thus gains the interest on the exercise price for the period up to the time he would otherwise have exercised it. So far, no one has been able to obtain a formula for the value of an American put option.

If we relax the assumption that the stock pays no dividend, we begin to get into some complicated problems. First of all, under certain conditions it will pay to exercise an American call option before maturity. Merton (1973) has shown that this can be true only just before the stock's ex-dividend date. Also, it is not clear what adjustment might be made in the terms of the option to protect the option holder against a loss due to a large dividend on the stock and to ensure that the value of the option will be the same as if the stock paid no dividend. Currently, the exercise price of a call option is generally reduced by the amount of any dividend paid on the stock. We can see that this is not adequate protection by imagining that the stock is that of a holding company and that it pays out all of its assets in the form of a dividend to its shareholders. This will reduce the price of the stock and the value of the option to zero, no matter what adjustment is made in the exercise price of the option. In fact, this

---

[11] The relation between the value of a call option and the value of a put option was first noted by Stoll (1969). He does not realize, however, that his analysis applies only to European options.

example shows that there may not be any adjustment in the terms of the option that will give adequate protection against a large dividend. In this case, the option value is going to be zero after the distribution, no matter what its terms are. Merton (1973) was the first to point out that the current adjustment for dividends is not adequate.

Warrant valuation

A warrant is an option that is a liability of a corporation. The holder of a warrant has the right to buy the corporation's stock (or other assets) on specified terms. The analysis of warrants is often much more complicated than the analysis of simple options, because:

(a) The life of a warrant is typically measured in years, rather than months. Over a period of years, the variance rate of the return on the stock may be expected to change substantially.
(b) The exercise price of the warrant is usually not adjusted at all for dividends. The possibility that dividends will be paid requires a modification of the valuation formula.
(c) The exercise price of a warrant sometimes changes on specified dates. It may pay to exercise a warrant just before its exercise price changes. This too requires a modification of the valuation formula.
(d) If the company is involved in a merger, the adjustment that is made in the terms of the warrant may change its value.
(e) Sometimes the exercise price can be paid using bonds of the corporation at face value, even though they may at the time be selling at a discount. This complicates the analysis and means that early exercise may sometimes be desirable.
(f) The exercise of a large number of warrants may sometimes result in a significant increase in the number of common shares outstanding.

In some cases, these complications can be treated as insignificant, and equation (13) can be used as an approximation to give an estimate of the warrant value. In other cases, some simple modifications of equation (13) will improve the approximation. Suppose, for example, that there are warrants outstanding, which, if exercised, would double the number of shares of the company's common stock. Let us define the 'equity' of the company as the sum of the value of all of its warrants and the value of all of its common stock. If the warrants are exercised at maturity, the equity of the company will increase by the aggregate amount of money paid in by the warrant holders when they exercise. The warrant holders will then own half of the new equity of the company, which is equal to the old equity plus the exercise money.

Thus, at maturity, the warrant holders will either receive nothing, or half of the new equity, minus the exercise money. Thus, they will receive nothing or half of the difference between the old equity and half the exercise money. We can look at the warrants as options to buy shares in the equity rather than shares of common stock, at half the stated exercise price rather than at the full exercise price. The value of a share in the equity is defined as the sum of the value of the warrants and the value of the common stock, divided by twice the number of outstanding shares of common stock. If we take this point of view, then we will take v^2 in equation (13) to be the variance rate of the return on the company's equity, rather than the variance rate of the return on the company's common stock.

A similar modification in the parameters of equation (13) can be made if the number of shares of stock outstanding after exercise of the warrants will be other than twice the number of shares outstanding before exercise of the warrants.

Common stock and bond valuation

It is not generally realized that corporate liabilities other than warrants may be viewed as options. Consider, for example, a company that has common stock and bonds outstanding and whose only asset is shares of common stock of a second company. Suppose that the bonds are 'pure discount bonds' with no coupon, giving the holder the right to a fixed sum of money, if the corporation can pay it, with a maturity of 10 years. Suppose that the bonds contain no restrictions on the company except a restriction that the company cannot pay any dividends until after the bonds are paid off. Finally, suppose that the company plans to sell all the stock it holds at the end of 10 years, pay off the bond holders if possible, and pay any remaining money to the stockholders as a liquidating dividend.

Under these conditions, it is clear that the stockholders have the equivalent of an option on their company's assets. In effect, the bond holders own the company's assets, but they have given options to the stockholders to buy the assets back. The value of the common stock at the end of 10 years will be the value of the company's assets minus the face value of the bonds, or zero, whichever is greater.

Thus, the value of the common stock will be $w(x,t)$, as given by equation (13), where we take v^2 to be the variance rate of the return on the shares held by the company, c to be the total face value of the outstanding bonds, and x to be the total value of the shares held by the company. The value of the bonds will simply be $x - w(x,t)$.

By subtracting the value of the bonds given by this formula from the value they would have if there were no default risk, we can figure the discount that should be applied to the bonds due to the existence of default risk.

Suppose, more generally, that the corporation holds business assets rather than financial assets. Suppose that at the end of the 10 year period, it will recapitalize by selling an entirely new class of common stock, using the proceeds to pay off the bond holders, and paying any money that is left to the old stockholders to retire their stock. In the absence of taxes, it is clear that the value of the corporation can be taken to be the sum of the total value of the debt and the total value of the common stock.[12] The amount of debt outstanding will not affect the total value of the corporation, but will affect the division of that value between the bonds and the stock. The formula for $w(x,t)$ will again describe the total value of the common stock, where x is taken to be the sum of the value of the bonds and the value of the stock. The formula for $x - w(x,t)$ will again describe the total value of the bonds. It can be shown that, as the face value c of the bonds increases, the market value $x - w(x,t)$ increases by a smaller percentage. An increase in the corporation's debt, keeping the total value of the corporation constant, will increase the probability of default and will thus reduce the market value of one of the corporation's bonds. If the company changes its capital structure by issuing more bonds and using the proceeds to retire common stock, it will hurt the existing bond holders, and help the existing stockholders. The bond price will fall, and the stock price will rise. In this sense, changes in the capital structure of a firm may affect the price of its common stock.[13] The price changes will occur when the change in the capital structure becomes certain, not when the actual change takes place.

Because of this possibility, the bond indenture may prohibit the sale of additional debt of the same or higher priority in the event that the firm is recapitalized. If the corporation issues new bonds that are subordinated to the existing bonds and uses the proceeds to retire common stock, the price of the existing bonds and the common stock price will be unaffected. Similarly, if the company issues new common stock and uses the proceeds to retire completely the most junior outstanding issue of bonds, neither the common stock price nor the price of any other issue of bonds will be affected.

The corporation's dividend policy will also affect the division of its total value between the bonds and the stock.[14] To take an extreme example,

---

[12] The fact that the total value of a corporation is not affected by its capital structure, in the absence of taxes and other imperfections, was first shown by Modigliani and Miller (1958).

[13] For a discussion of this point, see Fama and Miller (1972, pp.151–52).

[14] Miller and Modigliani (1961) show that the total value of a firm, in the absence of taxes and other imperfections, is not affected by its dividend policy. They also note that the price of the common stock and the value of the bonds will not be affected by a change in dividend policy if the funds for a higher dividend are raised by issuing common stock or if the money released by a lower dividend is used to repurchase common stock.

suppose again that the corporation's only assets are the shares of another company, and suppose that it sells all these shares and uses the proceeds to pay a dividend to its common stockholders. Then the value of the firm will go to zero, and the value of the bonds will go to zero. The common stockholders will have 'stolen' the company out from under the bond holders. Even for dividends of modest size, a higher dividend always favors the stockholders at the expense of the bond holders. A liberalization of dividend policy will increase the common stock price and decrease the bond price.[15] Because of this possibility, bond indentures contain restrictions on dividend policy, and the common stockholders have an incentive to pay themselves the largest dividend allowed by the terms of the bond indenture. However, it should be noted that the size of the effect of changing dividend policy will normally be very small.

If the company has coupon bonds rather than pure discount bonds outstanding, then we can view the common stock as a 'compound option'. The common stock is an option on an option on . . . an option on the firm. After making the last interest payment, the stockholders have an option to buy the company from the bond holders for the face value of the bonds. Call this 'option 1'. After making the next-to-the-last interest payment, but before making the last interest payment, the stockholders have an option to buy option 1 by making the last interest payment. Call this 'option 2'. Before making the next-to-the-last interest payment, the stockholders have an option to buy option 2 by making that interest payment. This is 'option 3'. The value of the stockholders' claim at any point in time is equal to the value of option $n + 1$, where n is the number of interest payments remaining in the life of the bond.

If payments to a sinking fund are required along with interest payments, then a similar analysis can be made. In this case, there is no 'balloon payment' at the end of the life of the bond. The sinking fund will have a final value equal to the face value of the bond. Option 1 gives the stockholders the right to buy

---

[15] This is true assuming that the liberalization of dividend policy is not accompanied by a change in the company's current and planned financial structure. Since the issue of common stock or junior debt will hurt the common shareholders (holding dividend policy constant), they will normally try to liberalize dividend policy without issuing new securities. They may be able to do this by selling some of the firm's financial assets, such as ownership claims on other firms. Or they may be able to do it by adding to the company's short-term bank debt, which is normally senior to its long-term debt. Finally, the company may be able to finance a higher dividend by selling off a division. Assuming that it receives a fair price for the division, and that there were no economies of combination, this need not involve any loss to the firm as a whole. If the firm issues new common stock or junior debt in exactly the amounts needed to finance the liberalization of dividend policy, then the common stock and bond prices will not be affected. If the liberalization of dividend policy is associated with a decision to issue more common stock or junior debt than is needed to pay the higher dividends, the common stock price will fall and the bond price will rise. But these actions are unlikely, since they are not in the stockholders' best interests.

the company from the bond holders by making the last sinking fund and interest payment. Option 2 gives the stockholders the right to buy option 1 by making the next-to-the-last sinking fund and interest payment. And the value of the stockholders' claim at any point in time is equal to the value of option n, where n is the number of sinking fund and interest payments remaining in the life of the bond. It is clear that the value of a bond for which sinking fund payments are required is greater than the value of a bond for which they are not required.

If the company has callable bonds, then the stockholders have more than one option. They can buy the next option by making the next interest or sinking fund and interest payment, or they can exercise their option to retire the bonds before maturity at prices specified by the terms of the call feature. Under our assumption of a constant short-term interest rate, the bonds would never sell above face value, and the usual kind of call option would never be exercised. Under more general assumptions, however, the call feature would have value to the stockholders and would have to be taken into account in deciding how the value of the company is divided between the stockholders and the bond holders.

Similarly, if the bonds are convertible, we simply add another option to the package. It is an option that the bond holders have to buy part of the company from the stockholders.

Unfortunately, these more complicated options cannot be handled by using the valuation formula (13). The valuation formula assumes that the variance rate of the return on the optioned asset is constant. But the variance of the return on an option is certainly not constant: it depends on the price of the stock and the maturity of the option. Thus the formula cannot be used, even as an approximation, to give the value of an option on an option. It is possible, however, that an analysis in the same spirit as the one that led to equation (13) would allow at least a numerical solution to the valuation of certain more complicated options.

Empirical tests

We have done empirical tests of the valuation formula on a large body of call-option data (Black and Scholes 1972). These tests indicate that the actual prices at which options are bought and sold deviate in certain systematic ways from the values predicted by the formula. Option buyers pay prices that are consistently higher than those predicted by the formula. Option writers, however, receive prices that are at about the level predicted by the formula. There are large transaction costs in the option market, all of which are effectively paid by option buyers.

Also, the difference between the price paid by option buyers and the value given by the formula is greater for options on low-risk stocks than for options on high-risk stocks. The market appears to underestimate the effect of differences in variance rate on the value of an option. Given the magnitude of the transaction costs in this market, however, this systematic misestimation of value does not imply profit opportunities for a speculator in the option market.

References

Ayres, Herbert F. 'Risk Aversion in the Warrants Market'. *Indus. Management Rev.* 4 (Fall 1963): 497–505. Reprinted in Cootner (1967), pp.497–505.

Baumol, William J.; Malkiel, Burton G.; and Quandt, Richard E. 'The Valuation of Convertible Securities'. *QJE* 80 (February 1966): 48–59.

Black, Fischer, and Scholes, Myron. 'The Valuation of Option Contracts and a Test of Market Efficiency'. *J. Finance* 27 (May 1972): 399–417.

Boness, A. James. 'Elements of a Theory of Stock-Option Values'. *JPE* 72 (April 1964): 163–75.

Chen, Andrew H.Y. 'A Model of Warrant Pricing in a Dynamic Market'. *J. Finance* 25 (December 1970): 1041–60.

Churchill, R.V. *Fourier Series and Boundary Value Problems*, 2nd Ed. New York: McGraw-Hill, 1963.

Cootner, Paul A. *The Random Character of Stock Market Prices*. Cambridge, Mass: MIT Press, 1967.

Fama, Eugene F. 'Multiperiod Consumption-Investment Decisions'. *AER* 60 (March 1970): 163–74.

Fama, Eugene F., and Miller, Merton H. *The Theory of Finance*. New York: Holt, Rinehart & Winston, 1972.

Lintner, John. 'The Valuation of Risk Assets and the Selection of Risky Investments in Stock Portfolios and Capital Budgets'. *Rev. Econ. and Statis.* 47 (February 1965): 768–83.

McKean, H.P., Jr. *Stochastic Integrals*. New York: Academic Press, 1969.

Merton, Robert C. 'Theory of Rational Option Pricing', *Bell J. Econ. and Management Sci.* (1973): in press.

Miller, Merton H., and Modigliani, Franco. 'Dividend Policy, Growth, and the Valuation of Shares'. *J. Bus.* 34 (October 1961): 411–33.

Modigliani, Franco, and Miller, Merton H. 'The Cost of Capital, Corporation Finance, and the Theory of Investment'. *AER* 48 (June 1958): 261–97.

Mossin, Jan. 'Equilibrium in a Capital Asset Market'. *Econometrica* 34 (October 1966): 768–83.

Samuelson, Paul A. 'Rational Theory of Warrant Pricing'. *Indus. Management Rev.* 6 (Spring 1965): 13–31. Reprinted in Cootner (1967), pp.506–32.

Samuelson, Paul A., and Merton, Robert C. 'A Complete Model of Warrant Pricing that Maximizes Utility'. *Indus. Management Rev.* 10 (Winter 1969): 17–46.

Sharpe, William F. 'Capital Asset Prices: A Theory of Market Equilibrium Under Conditions of Risk'. *J. Finance* 19 (September 1964): 425–42.

––*Portfolio Theory and Capital Markets*: New York: McGraw-Hill, 1970.

Sprenkle, Case. 'Warrant Prices as Indications of Expectations'. *Yale Econ. Essays* 1 (1961): 179–232. Reprinted in Cootner (1967), 412–74.

Stoll, Hans R. 'The Relationship Between Put and Call Option Prices', *J. Finance* 24 (December 1969): 802–24.

Thorp, Edward O., and Kassouf, Sheen T. *Beat the Market*. New York: Random House, 1967.

Treynor, Jack L. 'Implications for the Theory of Finance'. Unpublished memorandum, 1961. (*a*)

—–'Toward a Theory of Market Value of Risky Assets'. Unpublished memorandum, 1961. (*b*)

18 Convertible bonds: valuation and optimal strategies for call and conversion

M. J. Brennan and E. S. Schwartz*

I

The theory of option and warrant pricing has only of late been placed on a sound theoretical basis in a context of security market equilibrium [1,6]; closed form expressions have been derived by Black-Scholes [1] and Merton [6] for the value of an option when the underlying stock pays no dividend or the option is protected against dividends, and when the stock pays a continuous dividend which is proportional to the market value of the stock. Further research has extended this option pricing model to take account of jumps in security returns [3,8], and the basic option pricing model has been shown to obtain under certain assumptions, even in the absence of continuous trading opportunities [11]. More recently, algorithms have been developed [12] to solve the relevant dynamic programming problem when the stock does pay dividends and the option is not protected against dividend payments, so that the possibility of exercise prior to maturity must be considered for an American type option.

As yet however, little attempt has been made to apply the principles of the option pricing model to the most common type of convertible security, namely the convertible bond.[1] This security is considerably more complex than the

---

* The authors acknowledge the helpful comments of a referee of this journal, Jon Ingersoll, which have led to substantial improvements in the paper.
[1] In an independent and contemporaneous paper Ingersoll [4] considers the valuation of convertible bonds within the same framework as this paper. Several of his results correspond to ours. The major difference between the papers is that Ingersoll concentrates on deriving 'closed form' solutions for the value of a bond in a variety of special cases, whereas we offer a general algorithm for determining the value of a convertible bond.

warrant, not only because it pays a periodic coupon, but also because it involves a dual option: on the one hand, the bondholder possesses the option to convert the bond into common stock at his discretion, and on the other hand, the firm possesses the option to call the bond for redemption, the bondholder retaining the right to convert the bond or to redeem it. This call option is usually subject to some kind of restriction, a common one being that the bond may not be called for five years. The investor's optimal conversion strategy then depends on the firm's call strategy, and it appears at first sight that the optimal call strategy must also depend on the investor's conversion strategy, so that both optimal strategies must be solved for simultaneously. Fortunately, as we shall show below, the optimal call strategy is simply to call the bond as soon as the value of the bond if called is equal to the value if not called, so that the problem is considerably simplified.

Merton [6] has considered the related problem of valuing callable warrants on non-dividend paying stocks: callable warrants differ from convertible bonds in having no coupon payments, and in possessing no ultimate value save their conversion value; additionally, the assumption that the stock pays no dividends avoids the need to consider the possibility of voluntary conversion prior to expiration. Merton's analysis relies on the proposition that the value of a callable warrant is equal to the difference between the value of an equivalent non-callable warrant and the value of the firm's call option on the warrant. Under reasonable assumptions, a differential equation can be derived governing the value of the non-callable warrant and of the call provision, and hence of the callable warrant itself. The major difficulty appears to arise in the specification of appropriate boundary conditions; in particular in deriving the critical stock price above which the company should optimally exercise its call option: Merton shows how the critical stock price may be determined in the case of a perpetual warrant on a non-dividend paying stock.

This paper extends the work of Black-Scholes [1] and Merton [6] to the pricing of convertible bonds. The differential equation and boundary conditions governing the value of the bond are derived, and an algorithm is presented for solving the differential equation. The paper concludes with some examples designed to show the effect on the bond value of varying selected parameters.

Since numerical methods are employed to solve the differential equation, the valuation procedure is extremely flexible, and the model permits:

(i)   discrete coupon payments on the bond;
(ii) discrete dividend payments on the firm's common shares which may be a function of the value of the firm and time;
(iii) the investor's right to convert the bond into common shares at any point in time; simple changes in the appropriate boundary conditions allow for the possibility of changing conversion terms over time.

(iv) the corporation's right to call the bond, the investor having the right, if the bond is called, either to convert the bond or to redeem it at the call price. The right to call the bond may be restricted; for example the bond may not be callable for five years, or may not be callable until the stock is at a certain premium above the conversion price. These restrictions may be taken into account by appropriate modification of the boundary conditions;

(v) the possibility that the firm will default on the bond by bankruptcy either prior to, or at maturity. The model thus extends Merton's analysis of risky corporate discount bonds [7] to risky coupon bonds.

The model development also allows us to dispense with the 'incipient' assumption used in the above-mentioned papers [1,6], though not in Merton's [7] paper on risky debt; this is the assumption that the net supply of the risky security is zero.

In the interest of clarity and computational convenience, the simplifying assumption is made that the firm's outstanding securities consist solely of common stock and convertible securities; this assumption could be relaxed by further modification of the boundary conditions. Additionally, the risk free rate of interest is assumed to be not only known but also to be constant through time.

In the following section we consider the problem of optimal call and conversion strategies. Solution of this problem yields certain boundary conditions which must be satisfied by the solution to the differential equation governing the value of the convertible bond. This differential equation and the boundary conditions are considered further in Section III. Section IV describes the solution algorithm, and Section V discusses some numerical results.

II

A convertible bond can be valued only if the call and conversion strategies to be followed by the corporation and the investor respectively can be determined; for example, the bond value would in general clearly be affected if it were known that the firm would never exercise its call option, or that the investors would never convert prior to maturity. Thus, in deriving the call (conversion) strategy it is necessary to make an assumption about the strategy to be followed by the other party. The assumption we make is that each party, firm and investor, pursues an optimal strategy (to be defined below) and expects the other party to do the same. This assumption corresponds to the Miller-Modigliani [9] assumption of 'symmetric market rationality', and results in a pair of conversion-call strategies which are equilibrium in the sense that neither party could improve his position by adopting any other strategy. Then define:

$V(t)$	=	the aggregate market value at time t of the firm's outstanding securities including the convertible bonds.
$W(V,t)$	=	the market value at time t of one convertible bond with par value of \$1,000.
l	=	the number of convertible bonds outstanding.
$n(t)$	=	the number of shares of common stock into which each bond is convertible at time t.
m	=	the number of shares of common stock outstanding before conversion takes place.
I	=	the aggregate coupon payment on the outstanding convertible bonds at each periodic coupon date.
$i = I/l$	=	the periodic coupon payment per bond.
$CP(t)$	=	the price at which the bonds may be called for redemption at time t, including any accrued interest.
$B(V,t)$	=	the straight debt value of the bond; that is, the value of an otherwise identical bond with no conversion privilege.
$D(V,t)$	=	the aggregate dividend payment on the common stock at each dividend date.

Definition 1.   *The optimal conversion strategy is one which maximizes the value of the convertible bond at each instant in time.*

Definition 2.   *The optimal call strategy is one which minimizes the value of the convertible bonds at each instant in time.*

The aggregate market value of the firm's securities, $V(t)$ is assumed to be determined exogenously and by the Modigliani-Miller [10] theorem to be independent of the particular call and conversion strategies followed. Hence, by minimizing the value of the outstanding convertible bonds, the management will be maximizing the value of the firm's equity, which is equal to the difference between the aggregate market value of the firm, $V(t)$, and the value of the convertible bonds.

The conversion value of a bond is equal to the number of shares into which it is convertible times the value of a share if the bond is converted. Since, by the Modigliani-Miller theorem, conversion of the bonds cannot alter the aggregate value of the firm's securities, $V(t)$, the value of a share after conversion is given by the pre-conversion value of the firm, $V(t)$, divided by the number of shares outstanding after conversion has taken place. Since each bond is convertible into $n(t)$ shares at time t, the conversion value, $C(V,t)$ is given by

$$C(V,t) = n(t)V(t)/(m + ln(t))$$
$$= z(t)V(t), \qquad \text{where} \qquad z(t) = n(t)/(m + ln(t)). \quad (1)$$

Since, from Definition 1, it is optimal for the investor to convert should the value of the bond unconverted fall below the conversion value, we have the arbitrage condition:

$$W(V,t) \geqslant C(V,t). \qquad (2)$$

A stronger condition on the value of the bond may be derived from the following Lemma.

Lemma 1   *It will never be optimal to convert an uncalled convertible bond except immediately prior either to a dividend date or to an adverse change in the conversion terms, or at maturity.*

Proof

From Definition 1 it is never optimal to convert the bond if its market value exceeds its conversion value. But an uncalled bond can never sell at a price as low as conversion value except immediately prior to a dividend date or to an adverse change in conversion terms, since, if it did, the return on the bond up to the next dividend date or change in conversion terms would exhibit first degree stochastic dominance over the return on the underlying common stock. Therefore the bond will always sell above conversion value under these conditions, and the investor will never find it optimal to convert.

The stochastic dominance arises from the following consideration: if the bond is currently selling at conversion value, its rate of return up to the next dividend or conversion change date can never fall below the rate of return on the stock since the bond value can never fall below the conversion value by condition (2). However, if the value of the firm drops sufficiently, the priority of claim of the bond will cause its value to exceed the conversion value, so that the return on the bond will exceed the return on the stock under these conditions.[2]

Hence between dividend dates (2) holds as a strict inequality if there is no adverse change in conversion terms. This Lemma serves to simplify the

---

[2] Cf. Merton's [6] demonstration that a warrant will never be exercised except immediately prior to a dividend.

computational algorithm described below, since the possibility of conversion must only be considered at the discrete dividend dates, or when the conversion terms change adversely for the investor, or at call.

If a bond is called for redemption by the firm, the investor retains the option either of redeeming the bond at the current call price, $CP(t)$, or converting it and receiving an amount of shares equal in value to the conversion value, $C(V,t)$. Since by Definition 1, the investor will always select the more valuable option, the value of the bond if called, $VIC(V,t)$ is given by:

$$VIC(V,t) = \max[CP(t), C(V,t)]. \tag{3}$$

The firm's optimal call strategy is given by the following Lemma.

Lemma 2 *The firm's optimal call strategy is to call the bond as soon as its value if it is not called is equal to the call price.*

Proof

By Definition 2, the optimal call strategy is chosen to minimize the value of the convertible bonds. This is accomplished by calling the bonds as soon as their value if not called equals their value if called. For if the bonds were left uncalled at a market value exceeding their value if called, their value would clearly not be minimized; on the other hand, if the bonds were called when their value uncalled was below their value if called, calling would confer a needless gain on the bondholders and the value of the bonds would again not be minimized. Therefore, calling the bonds when their value if not called equals their value if called is indeed the strategy which minimizes the value of the bonds. Since the minimum value if called is the call price, the bonds will be called as soon as their value if not called is equal to the call price.

In the event that the conversion value exceeds the call price at the time the bond first becomes callable, the bond will be called immediately since by the proof of Lemma 1 the uncalled bond would sell for more than the conversion value which is then the value if called.[3]

---

[3] It was implicitly assumed in Lemma 2 that the bonds may be instantaneously called for conversion. A more typical arrangement requires the firm to give notice of its intention to call the bonds, introducing the risk to the firm that between the time notice is given and the time the bonds are actually called, the conversion value of the bonds will have fallen below the call price, so that the bonds will be redeemed rather than converted.

When notice of call is given the bonds will become non-callable bonds with maturity equal to the call notice period. This new bond value, which may be readily computed using the methods of Section IV, then becomes the 'effective call price' which should be used in Lemma 2.

An implication of this equilibrium call strategy in an efficient market is that the bond will sell at a price equal to its value if called when the call is exercised. Were this not the case, investors, knowing the optimal call strategy to be followed by the firm, could reap arbitrage profits from the difference between the pre-call bond price and the value if called. Note however that the firm's optimal call strategy cannot be inferred from the observation that the bond will sell at its value if called when the call is exercised, since this would be true of any, not necessarily optimal, call strategy, so long as the strategy is known to investors.

Lemma 2 gives rise to the following restrictions on the value of the bond:

(i) At time $t = t^\star$ when the bond first becomes callable, its value satisfies

$$W(V,t^\star) = C(V,t^\star), \qquad \text{if } C(V,t^\star) \geq CP(t^\star). \tag{4}$$

(ii) At any time when the bond is callable we have the call price constraint:

$$W(V,t) \leq CP(t). \tag{5}$$

Lemma 2 does not directly determine the values of $V(t)$ at which the bond will be called. These must be determined as part of the solution procedure.

III

Since W is a function only of V and t, it is readily shown (Cf. Black-Scholes [1] and Merton [6]) that if V follows the stochastic process

$$\frac{dV}{V} = \mu dt + \sigma dz, \tag{6}$$

where dz is a Gauss-Wiener process, then W must satisfy the stochastic differential equation

$$\tfrac{1}{2}\sigma^2 V^2 W_{vv} + rVW_v - rW + W_t = 0, \tag{7}$$

where r is the risk free rate of interest, and the subscript denotes partial differentiation.

Additionally, W must satisfy the following boundary conditions:

(i) At any time the aggregate value of the bonds outstanding cannot exceed the total value of the firm yielding the arbitrage condition:

$$lW(V,t) \leqslant V. \tag{8}$$

Since the common shares must have a non-negative value, the value of the outstanding bonds cannot exceed the aggregate value of the outstanding bonds and stocks. Setting $V = 0$ in (8), and recognizing that the bond value must also be non-negative, the bond value corresponding to a zero firm value is

$$W(0,t) = 0. \tag{9}$$

A further upper bound on W may be obtained by noting that the returns on the convertible bond are stochastically dominated in the first degree by the returns on a portfolio consisting of an equivalent straight bond and the maximum number of shares into which the bond may be converted over its remaining life. Hence W must satisfy

$$W(V,t) \leqslant B(V,t) + z^\star(t) V, \tag{10}$$

where $z^\star(t)$ is the maximum value of $z(\tau)$ for $\tau = (t,T)$.

The investor's conversion option ensures that

$$W(V,t) \geqslant C(V,t) = z(t) V. \tag{11}$$

(ii) The maturity value condition, corresponding to $t = T$, is:

$$W(V,t) = \begin{cases} z(T) V, & z(T) V \geqslant 1000 \\ 1000, & 1000l \leqslant V \leqslant 1000/z(T) \\ V/l, & V \leqslant 1000l \end{cases} \tag{12}$$

The above boundary condition reflects the fact that at maturity the bondholder receives the conversion value of the bond, $z(T) V$, if this exceeds the par value of the bond; he receives the par value if this exceeds the conversion value and if the par value of the outstanding bonds is less than the aggregate value of the firm; he receives a proportionate share of the value of the firm if this falls short of the par value.

(iii) When the bond is callable, the call price constraint is

$$W(V,t) \leqslant CP(t). \tag{13}$$

This follows from Lemma 2.

(iv) When the bond is not currently callable, the limiting firm value condition is:

$$\lim_{V \to \infty} W_v(V,t) = z(t). \tag{14}$$

For sufficiently high values of V the risk of default in the bond payments becomes negligible. The bond may then be regarded as a warrant to buy a fraction $z(t)$ of the firm with an exercise price equal to the present value of the riskless debt payments. (14) then follows from Merton's [6] demonstration of the corresponding proposition for a warrant.

(v) On the date of a dividend or an adverse change in conversion terms, the conversion condition is

$$W(V,t^-) = \max[W(V-D,t^+), z(t^-)V] \tag{15}$$

Where t^- denotes the time immediately before the event and t^+ the following instant. Equation (15) allows for the investor's right to convert immediately prior to the event.

(vi) On a coupon date when the bond is not currently callable

$$W(V,t^-) = W(V-I,t^+) + i. \tag{16}$$

The pre-coupon value is equal to the post-coupon value plus the value of the coupon.

(vii) On a coupon date when the bond is currently callable

$$W(V,t^-) = \min[W(V-I,t^+) + i, CP(t^-)]. \tag{17}$$

This follows from the condition

$$W(V,t^-) = \min[W(V-I,t^+) + I, VIC(V,t^-)], \tag{18}$$

together with the implication of Lemma 2 that $VIC(V,t) = CP(t)$ when the bond is called if an optimal call strategy is followed. Equation (18) itself follows from the observation that the firm's optimal strategy is to call the bond if the post-coupon uncalled value plus the coupon exceeds the value if called; by thus minimizing the value of the bond, the value of the equity is maximized, since the sum of the values is equal to the exogenously determined value of the firm.

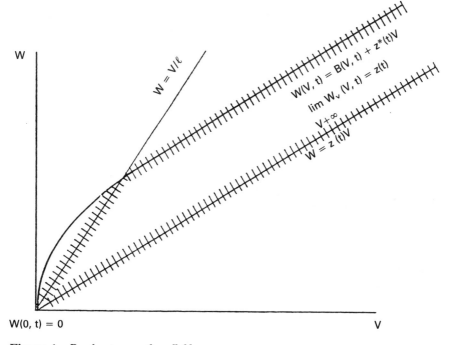

Figure 1 *Bond not currently callable*

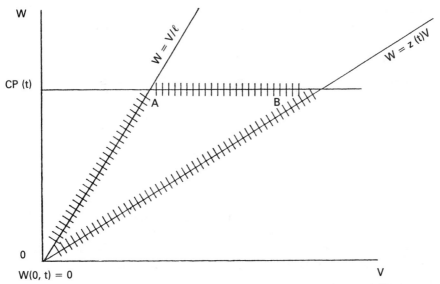

Note that when the bond is callable its value is bounded in the region OAB.
The upper bound (10) may cross OA above or below A.

Figure 2 *Bond currently callable*

Not all of the above boundary conditions need to be explicitly taken into account in the solution of the differential equation. The arbitrage condition (8) is automatically satisfied by the model. By Lemma 1, the conversion option condition (11) is automatically satisfied except at dividend or conversion term change dates when it is incorporated in (15).

The boundary conditions which must always be satisfied by the value of the bond when it is non-callable and callable are shown in Figures 1 and 2 respectively.

IV   The solution algorithm

Since there exists no known analytical solution to the differential equation (7) subject to the boundary conditions discussed above, it is necessary to resort to numerical methods to solve the equation. For this purpose it is more convenient to employ the variable τ, time to maturity, instead of the variable t, calendar time. (7) can then be re-written as

$$\tfrac{1}{2}\sigma^2 V^2 W_{vv} + rVW_v - rW - W_\tau = 0. \tag{7'}$$

Then, by writing finite differences instead of partial derivatives in (7'), the differential equation can be approximated by[4]

$$a_i W_{i-1,j} + b_i W_{i,\,j} + c_i W_{i+1,j} = W_{i,j-1}, i = 1,\ldots,(n-1), j = 1,\ldots,m, \tag{19}$$

where $a_i = \tfrac{1}{2}rki - \tfrac{1}{2}\sigma^2 ki^2, \; b_i = 1 + rk + \sigma^2 ki^2, \; c_i = \tfrac{1}{2}rki - \tfrac{1}{2}\sigma^2 ki^2$

$$W(V,\tau) = W(V_i,\tau_j) = W(ih,jk) = W_{i,j}$$

The symbols h and k are the discrete increments in the value of the firm and in time to maturity respectively. By reducing these step sizes, any desired degree of accuracy in the solution can be achieved, but at the expense of increased computational cost. The symbols n and m represent the number of steps in the time dimension and the firm value dimension respectively; the former is chosen to correspond to the maturity of the bond under consideration, while the latter must be sufficiently large for the limiting firm value condition (14) to be well approximated at the maximum firm value considered.

---

[4] See McCracken and Dorn [5] for a detailed explanation of the solution procedure.

With no loss of generality, it is assumed that $W(V,\tau)$ is the value of all the convertible bonds outstanding, convertible into a fraction z of the firm's shares.[5] Then the maturity value condition, (12), may be written in finite difference form as

$$W_{i,0} = \begin{cases} zV = zhi, & \text{for} \quad zhi \geqslant P \\ P & \text{for} \quad P \leqslant hi \leqslant P/z \\ V = hi & \text{for} \quad hi \leqslant P \end{cases} \tag{20}$$

where P is the par value plus accrued interest at maturity of the convertible bonds.

At any time prior to maturity, the zero firm value condition (9) applies and is written as:

$$W_{0,j} = 0, \quad j = 0,1,\ldots,m. \tag{21}$$

When the bond is not currently callable, the limiting firm value condition (14) applies and is approximated by

$$\frac{W_{n,j} - W_{n-1,j}}{h} = z. \tag{22}$$

For any given value of j, (19) constitutes a set of $(n - 1)$ linear equations in the $(n + 1)$ unknowns, $W_{i,j}$ $(i = 0, 1, \ldots, n)$. The remaining two equations come from the boundary conditions (21) and (22). The resulting set of $(n + 1)$ linear equations enable us to solve for $W_{i,j}$ in terms of $W_{i,j-1}$. Since $W_{i,0}$ $(i = 0, 1, \ldots, n)$ is given by (20), the whole set of $W_{i,j}$ may be generated by repeated solution of this set of equations, taking into account the boundary conditions imposed by the call and conversion options to be discussed below.

When the bond is currently callable, the limiting firm value condition (14) is replaced by the call price constraint (13), which, in the notation of this section, is written as

$$W_{i,j} \leqslant CP_j. \tag{23}$$

This boundary condition is taken into account by an iterative procedure described below. First, observe that since $W_{o,j} = 0$ from (21), the matrix of coefficients in the system (19) is tridiagonal, having zeros everywhere except on the main diagonal and the two adjacent diagonals. Then, by successive

---

[5] For clarity of presentation we omit the dependence of z on time to maturity, τ.

subtraction of each equation from a suitable multiple of the succeeding one, the system may be transformed into the simpler one

$$e_i W_{i,j} + f_i W_{i+1,j} = g_i, \qquad i = 1,...,(n-1), \tag{24}$$

where e_i, f_i, g_i are the coefficients of the transformed system.

Note that on account of the boundary conditions provided by call and conversion $W_{i,j}$ is undefined for $i > q$ where

$$q = CP_j/zh.$$

The symbol q corresponds to the value of the firm for which the conversion value of the bonds is equal to the call price. Therefore, when the bond is callable, the system (24) is reduced to $(q-1)$ equations $(i = 1, ... , q-1)$. The iterative procedure is as follows. Set $W_{q,j} = CP_j$. Solve equation $(q-1)$ of (24) for $W_{q-1,j}$. If $W_{q-1,j} > CP_j$ set $W_{q-1,j}$ equal to CP_j and solve equation $(q-2)$ for $W_{q-2,j}$. If $W_{q-2,j} > CP_j$ set $W_{q-2,j} = CP_j$. This process is continued until a set of $W_{i,j}$ is obtained which satisfy the boundary condition $W_{i,j} \leq CP_j$, and the differential equation. The value of $i(i = p)$ for which $W_{p,j} = CP_j$ corresponds to the value of the firm at which the bonds should be called, and $W_{i,j}$ is undefined for $i > p$.

On a dividend date, j_D, the conversion option gives rise to the boundary condition (15), which can be written as

$$W_{i,j_D} = \begin{cases} W_{i-D/h,j_D} & \text{for} \quad W_{i-D/h,j_D} \geq zV = zih \\ zih & \text{for} \quad W_{i-D/h,j_D} \leq zih \end{cases}$$

On a coupon date, j_c, the boundary condition (16) can be written as

$$W_{i,j_c} = W_{i-I/h,j_c} + I \tag{26}$$

if the bond is not currently callable, while if it is callable, (17) applies, and this can be written as

$$W_{i,j_c} = \begin{cases} W_{i-I/h,j_c} + I & \text{for} \quad W_{i-I/h,j_c} + I \leq CP_{j_c} \\ CP_{j_c} & \text{for} \quad W_{i-I/h,j_c} + I > CP_{j_c} \end{cases}$$

V   Comparative statics: some numerical results

This section reports the effects of variation in selected parameters on the relationship between the value of the convertible bond and the value of the firm. The parameters of the basic example, from which deviations are considered in the following examples, are given in Table 1.

Table 1 Data for basic example

Par Value of Bond	40
Semi-Annual Coupon	1.0
Quarterly Dividend	1.0
Convertible into 10% of the shares outstanding after conversion	
Firm Variance Rate	0.001 per month
Risk Free Rate	0.005 per month
Call terms:	none callable for 5 years
	callable at 43 for next 5 years★
	callable at 42 for next 5 years★
	callable at 41 for last 5 years★

★ plus accrued interest.

(i) Time to maturity

Figure 3 shows the relationship that exists at the time the bond is issued ($T =$ 20). At issue, for firm values above 150, the relationship corresponds closely to that derived from intuition and casual empiricism [2]; that is to say, the

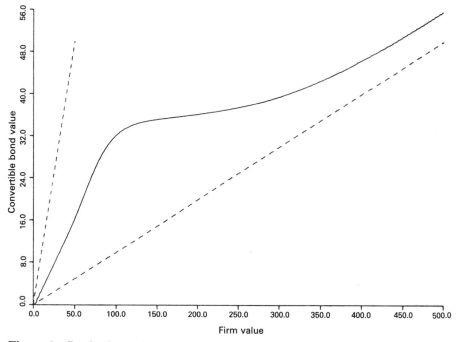

Figure 3 *Bond value at time of issue*

bond value reflects a premium above conversion value, and for lower values of the firm shows the influence of the 'bond value floor' or straight debt value. As many investors in convertible bonds have discovered to their chagrin, this floor value is itself variable, and for sufficiently low values of the firm declines rapidly, reflecting the possibility that the firm will actually default on the bond. As the bond approaches closer to maturity, the left hand section of the curve shifts further to the left, approaching the dotted line along which the bond value is equal to the firm value; this is a consequence of the fact that at low firm values the probability of default is high, and in the event of default the bondholders acquire the assets of the firm. On the other hand, with decreasing time to maturity the right hand section of the curve shifts further to the right, approaching the dotted line which represents the conversion value of the bond. This reduction in the conversion premium corresponds to that observed with warrants as time to maturity decreases.

Figure 4 shows the relationship which obtains at $T = 15$ when the bond is callable at 43; in this example the curve passes through the point at which the conversion value is equal to the call price. Since the bond is called as soon as it reaches the call price, this is the maximum value it attains.

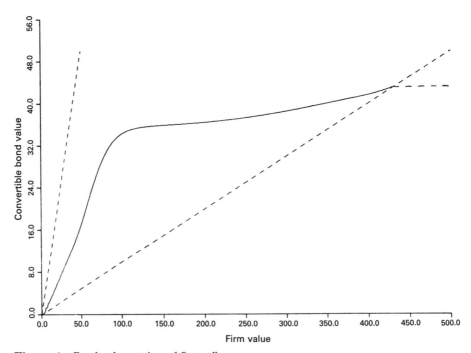

Figure 4 *Bond value at time of first call*

(ii) Dividend payments

Since convertible bonds, like warrants, are not protected against dividend payments by the firm, the effect of a higher dividend payment is to reduce the value of the bond. Figure 5 illustrates this effect at $T = 20$ for three different values of the dividend. The dividend actually has two distinct effects on the value of the convertible bond. First, it affects the straight debt value of the bond by increasing the probability of default and by reducing the assets available for the bondholders in the event of default. This is clearly visible in the relationships on the left hand side of the figure. Secondly, when the probability of default is small (i.e. for large values of V) the conversion premium is reduced. This latter effect is much smaller for two reasons: since the bond is callable at $T = 15$ the convertible bondholder is foregoing only 5 years of dividends; in addition, the right of the bondholder to convert limits the losses that can be imposed upon him by more generous dividend payments.

The convexity of the curves for $D = 1.00$ and $D = 2.00$ at extremely low values of V reflects a quirk of this model, which assumes that the same

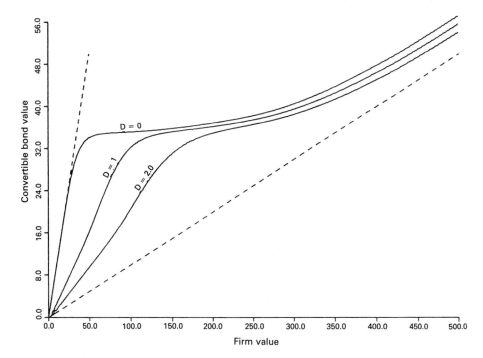

Figure 5 *Bond value at time of issue: effect of dividend payment*

dividend is paid whatever the value of the firm.[6] At sufficiently low firm values it will actually pay the bondholders to convert prior to a dividend before the assets providing security for their bonds are paid out from under them in the form of dividends. Realistically of course, indenture provisions would force a cessation of dividend payments long before this critical stage were reached.

(iii)   Variance rates

Figure 6 illustrates the relationships that obtain at time of issue for three different variance rates. As the figure indicates, an increase in the variance rate may increase or decrease the value of the bond. First, at very low firm values where default is almost certain whatever the variance rate, there is no effect. At

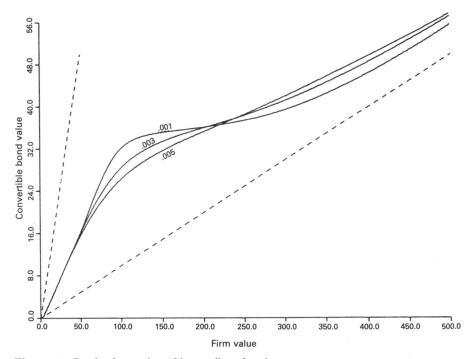

Figure 6   *Bond value at time of issue: effect of variance rate*

---

[6] The apparent discontinuity in the slope at extremely low values of V is a product of the discreteness of the solution procedure.

intermediate firm values, an increase in the variance rate both raises the expected loss through default as for a straight bond, and increases the expected gain from conversion. While the former effect predominates for firm values between about 50.0 and 200.0, for higher firm values the debt is almost risk free, and the convertible bond is essentially equivalent to a riskless straight bond plus a warrant with an exercise price equal to the straight bond value. It is then well known that higher variance rates will lead to higher warrant values, and this effect is apparent for high values of V.

(iv) Call dates

Figure 7 illustrates the effect of varying the date of first call on the value of the bond at time of issue. As would be expected, this has no effect on the value of the bond for low values of the firm where the prospect of conversion is remote in any event. At higher firm values, the bond value declines with the call deferral period so that at the first call date the upper portion of the curve is coincident with the dotted line representing the conversion value.

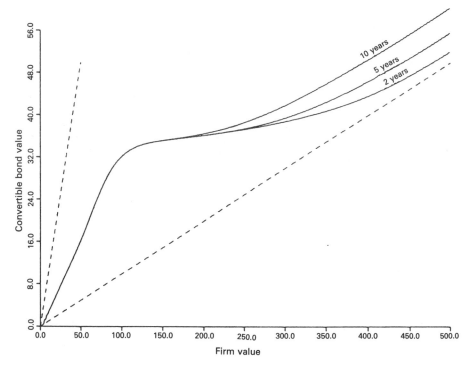

Figure 7 *Bond value at time of issue: effect of call deferral period*

(v)   Conversion terms

In Figure 8 the fraction of the firm's shares into which the bond is convertible is varied. The effect of this is to change the limiting slope of the relationship for high values of *V*.

The extreme case in which the conversion ratio is zero represents of course a straight bond, so that the vertical difference between the lowest curve and any of the others corresponds to the value of the conversion privilege.

While this paper is ostensibly concerned only with convertible bonds, it should be apparent that the analysis captures many of the most important aspects of risky coupon-paying straight bonds, and thus represents a significant generalization of Merton's [6] path breaking analysis of risky bonds, which was restricted only to discount bonds. A subsequent paper will treat the problem of valuing straight coupon bonds with risk of default, and examine in detail the effects of such common provisions as sinking funds, call privileges, and indenture restrictions on dividend payments.

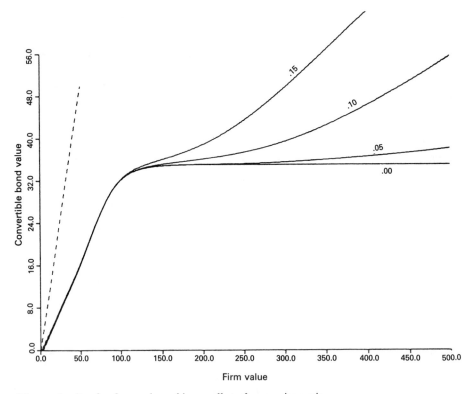

Figure 8   *Bond value at time of issue: effect of conversion ratio*

References

1 F. Black and M.S. Scholes, 'The Pricing of Options and Corporate Liabilities', *Journal of Political Economy*, Volume 81, Number 3 (May-June 1973).

2 E.F. Brigham, 'An Analysis of Convertible Debentures: Theory and Some Empirical Evidence', *Journal of Finance*, (March 1966).

3 J.C. Cox and S.A. Ross, 'The Valuation of Options for Alternative Stochastic Processes', *Journal of Financial Economics*, Volume 3, (January-March 1976).

4 J. Ingersoll, 'A Contingent-Claims Valuation of Convertible Bonds', unpublished manuscript, University of Chicago, (February 1976).

5 D.D. McCracken and W.M. Dorn, *Numerical Methods and Fortran Programming*, John Wiley & Sons, Inc., 1964.

6 R.C. Merton, 'The Theory of Rational Option Pricing', *Bell Journal of Economics and Management Science*, Volume 4, Number 1 (Spring 1973).

7 --'On the Pricing of Corporate Debt: The Risk Structure of Interest Rates', *Journal of Finance*, Volume 29, (May 1974).

8 --'Option Pricing When Underlying Stock Returns Are Discontinuous', *Journal of Financial Economics*, Volume 3, (January-March 1976).

9 M.H. Miller and F. Modigliani, 'Dividend Policy, Growth, and the Valuation of Shares', *Journal of Business*, Volume 34, (October 1961).

10 F. Modigliani and M.H. Miller, 'The Cost of Capital, Corporation Finance, and the Theory of Investment', *American Economic Review*, Volume 48, (June 1958).

11 M.E. Rubinstein, 'The Valuation of Uncertain Income Streams and The Pricing of Options', Working Paper No. 37, University of California, Berkeley.

12 E.S. Schwartz, 'Generalized Option Pricing Models: Numerical Solutions and the Pricing of a New Life Insurance Contract', Unpublished Ph.D. Dissertation, University of British Columbia, 1975.

Reproduced from Brennan, M.J. and Schwartz, E.S. (1977). Convertible bonds: valuation and optimal strategies for call and conversion. *The Journal of Finance*, **XXXII**(5), 1699–1715 by permission of the American Finance Association.

Index